REMEMBERING

Buddy

REMEMBERING
Buddy

THE DEFINITIVE BIOGRAPHY
JOHN GOLDROSEN AND JOHN BEECHER

OMNIBUS PRESS
LONDON · NEW YORK · SYDNEY

This book first published in
the United Kingdom in 1987 by GRR/Pavilion
This edition Copyright © 1996 Omnibus Press
(A Division of Book Sales Limited)

Text © 1975, 1979, 1987, 1996
John Goldrosen and John Beecher

Remembering Buddy is based in part on
a revised edition of *Buddy Holly – His
Life and Music*, first published in 1975

Text design by Peter Bridgewater
Cover design by Pearce Marchbank,
Studio Twenty, London

ISBN: 0.7119.5702.9
Order No. OP47838

Exclusive Distributors:
Book Sales Limited,
8/9 Frith Street,
London W1V 5TZ, UK
Music Sales Pty Limited,
120 Rothschild Avenue, Rosebery,
NSW 2018, Australia

To the Music Trade only:
Music Sales Limited,
8/9 Frith Street,
London W1V 5TZ, UK

The rights of John Goldrosen and John
Beecher to be identified as the authors of this
work have been asserted by them in
accordance with the Copyright Designs and
Patents Act 1988

Printed in the United Kingdom by
Staples Printers Limited, Rochester, Kent

A catalogue record for this books is
available from the British Library

Credits

Every effort has been made to trace the owners of copyright material used in this book. We gratefully acknowledge those who have assisted with the provision of illustrations and apologise for any errors or omissions. The publisher will be pleased to give proper acknowledgement in future editions. Where two names are shown the first is the original photographer and the second the copyright holder, or the person making the material available to us.

Front cover: Bruno/John Beecher Collection; 11: Lubbock News Agency; 12: John Goldrosen; 13; 15, 16; 17(r): Ella Holley; 17(1): Dave Stone; 20: John Beecher; 21: Lubbock High School; 22; 23: Larry Holley Collection; 24: Bob Montgomery; 25: Buddy Holly Memorial Society (BHMS) Collection; 26: Ben Hall; 27: Ella Holley; 29(l): Larry Holley Collection; 29(r): Rallo Henry/BHMS Collection; 30(t): John Beecher Collection; 30(b): Larry Holley Collection; 32: Dave Stone; 33(t): BHMS Collection; 33(c): Larry Holley Collection; 33(b): J. I. Allison; 34: BHMS Collection; 35: John Beecher Collection; 36: Decca-MCA Records; 37(t): Ben Hall; 37(b): The Billboard; 43: Larry Holley Collection; 45: Norman Petty/Vi Petty; 46(t): Jean-Pierre Chapados; 46(c): Vi Petty Collection; 46(b): John Ingman; 47: Louise Allison/J. I. Allison; 58: Ella Holley Collection; 68: The Cash Box; 69(t): Brunswick-MCA/Graham Harrison Collection; 69(b): The Cash Box; 71(l): Norman Petty/Vi Petty; 71(r): James Allison/J I. Allison; 72(l): J. I. Allison; 72(lc & c): Arsene/J I. Allison; 73: J. I. Allison Collection; 74: Larry Holley Collection; 75(1): Arsene/J I Allison; 75(c & r) : J. I. Allison Collection; 76(t): BGMS Collection; 76(b): J. I Allison; 77: Coral-MCA/Richard Weize Collection; 78: Nor Va Jak Music/MPL Communications; 79: J. I. Allison ; 81(l): John Beecher Collection; 81(r): J. I Allison; 81 & 85: Arsene/J. I. Allison; 86(t): John Beecher Collection; 86(b) & 87: Kriegsmann/J. I. Allison; 88(t): Melody Maker; 88(b): Martyn Wright/John Beecher Collection; 89(l): Ella Holley Collection; 89(r): BHMS Collection; 90 (tl & bl): Julian Levene Collection; 90(r): John Beecher Collection; 91: Flair Photography; 92(tl): Philip Gotlop/John Beecher; 92(tr): BBC Television; 92(l): Flair Photography; 93: The Billboard; 94: J I Allison/John Beecher Collection; 95: James Allison/J. I. Allison; 96: Song Hits; 97: The Billboard; 98: Dick Cole; 99: Coral-MCA/John Beecher Collection; 100: The Cash Box; 101: The Billboard; 102: John Goldrosen; 103: Dick Cole; 104(t): J. I.. Allison Collection; 104(b): Dave Skinner; 106: Maria Elena Holly Collection; 107(t): Steve Bonner Collection; 107(b): Louise Allison/J. I. Allison 108: Ella Holley; 113 & 114: The Cash Box 116: Ella Holley 119 (1 & r) : Eddie Randall /BHMS Collection ; 122: Bruno/John Beecher Collection; 125(b): Brunswick-MCA; 129(t): The Billboard; 128(l): The Cash Box; 128(r): Lubbock News Agency; 129: Bill Griggs; 131 & 135: Bruno/John Beecher Collection; 140: BHMS Collection; 141: Joanie Svenson/Don Larson; 142: Bruno/J Beecher Collection; 143: BHMS Collection; 116: Edwin Musser/BHMS Collection; 148(t): Bill Griggs; 148(b): Dave Skinner; 150: Variety; 151: George Tomsco; 158: J. I. Allison Collection; 166 & 167: Columbia Pictures; 171: Bill Griggs; 173: MPL. Communications; 175: Trevor Lailey; 176: J. I. Allison.

Colour section (between pages *116 & 117*): *page i,* clockwise from top left; Norman Petty/Vi Petty; Brunswick-MCA; Ronnie Keene/Trevor Lailey Collection; Don Guess/Derek Glenister Collection; *ii*; clockwise from top left: James Allison/J. I. Allison; James Allison/J. I. Allison; John Goldrosen; John Goldrosen; *iii*: James Allison/J. I. Allison; *iv*: Larry Matti.

Song Lyric Credits: The following is a list of copyright holders who have kindly given permission for copyright lyrics to be reproduced: Acuff Rose Music Limited, London for "Too Old to Cut the Mustard" by Bill Carlisle. International copyright secured. All rights reserved. Used by permission. Peermusic UK Limited, London for "I'm Looking For Someone to Love" by Buddy Holly and Norman Petty, "Listen to Me" by Charles Hardin and Norman Petty, "I'm Gonna Love You Too" by Joe Mauldin, Niki Sullivan, and Norman Petty, "Take Your Time" by Norman Petty and Buddy Holly, "Well All Right" by Norman Petty, Buddy Holly, Jerry Allison and Joe Mauldin, "Love's Made a Fool of You" by Buddy Holly and Bob Montgomery, "Everyday" by Charles Hardin and Norman Petty, "That Makes It Tough" by Buddy Holly, "Crying, Waiting, Hoping" by Buddy Holly, "Peggy Sue Got Married" by Buddy Holly, "That's What They Say" by Buddy Holly, "Learning the Game" by Buddy Holly and "You're the One" by Buddy Holly, Waylon Jennings, and Slim Corbin.International copyright secured. All rights reserved. Used by permission. Mayday Music (BMI)/The Benny Bird Co., USA and MCA Music Ltd., 77 Fulham Palace Road, London W6 for "American Pie" by Don McLean. © 1972. All rights reserved. Used by permission of Music Sales Limited. Tree Publishing Co., Inc. USA and Sony Music Publishing, 10 Great Marlborough Street, London W1 for "The Real Buddy Holly Story" by Sonny Curtis. © 1979 International Copyright Secured. All rights reserved. Used by permission of Music Sales Limited.

CONTENTS

PREFACE

Remembering Buddy was first published in Britain in 1986 by Pavilion Books, and in the United States in 1987 by Viking Penguin. That book was itself an updated and expanded version of my two prior biographies of Buddy Holly. The initial biography was *Buddy Holly: His Life and Music,* published in 1975 by the Popular Press (US) and Charisma Books (UK) and reprinted in 1979 in Britain by Granada Publishing; a revised edition of that original work was published in 1979 in the United States only by Quick Fox Press, under the title *The Buddy Holly Story.*

For this new edition of *Remembering Buddy,* the text of the book has been reprinted without alteration. The new edition retains the numerous photographs and illustrations of the prior edition, but in addition presents color photographs that were not included previously. The supplementary materials (including a session file, discography, chart file, and listing of tour dates) have been updated and reorganized for this edition. My thanks go to John Beecher, who selected and arranged the illustrations, and compiled all of the supplementary materials.

In the years since his tragic death in 1959, Buddy Holly has remained, without interruption, popular and influential in Britain. It is hard to think of any artist who has enjoyed such posthumous success in terms of both record sales and musical stature. By contrast, in the United States, Holly fell into obscurity in the 1960's, a period in which other American rock 'n' roll pioneers had to rely on foreign audiences to sustain their careers. By 1971, when I first began the research and travel that led to my initial Holly biography, leading rock music critics in America tended to be contemptuous of early rock 'n' roll artists, and those artists' recordings were often available in the U.S. only on imported collections. The last chapter of this book chronicles the changes in attitude which occurred in the 1970's. By providing source material for both the commercially successful movie *The Buddy Holly Story* (1978) and the informative and moving 1986 BBC Arena documentary (released in the United States on cable and home video as *The Real Buddy Holly Story),* the original version of this biography acted, I believe, as a catalyst for that change in outlook towards rock 'n 'roll in general, and Buddy Holly in particular. When the Rock'n'Roll Hall of Fame was established in 1986, Buddy Holly was selected as a charter member. Had the election taken place ten or fifteen years earlier, the American music industry might not have accorded Holly such recognition.

In the decade since the initial publication of *Remembering Buddy,* Holly's position as a rock 'n' roll icon has been solidified. His name is probably recognized more widely and across a broader age range than ever before. In Britain, the musical *Buddy* has been a hit in London for many years; the musical also enjoyed some success in New York, and touring companies of the Broadway production have played across the United States. Throughout America, the proliferation of 'oldies' radio stations and compact disc reissues of classic rock 'n' roll have made that music more available to both the casual listener and the dedicated fan than at any time since the decade of the 1950's itself. The unprecedented demand for the American postage stamp honoring Elvis Presley demonstrated that early rock 'n' roll now has a secure place in American popular culture. As a follow-up to the Presley stamp, the U.S. Postal Service issued a series of stamps honoring other rock 'n' roll and rhythm & blues greats; Buddy Holly was among the artists represented (along with Bill Haley, Clyde McPhatter, Ritchie Valens, Otis Redding, and Dinah Washington). To offer another, more offbeat indication of how well-known Holly's name and the facts of his life have become in recent years, consider the title and subject of a comic fantasy novel by Bradley Denton, published in 1991: *Buddy Holly Is Alive and Well on Ganymede.*

Holly has continued to influence and inspire successive generations of musicians representing a broad spectrum of musical genres. Most recently, country music performers, especially those with roots in popular music and in contemporary acoustic folk music as well as in traditional country music styles, have acknowledged the example set by Holly when he freely mixed musical styles and disregarded conventional boundaries. In the 1996 MCA/Decca tribute album *Notfadeaway,* such artists as Mary Chapin Carpenter, Nanci Griffith, and the Mavericks, who themselves have resisted categorization in their own careers, recorded their individualistic versions of Holly's compositions. The album was one more indication of the continuing breadth of Holly's appeal, and the enduring vitality of his music. It was one more reminder, as well, of how far ahead of his time Buddy Holly really was, in his vision of an American music that would transcend cultural boundaries.

Decades after Buddy Holly's death, his fans and musical descendants continue to draw inspiration from his ambition and commitment, and take pleasure from the music he created in his tragically short career. Though the music stands on its own, it can be

appreciated and enjoyed still more when connected to the details of Holly's life and personality, and placed in the context of the times in which he lived. In undertaking twenty-five years ago to write a biography of a then-underappreciated rock 'n' roll singer, I sought to provide this background. The re-publication of *Remembering Buddy* is intended to provide renewed access to the intriguing details of Holly's life and musical career.

John Goldrosen, June 1996

John Goldrosen has every right to be proud of his contribution to the re-establishment of Buddy Holly as a household name, especially in America. Without his book, there would have been a serious lack of research material for shows, films, liner notes—and of course for other books and articles. He was the first to interview in depth many of the people who knew Buddy Holly closely. He was also in many cases the last to do so, since several of Holly's friends and business associates have died since John set out to find out about the real Buddy Holly. It is unfortunate that at the very time when this book deserved to reach the wider market for anything relating to Buddy, *Remembering Buddy* disappeared from the bookshops both in England and in America. The failure of a previous publisher to exploit that market while still retaining the rights has delayed re-publication and made the book something of a rarity—so much so that even those who have sought to use it as source material for their own, sometimes fanciful, books have been unable to locate copies.

The publication in *Remembering Buddy* of a session file listing many unissued Buddy Holly recordings created much interest among fans and collectors. For many years it had seemed unlikely that any new Buddy Holly material would ever be released. Then, by the time we went to press in 1985, it became apparent that there were many unreleased recordings which had been forgotten or ignored by those who had been entrusted with Buddy's musical legacy. There was talk of several albums being released, but in fact only one emerged before legal wrangles prevented MCA from continuing and it seems unbelievable now that over a decade later, MCA has still not been able to release the tapes discovered in the Petty archives and in the possession of Holly's family and friends. While the parties involved—the record company, the Holly and Petty Estates and other artists whose recordings featured Holly as an instrumentalist—continued to argue over royalty terms and other demands, the bootleggers were quick to step in to exploit the now considerable market for Buddy Holly records. By obtaining copies of acetates and tapes which had been sold to collectors as a scam through a by-now ex-employee of MCA, the bootleggers, mostly in Europe and the USA, were able to provide the fans with what they wanted to hear. Some of the resulting albums were poorly packaged and show little regard for the feelings of Holly's family or fans; the producer of one CD even attempted to pass off a racist recording made some years after Buddy's death as an unissued Holly track. Other bootleggers have shown MCA how it should have handled the Holly catalogue, with good compilations, extensive notes, previously unseen photographs and attractive packaging. Little has been done to prevent the proliferation of the good or the bad and many stores now have more unauthorised product in their racks than legitimate releases. Unfortunately MCA's reissues of previously available recordings have remained patchy, with a few well-researched and annotated packages being heavily outweighed by the quickly compiled and ill-assorted compilations they have continued to release and license to others. It is to be hoped that this situation will change when it eventually becomes possible to legally release the unissued Buddy Holly tracks which remain in the vaults. A glance at the session files at the end of this book will give some idea of the amount of material involved.

In researching the additional material contained in the supplementary section I was again reminded of the bond that unites all Buddy Holly fans. Many religions could learn a lot from the gentle way Buddy's followers and friends still help the cause by bringing the word of Holly to new fans and by nudging those in the media to present and produce items which interest us all. The desire of many people to offer help and information and respond to requests has been most encouraging and I hope no-one will offended if they do not receive an acknowledgement in print. There simply are too many nice folks to thank and I hope that seeing the restoration of this work to the bookshelves will be some reward for their much appreciated assistance.

John Beecher, June 1996

JOHN GOLDROSEN first developed an interest in Buddy Holly and other rock 'n' roll artists as a teenager growing up in Massachusetts. He majored in history at Harvard College, where he produced radio shows on rock 'n' roll and traditional jazz. After finishing college, he undertook the several years of travel and research that culminated in the first comprehensive biography of Buddy Holly. Goldrosen holds a master's degree in regional planning from the University of North Carolina, and a doctor of laws degree from Harvard Law School. His hobbies include coaching soccer and running marathons.

JOHN BEECHER was born in Surrey. In 1957 he was made aware of the Crickets first record by a friend who also provided the fascinating information that their vocalist and Buddy Holly were one and the same. A quest for more facts eventually resulted in Beecher running fan clubs for Buddy Holly and the Crickets while in his teens; this led to a career in music publishing through a recommendation from Norman Petty. By the 1970s he had convinced MCA to allow him to repackage the Holly and Crickets catalogues, culminating in a co-operation with Malcolm Jones to produce the award-winning *Complete Buddy Holly* box set. He now lives in Gloucestershire where he releases rock 'n' roll material on Rollercoaster Records.

INTRODUCTION

In Search of the Singer

For Lycidas is dead, dead ere
his prime
Young Lycidas and hath not
left his peer
Who would not sing for
Lycidas? He Knew
Himself to sing, and build the
lofty rhyme

JOHN MILTON, LYCIDAS

I never saw Buddy Holly perform, and I can't remember hearing his songs before his death in 1959. (I was eight years old at the time, but that's not much of an excuse—one friend of mine was seven when he bought a copy of "Peggy Sue". But I do remember just where I was a couple of years later when I first heard one of Holly's songs—the tune was "Oh Boy!"—and how the name and the song stayed in my mind even though my interest in popular music was then minimal. The "British Invasion" of 1964 which revived American rock'n'roll rekindled my interest in Holly and his contemporaries, to whom the British groups were so indebted for their sound and, often, their material. Like so many other fans, I found that the age of Holly's records was unimportant, All I knew was that the songs spoke to *me* right then. All my feelings and experiences, both good and bad, seemed to have been expressed within the variety of Holly's style and matter. Long before the rock'n'roll revival craze of the early 1970's, I had decided that contemporary rock music offered nothing so exciting, moving and meaningful as the music Buddy Holly had composed and recorded years before.

When we fans wanted to go beyond the records—when we wanted to learn more about the background of Holly and other rock'n'rollers of the 1950's—we found little information available. In the United States, early rock'n'roll was treated as frivolous music both at the time it was popular and for over a decade thereafter, so there was little firsthand information about those early artists. No one had reviewed Buddy Holly's concerts for the *New York Times*, and there had been no young journalists around waiting to interview him backstage to record his own thoughts about his music. Whatever films of his performances might have existed were buried in the vaults of television production companies, and unavailable to the public. Holly had never appeared in a commercial motion picture. What little did appear in print on him was often contradictory or biased, and failed to answer the questions most important to the fans.

There was nothing for a fan to do but save up some money, set aside a year or two, and set out in search of the answers. This book was the product, then, of a twenty-thousand-mile cross-country drive to contact the people and visit the places that were part of Buddy Holly's life.

The image of Holly which emerged was an intriguing and complicated one. Holly presented different sides of himself to different people, and never revealed himself totally to anyone. Only after talking with many of those who knew him best could the pieces be fitted together, and the conflicting accounts and legends be weighed. As it turned out, the Buddy Holly story was indeed one which deserved to be told. This book incorporates much material that has come to light in the years since my original research, but the picture of Holly which emerges in these pages is, I think, largely unchanged: the more I learn, the more I am confirmed in my impression of him as a decent human being and a gifted and influential musician.

In revising my book for this new edition, I have done additional research, and have been assisted by others who have also dedicated themselves to uncovering as much information as possible about Holly. Particularly noteworthy have been the efforts of Bill Griggs, founder of the Buddy Holly Memorial Society. Since its inception in 1976, the BHMS has served as a communications link for Holly fans worldwide. The BHMS newsletter, *Reminiscing*, has published numerous interviews with people I had not myself contacted, as well as photographs and other documents. The BHMS has, in effect, served as a library and research centre for writers, radio and television producers, and recording industry personnel, and has therefore been

an important catalyst in the revival of interest in Holly over the past decade. I am grateful to Bill Griggs for his assistance, and for permitting me to draw upon the interviews published in *Reminiscing* for use in this book.

In the years since the original edition of this book was published, several people quoted in it have died, including Norman Petty, 'Hipockets' Duncan, and Holly's father, Lawrence Holley. I have not altered this edition to accommodate their deaths: they speak through these pages, as before, in the present tense, like Holly's music.

Without the assistance of those who were so generous with their time and recollections, I would have found it next to impossible to write a biography of Holly. I am especially grateful to Holly's parents, Ella and Lawrence Holley; his widow, Maria Elena Holly, and the original Crickets, Jerry Allison, Joe Mauldin and Niki Sullivan. They spent many hours discussing the details of Buddy's life and gave me access to tapes, clippings, and photographs in their possession—without demanding any control whatsoever over the final content of the book.

Another invaluable source of information has been tapes of the memorial shows broadcast each year on the anniversary of Holly's death by Lubbock's KLLL Radio; the KLLL shows often included interviews with Holly's friends, family members, or fellow performers.

All the following also offered their own memories of Buddy Holly and the rock'n'roll era, or helped put me in contact with Holly's acquaintances. Resolving any conflicts among the various accounts was my own responsibility, and as with any such work, the author must be held accountable for any errors of fact or judgement. Those whose help should be acknowledged include: Sonny Curtis, 'Pappy' Dave Stone, Dick Jacobs, Bob Montgomery, Ben Hall, Norman Petty, 'Hipockets' Duncan, Larry Holley, Scotty Moore, Don and Phil Everly, Tommy Allsup, Mrs Jo Walker of the Country Music Association, Ralph Peer II, Larry Welborn, Don Guess, George Atwood, Daniel Dougherty, Bob Linville, Bill Hall, Carroll Anderson, Bud Andrews, Jerry Coleman, Murray Deutch, Bob Theile, Owen Bradley and Luke McDaniel.

In addition to Bill Griggs and John Beecher, numerous other Holly fans and collectors have, throughout the years, offered both practical and moral support. I thank all those who have made information available to me, either directly or through their contributions to the BHMS newsletter. Other information was derived from the newsletters of the British Buddy Holly Appreciation Society. Among those who deserve special mention are Joan Turner, Steve Bonner, Wayne Jones, George Denham and Malcolm Jones.

Finally, my thanks are due to my family and friends, for their support and encouragement.

John Goldrosen
Whitman, Massachusetts
May, 1986

CHAPTER ONE

HOME TOWN: LUBBOCK, TEXAS

Over a quarter-century has now passed since Buddy Holly's life ended with such suddenness one wintry night in Iowa. Only middle-aged rock 'n' roll fans can remember seeing and hearing him live or on television. For younger generations, he is a semi-legendary voice on a record, or a face in a photograph or in a grainy television film from a distant era. And yet, though Holly's life ended long ago, his career has lived on through the continuing popularity of the recordings he created, the music that was the devotion of his short life.

When someone asks "Who was Buddy Holly?" the music furnishes the most immediate answer. And yet, it is not enough—the music only raises more questions. Where did Buddy Holly and his music come from? Why does his music have the sound it does? How much was his own creation and how much drawn from his musical environment? If the melodies and lyrics suggest something to you or make you feel a certain way, how can you be sure that this is how he meant it to be? What sort of person was he, and what drove him to become a musical performer? What were his successes and failures in life, and what were his goals for the years that never came?

When I first decided to seek answers to these questions some fifteen years ago, the answers were not to be found in any ready source—at least, there was hardly anything in print based on reliable, first-hand knowledge. In search of the answers—in search of the singer—it was necessary to put aside what I had read and heard before, and instead to seek out those who had known Buddy Holly and worked with him. And the search brought me to the city which was his birthplace and lifelong home.

When Buddy Holly was born in 1936, Lubbock, Texas had just twenty-five thousand inhabitants—only one-seventh of its present population—and had existed as a permanent settlement for only forty-five years. Its economy was based on a college—Texas Tech, a state school which the young community had won for itself in 1923—and on cotton, which had come to be widely planted in the region during the same decade. There was not much large-scale industry; the college provided jobs in the construction trades and student business for small retailers, while the farms produced a demand for agricultural supplies and implements. Even when the small town grew into a good-sized city, it still looked to the college and the farms for its prosperity, and kept the appearance and attitudes of a rural community.

Lubbock lies three hundred miles west of Dallas on a broad plateau that offered an unbroken sea of grass to the view of the first settlers. They did not arrive until the 1890's; the growth of the region since then has been so rapid that ambitious goals and optimism about reaching them come naturally to the inhabitants. The census figures alone tell a story. As late as 1920, Lubbock had just four thousand residents; a decade later, there were twenty thousand people there; by 1950, the population had reached seventy thousand; and today, the city has over one hundred and seventy thousand people.

It's only natural, too, that the town should present a strong sense of individual and community pride. From the moment the town was founded in 1891, its citizens have always believed that Lubbock was destined to become the central city of west Texas. Whether or not destiny had anything to do with it, their faith was justified. At the start, this was just another of the tiny frontier towns dotting the area; now it is the largest city for three hundred miles around and has earned the title of "Hub City of the South Plains". Explaining how this happened isn't easy, but the community believes, with

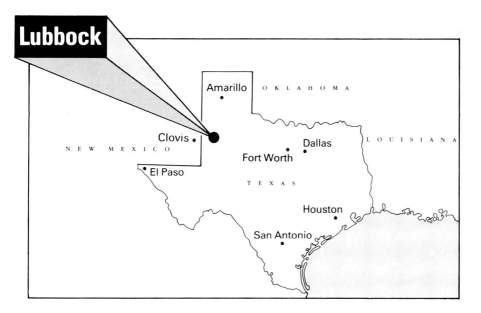

some justification, that the growth was due to the town's efforts on its own behalf. Town leaders rarely fought each other, but instead concentrated on winning the town's battles for railroads and colleges; when the battles were won, Lubbock's primacy was practically assured. This competitive spirit still dominates the town's outlook on life and success—whether in business, sports or culture.

Despite this expansive optimism—or is it because of it?—Lubbock remains conservative in thought and morals. "This isn't just the Bible Belt," jokes one resident, "it's the *buckle* of the Bible Belt." The three leading religious denominations are Baptist, Church of Christ and Methodist, and the congregations at their main Lubbock churches rank among the largest anywhere for those sects. The total number of all religious groups must run into the hundreds, which explains why Lubbock has the nickname, "the City of Churches". The town has no wild frontier past to look back on; organized religion asserted itself early, and the town grew partly on its reputation as a good place to bring up a family. Prohibition was not repealed until 1972. Until then, no package stores were allowed within the city limits and no liquor could be sold by the drink except at "private" clubs. As in other Southern towns with similar regulations, the result was a string of clubs, honky-tonks and liquor stores lying just beyond the town line along the highways leading out of the city.

Lubbock is also linked to the older South in its history of racial discrimination. "Lubbock is farther south than Georgia," said one citizen laconically, in explaining the state of race relations in the town. Blacks and Hispanics each make up about ten per cent of the population, with Hispanics, who have only appeared in sizeable numbers since the 1950's, on the increase. Until recent years, school segregation was fairly complete. Even now, the residential patterns are obvious: whites move out into the new subdivisions on the west and south sides, while the older, less desirable neighbourhoods in the north and east quarters are left to the other racial groups. Actually, there is probably less contact between the races—and certainly more ignorance about the existence of a racial problem—than there is in the older parts of the South. When Buddy Holly was growing up in Lubbock, he had only limited contact with local blacks and their music, in contrast to the experience of Elvis Presley, Jerry Lee Lewis or Carl Perkins.

9

Because Lubbock's rapid growth occurred after 1920 when Congress limited immigration, there are few foreign-born or first-generation American citizens among the town's Anglo population. The diversity of ethnic groups to be found in Eastern cities is missing here; most of Lubbock's settlers came from the older sections of Texas.

All the same, there are social divisions within the white population, and a person's cultural tastes can depend on his social status. Lubbock supports theatre groups and a symphony, and plays host to theatrical road companies, ballets, chamber groups, and pop and rock music shows—all of which receive attention and support from the city newspaper, the *Avalanche-Journal*. But when a country music show comes to town, it receives less publicity. At least until recent years, country music has been thought of in Lubbock as music for poor people and, as a result, the "better" element in town—and anyone who wants to be considered in that class—has avoided any association with country music. (The reaction is a common one wherever country music is popular—even in Nashville.) Anyone caught listening to it feels compelled to make excuses: "I just had the radio on, I wasn't really *listening* to it."

However invisible it may be to the public journal, country music does still flourish in Lubbock, as it did when Buddy Holly was growing up there. Since the 1930's, live country music "jamborees" have been a Saturday night feature in the cities and small towns of west Texas. Often sponsored by radio stations, these musical get-togethers offer local artists opportunities to perform, compete, and share styles and techniques with each other. Most of the numerous clubs and honky-tonks in the area feature country music, whether performed live by bands or played on jukeboxes.

In the southwest, country music has always been dance music, not just music to sit and listen to. It was here that, in the 1930's and 1940's, country bands began to use steel and electric guitars, tenor banjos, string basses, and occasionally drums to provide more rhythm and a louder sound. It was here, too, that "honky-tonk" vocalists and the famous "western swing" bands of Bob Wills and Hank Thompson first became popular. All this went largely unnoticed in the North, and was not entirely welcomed by the older parts of the South, where more traditional instrumental and vocal performers had been popular before. It was only grudgingly that the Grand Ole Opry allowed Bob Wills to use drums when he appeared on the Opry in 1945, and it was some time after the start of the rock 'n' roll era before the Opry routinely allowed drums on its stage. But in the southwest, the assumption that country music was dance music, and the concept of country vocalists as lead singers for small rhythm groups, were familiar to country music fans of all ages well in advance of the rock 'n' roll movement.

These assumptions partly explain why the west Texas area produced more than its share of rockabilly artists, songwriters, sidemen and producers. The gap between country vocalists and combos of the 1940's and early 1950's and rockabilly performers who appeared just afterwards was not all that great; at the least, a young performer trained in these country music styles could move into rock 'n' roll. The same held true for performers raised on rhythm & blues traditions, but not for those raised in a pop music environment. Moreover, no matter what established country music stars thought of the young rockabilly intruders into the recording world and of their effect on country music, rockabilly performers were accepted as country singers in the southwest—and given the support and encouragement of local country music fans and musicians there. In a town such as Lubbock, the major opposition to the new music actually came from the elements in the population

● *Texas Technological College in the 1950's*

that had never cared for country music either.

Obviously, the brand of music popular in west Texas encouraged young country performers trying to make a career out of their music; but so too did the prevailing attitude toward music in general—and who should play it. Americans, a nation of spectators in sports, are often the same in the arts. An American may listen to music on recordings or at concerts, and maybe play an instrument privately but without getting too far with it—too sharp a line is drawn between "professionals" and "amateurs". In most places, music has ceased to be a family activity. In the Lubbock area, however, interest in music is more personal, and performers of all ages take more pride in their talents and set high goals for themselves. Each high school has a band, orchestra and chorus, and the junior high schools face a large demand for classes offering instruction in all band instruments.

When asked why so many musicians have come out of the area, the musicians themselves find the question difficult to answer. One replied, "Well, there isn't anything else out there to do *but* pick." Isolation and boredom may have something to do with it but Lubbock does have movies, radio stations and television, just like any other American city of similar size. The answer lies in the way the whole community approaches music. Among a part of the population, popular music is encouraged as much as "serious" music, and even in preference to it. Among country musicians especially, music is a strong force in family life. Furthermore, the performers share the area's sense of pride and desire for improvement. Explains one musician who was a contemporary of Holly's:

"Lubbock has always had this attitude that you move ahead by being just a little better than someone else. It was the same for the musicians—there was this sense of pride in improving, in being good. There was competition and people you could learn from; and once you started, you felt like you had to reach up to the level already established."

As a result of its geographical isolation, Lubbock attracts a number of concerts and shows out of proportion to its size. In more crowded areas of the nation, any city of Lubbock's size is usually so close to a much larger metropolis that local cultural life is stifled by the competition of the big city. But because it is three hundred miles from any larger town, Lubbock remains an independent market—and its residents, lacking steady access to such entertainment, turn out well for visiting one-night shows. The city boasts convention and auditorium facilities superior to those of cities several times its size. So an aspiring musician not only has the opportunity to play regularly at local functions, but also the chance to hear and see his models in person.

For all their pride in the town's growth and importance, Lubbock residents cling to the city's small-town past and all the good and bad that it implies. Lubbock has grown too fast to realize how large it is. Besides, its citizens are largely immigrants from small towns and farming communities who have not left all their habits behind; friends and strangers still say hello to each other when they pass on the street. The city itself has nothing rural to it. The population is strangely crowded together; house lots are small, and with the flat land almost entirely usable for buildings, adjacent houses are often just a few feet apart. There are no real suburbs, since the city limits contain almost all of the residential sections.

Beyond the city itself are only open fields of cotton and feed lots for cattle raising. The flat terrain stretches endlessly under a warm, blue sky to sharp, distant horizons, visible clearly in the dry air. The land rarely leaves a neutral impression; to some, it is unbearably boring, while others find it exhilarating: "There's just something about it," is all they can say. And if it strikes you that way, then you can understand the confidence and urgent ambition that so many of the inhabitants possess. The land offers no boundaries to the sight; it promises opportunity and provides the urge to be on the move, outwards and upwards. A countryside bare of trees and mountains offers no cover and hides no secrets; and so the people too are outspoken, unafraid to bare themselves to outsiders, and eager to learn the stories of newcomers and strangers. In fact, few families have lived here more than a generation or two, and so all are newcomers of a sort. It is a country where the frontier has been settled only yesterday, where an elderly schoolteacher remembers the hitching post outside her school and the sons of cowboys who rode to

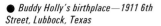

● *Buddy Holly's birthplace—1911 6th Street, Lubbock, Texas*

class each morning. The frontier is now a memory, but not a distant one, and the old American faith that hard work and determination bring success has not yet been tarnished by doubt.

It was in this town and among such people that Buddy Holly grew up and formed his hopes. When the building of Texas Tech in 1923 and the spread of cotton farming to the West Texas plains created an economic boom in Lubbock, thousands left the poorer towns and villages of east and central Texas and sought work in the young city. Among the newcomers were Lawrence and Ella (Drake) Holley.[1] Mr. Holley had been raised on a farm near Honey Grove, a small town close to Paris in northeastern Texas. As a young man, he moved west to Vernon and became a short-order cook. In Vernon he met Ella and the two were married in 1924. The promise of employment in Lubbock, the opportunity to be part of a new and growing town, and the move of Mrs. Holley's own family to Lubbock all led the Holleys to go there themselves the year after they were married.

Even in the years of the Depression there was work for Mr. Holley, but the family never had more than just enough to make ends meet. "I guess we were poor—but of course, we didn't *know* that we were poor," Mrs. Holley recalls now. And although she will not talk of it herself, Buddy's friends are quick to point out that the Holleys, in spite of their low income, always managed to come up with the money for what they thought was important for their children—including musical instruments and lessons.

During the first few years after his arrival in Lubbock, Mr. Holley worked as a cook and a carpenter and, through most of the 1930's and 1940's, he was employed as a tailor and salesman in a clothing store. The Holleys lived in rented houses, moving almost yearly. Their first child, Larry, was born in 1925; a second son, Travis, followed in 1927; and their one daughter, Patricia, was born in 1929. The family was living in a one-storey house at 1911 Sixth Street when their last child was born on September 7, 1936. He was named Charles Hardin Holley, after his two grandfathers Charles Drake and John Hardin Holley. Though his birth certificate carried his official given name, Mr. and Mrs. Holley decided right then that "it was too long a name for such a little boy". They decided to call him Buddy, a popular nickname for the youngest in a family, and it was by that name that he was known throughout his life.

● *Charles Hardin 'Buddy' Holley at 12 months*

[1] *The difference in spelling between the last name of Buddy Holly and that of his parents arose when the family name was misspelled on Holly's first recording contract in 1956. Holly did not bother to have the error corrected; perhaps he preferred the simpler spelling anyway, since his family name was likely to be frequently misspelled in the same accidental manner if he chose to keep the original spelling. For the sake of consistency, throughout this book Buddy's last name has been spelled "Holly" and that of his parents "Holley".*

CHAPTER TWO

GROWING
· UP IN ·
LUBBOCK

There were no musical virtuosos among Buddy Holly's kin; but as a young child, he was surrounded by a family in which—like many other families in that part of the country—practically everyone played some instrument or sang, on an amateur basis. At family get-togethers, he would have heard his mother singing duets with her twin sister, sometimes joined by Buddy's sister Pat. He would also have listened to his oldest brother Larry, who played the violin and the guitar, and to his other brother Travis, who played the guitar, accordion and piano. (Buddy's father was the only family member who didn't join in the music—"*Someone* had to listen," he would later joke.)

Even so, Buddy did not show a strong personal interest in music until he reached his teens, although his first appearance on stage was at the age of five. This was when his brothers were preparing to enter a talent show at the nearby town of County Line, with Larry playing violin and guitar and both joining on the vocal. Mrs. Holley suggested that they take Buddy along and let him sing a number, too. "You know how they felt about *that*," she recalls. "Said they didn't see why their kid brother had to tag along, and so on. But after arguing about it a while, they gave in." Mr. Holley had given Buddy a small toy violin—and greased the strings so that Buddy could play with his toy without bothering others. At the talent show, Larry and Travis played their own number, and then Buddy carried his violin onto the stage and, accompanied by his brothers, sang a song his mother had taught him called "Down the River of Memories". His brothers failed to win anything for their duet, but to their surprise and chagrin, Buddy won a five-dollar prize for his performance.

But that was an exception, and it was several years before Buddy, spurred on a little by his parents, showed any desire to sing or play an instrument. A fanciful account of the origins of Buddy's music was later offered in record company publicity write-ups, and set down in the liner notes to his first solo album:

> *Buddy's interest in music began at the age of eight, at which time he enthusiastically took up the violin. Unfortunately, his enthusiasm was not shared by those who heard his rather squeaky efforts. Soon, after he had driven everyone within earshot wild, he switched to the guitar—an instrument which proved to be a natural for him. At fifteen, Buddy began singing and accompanying himself on the guitar.*

Actually, Buddy did not play the violin or any other instrument until he was about eleven years old. At that time, his mother suggested that he take up the piano. She explains, "Larry and Travis already played a couple of instruments, and I thought it was about time Buddy learned to play something too." Mrs. Holley doesn't remember Buddy having much feeling about it one way or the other: "He was kind of quiet then—mostly kept his thoughts to himself. We asked him to try this, and so he agreed."

Buddy took lessons from a teacher connected with the Lubbock school system. Though his family did not notice any marked interest on his part, he must have applied himself quietly to the subject, or else have had a natural aptitude for it, for after just a few months his teacher reported to the Holleys that Buddy was one of her best pupils—he learned quickly, and could play some pieces by ear. But after only nine months of piano, Buddy told his parents that he wanted to stop taking lessons and, typically, he did not bother to explain why. In fact, he continued to play piano on his own throughout his life, though he never felt he played well enough to do so publicly. Even during the time he was taking lessons, his interest ran to popular rhythms— his brothers describe him playing boogie-woogie figures after his nine months

of lessons. Years later, when he was a national star, he would sit with his family and hometown friends and accompany himself while singing his new songs, or when playing some of his own favourite recordings by artists such as pianist Fats Domino.

When Buddy dropped piano, it went without saying that he was going to take up something in its place. He told his parents that he wanted to learn how to play the guitar. They arranged for him to take lessons on steel guitar but after about twenty lessons Buddy got more specific about what sort of guitar he wanted to play: "The kind Travis has"—the standard acoustic guitar. His obliging parents got him one. Buddy learned a few chords from Travis and then learned on his own. Apparently, it didn't take too long for him to become reasonably proficient; before the year was out, he was playing his guitar on the bus to school and entertaining his friends with country tunes, his favourite being Hank Williams's "Lovesick Blues".

Buddy was in the sixth grade then. In the fall of 1949, he entered Hutchinson Junior High and met another young guitarist, Bob Montgomery, who was also entering the seventh grade. The two became close friends and musical companions, practising and performing together and sharing their musical tastes, which came to be quite varied.

The foremost country singer and songwriter of the time, Hank Williams, was probably the most profound early influence on Holly. Williams achieved prominence when he joined the Louisiana Hayride, a weekly live country music show that was broadcast over KWKH, a fifty-thousand-watt Shreveport, Louisiana station, easily audible at night in Lubbock. Williams moved to the Grand Ole Opry on WSM in Nashville in 1949 and had his first major record hits the same year. He remained the most significant performer in country music until his sudden death at the age of twenty-nine on January 1, 1953.

Williams's impact on adolescent country music fans such as Holly was much greater than that of other country singers whose styles and messages were more directly oriented to adult audiences. The songs of Hank Williams carried an intense personal touch; they revealed his life through his music. Other country singers were "sincere" in their singing—they could assume a role convincingly—but Williams wasn't even assuming a role, he was living it. There was a sense of romantic legend in his hard and sad life—a life which contributed much to his music, but also seemed to lead inexorably and inevitably to his early death. Even at the peak of his career, he was still a mysterious loner, a bit of a rebel against the conventions of his field. All this made him much more a figure of interest to some adolescents than other country stars were. His reaching tenor vocal style, haunting melodies and plaintive lyrics, as well as the example of his individualistic career, all left their mark on young country performers.

When it came to performing as a team, Holly and Montgomery were more directly influenced by other country instrumental and vocal styles—especially bluegrass. Bill Monroe had established this traditional string band style in its modern form just before World War II, but it was in the late 1940's that bluegrass gained its greatest popularity among country music fans. Though most bluegrass musicians hailed from the eastern South, the style was not alien to areas like Texas where fiddle music was popular. In any case, Holly and Montgomery could listen to records played on the local country music radio shows, or to Bill Monroe and the Bluegrass Boys and Monroe "alumni" such as Lester Flatt and Earl Scruggs when they appeared on the Grand Ole Opry. The high tenor harmonies in bluegrass vocals were attractive to the

● *Buddy at 2½ with his father*

● *4 years old*

● *Buddy at 5—very much a 'Lubbock Westerner'*

● *Buddy at 7 with his cousin, Sam Modrall*

two young musicians (whose voices had not yet changed), and so too were the brilliant and exciting instrumental patterns created by the bluegrass bands. Holly in fact learned to play banjo and mandolin, though he concentrated his attention on the guitar. Holly and Montgomery were also fans of country duet teams—the Louvin Brothers and Johnnie and Jack were two favourites—whose close harmonies resembled those of the bluegrass singers though their instrumental patterns were simpler. This was the style Holly and Montgomery imitated most closely on the demonstration recordings made during their high school years which later appeared on an album, *Holly In The Hills*.

By the early 1950's, Holly and Montgomery were expanding their interests to music outside the country vein. The clear channel stations in Nashville, Shreveport and Dallas (KRLD) were bringing them live country music on the Grand Ole Opry, the Louisiana Hayride and the Big D Jamboree respectively; but the pair were also using the radio to listen to black music. At the time, rhythm & blues and blues were not being played on any local Lubbock station and there was very little contact between whites and blacks in the town. All the same, there was, even then, an audience for such music among whites in the Lubbock area. Holly, Montgomery and others with similar tastes found a more distant source for the sounds they could not hear in Lubbock—"Stan's Record Review", a radio show sponsored by Shreveport record-shop owner Stan Lewis and hosted by a disc jockey named Frank "Gatemouth" Page, was broadcast nightly at 10.30 on KWKH. Holly listened closely to the vocal and instrumental styles he heard on the radio (he and Montgomery were too poor to buy many records) and adapted them to his own playing years before the beginning of the rock 'n' roll era or the advent of Elvis Presley.

Rhythm & blues groups such as the Clovers, the Dominoes, and Hank Ballard and the Midnighters were the ones which attracted increasing attention from whites in the early 1950's; but interestingly enough, Holly and Montgomery were more interested in what was known as the "root blues", performed by figures such as Lightnin' Hopkins, Muddy Waters, Little Walter and Howlin' Wolf. At first, the two held a purist attitude towards the rhythm & blues groups, even though they still enjoyed the music. Montgomery explains: "Blues to us was Muddy Waters, Little Walter, and Lightnin' Hopkins, and we didn't really think of the Drifters or the Clovers as being *blues* singers—because they *weren't*. They were pop artists, as far as we were concerned."

Few of Holly's white contemporaries, in Lubbock or elsewhere, shared his interest in black blues styles—but among this minority were many who later became rock 'n' roll musicians. Although rhythm & blues records did not begin to attract a wider white audience until 1954 or so, musical tastes had stopped running strictly along racial lines well before then, particularly in the South. The existence of segregation did not mean that blacks and whites were ignorant of each other's musical idioms. The white musicians who were to enter the rock 'n' roll field constituted a sort of *avant-garde* among their contemporaries, taking a serious interest in black music five or ten years in advance of the popularization of rock 'n' roll. Scotty Moore, Elvis Presley's lead guitarist for many years, was as familiar with black artists such as Roy Hamilton, Howlin' Wolf, Junior Parker and Lowell Fulson as he was with country music. "I'd always enjoyed R & B," he says. "It was just something we grew up with in Tennessee." The reason why he had a country band before teaming up with Presley was simply that a white band could get more

● *Buddy at 13—about the time he made his first recordings*

● *Buddy, Larry Welborn & Bob Montgomery at KDAV in 1955*

jobs playing country music than it could playing rhythm & blues.

Ironically, Buddy and Bob, who were so ahead of the crowd in their taste for black music, were considered old-fashioned by Lubbock teenagers for their interest in bluegrass and country & western. Bob Montgomery remembers that "at that time, kids who listened to country & western much wouldn't admit it to the other kids, because it was 'hip' to like other things." A Lubbock disc jockey who was himself a teenager puts it more bluntly: "The kids would listen to *anything* else rather than listen to country & western. But before rock 'n' roll, they really didn't listen to anything at all."

As far as most of the teenagers in town were concerned, country music had little to do with them. They had reason to think so. Although postwar country songs frequently offered more graphic, realistic lyrics than the pop music of the time, country music was still directed entirely at an adult audience. Country singers sang of marriage, adultery, religious salvation, the beer and blood of honky-tonk life and other subjects without direct significance to most teenagers. The performers, too, were adults. Before the rock 'n' roll years, most country singers reached their thirties before they managed to work their way out of the provinces and gain national recognition. The same stars dominated the field from the end of World War II into the early 1950's—new, younger stars were rare, Hank Williams being a prime exception. The middle-aged singers, producers and songwriters became entrenched, aided perhaps by the disrupting effect World War II and the Korean War had on the development of younger performers. Those who were in control were satisfied with the size and the make-up of their audience, and called that time "The Golden Era of Country Music". But they failed to see the danger signals—they ignored the loss of the potential younger listeners. And they did not consider what would happen to their own field if younger stars ever broke through the traditional barriers.

Not that Holly and Montgomery had to hide their interests from their friends to avoid becoming social outcasts. Even though young people thought so little of country music then, Buddy and Bob could still entertain their peers without embarrassment. Whatever his brand of music, a musician enjoyed a high status in that society. "If you were a musician," explains one who was, "you were something special." And if you played an instrument in such a town, you grabbed every chance you got to perform for others. Holly and Montgomery started with school functions—assemblies, parents' night open houses and the like. Stage fright was not a problem for them—they already played well enough to please, and their brash personalities were not cowed by the audience they might be facing. One time, the two were invited to appear on a parents' night programme at their junior high school. No one thought to ask them what they intended to sing, and it was left up to them to introduce their song. When their turn came, they strode to the microphone and announced that they wished to dedicate their number to one of their teachers. The tune was a country novelty song made popular by the Carlisle Brothers, "Too Old to Cut the Mustard":

> . . . used to fight the girls off with a stick,
> But now they say, "He makes me sick!"
> Too old, too old,
> He's too old to cut the mustard anymore. . . .

"We were as surprised as the teachers were," says Mrs. Holley. "Oh, we were so embarrassed—we felt like sinking right into the ground. Looking back on it now, it's pretty funny, really. But we thought they would get kicked out of school or something. Nothing happened, though. But that's what they were like, you know."

Into their high school years, the pair continued to seize any opportunity to play in public. Live music was an important part of local business promotions and offered Buddy and Bob a chance to perform and be seen. When a new food market was about to open, or a car dealer made plans to expand his used-car lot, or a department store scheduled a sale, a celebration was planned to attract public attention. The word passed among the local musicians, and the eager ones sought a place on the programme—and a chance to be mentioned in the newspaper ad as the "live entertainment". Buddy and Bob played when they could, sometimes for nothing, sometimes for as much as five or ten dollars. As Montgomery puts it, "We played anywhere we could get to a microphone."

In the autumn of 1953, when Montgomery and Holly were high school juniors, they got their first chance to perform on the radio. Before that time, the existing Lubbock stations had offered "block programming"—half an hour of this, an hour of that—most of which was supplied by the national radio networks. Then, in 1953, Dave Stone, a disc jockey on station KSEL, obtained the licence for a new daytime station in Lubbock. Stone decided to devote the new station's entire airtime to country & western music. He was joined in this venture by two other KSEL announcers with a taste for country music, "Hipockets" Duncan and Ben Hall. The new station, KDAV, began operation in September 1953 and, to the best of anyone's knowledge, it was the first full-time country music station in the United States.

While on KSEL, Stone and Duncan had hosted the Saturday night "KSEL Jamboree", which had featured a bill of live local talent sometimes headed by a visiting name act or two. The Jamboree had at times attracted live audiences numbering in the thousands. The two men decided to bring the concept with them to KDAV. Since that station was limited to daylight operation, they scheduled the live show for Sunday afternoons and called it the "Sunday Party". The show went on the air a few weeks after the station began broadcasting.

KDAV had announced that anyone who wished to perform could come down to the station that Sunday. Buddy and Bob showed up, of course, along with other acts of varied ages. Besides his interest in the radio station, Hipockets Duncan was also involved in booking and promoting talent, and so was alert to any new possibilities that he came across. Holly's very first appearance on the Sunday Party caught Duncan's attention.

"I could see right away that Buddy had it," Duncan says, "a lot of grit, a lot of determination—he just had more drive than the other youngsters there. He had a lot of talent, that's true. But then, everybody has a talent of some sort or another. What Buddy had was the determination to develop that talent."

Duncan encouraged Holly, Montgomery and a younger bass player named Larry Welborn to form a trio, and the group was given a regular half-hour slot on the Sunday Party, at 2.30 P.M.—like the Grand Ole Opry, the Sunday Party was divided into thirty-minute segments hosted by a regular act. The trio's segment was named "The Buddy and Bob Show", and it was by that title that the group came to be called. Sometimes they were referred to as Buddy, Bob and Larry, but Buddy and Bob fitted the name pattern of the time set by country acts such as Flatt and Scruggs, Johnnie and Jack, and Jim and Jesse.

Most of the time they sang country duets in the harmony styles of Johnnie and Jack or the Louvin Brothers. On solo passages Bob usually sang, while Buddy played a guitar break. Occasionally, though, the trio played blues or rhythm & blues tunes, usually with Buddy performing the lead vocal. In 1954, one of Holly's favourites was the suggestive "Work With Me, Annie", a tune that was a great rhythm & blues hit for Hank Ballard and the Midnighters but which was banned from most white pop stations because of its descriptive lyrics. Apparently, no pop station in Lubbock would play the recording either; but Holly sang the song more than once on KDAV, which was proud of its status as Lubbock's first all-country station. The pattern does have a certain logic to it. Though country songs were rarely as explicit in dealing with sex as was "Work With Me, Annie", the earthiness of their lyrics might likewise have surprised pop listeners used to the bland sentimentality of Tin Pan Alley offerings. And conversely, at least some country fans, especially young adults, were interested in rhythm & blues but disliked standard white pop music. Buddy's brother Larry was that way himself. "When I was in the army," he recalls, "during World War II and right afterwards, they'd play a lot of pop music—slow ballads and syrupy-sweet songs with slick vocalists like Sinatra and Vaughn Monroe. Boy, I couldn't stand that stuff. Because I liked music with a beat—like country music and black music."

The "Buddy and Bob Show" gave the team more exposure and they continued to grab whatever jobs came along. Hipockets Duncan noticed that people were often ready to take advantage of young musicians who were so willing to perform. "There was one fellow in Lubbock," Duncan remembers, "who would throw a party and 'invite' the boys, and tell them, 'Say, bring your instruments along and join in.' Sure enough, those kids were so eager to play, they'd wind up playing all night, and that guy would have entertainment for his party without paying anything for it."

To prevent such cheating, the boys agreed to let Duncan serve as their manager. The contract was signed with the understanding that when the boys became successful enough to travel outside the west Texas area, Duncan would end his role. Both sides to the agreement were equally sure that such a provision was necessary: the word "if" wasn't part of their vocabulary.

● *Hipockets Duncan in 1978*

The boys fully expected to make a career out of music and to become stars on stage and on record. When asked, "At what age did you and Buddy decide that you wanted to be professional musicians?", Montgomery laughed and replied, "Oh, we always planned that, both of us. We never really considered anything else."

Even so, during his high school years, Buddy did prepare for a non-musical career, just in case. He took courses in printing and drafting and worked part-time during his junior and senior years at Panhandle Steel Products as part of the high school's vocational education work-study programme. His parents admit that he may have enrolled in the programme partly because it offered the chance to spend less time in classrooms. By everyone's admission, Buddy was just an average student; he was never in any academic difficulty, but he was hardly outstanding, either. He doesn't seem to have left any more of an impression on his teachers than they left on him. One teacher still at Lubbock High recalled, "I taught him once. But to be honest, it was only after the news was in the paper about his death that I remembered that he had been in my class. He was a quiet kid—wasn't any great student, but didn't cause any trouble either, you understand. So I really don't remember anything about him."

"To Buddy, school was like prison," says Mrs. Holley. "But that was the way most of the kids felt then. They still do, don't they? I never saw him study at home. Every fall I'd say to him, 'Now Buddy, this year it's going to be harder, you know—you're going to have to start bringing your books home sometimes.' And he'd make some kind of promise to do that. But he never did; and he got by all right in school, so I guess he never had to."

The description of his school activities in the high school yearbook shows that they were related to his job or to the arts. He belonged to the Vocational Industrial Club of Industrial Cooperative Training, Chapter 95, and was its vice-president his senior year. (Montgomery also belonged to the club, and held an office the same year—the pair was intact in non-musical activities too, it seemed.) Holly sang for two years in the high school's mixed *a cappella* choirs—the sophomore Choralaires, and the junior-senior Westernaires. (Holly didn't participate in the group during his senior year, probably because of his job.) He belonged also to clubs for students interested in art and in classical and semi-classical music; of course, as any high school graduate knows, membership in such clubs doesn't necessarily mean productive participation. The only academic achievement by Holly that might be mentioned is a pin he won from a Fort Worth newspaper in a journalism contest. The Holleys know almost nothing about it. Buddy came home one day, handed his mother the pin and told her to put it away somewhere, and didn't tell his parents anything else about it. They never thought to ask, and they still don't have the faintest idea what he did to win the prize.

Together, Buddy, Bob and Larry did win one school prize for their music. Lubbock High School students and teams are called the Westerners; once a year, up through the 1950's, the school held a "Westerner Round-Up Day" with appropriate dress and music. During Buddy's junior year, the trio entered the song contest at the Round-Up, performed a tune Montgomery had written called "Flower Of My Heart" and won the contest (and individual prizes of Westerner belts). It was small glory, but still, it meant something.

Music was foremost among Buddy's activities, but he exhibited related talents and interests, too. The dexterity and coordination he showed in playing musical instruments were also exercised in handicrafts, in particular leather work. He would make pocketbooks, wallets and other articles as gifts

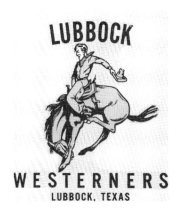

LUBBOCK

WESTERNERS
LUBBOCK, TEXAS

for his friends and family. In late 1956, when Buddy was still a struggling artist, leading country star Marty Robbins saw Buddy's leather work and asked him to make some wallets—for distribution to Robbins's fans. Buddy at first agreed, but later decided that he was too busy for the job, no matter what price he was offered. His most ambitious project was a leather cover that he made for his Gibson acoustic guitar not long after his first record release in 1956. Buddy had seen the cover Elvis Presley had on *his* guitar and decided that he had to have one for his own. (Of course, Elvis could *buy* his.) After cutting, shaping and tooling the leather, Holly traced designs on it, and coloured the leather in blue and black. At opposite ends, he inscribed the titles of the cuts on his first record ("Blue Days, Black Nights" and "Love Me") and the name of his state, putting his own name on the body of the guitar. He showed his interest in design and arrangement in other ways, too, making a few paintings and spending hours making architectural plans for hypothetical houses.

In the summer, his father would call on his manual abilities for more mundane tasks, such as helping in the residential construction business Mr. Holley and his two older sons had recently formed. "He could lay tile real well," Mr. Holley recalls with pride. "He was fast and neat—good with his hands." When Mr. Holley didn't have work for Buddy and his musical friends, Buddy's uncle, a bricklayer, could put the boys to work mixing mud and carrying bricks—no soft job, to be sure, in the west Texas summer sun.

Though Texas is even more devoted to sports than to country music, Buddy was not particularly sportsminded himself. He lacked the build for football, although he did play that and baseball informally with his friends. He sometimes went on fishing trips in the hills of New Mexico with his older brothers, and hunted rabbits in the fields around Lubbock.

Music dominated all. Besides the performances of the Buddy, Bob and Larry team, there were jam sessions with other local youths or occasional dates playing with the area's larger country bands, including one led by KDAV announcer Ben Hall. Bob Montgomery remained Buddy's closest companion. Often they would be at one or the other's house, listening to the radio or practising by themselves. But both were filled with nervous energy, an urge to be going somewhere, to be doing something. More of their time was spent "cruising", driving an old car around town and to the drive-in restaurants where Lubbock teenagers hung out, searching for action or activity in a town that offered very little. In the early 1950's, television was a novelty and a popular rage (perhaps one reason why teenagers didn't listen much to the radio); but it was a sign of Buddy's restlessness and impatience that he almost never watched TV and couldn't see why anyone would spend time sitting quietly, entranced by a tiny screen. "I'll go into somebody's house," he told his parents once, "and they'll be sitting watching TV—they don't look up or anything. And if they're eating, they practically put the food in their ears. I just can't understand it." The only time the Holleys can remember their son staying home to watch TV was once in 1956—when Elvis Presley made his first appearance on *The Ed Sullivan Show*.

Buddy's impatience marked his method of practising his music. He rarely practised songs steadily and thoroughly, at least not when he was playing alone. Sometimes when he was at home, he would mention a song or an instrumental and wonder out loud if he could play it. After playing a few bars and running through some chord progressions, he would stop and say with satisfaction, "Yup—I can play it", and go on to something else. And of couse, he *could* play it.

● *Buddy at 18, on a family trip to Colorado*

"The shy Texan" was the catch phrase applied to Buddy Holly years later, but those who knew him well have other memories. He was indeed often shy with strangers, even when he had gained national stardom. Maybe, though, there was more of caution than of shyness in his manner. His close boyhood friends remember that Buddy was brash, determined, aggressive and a bit high-tempered. There was nothing shy or reserved about the way he drove a car: he piled up a good number of tickets, mostly for speeding, and lost his licence for a time as a result. And when he had to deal with other people, he was often overbearing. He wanted everything done just right—and he was sure that he knew the right way of doing it. "He used to have his friends over to our house to play and practise," says his mother, "and one time he was really fussing and arguing with them about how something should be done. When the session was over and they all left, I said to him, 'Now Buddy, they're just kids—you can't yell at people like that, you've got to get along with them.' And he said, 'Mother, they just don't care—they don't take it seriously enough. But it's gotta be right, and so I have to get after them to play it like it should be played.'"

Larry Holley remembers that it took Buddy a while to grow up. "He was the youngest in the family, of course, and by the time he was a teenager he was the only one at home. He was pretty spoiled, to tell the truth. For a while he was awfully sassy to his parents. So one day—he was maybe seventeen or eighteen at the time—I just took him aside and told him, 'Now look, they're my parents too, and I'm not going to have you talking to them like that. I want that to stop, right now.' And after that, he really changed. Oh, he was just as determined in what he did and what he thought. He always did things like he wasn't going to have much time to do them. But he acted more respectful to his parents, and held his temper better, and was a little more considerate to other people."

Buddy was always close to his parents and to the other children in the family. Not every young musician at the time had parents who encouraged his music and even shared his tastes. "We never minded having him practising at our house with his friends," says Mrs. Holley. "He was trying to be a success, so of course we were all for him. Anyway, I liked the sort of music he was listening to. Especially those black gospel singers—some of those songs were so pretty. He liked Ray Charles a lot. He had one record by Ray Charles, 'My Bonnie'—I still have it at home—and he'd play that and sing it, and I'd join in and sing along with the girls' chorus part on it. You see, some of those parents were really down on their kids, and made fun of their music—but the music Buddy was playing wasn't so very different from what we were used to, as far as we were concerned."

It was a very religious family, and one in which the "Protestant ethic" of morality and success through hard work was stressed. The Holleys were fundamentalist Baptists. According to their faith, one is not born into the church; instead, each person must arrive at his or her own personal acceptance of Christ as Saviour. His parents say that Buddy was fourteen when he "came to know the Lord" and was baptized. Buddy's father and older brothers served as officers of the Tabernacle Baptist Church in Lubbock; their church, not just their faith, was an important part of their lives. Services at the church avoid both the emotionalism of the pentecostal sects and the formal ceremony of more organized faiths. The church music consists of simple tunes—songs, really, not hymns—meant to be sung always by the entire congregation without the leadership or domination of a choir. Sometimes the songs are written in parts, and the congregation follows the familiar phrases with

everybody singing what suits them. When you attend such a service and sing the songs, you are reminded of the background vocal patterns incorporated later into Holly's records.

His fellow musicians confirm Buddy's faith. Crickets' drummer Jerry Allison says, "Oh yeah, Buddy was very religious. I mean, when we were playing together, he didn't go to church every Sunday or preach to everybody; but I knew that he felt very deeply about his convictions."

"We were against drinking alcohol or smoking cigarettes," says Mrs. Holley, "and Buddy didn't hold to that strictly. When he started smoking, he'd do it on the sly, thinking I didn't know, and finally I said, 'If you're going to smoke, don't bother hiding it, just come out here in the living room and do it there.' He drank, but not too much; at least I can only remember him being drunk once. It was when the Hank Thompson band came to town once in 1956. Buddy had toured with them a few months before, so some of the fellows rang him up and got him out of bed and told him to come on down. And when he came back it was pretty clear that he was drunk and he just said, 'Mom, I'm sorry.' I wasn't really mad at him—I was mad at those fellows in the band."

She adds, "I didn't always see that much of Buddy—he was always on the go, running around with his friends. But when he came in at night, I'd fix up some peanut butter-and-jelly sandwiches, and we'd sit in the kitchen and talk about things—we called it our 'jam session'." Is this all just the way a mother wants to remember it? No, it doesn't seem so—Buddy's friends still describe his parents with affection, and never fail to mention the Holleys' close relationship with Buddy. (It's strange that, while rock 'n' roll is associated with adolescent rebellion in everyone's mind, many top rock 'n' roll singers received strong support from their families—for starters, take the cases of the Everly Brothers, Jerry Lee Lewis and, especially, Elvis Presley.)

But there is another side to the story, too. It's hard to pin down because

● *Buddy, Don and Bob*

it's not obvious in anything Buddy said or did but one has the impression, from following Buddy's story, that he shared the teenager's fear that his parents did not really understand his hopes and concerns. One boyhood friend of Buddy's offers this explanation:

"Buddy was never really convinced that his parents cared about what he was doing; he felt like he had to prove himself to them, over and over. And I guess that's the way he was about a lot of things. He could be confident, even arrogant; but really, he was so determined to be successful because he was so afraid of failing. He wanted to be liked—it wasn't just a matter of making a lot of money. And so every record had to be a hit, and when he had one, he had to try for another and prove himself again. He could never be sure. Funny how his songs are like that, too."

Physically as well as emotionally, Buddy matured late. His physical appearance always led people to underestimate his age. His high school senior picture makes him look closer to sixteen than to nineteen years in age. As a boy, he had been of average build, even overweight at times; but by the time he graduated high school, he was thin and lanky, though he had not yet reached his adult height and weight: an inch under six feet, and only 145 pounds. He had a boyish face and voice, and brownish-black hair that was just beginning to curl. (Holly's hair was naturally dark. Album covers that show him with light hair are either touch-ups of black-and-white shots or colour photos taken with filters.)

And of course, he wore glasses. Though boyhood pictures of Buddy indicate that his eyes were weak, his nearsightedness was not discovered until he was about fifteen, when a routine school eye exam showed that he needed glasses badly. His wearing of glasses became a bit of an issue when he began to perform as a rock 'n' roll singer before young audiences. After all, who had ever heard of a singing star with glasses? For a short period in the early part of 1956, Holly tried contact lenses, but found them uncomfortable and awkward. On one tour later that year, he did attempt to perform without glasses, but that experiment ended one night when he dropped his pick and had to get down on his hands and knees to search for it. Thereafter, Holly was willing to take off his glasses for publicity photos, but he stubbornly spurned the advice of those who suggested that he remove his glasses when he sang. He told his mother, "They just want me to fall right off the stage, that's all. If people are going to like me, they'll just have to like me with my glasses on." And by the time Holly was established, he had made his glasses such a distinctive feature that some singers even tried to look more like him by wearing glasses that they themselves didn't need.

There was school, and there was music—and there was a girl named Echo McGuire. The two had met when Buddy was about fifteen and had dated steadily through high school. Although they had planned to get married after high school, they found themselves moving in different directions as their high school days were ending. Echo respected Buddy's interest in music, but was not personally comfortable with it. She explains, "I came from a very conservative church background, and I didn't even dance. So when Buddy would play for dances, I did not go. He accepted that as the way I was, but it was a separation between us."

In the autumn of 1955, Echo began to attend a Christian college in Abilene. She and Buddy continued to see each other at weekends, but she gradually came to realize that his life as a musical performer was not one she could be happy sharing. She says, "Deep down inside, I probably knew it was the type of life I couldn't be a part of. When he started to make records and become known as a musician, I shared in his excitement, but I think I realized that this was going to come between us. I could see the direction that he was going in, and it just wasn't what I wanted for myself. It wasn't that I loved him less or fell out of love with him; I think I still loved him, but I couldn't see myself in that position."

Echo transferred to a college in Nebraska in 1956. She and Buddy continued to correspond, and he came to Nebraska once to see her; but by late 1957, she had become engaged to a classmate, whom she married in early 1958.

● *Buddy and Echo*

Country & western, western swing, bluegrass, blues, rhythm & blues, black and white gospel music—all these had a place in Buddy Holly's musical background. It may seem a long way from the Louvin Brothers or Flatt and Scruggs to the music of the Crickets; and yet, such was the music Holly was listening to and playing with Bob Montgomery, even while the two were adding rock 'n' roll tunes to their repertoire. It is reasonable then to think that even Holly's later styles were influenced by the music with which he had grown up.

As a solo vocalist, his early style owed much to both country and blues performers. Hank Williams was an important model. Williams's quavering tenor voice and his distinctive country habit of rising to a required pitch instead of sounding it cleanly had their influence on Holly's own style. Holly's famed "hiccup" is related to Williams's yodelling technique, which Holly had been fond of imitating. Of course, other country singers shared these traits, so Williams may not have been the only one to influence Holly. Hank Snow was another favourite of Holly's; the pleasant strong tone of Snow's singing, the fast tempo of his rhythmic train songs and the guitar playing featured on his recordings made Snow another considerable influence on the development of rockabilly artists. And the self-confident lyrics in such Snow songs as "I'm Moving On" and "Golden Rocket" ("You trifling women can't keep a good man down. . . .") found their echo in such Crickets classics as "That'll Be The Day" and "Think It Over."

Hank Williams and other country singers were themselves so influenced by the blues that it is hard to say just where their influence on Holly leaves off and that of black blues performers begins. Holly was quick to imitate the styles of blues and rhythm & blues singers, and did so long before he ever heard of Elvis Presley—in fact, the first time that Larry Holley heard a Presley recording, he turned to his wife and said, "You know something? That boy sounds a lot like Buddy!" According to Larry Welborn, Elvis's example did influence Holly to use a blues style on such fast-paced tunes as Presley's "That's All Right", in addition to the slow and medium-paced songs ("Work With Me, Annie" for example) which Holly was already singing in that manner.

Holly never explained what lay behind his music, or how he developed the sense of rhythm and texture that characterized it; but bluegrass undoubtedly had a lot to do with it. Although in Holly's rock 'n' roll recordings the vocal harmonization and instrumental ensemble style of bluegrass are not evident, something of the spirit of bluegrass remains. The fast, driving rhythms, offbeat chordal shifts and country-based harmonic patterns of Holly's songs (and the bar-by-bar chord changes often involved) owe much to bluegrass. Though the steady, flowing guitar effect typical of Holly's songs has no particular parallel in bluegrass, it did aim at the same feeling of unrelieved rhythmic excitement that is created in bluegrass performances.

● *Buddy (right) on stage with Ben Hall and Weldon Myrick*

KDAV announcer Ben Hall, with whose country band Holly sometimes played in those years, remembers that Holly was then already using the driving rhythm guitar sound of "Peggy Sue" when he played rhythm guitar on fast-paced bluegrass and fiddle tunes. The full texture of Holly's songs likewise has its precedent in the polyphonic effects of bluegrass music. As in bluegrass, Holly's music does not rely on sudden shifts between loud and soft passages to create excitement; instead, tension is built through the conflict of rhythmic patterns and the varying blend of voices and instruments. This is not to say that Holly was imitating bluegrass consciously; rather that some of it simply rubbed off on him.

One influence to which Holly was apparently not exposed was Mexican music. Some critics have thought that the unusual rhythmic patterns found in Holly's songs were derived from a firsthand exposure to Latin music. However, Lubbock is several hundred miles from the Mexican border, and the culture of the Hispanic community in Lubbock itself was isolated from that of the whites. Spanish instrumentals were part of the repertoire of western swing bands at the time; but while Holly's parents do recall him playing such tunes occasionally, they don't remember him showing any deep interest in Mexican music. The calypso and "chalypso" (cha-cha plus calypso) sounds which fed into the popular music world in 1956 and 1957 and the various Latin dance beats popular earlier in the decade probably had more of an influence on Holly's rhythms.

The term "Tex-Mex sound", often used to describe Holly's recordings, was therefore rather misleading. The term had been used before the rock 'n' roll era to categorize Spanish language music of the Texas-Mexico border areas. As applied to Holly's recordings, though, the abbreviation stood for Texas and New, not Old, Mexico. It was a convenient way of categorizing Holly, who didn't seem to fit the existing categories, and it did suggest that there was something distinctive to the brand of rockabilly played in the area. But although there are still country musicians there who can play excellent rock 'n' roll when given the opportunity, they do not play the same way Holly did. Holly's environment was important to the spirit and style of his music—it made a difference that he was born and raised in Lubbock, and not New York City or Pittsburgh. But even those who played with Holly and who grew up surrounded by the same musical influences are quick to give Holly the credit for the innovative quality of his music. "It just came from inside of him," they say, unable to explain its derivation otherwise. They are the first to admit that Holly's style was unique, and not just an example of a broad regional sound.

In 1954, questions about rock 'n' roll style still lay in the future. Holly, Montgomery and other young musicians played their country music and, if they had high ambitions, waited for the break that would give them a chance to become recording stars. Meanwhile, change was coming to the music industry. Before Holly had graduated from high school, a demand had been exposed, one which was gradually filled by the type of singer Buddy Holly was and the sort of music he was able to play.

INTERLUDE

MY

AUTOBIOGRAPHY

I was born one fall day, a certain particular one, because it was Sept. 7, 1936 and school for that year was starting. It also the first Monday of the month and Dollar Day, and also Labor Day, so you see, it was very eventful in more ways than one. Mr. and Mrs. L. O. Holley were the happy parents of this bouncing, baby boy, or so I'm told, because I was a little young then to be remembering it now.

My life has been what you might call an uneventful one, and it seems there is not much of interest to tell. I was born here in Lubbock and except for a year and a half when I moved to the Roosevelt School District, I have lived here all my life so far. I don't remember too much of this period of my life up until the time I started to go to school at Roscoe Wilson when I was seven. Since then I remember most of the more important events of my school days. It was during the 4th grade that I moved to Roosevelt and continued to school there until I finished the 6th grade. I then moved back to the Lubbock School Dist. and started to Junior High School at J. T. HUTCHINSON. It was great to be back among my old grade school friends and everything clicked right off. It was really a joy to me to become a westerner of Lubbock Senior High School. Little did I know what the last nine weeks of my sophomore year held in store for me. This will make the second time I have given my English theme for my test; I got kicked out of Plane Geometry class in the last week of school; I am behind with my Biology work and will probably fail every course I'm taking. At least that's the way I feel. But why quit there? I may as well go ahead and tell all. My father's out of town on a fishing trip, and he is really going to be proud of my latest accomplishments when he gets back. As of now, I have these on the list. When I was driving our pickup Sunday afternoon against a hard wind, the hood came unfastened and blew up and now it's bent so that it won't fasten down good. Before I got home, I stopped at a boy's house and he knocked a baseball into the front glass, shattering it all over me. As if that wasn't enough, I had an appointment to apply for a job with a drafting firm yesterday afternoon and when my mother came after me, she let me drive on towards town. I had bought a picture of the choir and she was looking at it. She asked where I was, and I pointed to my picture. Just as I looked back up we hit the back of a Chrysler and tore the front end of our car up. So you see, I hope my father gets to catching so many fish that he will forget to come back for a little while.

Well, that's enough of bad things for a while. I have many hobbies. Some of these are hunting, fishing, leatherwork, reading, painting, and playing western music. I have thought about making a career out of western music if I am good enough but I will just have to wait to see how that turns out. I like drafting and have thought a lot about making it my life's work, but I guess everything will just have to wait and turn out for the best.

Well, that's my life to the present date, and even though it may seem awful and full of calamities, I'd sure be in a bad shape without it.

FINIS
FINALE
In other words,
THE END

(The complete text of an assignment Holly wrote for his sophomore English course in the spring of 1953.)

CHAPTER THREE

TO NASHVILLE AND BACK

By 1954, a pop station in Lubbock, KSEL, was playing rock 'n' roll regularly, for an hour in the afternoon after school let out. The audience was largely white, but the songs played were mostly rhythm & blues recordings by black performers. Lubbock's white teenagers favoured the original versions of rock 'n' roll hits by black artists over the cover versions by whites that often captured the market for the songs elsewhere. Joe Turner, Little Richard and Fats Domino had hit records and successful personal appearances in Lubbock when their audiences were more limited nationally and their songs were providing hits for Bill Haley and Pat Boone. Black vocal groups like the Clovers and the Drifters were also early favourites in Lubbock.

None of this had the social implications one might expect. It's true enough that the popularization of rock 'n' roll and the growth of the civil rights movement both occurred in the years after 1954, and it's tempting to think of this as more than just a coincidence. But this may just be wishful thinking, or a natural inclination of those who have always supported racial equality to assume that anyone who liked black music lost his prejudices against blacks in general. That didn't happen in Lubbock, nor did it happen elsewhere. Unlike some other cities in the South, Lubbock's auditoriums did allow integrated seating, and shows by black artists were attended by large numbers of whites. But one disc jockey remembers that, even at such shows, whites usually sat together in the orchestra, while blacks watched the show from the balcony.

Music did, however, provide a way to break down the barriers, for those who wanted it to. Larry Holley recalls an incident from 1956:

"We went to get a load of tile in San Angelo (Texas), Buddy and I, in an eighteen-wheeler. There was a little coloured beer joint just outside of town. We were hungry and wanted some hamburgers, so we went in and sat down. They had a three-piece coloured band playing. Buddy went up and started talking to them, and they knew from how he talked that he was a musician. One of them said, 'Hey, man, why don't you play one!' Buddy said, 'Don't mind if I do!' He picked up that electric guitar, and as soon as he touched it, the sound was completely different. He played 'Sexy Ways', and everyone looked up. Somebody made a phone call and people started coming in, and it wasn't long until that place was packed. They wouldn't let him quit. That place was dead when we got there, but it was rocking when we left."

As more young whites turned to rock 'n' roll, the Buddy and Bob Show began to attract a larger audience. At first, the boys' listeners had been mostly young adults and older country fans; now, requests were coming from teenagers too, and Holly performed rhythm & blues tunes more frequently. The show even became a live attraction. On Sunday afternoons, the KDAV studio, located in the open country south of the settled parts of town, became a gathering place for Lubbock teenagers, who would drive down, park their cars in front of the station with radios playing, and watch the performers through the studio windows.

By 1955, Buddy was getting requests to sing the material of another white singer—Elvis Presley. Billed as "the Hillbilly Cat", Presley became popular in the South and southwest a year before the rest of the nation discovered him. Presley's first hit, "That's All Right"/"Blue Moon of Kentucky", was released on Sun Records in August 1954, and became a sizeable hit on country stations such as KDAV. Even in areas where country music was popular, Presley's audience to begin with was an adult one because few teenagers listened to the country & western stations that were playing his records.

Early in 1955, KDAV booked Elvis into the Cotton Club, Lubbock's leading country dance hall. For this appearance, Elvis got thirty-five dollars—out of which sum he had to pay his sidemen, Scotty Moore and Bill Black. Hipockets Duncan remembers that appearance:

"To a lot of the people there, Elvis was a novelty—a country singer performing black music, and doing all those motions too. And so maybe they thought it was funny at first—but if you looked at the women, well, you could see that they were eyeing Elvis and they knew what it was all about; and I think that even made some of the men a bit jealous. But you know, he was just a quiet, polite kid. A bit later, one of those Hollywood magazines paid some writer a few thousand dollars to come up with a story about Elvis's trips to Lubbock, and that writer invented a pack of lies—said Elvis had been caught making love to the police chief's daughter, and had had his Cadillac firebombed by the girl's boyfriend on his next trip to Lubbock, and so on—every bit of it complete fiction. Elvis didn't even smoke or drink when I knew him then. Between sets that night, he just sat in a corner, drinking a Coke. And Buddy and Bob were there that night—I don't know what the age limits were there, but they came down all the time to see the shows. And so they went over to talk with Elvis. Later Buddy said to me, 'You know, he's a real nice, friendly fellow'—I guess Buddy was surprised that Elvis was so normal and would talk to him so easily, because Buddy thought of Elvis as a big star and really admired him. Elvis was enough of a star to be paid to play at the grand opening of the local Pontiac dealership the next day. Buddy and his trio played there, too. And when the next KDAV Sunday Party rolled around, Buddy was singing Elvis's songs."

It was still a while before Presley's popularity among teenagers began to match his appeal to adults. He soon began performing on the Louisiana Hayride and touring on country package shows, but these attracted primarily adult audiences. On his next visit to Lubbock, Elvis appeared on a show with Ferlin Husky. Buddy, Bob and Larry opened the show, and Elvis was the next act—the first of the touring acts to come on stage, and hence the least important. Larry Welborn recalls, "After the show, we had to help Ferlin

● *One of a series of early publicity pictures*

● *Holly, Montgomery, Welborn and Curtis at Rallo Henry's store opening in Lubbock. The announcer is Hipockets Duncan*

● Buddy and Bob

Husky climb through a dressing room window to get away from all the autograph hunters. But Elvis had no trouble just walking right out of the auditorium." In fact, when the tour bus had come into town that afternoon, Montgomery and Holly had met it at the edge of town and driven Elvis off in their car for a guided tour of Lubbock; a year later, that might not have been too safe to do.

Led by Presley, the country-rock sound of Sun Records was gaining in popularity. Dave Stone and Hipockets Duncan boosted Elvis's records on their station. To them, Presley was country, and they could sense that his style was the coming thing in country music. Stone even added a daily "Rock 'n' Roll Hit Parade" to the KDAV schedule. Buddy and Bob steadily performed more rockabilly, both on their radio show and in the other engagements they played. Their calling cards now read "Buddy and Bob—Western and Bop", and it was more of the latter they were called on to play at both teen-age shows and country dates. Once, they played intermissions at the Cotton Club during an appearance by Hank Thompson and the Brazos Valley Boys. The trio played all rockabilly—apparently, the audience was ready to accept this new dance music alongside the older western swing of Hank Thompson.

Holly and Montgomery were now out of high school—and still looking for their break. During 1954 and 1955, they cut several "demo" (demonstration) records with the hope, Montgomery says, of interesting a record company in offering them a contract. They gave the demos to a local promotion man for Columbia, who promised to "send them to some people". Whether he actually did or not, nothing ever came of that. The boys were a bit ignorant about the whole process, anyway. Montgomery explains, "We thought if you got a record contract, you were automatically rich. We had seen the country artists come through in their Cadillacs with Tennessee licence plates and we thought all you had to do was to get on a record and you had it made."

Holly and Montgomery also took advantage of the contacts they had with other musicians and lined up appearances on shows outside the immediate Lubbock area. Once, they appeared on the Big D Jamboree, the live country music show broadcast over KRLD in Dallas. Sid King, a Dallas country musician about the same age as Holly who had a band called the Five Strings, recalls how that came about:

"We worked Lubbock several times, and we got to know Buddy. When we'd play the Cotton Club, he used to come up and sit in with us, him and Bob Montgomery and Larry Welborn. We were recording then for Columbia and our records were being played; and of course, he hadn't even made a record, so he thought we were big deals. A couple of times, he invited us for dinner, over to his house. Now, we were regulars on the Big D Jamboree, so one time I said, 'Well, Buddy, why don't you come on up, and we'll get you on the Jamboree.' And we must have told him what week we'd be on, 'cause we didn't play every Saturday, we only worked there once a month. Well, you couldn't say something like that to Buddy, 'cause he'd be there the next day. And that's kind of what happened—he didn't even call us or anything, he just showed up, him and the others. He came in on Friday night and he spent the night in my house. And so I introduced him to Johnny Harper, who was the talent coordinator on the Jamboree, and they put Buddy on the show that night. He did two or three songs, and I think he encored."

Larry Holley remembers that the trio sang "Down The Line" that night, and Sid King confirms that Holly performed rockabilly on the show. King says, "He was on an Elvis Presley kick—he just idolized the guy. And I

mean, he sounded exactly like him. He did the Presley things on the Jamboree."

Holly did not get paid for the appearance on the Big D Jamboree, but it was the exposure he wanted. King remembers another long trip Holly made, just for the chance to play:

"Me and my band had done a show in Wichita Falls. We told Buddy about the show, and darned if he didn't drive up there the very next week. Now, we hadn't gone back there, because the promoter was supposed to send us some money, but we never did get paid. Well, Buddy went up to the promoter, and he said, 'Sid King told me to come down, said you might use us on the show.' And the guy said, 'Well, Sid and his boys didn't show up, so we'll just let you play in their place.' And Buddy said, 'Will I make the same money they did?' And the guy said, 'Yeah.' Which was zero!"

Another time, Holly, Montgomery and Welborn drove all the way to Shreveport, Louisiana, in an unsuccessful attempt to get on the Louisiana Hayride. When Elvis Presley had come to the Cotton Club, he had told the boys that if they came on down to the Hayride, he'd be sure to get them on the show. "Of course, we had always dreamed of appearing on the Grand Ole Opry and the Louisiana Hayride," Larry Welborn recalls, "and so one weekend, we decided to take Elvis up on his offer. But there was one little thing we forgot to check out. We drove all the way to Shreveport and went to the show and told Horace Logan, the Hayride programme director, that 'Elvis sent for us.' But Elvis was out on tour that weekend. Heck, we couldn't even get in the door."

Months later, though, the dream actually came true for Buddy Holly—a record contract with one of the Nashville majors. The details of how Holly won his first recording contract are coloured by legend and obscured by the subsequent deaths of several leading figures involved.

Contrary to popular legend, it was not a show with Elvis Presley that led to Buddy Holly's first contract. According to KDAV owner Dave Stone, neither Elvis nor Colonel Tom Parker had anything to do with it. The decisive event was an appearance Holly made on a show which KDAV booked into Lubbock on October 14, 1955. Bill Haley and the Comets headlined the show; also on the bill was country artist Jimmy Rodgers Snow, Hank Snow's son. Travelling with the show was Nashville talent agent Eddie Crandall. Stone thought that putting Buddy, Bob and Larry on a bill that included both country and rock 'n' roll artists might impress upon Crandall the range of Holly's talents and possibilities. On such shows, Buddy sang some rock 'n' roll tunes solo and did country duets with Montgomery as well, so that Crandall would get to hear the variety of Holly's style. Where the story involving Presley and Parker originated is anyone's guess. Presley appeared in Lubbock the night after the Haley show, and Hipockets Duncan recalls struggling successfully to get Buddy's trio placed on the already crowded bill (which, according to a newspaper ad, included country artists Jimmy Newman, Bobby Lord, Floyd Cramer, and "sensational new star" Johnny Cash). Parker was not yet Presley's full-time manager, however, and it seems doubtful that the Colonel was in Lubbock that night. The proximity of events would explain, though, why some thought the show with Presley had been the one that brought Holly to the attention of people in Nashville.

Eddie Crandall got to see Holly perform even more just two weeks later, when Marty Robbins, whom Crandall managed, played Lubbock at the end of October. Larry Welborn remembers that the Buddy and Bob trio opened

Nashville, Tenn.
December 2,1955

Mr. Dave Stone:
Radio Station KDAV
Lubbock, Texas.

Dear Dave:

This will confirm our telephone conversation of last evening.
Sorry I called you so late last night.

Dave I'm very confident I can do something so far as getting
Buddy Holly a recording contract. It may not be a major, but
even a small one would be beneficial to someone who is trying
to get a break.And he's got to get a start somewhere. Anyway,
I'll see what I can do. ....But remember, give me exclusive
rights in his behalf for a period of time, so I can see what
I can do. Anotherwords, don't let anyone else try to negotiate
for him directly or indirectly, until I'm given a chance to see
what I can do.

Col. Parker suggested I try and help Buddy as he's pretty well
tied up....And with your friendship, I'll try my darndest to
help him.

Marty Robbins also thinks Buddy has what it takes. So, all we
can do is try....O.K.?

Please say hello to your wife and daughters.

I'll keep in touch with you as often as possible.

Always your friend,

OFFICE:
319 7th. Ave. North,   exclusive management:
Nashville, Tenn.   Marty Robbins
PHONE: 4-4762   George Morgan
                            Cowboy Copas

WESTERN UNION
TELEGRAM

3AC11 CTAQ43
CT NVAO55 N= PD=NASHVILLE TENN 3=
DAVE STONE=
  RADIO STATION KDAV LUBBOCK TEX=
HAVE BUDDY HOLLY CUT 4 ORIGINAL SONGS ON ASCETATE DONT
CHANGE HIS STYLE AT ALL GET THESE TO ME SOON AS POSSIBLE
AIR MAIL SPECIAL=
  EDDIE CRANDALL 319 7 AVE NORTH=

● *Eddie Crandall was keen to promote
Holly in Nashville*

the show and also joined Robbins and his group afterwards for an all-night jam session at the Cotton Club; Welborn believes that Crandall was there that night. Crandall was indeed impressed by what he had seen of Holly during these two visits to Lubbock. When Crandall returned to Nashville, he set out to do what he could for the young singer. On December 2, he wrote to Dave Stone:

> *Dave, I'm very confident I can do something as far as getting Buddy Holly a recording contract. It may not be a major, but even a small one would be beneficial to someone who is trying to get a break. And he's got to get a start somewhere. Anyway, I'll see what I can do. . . . Marty Robbins also thinks Buddy has what it takes. So, all we can do is try. . . . O.K.?*

The next day, Crandall sent a telegram, asking Stone to have Holly make four demos and send them to Nashville. Crandall thought to add an instruction: "Don't change his style at all."

Crandall spoke with Colonel Tom Parker, but the Colonel was busy— Parker had just become Presley's official manager, and was in the midst of negotiating the sale of Elvis's Sun contract to RCA Victor. Crandall also spoke with Jim Denny, who had for some time been a booking agent for the Grand Ole Opry and was now moving out on his own as a talent agent and a music publisher. Denny agreed that Holly had potential, and he took on the task of getting him a contract.

At the time, Decca, RCA Victor and Columbia were the three major record companies with country & western divisions in Nashville. Denny had no luck with Columbia, which was then uninterested in rockabilly, but found a more receptive listener in Paul Cohen, Nashville A & R (Artists and Repertoire) director for Decca. With RCA Victor having just signed Presley, Decca was open to the idea of giving a contract to a similar rockabilly singer.

One night in mid-January 1956, Denny called Dave Stone's home. Stone was out, and so Denny spoke to Stone's wife, Pat, about Holly's physical appearance and personal habits. Satisfied with what he was told, he asked Pat Stone to find Holly and have the singer call him; Decca was ready to offer Holly a contract.

Holly was of course elated at the offer—but there was one hitch. Decca was only interested in him, and not in the Buddy and Bob duo. When Buddy asked about bringing Montgomery to Nashville, too, Denny told him, "Well, you can bring him along if you want, but he can't sing on the records. We want one singer, not two."

The development should not have surprised Buddy. During the previous year, he had been singing more and more solo rockabilly numbers, whenever the trio performed. Still, for years, he and Bob had played together, planned together, and thought of winning a contract together. At first Buddy thought of turning down any offer which did not include Montgomery. But Montgomery soon talked him out of that; Bob argued that since a recording contract and a career in music was what they had hoped for, for so long, Buddy should seize the opportunity given him. Mrs. Holley recalls, "Bob said, 'You've got your chance—now go ahead!' And so Buddy did."

The contract offer did lead, though, to the break-up of the trio. Bob undoubtedly felt that he would now do better on his own. His voice was suited for country and not rock 'n' roll. And he did not want to be just a sideman. In the early days of the Buddy and Bob team, they had performed about three country duet tunes (on which Bob normally sang the solo passages) to every blues tune (on which Holly sang mostly solo); but now Buddy had developed into a solo artist, and Bob's role could only have been a limited one. Larry Welborn was a couple of years younger, still in school, and not ready for the travelling life of a professional musician which Holly now envisioned. Welborn went off on his own and began to play lead guitar for a young local rock 'n' roll group, the Four Teens. All three remained good friends. Montgomery did in fact go with Holly to Nashville once to watch a session, and the two later wrote several songs together; and Buddy lent his own guitar to Welborn for him to play when he was starting his new group. When the trio was dissolved, Hipockets Duncan ended his formal relationship with Holly, too. He simply called the boys together one day and tore up their contract, as he had promised to do when their activities began to expand beyond the Lubbock area.

As Buddy had never limited his playing to the appearances of the trio, but had also played gigs with several local country bands, he now drew on the area musicians he had known for some time to accompany him on his first Nashville session. On the Sunday Party and in playing with Ben Hall's band, Holly had met Sonny Curtis, a talented musician just a year or two older than Buddy. At that time, Curtis was mostly playing the fiddle, but he was also a fine guitar player, familiar with the Chet Atkins guitar style which had influenced Scotty Moore's lead guitar playing on the early Elvis Presley records. Holly was impressed with Curtis's playing; indeed, Larry Welborn says that Curtis was a more proficient guitarist than Holly at the time, and that Holly owed much of his technique, though not his "feel", to what he learned from Curtis. Holly asked Sonny to play lead guitar on the forthcoming recording session. For a bass player, Buddy turned to Don Guess, a musician of about the same age with whom Buddy had played off and on since their junior high school years.

Also part of Holly's new group was a drummer, Jerry Allison. Allison had actually joined Holly in mid 1955. The original Buddy, Bob and Larry trio of two guitars and a stand-up bass had fittingly, if inadvertently, matched the instrumental line-up of Elvis's original band. Once Presley's Sun recordings began to include drums, Holly was quick to move in the same direction.

Jerry Allison was two years younger than Buddy and still a senior at Lubbock High. The two were long-time friends, having first met when Allison's family moved to Lubbock in 1950 from nearby Plainview and Jerry entered Buddy's junior high school. Allison now had several years' experience playing drums in all sorts of dance bands—jazz, pop and country. Like Buddy, his tastes ran to rhythm & blues and rockabilly, and Allison was as ready as Holly to form a band playing their own kind of music. Holly and Allison practised together often in the winter of 1955–56—"Jerry's drum set sat in our living room for the longest time, it was almost part of the furniture," says Mrs. Holley. "Of course, they needed a place to play, so we didn't mind." Unfortunately, when Buddy went to Nashville in late January to cut his first records, Allison was unable to go along, because he was still in school.

Before going to Nashville, Holly bought some new equipment for himself and his band. During his high school years, he had bought a small amplifier and a pick-up for his Gibson and, in 1954, he had purchased an inexpensive electric guitar. Now that he was going to Nashville, he was determined to go first-class. Larry Holley recalls Buddy's reasoning:

"Buddy came to me and asked me for a loan so he could buy a new guitar and amplifiers. Well, I had my own business by then and I was doing all right and had the money, so I was glad to help him out. I asked him how much he needed, and he said a thousand dollars. I didn't mind giving him

● *Allison, Curtis & Holly in 1956*

● *Don Guess, Holly & Allison*

● *Off to Nashville—Buddy, Jerry and Bob*

Holly recording in Nashville

that much, but I wondered if it was wise to spend money that way—I think six hundred dollars went for the guitar alone. So I questioned him about it, and he said, 'No, I know what I'm doing. I'm going to be a star now, and everything I do has got to be the best, and my guitar has got to be the best.' And I gave him the money—I didn't doubt that he'd be able to pay it back eventually, when he got big. That was when he bought that Fender Stratocaster, the one he used on all his records and in his concerts." (Actually, this original Stratocaster had to be replaced in mid-1958, when it was stolen from a parked trailer while the Crickets were on tour.)

"As I remember," says Sonny Curtis, "we left for Nashville in a bit of a hurry. Buddy was driving a new 1955 Oldsmobile then; his family had traded in their old car and sort of given him this new one as a graduation present, but he was supposed to make the payments on it. So he was trying to stay one step ahead of the collection agency, and I think that's why we left so quick. There was Don Guess and Buddy and me, and we strapped Don's bass to the top of the car. It was a long trip; and on the way back we were practically broke. I remember we stopped at an aunt of Buddy's in east Texas, so we could get a decent meal."

When the Texans arrived at the Decca studio in Nashville, Holly found that although Decca was willing to let him use Curtis and Guess on the session, they did not want Holly to play his own rhythm guitar—they argued that the instrument would feed into the vocal microphone and interfere with the quality of the recording. Nor did they think that a rock 'n' roll style of drumming was necessary on the session. (According to personnel sheets for the session, studio guitarist Grady Martin and drummer Doug Kirkham joined Curtis and Guess in backing Holly on the recordings made that day.)

Buddy accepted Decca's decision. He was ready to do whatever was asked of him, and whatever it took to get started in the business. It was reasonable for him to assume that the people he was working with knew what they were doing and what was proper for his recordings. Decca was a major label, and had for years been a leader in the country field with such acts as Red Foley, Ernest Tubb and Kitty Wells. Paul Cohen had been one of the pioneer A & R men in Nashville, and Owen Bradley, Holly's producer, was a primary figure in the growth of the Nashville recording scene.

But that was just the problem. The company and the men who were in charge of Holly's first recordings were involved in country music too deeply and too successfully to cope with rock 'n' roll. Decca's one rock 'n' roll star in the 1950's was Bill Haley, and he was not connected with the Nashville office of the firm. The Johnny Burnette Trio, a classic rockabilly group whose records were issued by Decca's Coral subsidiary, were signed through the New York office, though most of their records were made at Bradley's studio in Nashville. The other country-based rock 'n' roll stars had started with Sun Records in Memphis, two hundred miles and a world away from Nashville, or with more obscure labels in Texas and Louisiana. Some, including Jerry Lee Lewis, had been turned down by the Nashville companies they had first sought out.

The world of country music offered a mixed reception to rock 'n' roll. On one side were some younger musicians like the Sun artists who considered

their music to be an extension of country music or a mixture of it with other forms—but not a wholesale abandonment of country music. On the other side, though, were the established record companies and some major artists who saw the new music as related to country music only in the way that heresy is related to orthodoxy. Certainly, part of their opposition was a matter of self-interest—they had dominated the field for some time, and new artists and independent record companies were a threat to their security and prestige. The split in Nashville lingers to this day. Some remember the late 1950's as a disastrous time for country music but, at the same time, many of those prominent today in country music came to Nashville after beginning their recording or producing careers in rock 'n' roll. I once found myself in a Nashville office with two men—one, an important producer and publisher who had been an independent rock 'n' roll producer in east Texas fifteen years before; the other, a "picker" who, when asked for his memories of rock 'n' roll, answered, "Remember it? I'm still trying to *forget* it!"

Country music fans were also split. Elvis Presley was the first centre of controversy. "Letters to the Editor" columns in country music fan magazines were filled with attacks upon, and defences of, Presley's credentials as a country singer. When someone didn't sound like a traditional country singer but sold records in country markets and was a hit with country audiences, what was he? Elvis, at least, was given a mark of approval by being invited onto the Louisiana Hayride and (grudgingly) the Grand Ole Opry; but later there were rockabilly stars who had number one hits on the country charts but were not allowed to appear on the Opry. Amid this confusion, the record companies, producers and artists attempted to come up with recordings that would sell to both country and rock 'n' roll audiences—and sometimes created tunes that were not enough of one or the other to sell in either market.

Although Holly's recordings on Decca have since been described as country & western, they were not really intended to be so at the time—at least, they were intended to appeal to rock 'n' roll audiences as well. This was 1956, not 1953; Presley was having his first million-sellers on RCA Victor, and rock 'n' roll was becoming a national phenomenon. Holly was already well familiar with the songs of Presley, Domino, Little Richard and other rock 'n' roll performers. Decca apparently wanted Holly to be a rockabilly artist along the lines of Elvis Presley—that is, such was the intent, if any attention at all was really paid to the question of Holly's potential appeal. His records received little promotion of any sort in any market.

The confusion was not eased any by the tense and uncertain atmosphere at the sessions. Nashville was a closely knit society, and teenage rockabilly musicians from West Texas were not part of it. Decca personnel were not deliberately unfriendly—after all, Holly was under contract to them and any success he gained would have been to their profit. But Holly and his friends could easily sense what the unspoken attitude was: they were inexperienced, "hick" musicians with nothing special to offer a large, old, sophisticated record company. The cultural gap could not have been much wider if the boys had gone to Los Angeles or New York to make their first recordings. Jim Denny was astonished when he discovered, shortly before the first session was about to begin, that Holly and his comrades did not belong to the musicians' union—a requirement for anyone playing on a recording session in Nashville. Holly, for his part, was young and brash and overconfident, not yet aware of the difference between having a record contract and having hit records. He rubbed some people the wrong way. At Cedarwood Music, the publishing company founded by Jim Denny, a secretary will tell you bluntly,

"All I remember about Buddy Holly is that I didn't like him."

Sonny Curtis offers his memories of those sessions:

"In Nashville, we just stayed at the motel and didn't hang around with anybody. Just sort of hung with ourselves. Or hung up at Marty Robbins's office and chased chicks. I don't think anybody there was really very interested in Buddy. I don't think they thought about him being a big star, or wanted him to go in any particular direction. They just made a contract and were going to record him. Best I remember, nobody messed with us at all, or told us how they wanted it to sound—they just turned on the mikes and let us go. They weren't really into rock 'n' roll, and they didn't know what to do—they knew it was happening, and they just wanted a rock 'n' roll artist. And they didn't have a clue as to how rock 'n' roll should sound, because everything in Nashville was still basically country—this was even before those Nashville guys got into rock 'n' roll. So they wanted a rock 'n' roll group and they left it all up to us, but we didn't know anything about how you did it, about how to make a recording."

Jerry Allison, who made it to the next session, adds, "Back on those dates, I don't even remember which guy was Paul Cohen and which guy was Owen Bradley or who the engineers were. It was like, they were biggies and we were just dips. We didn't groove with them or anything. We were sort of just afraid of them."

Owen Bradley, the producer of Holly's Nashville records, offers his explanation of what happened at Holly's sessions:

"When Paul Cohen sent Buddy over, Paul said he wanted it country—at least, that was my understanding. And it was my job to please Paul Cohen. We had been very successful with a country formula; we were all into country, and it's hard to change patterns. Buddy couldn't fit into our formula any more than we could fit into his—he was unique, and he wasn't in a pattern. It was like two people speaking different languages. Or you could say it's like comparing different flavours of ice-cream. Buddy was an unusual flavour that we just didn't understand. Our musicians were fantastic at what they were doing, but they just didn't know how to do what *he* was doing. I remember Buddy wanted the drummer to do something, and the drummer just couldn't do it. Buddy was trying to make sort of a rock 'n' roll record, and he should have had guys with a black feel—our guys had a country feel.

"He was a very nice guy, very easy to work with. I think we gave him the best shot we knew how to give him, at the time. But it just wasn't the right combination; the chemistry wasn't right. It just wasn't meant to be. We didn't understand, and he didn't know how to tell us."

Nashville didn't know what to do with Buddy Holly, and even if it had been ready to listen to Holly's own suggestions, Buddy probably could not have explained to them just what they *should* do. Whenever Holly had a clear idea of how he wanted something done, he could be very stubborn about insisting upon it. However, he had not yet arrived at his own distinctive style, nor did he understand the commercial complexities of the record industry. Playing live at West Texas dances was one thing; making a record that would catch the ears of disc jockeys and listeners was another. Besides, despite his brash exterior, Holly was self-conscious and uncomfortable in the presence of the more experienced producers and musicians. He was somewhat awed by the reputations of those with whom he worked and occasionally followed their advice too readily. For example, because singer Webb Pierce told Buddy that the way to be successful was to sing in a high voice, Holly sang above his own range on some recordings and wound up out of pitch.

Holly was allowed some leeway in the material he chose to record. Paul Cohen and Owen Bradley determined the arrangements for the sessions and decided what was to be recorded and released, but they did choose most of the songs from tunes offered to them by Holly and his group. The arrangement suited all, since Holly got to sing songs of his own choice, while Jim Denny could have the new songs published by his Cedarwood Music publishing firm. Anyway, no established songwriter would have wanted to waste songs on an unproven artist if the tunes could be saved for bigger names.

Holly was starting to write some songs himself, but for his first recordings, he turned as well to the efforts of other musicians and songwriters. When Holly got word of his record contract, he called KDAV disc jockey Ben Hall to ask him if he had a song Holly could cut on the forthcoming session. By a happy coincidence, just a couple of weeks before, Hall had written a song with Holly's style specifically in mind, hoping that Buddy would get the chance to record it. "Blue Days, Black Nights" became Holly's first recording and his first release.

Looked at in isolation, "Blue Days, Black Nights" is a good record. The arrangement is simple and uncluttered, and Holly has the vocal choruses to himself. The melody is country but with blues inflections (particularly in the refrain phrase), and is a good vehicle for the vocal slides and stops which already marked Holly's style. Still, there are flaws, especially when the record is considered in relation to the markets of the time. The recording falls into a curious grey area between older country and the developing rock 'n' roll forms. The unrestrained vocal goes beyond country standards, but the beat is not emphatic enough for rock 'n' roll. Although Don Guess's bass playing lends an emphatic rhythm to the tune, it is under-recorded by rock 'n' roll standards. The lead guitar solo by Sonny Curtis is technically perfect but lacks the drive of guitar breaks on the early Sun recordings of Elvis Presley, Carl Perkins, Roy Orbison and others. The use of echo only emphasizes the fact that this is a studio recording: the system involved a tape delay rather than a separate "live" chamber, such as that used by Sam Phillips in Memphis and on Holly's later recordings with Norman Petty in Clovis, and hence sounds more artificial. Overall, the record lacks the immediacy of Holly's later recordings. He puts feeling into the vocal but he remains remote, performing before the listener without truly communicating with him.

The flip side of the single, "Love Me", was written by Holly and Sue Parrish, another local Lubbock songwriter. It is one of Holly's less memorable recordings. With a rocking band, he could have given some excitement to the song by working the rhythms of the lyrics against those of the band; but here, he is left stranded, and there is little to the song. The recording does at least demonstrate that some of the marks of Holly's style were developed well before the Crickets' recordings that made them famous.

Two other tunes, "Don't Come Back Knockin'" and "Midnight Shift", were recorded at this same session. "Don't Come Back Knockin'" was also written by Holly and Sue Parrish. It was a stronger and less cliché-ridden effort than "Love Me", with a blues-based melody, a vocal that delivered the hurt but defiant tone of the lyrics, and a stronger accompaniment with prominent rhythm guitar playing by Grady Martin.

"Midnight Shift" was, for many years, as obscure in America as most of these Decca recordings were. In England, however, the song was released as a single in the spring of 1959 and made the top thirty. More recently, rock critics have given it much attention, one describing the recording (in particular, Holly's vocal) as "early Dylan". The song was written by Luke

● *Ben Hall's lyric sheet for 'Blue Days—Black Nights'*

McDaniel, an Alabaman, who had himself recorded as a country and rock-abilly artist for King (he later did one session as well for Sam Phillips at Sun). McDaniel wrote the song in late 1955 and took it to Nashville where he made a voice and guitar demo of it for Buddy Killen of Tree Publishing. McDaniel chose a pseudonym, "Earl Lee", for the songwriter credit. "I was under a writing contract to Acuff-Rose Publishing at the time," he explains. "And of course, they didn't handle that kind of material—they were strictly country, heartbreak country, if you know what I mean. So I used another name, and put the song into Tree Publishing." The second name on the song, "Jimmie Ainsworth", was also a pseudonym—for a friend of McDaniel's named Jimmy Rogers who did not actually participate in writing the song. "We were travelling in his automobile," says McDaniel, "so I put his name on the song."

McDaniel intended "Midnight Shift" to be done in a rockabilly style. "I started off country," recalls McDaniel, "but I was doing rock on my flip sides, even before Elvis came on—except we didn't call it rock, it was just the old-type Saturday night blues that we had been doing." The name of the woman in the song was not intentionally derived from Hank Ballard's "Annie" songs; McDaniel says, "I did not have any other song in mind at the time that I wrote 'Midnight Shift'. I was just picking up things of what women would do when they begin to slack off from a true marriage—you know, things begin to pop up in your life, and so I put them into the song."

McDaniel never met Holly; it was Killen who somehow got the song to Jim Denny. Sonny Curtis remembers Denny playing the demo for Holly at the session: "Some old boy just had his acoustic guitar and sang on the demo. It was a really good demo, and we all just loved the song."

Holly's first single was released in April 1956. Although it was not a complete flop, it didn't exactly blaze up the charts, either. A few months later, Decca estimated sales at nineteen thousand copies, but that estimate was undoubtedly optimistic. Holly was obviously straining to be positive when he wrote to a booking agent, "I have talked to some friends that were travelling up around the northeastern part of the country, and they said my record was very popular around Washington, D.C. and through Missouri." Sonny Curtis and Jerry Allison remember the thrill everyone got when they stopped at a bar on the way to Nashville for their next session and found "Blue Days, Black Nights" on the jukebox.

The uncertainty of the record's classification didn't help its success. Whatever Decca's original intention in signing Holly, his record was treated as country; *Billboard* covered it in its "Reviews of New Country & Western Records" column. The reviewer gave the single a good rating and added an offhanded sort of compliment in his comment: "Cedarwood succumbs to rock 'n' roll, too. If the public will take more than one Presley or Perkins, as it well may, Holly stands a strong chance." The record was not close enough to rock 'n' roll to be played on pop stations; programmers were unlikely to pay much attention to records which did not readily seem to fit the musical categories of their stations, especially when the artist was an unknown. Anyway, there was little or no promotion of the record, and due to the independent character of Decca's Nashville division, it is unlikely that the single was even distributed to other than country stations.

For Holly and his friends, getting out on record was quite a thrill, at least until the realization sunk in that the record was going nowhere and they were still broke. Only Ben Hall recalls Buddy ever expressing any dissatisfaction with the recording; Hall remembers that Buddy thought the absence

of Allison on the recording had weakened it considerably, and hoped to re-cut the song with Allison present before putting it on any intended album.

Twice during 1956, Holly managed to get booked on extended package tours travelling outside his native area, and thereby gained some needed experience in facing the public. In April and May, Holly and his band toured through the southeastern states on a show which included Sonny James, Faron Young, Tommy Collins and Wanda Jackson. Holly, Curtis and Guess opened each programme, doing a short set of their own tunes before stepping back to act as sidemen for the acts on the tour that lacked their own road bands.

"We were a little 'green'," Holly later wrote to a friend in a bit of under-statement. "We were pretty terrible," says Sonny Curtis more directly. "Our portion of the show was very amateurish—we couldn't get it together. We opened the show, and they'd open up the curtain and Buddy would have his back to the audience and be messing with his amp."

In the autumn, Holly made another three-week tour, accompanied this time by Curtis, Guess and Allison; this show was headed by Hank Thompson and included Cowboy Copas, Hank Locklin, Mitchell Torok, Wanda Jackson, Glen Reeves and George Jones. On such tours, Holly and his band had to vary their style of accompaniment, depending on how close the lead singer came to their own rockabilly style. At times, there was some rivalry with the more strictly country acts—especially George Jones, then just begin-ning to gain prominence in the country field, and steadfast about staying in it. Jones made no secret of his dislike for the dress and style of Holly and Glen Reeves; Curtis recalls, "Reeves was into rock 'n' roll and he wore green coats and all that—sports coats instead of cowboy boots. Turned George Jones right off." Holly's group would sometimes retaliate by break-ing into a rockabilly beat while backing up Jones. "You'd like it if you could do it," they said before one show; and so Jones went on stage that night and performed nothing but rockabilly, in fine fashion. Or so the story goes.

The tours helped Holly to polish his stage manners, and gave him and his companions a welcome taste of what it was like to be professional musi-cians. Don Guess recalls what the tours meant to him:

"On our early tours, we were wide-eyed youngsters from Lubbock and the music business was just fantastic to us. Actually, we could not really absorb what was happening to us on these tours. We had Buddy's car, and we carried the bass fiddle right on top of it—and I remember, one of those guys that was touring with us, Faron Young, we pulled into some town in Florida, and he was out in the street, and he said, 'Gee whiz, look at those hillbillies.' It sort of tickled us, and it was a compliment, too, actually."

But the first record hadn't created much of a stir, and bookings were few and far between. Hipockets Duncan had recently left KDAV and moved to Amarillo to run a club and a restaurant there. "One day," he remembers, "I got a call from Buddy—'Hipockets,' said Buddy, 'we're hungry.' Their record wasn't doing too much, and they just weren't getting bookings. So I booked him into my club, the Clover Club, for Friday nights for a teenage dance—we closed down the bar. I couldn't pay him much, but of course we had the restaurant so the boys would eat there and get a good meal. They'd come up on Friday and play and stay overnight, then go back to Lubbock. And we had maybe a thousand teenagers there on average after it got going.

"There's a lot of people think Buddy just skyrocketed to fame overnight, and that's just not true—there were plenty of hard times to go through before that. But he wouldn't let it stop him—on a number of occasions he could have said, 'Well, I quit,' because of things that happened to him. But he didn't give up; and he didn't forget other people either—he had a big heart, and he was a buddy to a lot of people. Once up at the Clover Club, a young man named Earl Sinks came in to see me, and he wanted to know if there was any chance that he could sing with Buddy's band—to get a little recognition for himself. So I went up to talk with Buddy about it, and he said, 'Tell him to come right on up, he's welcome.' So that was his attitude, even though he was still trying to make a name for himself. And by coincidence, this fellow Earl Sinks later sang lead with the Crickets on a few records after Buddy got killed."

At the Amarillo dances, Holly and his band could play rock 'n' roll exclusively. They also began to play rock 'n' roll more regularly in Lubbock on Saturday nights at a youth centre's teen dances. Before this, there had been little opportunity for Lubbock teenagers to dance to their own music. The town did not provide any place for them to use, and dancing was prohibited at rock 'n' roll concerts in the town's auditorium and coliseum.

An appearance at the Cotton Club on a show with Little Richard brought Holly and his friends their first mention in Lubbock's daily newspaper. The headline read: "Teenage 'Bop' Clubs Worry City Officials."

"Oh yeah, I remember that," says Jerry Allison. "They talked all about knife fights or something; and I think it said, 'while three young musicians frantically belaboured "Hound Dog",' I think that's how they put it, about what the band was doing." Sonny Curtis adds, "It had the kids doing the dirty bop, and it had their eyes all blacked out—I remember that. There was a picture and an article and everything."

Mrs. Holley also remembers it well: "Buddy came home one day all excited and said that the newspaper had sent a reporter down to the youth centre to do a story on Buddy and the boys. And I was sort of suspicious, wondered what they were up to. Sure enough, when the story came out, it was really slurred—they just wanted to put the boys down and play up any trouble they could find at the centre. Which wasn't fair, because it was the first place the kids had had for their own; and when Buddy was playing there, if there was any trouble, like fights or beer being brought in, he'd take charge a bit and tell the kids, 'Look, we've got to stop this or the police will be coming in here to shut us down.' Anyway, that article made me really mad, and I wrote the paper a letter. I said that they wouldn't have reported any of these things if they had happened at the country club. And I told them that Buddy and his friends were just poor boys trying to make it all on their own, doing the best they could to work their way up in the world. And that's what this country is supposed to be all about, after all. Well, they did send another reporter over to do a more factual story on Buddy, telling about his contract and all. But even when he was a big national star, the rich people here never paid any attention to him."

The rock 'n' roll Holly was playing at the time comes across best on the recordings he made with his own full band at his second Nashville session, in July 1956. Decca did not release these cuts until a year later, after Holly had left Decca and become a success with the Crickets. Holly's Nashville recordings were then rushed out in an album with the deceptive title *That'll Be The Day*—deceptive because the version of the song on the Decca album was not the hit version which had sold several million singles by the time the Decca album came out. On this album, Holly's band was labelled the Three Tunes; actually, his band had no set title at that time. On the springtime package tour, the two band members who had accompanied Holly were called

the Two Tones. Most of the time, however, when the act appeared on its own, it was just billed as "Buddy Holly". Just as Buddy and Bob had chosen their duet title after other country acts of the day, and Holly was later to use the group title of the Crickets when group titles were popular, so in 1956, when stars like Domino and Presley went by their own names, Holly's band didn't require a title.

The July session almost didn't come off. Holly drove to Nashville with Curtis, Guess and Allison, now out of school. The one item the group lacked was a bass. Guess, who had played acoustic and steel guitar before joining Buddy, had never actually bought a bass. As strapped for cash as the rest of the group, he had rented one instead from the Lubbock school system for about six dollars a year. Now it was July, the school year was over, and Guess had lost the use of the bass. Curtis and Allison recount what happened:

Curtis: I remember Owen Bradley real well 'cause he gave us a big hassle—

Allison: About getting that bass. He wanted to go waterskiing—and he gave us twenty minutes to round up the bass.

Curtis: We were gonna use somebody's bass, but when we arrived at the session, it wasn't there. It was up at WSM—Lightning Chance's bass, he's a big old bass player in Nashville. And we had to go up there real quick and get that bass. Or we weren't going to get to record that day.

Allison: Or the next day, I don't think.

Curtis: Or ever again!

The engineering on Holly's first single had at least been technically proper, even if it failed to match the earthy rock 'n' roll sound Sam Phillips was producing at Sun. By contrast, the production of the five July masters was poor by any standard. Obvious flaws in the recordings were allowed to stand, instead of being corrected in additional takes. Instruments are poorly balanced and the echo effect is extremely overemphasized. All the same, Holly's early rock 'n' roll sound still comes through better on these masters than on those cut at his other Decca sessions.

Probably the two best of the July recordings are "Ting-a-Ling" and "Rock Around With Ollie Vee". The first, written by Atlantic producer Ahmet Ertegun, had been a rhythm & blues hit for the Clovers in 1952. Holly's version is quite different from the original. At the same time as he moves the tune forward into the rock 'n' roll era, he actually gives it more of a basic blues sound than it had had on the Clovers' version. Jerry Allison comments:

"We used to sit around and listen to blues pickers like Lonnie Johnson. Like there was that song called 'Jelly Roll', and the style of guitar that Buddy played on 'That'll Be The Day'—that was the sort of guitar that that old blues picker played. So that's probably how he got that; and I think he played exactly the same lick on 'Ting-a-Ling'."

"Rock Around With Ollie Vee" was written by Sonny Curtis and features him on lead guitar. It is faster in pace and equal in excitement to "Ting-a-Ling"; Holly's vocal has the freedom and variety of his finest recordings. Allison's drumming provides the emphatic beat that is so lacking on the songs recorded with Nashville musicians. "Ollie Vee" is not far removed from the frenetic performances of "Oh Boy!" and "I'm Looking For Someone To Love", recorded by the Crickets a year later.

Somewhat similar in tempo but closer to country melodic and harmonic patterns was a song written by Holly, "I'm Changin' All Those Changes".

"Girl On My Mind" (written by Don Guess) has the slow but emphatic beat of rock 'n' roll ballads; its major flaw is Holly's strained vocal, an instance of his unwisely following the advice and example of others on how to sing. He was too ready at this point in his career to imitate Elvis Presley or Tony Williams (lead singer for the Platters) instead of adapting songs to his own style. Sonny Curtis played lead guitar on both of these tunes.

The fifth song recorded at this session had been written by Holly and Allison, with the indirect assistance of actor John Wayne. In 1956, Wayne starred in the classic Western *The Searchers*. Wayne's catch phrase throughout the picture was "That'll be the day!", which Wayne snarled in disagreeing with the opinions or threats of other characters. The saying became a byword among those who saw the film, including Holly and his friends. The day after seeing the film, Buddy and Jerry constructed a song around the phrase, a song which embodied the toughness, cynicism and bluster that Wayne had put into the line. It was the first time they had ever written a song together.

"We had been practising in my bedroom," says Allison. "Buddy said, 'Let's write a song.'

"I said, 'That'll be the day!'

"Buddy said, 'Yeah, that sounds like a good idea!'"

"That'll Be The Day" became the first hit for the Crickets on the Brunswick label in the summer of 1957; the earlier recording of it is quite different and definitely inferior. The Decca version lacks the ease and the humour of the Brunswick recording. The beat is more rigid. Holly's vocal, harsh and a bit overbearing as he compensates for the lack of background voices, is pitched too high for his own voice. His guitar solo is inadequately supported by the rest of the band, which is under-recorded. Finally, the echo effect is way overdone.

Despite the flaws, Buddy and the others were convinced from the start that they had a potential hit song in "That'll Be The Day". Others present had different opinions. Jerry Allison says, "It seems like Owen Bradley said that that was the worst song he'd ever heard." Sonny Curtis adds, "Yeah, all the engineers thought that was the worst one. But there was this one kid there, swept up the studio, I think. And we got that kid out in the alley and said, 'Hey, which one did *you* like?' and he said, 'Man, I like "That'll Be The Day"!' And we said, 'Yeah, you're so right.' I remember when it was number one in the country. Owen Bradley had a record out of 'White Silver Sands' that was number one hundred, and I went ahhh!"

Much to Holly's disappointment, Decca did not release any of the July masters, and seemed in no hurry to release anything of his again. Holly apparently thought that he could come closer to the sound Decca wanted if he did a session using all regular studio musicians. Sonny Curtis explains, "I think Holly went through a period there when he was kind of in awe of all those studio musicians. He wanted to get that type sound. I think he thought, 'Boy, if I had that really good slick band behind me, it'd really sound good'. And then after it happened, he changed his mind."

Decca agreed to cut Holly once more, and Buddy went back to Nashville in November for the Disc Jockey Festival (the ancestor of the current October DJ Convention) and for a last session with Decca.

Three songs were recorded. One was a remake of "Rock Around With Ollie Vee", done this time with a studio band whose guitars and saxophones lent the recording a Bill Haley sound. (This version of the song was released on a single the following year, but was not put on the Decca *That'll Be The Day* album.) The other two songs, released in December on Holly's second single, were both written by Don Guess. The "A" side, "Modern Don Juan", is a happy up-tempo tune along much the same lines as "Blue Days, Black Nights", but is superior to the early recording in several ways. Overall, it has a more unified sound, with repeated identifying riffs on saxophone (played by Boots Randolph) and lead guitar (Grady Martin). Holly's vocal is enthusiastic and shows a developing sense of timing. "You Are My One Desire", the slow ballad on the flip side, provides a dramatic vocal which is free of the strain shown by Holly on "Girl On My Mind". Both songs are a bit closer to rock 'n' roll than the first release had been—closer, but still not there. Compare the instrumental accompaniments on "You Are My One Desire" and "Girl On My Mind", or the two versions of "Rock Around With Ollie Vee", and it is obvious that the Decca studio musicians, for all their skill and experience, could not match the rock 'n' roll feel of Holly and his band.

The new single, released around Christmas time, followed the course of "Blue Days, Black Nights". "Modern Don Juan" received an acceptable review from *Billboard*, was treated as a strictly country & western disc, got no promotion and did not sell. By then, Decca was only going through the motions anyway, since it was about to drop Holly's contract. Like most artists signed by major record companies at the time, Holly had a five-year contract with Decca, with the company having the option each year of continuing or dropping the contract; Decca could see no reason to keep Holly on its roster.

Holly was probably just as happy to be leaving the label. There was some personal animosity involved. Holly got along well with Owen Bradley and Jim Denny, but he clashed with Paul Cohen. Cohen told Holly that the Texan didn't have the voice to be a singer and should forget about a musical career; according to Norman Petty, the producer who was to handle most of Holly's future recordings, Cohen called Holly "the biggest no-talent I have ever worked with". Producers and musicians who recorded with Holly generally describe him as easy to work with at sessions, but it all depended on who was involved—sometimes, sparks could fly. Don Guess remembers: "Buddy was very temperamental at times. He definitely wanted his own way. He did make suggestions at the sessions—he told them what he wanted and how he wanted it to sound, and sometimes they disagreed with him. Jim Denny and his wife, Dollie, had a lot to do with holding Buddy down as far as his temper was concerned in sessions."

"Holly was likely to get in a hassle with somebody," explains Jerry Allison. "He always knew just what he wanted—and if somebody didn't do it like he wanted it done, there would be a conflict. Buddy wasn't ever meek."

Now, Holly was waiting for his Decca contract to expire, but he didn't have anything better to look forward to. He had received some encouragement from artists he talked to at the November country music convention. "They told him to try again," says Mrs. Holley, "but they said he had to get out of Nashville, because they just weren't ready for him there." If he had learned anything during the course of the year, it was that the road to success for a young Texas singer did not necessarily run through Nashville.

The association with Decca was an unsuccessful and unhappy one for Holly. However, looking at it now in the light of his subsequent career, it was actually for the best that he failed with Decca. He was to have much more independence with Norman Petty and Coral/Brunswick Records than he would ever have had with the more conservative and tradition-bound Decca and its producers. Besides, the year's delay was beneficial to Holly.

Too often, a young and inexperienced artist has been pushed before the public too quickly, before he has fully developed his musical abilities or mastered the art of holding a live audience's attention and sympathy. During 1956, Holly gained some experience he badly needed in singing as a solo artist and in performing on stage before unfamiliar audiences. The year gave Holly time to play different sorts of material and blend different styles in the songs he wrote and performed. He could see now that it was one thing to sing before a small audience, and another to arrange and record a song so as to make a hit record out of it. By 1957, he had developed a more distinctive style and had started to write his own songs, instead of relying primarily on others for his material.

While Holly was maturing as a performer, he was also losing his youthful naivety about the music business. His experiences with Decca taught him much about the capricious nature of the recording industry and the people involved in it. He knew now a little better how to deal with such problems in the future. He had also matured as a person. His temper and occasional overconfidence had been cut down to a more reasonable level, but his will was unbroken. From this point on, he could direct his course more surely. Had he become a sudden star in 1956, Decca or Jim Denny could have claimed the credit for Holly's success, and he would have had little basis on which to protest the judgement of others as they charted his career. Now though, he was less likely to be trapped in such a position.

All that can be seen in retrospect. But for Buddy Holly, the late autumn of 1956 was the most discouraging time of his life. He had had his chance to become a recording star, the chance he had dreamed of through adolescence. Now, a major record company had pronounced him a failure, and he had no evidence to contradict that.

Before long, though, Holly rebounded from his discouragement. The advice of those who had told him to give up his career only caused him to try harder. Singing was his chief joy, what he most wanted to do in life. Observes one Lubbock acquaintance: "Buddy was a pretty intense person — and moody. I think his music helped him get 'up'—it was a release for him." Larry Welborn adds, "Offstage, he was quiet—not wild at all. But he was very uninhibited when he performed. He didn't worry about how he looked to an audience. Not that he didn't care, I don't mean that—what I mean is, he didn't hold anything back. And that was what made him so good."

Music was more than just a career to Buddy Holly; it was his way of proving his worth. He could not give it up yet; and he was not to be deterred by the pessimists, such as one Lubbock adult whom he overheard saying, "That Buddy Holly will never amount to anything!"

Within weeks of his last session in Nashville, Holly drove up to Clovis, New Mexico, just ninety miles from Lubbock, to see Norman Petty.

CHAPTER FOUR

THE CRICKETS

In the early years of rock 'n' roll, when major record labels were often both ignorant of the new music and reluctant to promote it, independent producers were responsible for many artistic and commercial successes. Norman Petty has come to be recognized as one of the most important of these producers, thanks to his association with Buddy Holly and with other lesser-known rock 'n' roll artists.

Petty, born in Clovis, New Mexico, in 1927, played the piano and other instruments from a young age. As a child, he was exposed to folk, country and western-swing music, and later became familiar with pop and classical instrumental music as well. During his high school years, he worked for a local radio station and gained the technical know-how which he used later in constructing his own studio and producing records. Petty married in 1948; months later, he and his wife Vi, a classically trained pianist, began to devote more of their time to music. The Norman Petty Trio was formed, with Petty as organist, Vi Petty as pianist and a friend named Jack Vaughn as guitarist. His band featured the sort of sweet instrumental mood music played at country club dances and similar affairs, with little resemblance to either rhythm & blues or country & western. Besides performing in person, the Trio began to make recordings. Their version of "Mood Indigo" was a moderate hit in 1954, while Petty's own composition, "Almost Paradise", brought him sizeable returns in 1957, both from the Trio's recording and from the writer's royalties on the very successful version by Roger Williams.

In 1955, after the success of "Mood Indigo", Petty established his own studio. His original purpose was to free his group from dependence on other studios and producers. Soon, though, he found that there was a demand in the area for a well-equipped studio. Petty had the equipment, musical training and ability, and technical competence to make good records. Before long, he found that his recording work was more than just a sideline to the Trio's activities. In addition, he established a publishing firm, Nor Va Jak Music (a title formed from the names of the Trio members: Jack Vaughn later dropped out of the picture). Petty gradually increased his activities as a publisher and producer, recording new artists, publishing their songs and selling the masters to established labels.

By 1957, Petty had connections with major music firms. His Trio was under contract to Columbia Records, and Petty was friendly with Columbia's A & R director, Mitch Miller. Petty had a tie as well with Murray Deutch at Peer-Southern Music, the firm which had published Petty's "Almost Paradise": Petty had entered into an agreement whereby Peer-Southern acted as Nor Va Jak's selling agent, giving Petty the benefit of Peer-Southern's worldwide operations. Thus, unlike many independent producers, Petty was known and respected in the New York music business, and had less difficulty than others in finding someone to listen to the masters that he had produced and wished to sell.

Aspiring musicians in the area knew about the quality of Petty's equipment and the extent of his connections. They were attracted, too, by Petty's policy on studio rates. While most studios charged by the hour, Petty instead charged a group for a session or a record, without setting time limits on the studio work involved. This policy derived from his own experience as a recording artist: a major impetus for the creation of his studio had, after all, been his desire to free his Trio from the constraints of standard studio practices. "I learned rather young," he later told an interviewer, "that creativity didn't come by the hour, so we simply expanded that idea when we started recording other people in the studio." His theory was that a group

● *Norman Petty's Recording Studio*

● *The Norman Petty Trio*

● *The control room at Norman Petty's studio with some of the equipment used in the 1950s*

would produce a better record—a record which would sell well enough to establish the song as a standard in his publishing catalogue—if it was allowed to take as long as it needed. He was willing to take a loss on the studio (usually just a paper loss, since all that was involved was his own time), in exchange for the large returns on publishing royalties for the original record and later versions of the same song.

Because of the open-ended procedures in use at Petty's studio, the record-keeping and documentation which are normally available for union-regulated studios in Nashville or New York do not exist for Holly's Clovis sessions. Consequently, there is no simple way to determine with certainty the dates when recordings were made, or the musicians who played on specific cuts. The story of the recordings must be pieced together from the accounts of the participants, whose memories are sometimes contradictory. In some cases, dated demos exist, but even these show only the date that the demo was made, not the date of the actual recording session. Nor are the release dates of singles decisive in determining the order of recordings, since the songs were sometimes chosen from a stockpile of recordings made six or nine months before. Thus, only approximate dates can be offered for some recordings, based on the varied guesses of the musicians involved.

Petty's studio had been one of the three or four studios used by Holly and his friends for cutting demo records in 1956. Petty and Holly became slightly acquainted at the time; by late 1956, Petty was aware of Holly's impending departure from Decca. When Holly came to see Petty to discuss making some professional demos, the producer told Buddy to go back to Lubbock, form a group and rehearse some songs, and then return to make the demos.

"My first impression of him," Petty later told an interviewer, "was of a person ultra-eager to succeed. He had the eagerness of someone who has something on his mind and who wants to do something about it.

"He wore a T-shirt and Levis. Really, he was unimpressive to look at, but impressive to hear. In fact, businessmen around here asked me why I was interested in a hillbilly like Holly, and I told them I thought Buddy was a diamond in the rough."

Many fans have wondered why Holly never sought out Sam Phillips at Sun Records after the year with Decca—or before that. (There have even been rumours that Holly did make records with Sun, but in fact that never happened.) One explanation is that Clovis is a lot closer to Lubbock than Memphis. Perhaps if Petty had been unable to do anything, Buddy would next have made his way to Memphis.

Larry Welborn offers a broader explanation of why this didn't happen earlier: "Buddy may have thought of going to Sun Records—I really don't know. But at least back when I was playing with him, he wouldn't have thought of going to Memphis himself to seek a contract. You see, there was this idea everyone had at that time, that you just didn't do something like that—you waited for someone to discover *you*. You just kept playing and hoped that there was someone out there in the audience noticing. Which, after all, was the way Buddy got his first contract with Decca."

By the end of 1956, Holly had the problem of putting together a new band. Don Guess had dropped out shortly after the autumn tour with Hank Thompson. The circumstances are forgotten now, but Jerry Allison thinks it had to do with Don being unable to afford his own bass. Not long after, Sonny Curtis also left the group. Allison explains:

"The reason that we changed people was usually something personal—like

Sonny didn't particularly like to play rhythm guitar, he liked to play lead guitar. So when Buddy got to wanting to play lead, Sonny said, well shoot, I don't want to play rhythm, so I just won't play those gigs."

Sonny Curtis points out another reason:

"I wasn't getting along with Holly that well—we sort of had a conflict of personality. But the main reason I quit was because we weren't making any money. So I was playing around with different people, just whoever needed a guitar picker. I got a gig with Slim Whitman, and then one with the Phillip Morris Country Music Show down in Nashville. And then I moved from there to Colorado Springs and picked in a club, and that was about the time Buddy and the Crickets made it with 'That'll Be The Day'."

As in the years before 1956, Holly's band had not been a set group. "There wasn't really any steady group," Jerry Allison explains, "it was just whatever came up and whoever was hanging around at the time and was available to play." Buddy was ready enough to practise or perform with anyone who asked him. As a result, there are dozens of people around Lubbock who claim to have played with Buddy Holly, and most of them are telling the truth. For some time in late 1956 and early 1957, though, Holly and Allison performed regularly at the Lubbock youth centre without any other accompaniment—just a solo vocal backed by an electric guitar and drums, rockabilly down to the bare essentials. Holly and Allison were good enough to pull it off, and the experience forced the two to develop the intuitive team-work that characterized their later records. Sonny Curtis recalls:

"Boy, that was some good stuff, when Allison and Holly were just picking by themselves—that really felt nice. And that's how they got to picking together so good—they simply had to fill up every hole."

"Sure made the money go farther, too," adds Allison—and that may have been one good reason why Holly and Allison didn't search immediately for another guitarist or a bass player.

By January, though, the two were looking for other musicians and vocalists to join them on the demos that they were now planning to cut at Petty's studio. One person they met was Niki Sullivan, another Lubbock resident who was a year younger than Holly. Sullivan played rhythm guitar, and had much the same musical interests as Buddy. (Strangely enough, Holly and Sullivan were third cousins, but only found this out when a number of their mutual relatives showed up for a Crickets appearance in Waco, Texas, in late 1957.)

Sullivan traces his own interest in music back to 1949, and Hank Williams's "Lovesick Blues":

"I listened to that song *all* the time. My father had a guitar around the house that I had never touched, but when that song came out I was so intrigued by it, that I asked my father how to play the guitar, and he showed me about four or five chords so I could sing and play along to 'Lovesick Blues'. And then I got involved with steel guitar, and took some lessons. My parents sent me to a steel guitar school here in Lubbock, but I detested reading music, and so I dropped out of the school and eventually drifted away from steel guitar, and went back to the rhythm guitar."

Sullivan remembers that he lost interest in music for a time in favour of golf. It was rhythm & blues and rock 'n' roll that rekindled his interest in music:

"I started listening to rhythm & blues in high school. I can remember in my junior year, the Midnighters were very popular—where I ate lunch, they had those records on the jukebox, like 'Work With Me, Annie'. And

● *A rare freeze-up in Lubbock, winter 1956, led to an accident with Jerry's car*

we listened to KWKH in Shreveport, Louisiana, and XERF in Del Rio, and by 1954 or so, there were radio shows on KSEL. And then when Elvis Presley came along, I was just awestruck by Presley. That's when I started to pick up the guitar again. And I started standing in front of a blank wall—I didn't have a mirror in my room—and I imitated Elvis Presley in my imagination, playing the guitar. I borrowed all of his Sun recordings from my friends.

"Now, Buddy was the closest thing to Elvis Presley we had. I can remember him sitting in a black car parked on the west side of the high school, playing his guitar. And he'd burn a little rubber with some of his friends, making the circle around the drive-ins. He would stop and have a Coke or a hamburger, and there would always be a crowd of people over at the car, listening to Buddy play. So then *I* started riding around with friends, and we'd go to the Village Drive-In, which was close to the Hi-D-Ho Drive-In where Buddy liked to hang out, and I'd sit out on the car and play, to get out and be seen."

Sullivan's involvement with Holly and Allison seems almost to have been a matter of accident. One day in late 1956, a mutual friend named Bobby Peeples who was on his way over to Holly's house with a tape recorder, asked Niki to come along and suggested he bring his guitar. "When we got there," says Niki, "Bobby mentioned to Buddy that I had a guitar out in the car, so Buddy said, 'Well, why don't you go ahead and bring it in,' so I did. Jerry was there, too, and we jammed around."

Sullivan kept practising with Holly and Allison, off and on. "It was sometime early in February," he recalls, "that Buddy explained to me that he wanted to try something in Clovis. I don't remember Buddy ever suggesting that we actually form a group—so much of everything was just off the cuff, just 'Let's do it'. It was just put to me that we were going to go over to Clovis and make some demos."

By this time, a pair of records recorded the previous spring at Petty's studio had become national rock 'n' roll hits. A West Texas group called the Rhythm Orchids had recorded several masters in Clovis, which they eventually sold to the newly formed Roulette Records. Roulette put out two separate records under the names of the two different vocalists in the group, and wound up with two million-selling singles—Buddy Knox's "Party Doll" and Jimmy Bowen's "I'm Sticking With You". Petty was involved in the Bowen and Knox recordings only as a producer; the deal with Roulette was made by the Rhythm Orchids on their own.

Holly and Allison did not plan to have Petty arrange a contract for them: they believed they had their own contact with Roulette Records in New York. Jerry Allison goes through the complicated story:

"Donnie Lanier was Buddy Knox's lead guitarist, and Lanier's sister worked for Roulette. She had this cousin in Lubbock named Gary Tollett, and she wanted to see if she could get him on Roulette, just like she did Buddy Knox and Jimmy Bowen and the Rhythm Orchids. So there was this other sister who lived in Lubbock named June Clark, and she called Sonny Curtis, and told him that she wanted to cut some demos with this cousin of hers, and asked, do you know a good drummer? And so Sonny said, yeah, call Jerry. So she called me and said, Sonny Curtis told me to call you; I want to cut some demos with this cousin of mine to send to New York, and do you want to play on this? And I said, yeah—but you shouldn't use Sonny, you ought to use Holly. For guitar. And so that's how that thing got started. And so Sonny and I—I mean, we live close to each other, and we're still real good old buddies, and have been for thirty years. But Buddy and I were rock, and he was kind of singing just country, and we played together some, but just had different musical tastes or whatever. So we got together to rehearse with this cousin, Gary Tollett, and to cut some demos with him. And we said, hey, if we cut some demos we could use someone to send ours to. And June Clark said, sure."

Holly and Allison did in fact play on several demos recorded by Tollett at Clovis, but none of these has ever been commercially released. One demo ("Go Boy Go"/"Gone") is dated March 1, 1957. In an interview with Bill Griggs of the Buddy Holly Memorial Society, Tollett said that this demo was sent to New York and led to a contract for Tollett on Gone Records (which was associated with Roulette), but that his only release on Gone, "Pretty Baby"/"Love Is Dynamite", was recorded in New York with staff musicians. (The record was released under the name of Gary Dale.) Another unreleased Tollett demo on which Holly played was recorded at Clovis in July 1957, and consisted of "Look to the Future" (written by Niki Sullivan) and "Honey Honey".

In return for Holly's assistance on Tollett's demos, Tollett and his wife, Ramona, readily agreed to join with Niki Sullivan in singing the background vocals on Holly's planned session. Holly still needed a bass player, and he invited his old friend Larry Welborn to play on the recording date.

Gary Tollett recalls practising several times with Holly, Allison and Sullivan, often at the home of June Clark and her husband in Lubbock: "We met and we would play for hours on end in the evenings at their house, rehearsing different numbers. That's where 'That'll Be The Day' got started, the new recording, the one that made the hit." Niki Sullivan also remembers the practising that preceded the trip to Clovis:

"We worked on 'That'll Be The Day' several times, just for me to learn the parts and everything, because I had never heard it played publicly. Everything we played was in the key of A. Buddy decided on the vocals and the arrangements—he was in total charge of everything. Whatever changes were made from the way it had sounded in Nashville, Buddy made those changes. The last night, we were over at June Clark's house; we worked on background vocals especially." Sullivan says that June Clark also came to the session and sang on the Holly recordings; however, the Tolletts and Larry Holley don't remember Clark being there, and Sullivan may be thinking instead of the sessions for Tollett's demos.

Sullivan recalls that "I'm Looking For Someone To Love" was written that last night of practice, to provide a flip side for "That'll Be The Day". It was just a few days later that the group went to Clovis for its session. Sullivan says, "I was working at the time, delivering flowers, and I called in sick so I could go up to Clovis. It seems to me we went in Buddy's car, that black and white Oldsmobile. We stopped on the way to visit someone's relatives, and then went on to the studio; we got there in the evening."

The session began on the evening of February 24, 1957 and ran into the early hours of the next morning; thus, February 25 is considered to be the official recording date for "That'll Be The Day" and "I'm Looking For Someone To Love". Each of the participants remembers the session a little differently. Larry Welborn recalls most of all the work that went into the records:

"We had worked on 'That'll Be The Day' for a long time, along with those singers. But even when we went up to Clovis, it seems to me like we spent twelve hours on it—just recording it over and over. Buddy had worked out the arrangement ahead of time—he was responsible for that. But Norman

Petty had us run through it again and again, trying to make sure it was perfect. He'd stop us when he heard a bad note, or if he thought Buddy was a bit off-key."

By contrast, Allison recalls having a relaxed attitude about it:

"We were cutting 'That'll Be The Day' just as a demo to send to New York, to see if they liked the sound of the group—not for a master record. So we just went in and set up and sort of shucked through it. I think we cut it two times. And of course, all of it at one time, voices and instruments— it was mono. So we just cut it and said, that's good enough for a demo. And we didn't try to get it perfect, because we never suspected that record would come out."

Gary Tollett offers still another point of view:

"It was a long drive over there to Clovis. We had to go after work or school. When we got there, we had to rehearse again, and we started recording about 9.00 as I recall. We worked on "I'm Looking For Someone To Love" until about midnight. For some reason, most of us thought that "I'm Looking For Someone To Love" might be the 'A' side, and we worked on that real hard. Then, after we got it done to what we thought was our best, we started working on 'That'll Be The Day'. Surprisingly enough, we didn't work nearly as hard on 'That'll Be The Day'. I recall we probably made about three or four takes of that and said that we were gonna quit, 'cause by this time it was about 2.30 or 3.00 in the morning and we all had to pile in the cars and go back to work or back to school. . . . We just had a good time, not dreaming that we would be cutting a master record. Buddy, of course, ramrodded the whole thing. It was his show and his record, and we did it his way. He was always in charge of it, and that was perfectly all right with us, we were over there to help him."

Niki Sullivan remembers most of all the good feeling that prevailed during the recording of "That'll Be The Day":

"It did take two hours, maybe three—it didn't take that long to do the actual song, but there was a little problem in setting up and getting the balance and everything right, to where it would sound like a decent demo. I was standing with the other singers, with Gary Tollett on my left, and June Clark and Ramona Tollett facing me, all singing into one microphone. I was playing rhythm guitar, but it wasn't miked, so if it had been picked up at all, it would have been through our singing mike. And I don't remember how we got in the mood, but I definitely remember it being a very fun thing, laughing and cutting up, and I know even when we were singing background, we smiled a lot."

Sometimes Holly's songs were recorded in just one or two takes, but there were times when Petty and the Crickets spent hours on a single song. The sound and "feel" of the tune were either worked out in advance by the Crickets at practice sessions back in Lubbock or quickly determined at Petty's studio by running through the new song a few times. Then, the group played the song over and over again, repeating it in almost identical fashion to make sure that the balance was right and there were no mistakes in the performance. Sometimes, in the opinion of the musicians, Petty sought to "polish" the sound of the group more than was necessary or desirable—Petty's metaphor for Holly—a diamond in the rough—might indicate how he conceived his role. But Petty disputes any impression that he imposed his standards on the groups which recorded for him:

"I don't recall anybody being forced to do anything over and over. Most of them would say, 'Well, what do you think?' They were uncertain and relied on my better judgement. If I felt that they could actually do better, we tried it, harder and longer, and they usually came out much better. But it was not at my insistence. I don't recall anything being done over and over until *I* felt that it was the best. It was usually either that mistakes were obvious, or the musicians got tired and would go back and start again. I wasn't really 'polishing' Buddy. It was the others who would have problems getting with what Buddy was trying to do. I was just paid for sessions—if a group was satisfied with two takes, 'bye', because I was paid the same whether it was an hour or just fifteen minutes."

In any event, Petty's trained ear and open-ended studio schedule prevented any obvious flaws caused by accident or haste. But the apparent spontaneity of the recordings was not just an illusion. The few songs which Holly cut in New York in 1958 with Coral music director Dick Jacobs were recorded more quickly. "On the songs I produced," says Jacobs, "we cut two or three takes at the maximum—and as far as Holly's performance went, we could have stopped after the first take."

Even if the first Clovis recordings were meant to be demos and not masters, neither Holly or Petty were likely to make much of a distinction when recording the material. They were both perfectionists in the studio, and this as much as anything explains the fruitfulness of their association: Holly had found someone willing to give the time to see things done right, and Petty had found someone worth the extra effort. The two cuts recorded that long night in Clovis were certainly among the finest to come out of Holly's sessions there.

"I'm Looking For Someone To Love" follows a twelve-bar blues pattern. However, like such other Holly recordings as "Peggy Sue" and "Oh Boy!", this tune has a bright, happy sound which makes it blues in form but something else in spirit. The lyrics are a bit autobiographical. Like the singer in the song, Holly had been "playing the field" since breaking up with his early girlfriend, Echo. Mrs. Holley reluctantly mentions:

"After Buddy and Echo split up, Buddy seemed not to care who he went with much. He just decided to get him a girl. Of course, he was starting out singing, and getting pretty popular around here by that time, so he could get a lot of girls, you know. But, I'm sorry to say, he went with quite a few that weren't just—you know, he met them at these dances and places like that, and they weren't—they didn't have too good a reputation, maybe. I wouldn't have wanted him to marry them, I know that."

The singer's confident tone does not disguise his disappointment over the turn of events. Though he says, "Well, if you're not here, baby, I don't care," the slant of the lyrics casts doubt on his proclaimed indifference:

Staying at home,
Waiting for you,
Just won't get it
'Cause you say we're through,

Well, I'm looking for someone to love,
I'm a-looking for someone to love,
Well, if you're not here,
But baby, I don't care,
'Cause I'm looking for someone to love.

Playing the field
All day long,
Since I found out
I was wronged,
   Well, I'm looking for someone to love. . . .

Caught myself
Thinking of you,
You can't love me
And another one, too,
   Well, I'm looking for someone to love. . . .

The remaining verse was just for fun—"Drunk man, street car, foot slip, there you are!" was a saying of Mrs. Holley's, and Buddy decided to put it on a record.

The whole recording is an excellent example of the Crickets' "total sound". Jerry Allison's drumming perfectly accents the melody and the vocal, while the vocal background functions as an instrument in itself. Holly takes two full instrumental choruses, after the second and third verses, playing figures that he sometimes had simply picked up from other guitarists in the rhythm & blues and country fields, but which had not yet been presented so thoroughly in rock 'n' roll recordings. His vocal has hints of the hiccuping style used more dramatically on "Peggy Sue". The catch in the voice was an effect common to many vocalists with country backgrounds—not *everyone* who sounded like Holly was imitating him—but when presented to new audiences in Holly's controlled fashion, it was a novel and attractive sound.

Like many of Holly's flip sides, and album cuts, "I'm Looking For Someone To Love" might have been a hit record on its own; but it was a definite "B" side when coupled with "That'll Be The Day". Holly's and Allison's faith paid off. With a careful arrangement, a proper balance of instrument volume levels and a natural unstrained vocal performance, the new version was free of the flaws in the earlier Decca recording. As with the flip side, the sound can be summed up as "unified". According to Norman Petty, when Buddy liked or disliked something strongly, he said it gave him "the all-overs"—an accurate term expressing the spirit and effect of his own recordings. It isn't just Holly's vocal or the melody or the lyrics or any one instrument that makes "That'll Be The Day" a success. What is most important is that all the elements mesh so perfectly—as they had not on the Decca recording. Consider just the instrumental chorus: first there are the blues runs of Holly's treble strings, falling in pitch and then returning upwards in the fourth bar to a crescendo which Allison supports with a heavy triplet rhythm on drums and cymbals; then the sound subsides for four bars while the stand-up bass, bass drum and bass guitar strings dominate the sound. And at the expected moment, Holly's treble lead guitar comes back to the fore for the perfectly timed and syncopated phrases of the last four bars. The chorus builds and captures all the excitement that is dissipated in the Decca recording.

Jerry and Buddy still had to decide what name to put on the records with which they hoped to win a new contract. It seemed at the time that the name "Buddy Holly" would, if used, get them in trouble. Although Holly's option had not been picked up by Decca, the company had not yet formally granted him his release. Besides, there was a standard provision in his contract with Decca forbidding Holly from re-recording for another label material he had already recorded for Decca, for a period of five years. This clause, of course, covered "That'll Be The Day", even though Decca had not released their master of the song and had no inclination to do so. According to Allison, Holly actually called Paul Cohen and asked permission to re-record the song, but Cohen refused. Holly and Allison were determined to make "That'll Be The Day" a hit, and were prepared to go ahead and ignore the prohibition. Obviously, though, the records could not carry Holly's name until things were straightened out. And so, the two decided to come up with a group title to disguise the personnel on the record.

There are several legends about the naming of the Crickets. One of the incorrect stories is worth telling—although it is not the true explanation for the origin of the title, the story is at least based on an actual incident. Later in the summer of 1957, while the group was recording "I'm Gonna Love You Too", Norman Petty heard the occasional chirping of a cricket on the sound returning from the echo chamber. Several takes were ruined by the cricket before all present put down their instruments and searched the chamber for the insect. When Petty and the musicians entered the room, the cricket stopped chirping, and no one could find the insect. The session was resumed, but once again, the chirping interrupted the takes. After another unsuccessful search, Petty and the boys went ahead and recorded the song a few times anyway. In playing back the tape, Petty noticed one take where the cricket only joined in at the very end of the song, chirping four times at the right tempo as the record faded away. Petty decided to leave the chirps on the record, as a sort of gimmick; and so, the legend goes, the Crickets got their name.

Actually, while the incident described did happen, the name had been chosen before then. There was nothing so dramatic about the choice. Early rock 'n' roll groups offered myriads of titles based on birds, jewels, astronomical objects and flowers; perhaps thinking of an earlier rhythm & blues group, the Spiders, the group decided to consider an insect for a name.

"We were at Jerry's house," says Niki Sullivan, "and everything we thought of had been used or didn't fit. So Jerry got an encyclopedia, and somehow we got started on insects. There was a whole page of bugs. We thought about 'grasshopper', and quickly passed that over. And we did consider the name 'Beetles', but Jerry said, 'Aw, that's just a bug you'd want to step on,' so we immediately dropped that. Then Jerry came up with the idea of the Crickets. He said, 'Well, you know, they make a happy sound, they're a happy type of insect.' I remember him saying too, 'They make music by rubbing their legs together,' and that cracked us up. So we kept going and tried some other names, but finally we settled on the Crickets. You know, though, we really weren't happy with that name. In fact, at some point, we were laughed at—might have been the Cotton Club, just after our record was released. People kidded us about the name, about how dumb it was."

The Crickets themselves developed an attachment to the name and the creature that inspired it. "We were on tour down in Corpus Christi in the autumn of 1957," says Niki, "and we got to this motel about two or three in the morning. Well, we walked into the motel room, and I had never seen so many crickets in my life. There were about fifteen million, in the beds, under the pillows, on the floor, everywhere. So we immediately closed the door and went back to the office, but they said, 'Sorry, nothing we can do about it—it's just that time of year.' And that was the only room they had. So we went back to the room, and it was Jerry who said, 'Don't kill any of the crickets! It'd be a bad omen.' So we swept the crickets out the door, or put them on a sheet and threw them outside—just anything to keep from killing them. But I know that when we finally got to bed that night, I slept with my mouth closed."

Shortly after making the first two Clovis recordings, Holly and Allison found their permanent bass player—Joe B. Mauldin, then just sixteen and still in school at Lubbock High. Joe had known Jerry in school, but not Buddy, although Buddy had unknowingly influenced Joe to become a rock 'n' roll musician.

"When I was very young," Joe B. recalls, "my mother started me taking piano lessons, and I took lessons for about six years. It was a drag the whole time because I didn't enjoy it at all. Of course, she had me studying classical music. And after I got into junior high school, I guess I was thirteen years old, I wanted to play steel guitar, so my mom bought me a steel guitar, and I took lessons for a while. And kinda faked it for a while. And I took some trumpet lessons while I was in junior high, and tried to get involved with the school band. But that never panned out either—I think I lost my trumpet or something. And then I was out of music, outside of singing at school functions and what have you. I had liked pop music more than country—Johnny Ray was my idol—when I was in grade school. And then I got interested in rhythm & blues, and I listened to Stan's Record Review—came on at 10.30 at night, and we could just barely tune it in on our car radios. But the little group of guys that I ran around with, we used to always make sure that we'd listen to Stan's Record Review.

"I had known of Buddy and seen him play when it was just Buddy, Bob and Larry. This was back before I had any conception that I might be a musician or get into the record business. And I remember one day, my mother and I were walking down the street in downtown Lubbock—this would have been in the fall of 1955—and we passed a tyre store. Buddy, Bob and Larry were doing a show there, a promotion thing for this tyre store, and were up on a big trailer truck playing. And as we walked by, my mother said, 'Look, there's Elvis Presley!' So I had to explain to Mother who it really was. So she wanted to stop and watch for a few minutes, and we did. And I guess that's what got me really interested in music. You know, seeing a hometown boy playing the kind of music that I liked myself. And I happened to think right then, 'Boy, wouldn't it be fun if I could get in his group—wish I could play an instrument good enough.'"

Not long afterwards, Joe B. met a young singer and rhythm guitarist named Terry Church (who later recorded under the name Terry Noland), and Church showed Mauldin how to play a few notes on a bass fiddle. Church and Mauldin soon joined with Larry Welborn and a drummer, Brownie Higgs, to form the Four Teens. Joe was still bass player for this group when he was approached by Allison and Holly.

"Buddy and Jerry came by one day," he recalls. "They had a job in Carlsbad, New Mexico, to play a dance, and they needed a bass player for that night, and so I accepted the job, and went to Carlsbad with them and played the dance. And on the way back, Buddy asked me if I wanted to play regular with him. And become one of the Crickets. One of the things that Buddy laid on me to play with the group, he said, 'We've cut a record called "That'll Be The Day", and it's gonna be a stone hit. And we're gonna get rich.'

"Well, I'd heard this a million times before, from all kinds of people. So I said, 'Man, what makes you think that? It's not even out yet—how do you know it's going to sell?'

"He said, 'Oh, that's all right, it'll be a hit. And we're gonna get rich.'

"And I said, 'Well, how long do you think *that's* going to take?'

"And he said, 'How long did it take Elvis?'

"So I laughed at him. But the next day, I agreed to play regular with him."

The Crickets, now a full foursome, returned to Clovis and cut two more tunes to send to Roulette—a simple rock 'n' roll ballad which Joe and the Four Teens had written called "Last Night", and a loosely paced version of "Maybe Baby", a big hit for them a year later after they revised the arrangement and recorded the song again. (The unusual, alternative version was not released at the time, but is now available on compilation albums.) They saw no point in re-recording "That'll Be The Day" or "I'm Looking For Someone To Love" just because Mauldin had joined the group on bass. As a result, Larry Welborn actually played on the Crickets' first record. "Of course, all I got back was my expenses up and back from the session, which Buddy paid," Welborn remembers with a laugh.

While waiting for a reply from Roulette, the Crickets tried to gain a spot on Arthur Godfrey's *Talent Scouts*, a nationally broadcast television showcase for amateur talent, with the idea that this would help their chances of winning a record contract. Joe B. explains, "We were thinking that this was a good chance for some network exposure, television exposure. It seemed as though anybody that was on one of those big talent shows—Arthur Godfrey or Ted Mack—they always got record deals." The Crickets drove up to Amarillo, the nearest place they could audition for the Godfrey show.

"We got on the audition," says Mauldin, "and I think we played a Little Richard song, and some of our own stuff. When we finished, the guy that was in charge of the audition said, 'Oh my gosh, what is music coming to.' So we kind of knew right away that we weren't going to get on the show."

(The Godfrey show did not exactly have its finger on the pulse of American pop music: in 1955, Elvis Presley had flunked *his* audition for *Talent Scouts*.)

Despite their contacts at Roulette, the Crickets were turned down by the record company, which apparently felt it already had what it wanted in Buddy Knox, Jimmy Bowen and Jimmie Rodgers. Roulette, Allison remembers, was more interested in the songs on the demos. "Buddy Knox and Jimmy Bowen, and I think the guitar player Donnie Lanier, were going to record the songs. Of course, we were in touch with them because of Lanier's sister. And we said, please don't record the songs, because we're trying to get a deal ourselves. So they didn't put them out."

At some point, Norman Petty became involved in trying to land the group a record contract. Holly and Allison certainly knew that Petty had contacts with Peer-Southern Music and Columbia. Petty says that his efforts were made at their request. "They asked me to take it into New York to sell," says Petty. "I didn't say, 'Well, I'll take it in for you.' They said, 'Will you take it in?'" Whether or not Petty knew of the Roulette connection, and whether he began his efforts before or after Roulette turned the group down, is disputed. The Crickets say that Petty knew that they planned to submit the record to Roulette—that was, after all, the reason for making the demos in the first place, to take advantage of their supposedly being "in" with the company. They say that Petty offered to try to place the record, even while the approach to Roulette was being made. Petty remembers it differently: "I didn't know they were even considering the Roulette angle at all. That was not my impression. Had I known they wanted to do that, I would not have taken the record. Because it's always a difficult thing to do, to have five people working on the same thing."

According to Petty, he personally took the tape of "That'll Be The Day" to New York and played it for Bob Thiele, A&R director for Coral Records, at a meeting arranged by Murray Deutch of Peer-Southern. (Coral was a subsidiary of Decca—a coincidence which Holly would later recall with some amusement: "They kicked us out the front door, and so we went in the back door.") Thiele and Deutch remember the sequence of events differently; Thiele, in fact, does not remember even meeting Petty until a trip which Thiele and Deutch made to Clovis several months later.

Deutch offers his account: "Norman sent me the tape of 'That'll Be The Day', and I went nuts about it. I don't know quite what it was, it was just my instinct—the song had an intonation I had never heard before. Now, after 'Almost Paradise', we had set up a deal whereby the publishing rights were split fifty-fifty between Peer-Southern and Nor Va Jak, and our firm acted as the administrator. So I made a deal with Petty: if I could get Holly and the Crickets a record contract, then he would give Peer-Southern fifty percent of the publishing on 'That'll Be The Day'.

"But then, I couldn't sell anybody on what I believed in. I went to Jerry Wexler at Atlantic, Mitch Miller at Columbia, Joe Carlton at RCA—everybody turned it down. So then I tried Bob Thiele at Coral. Dick Jacobs, the music director at Coral, had had a hit the year before with one of our songs, 'Petticoats of Portugal'. But Bob turned me down for two weeks. Finally, I asked him, as a favour to me, to press just a thousand copies, just so I could get the publishing rights to the song. Because I was sure it could be a hit."

Thiele's delay was actually caused by opposition within his own company. Coral had in fact been the label for which the Johnny Burnette Trio had recorded, but their releases had been commercially unsuccessful (though they are now considered classics by rockabilly fans). Whether for reasons of taste or commercial judgement, top executives were now reluctant to sign another rock 'n' roll artist. Thiele recounts:

"I liked the record from the start. I was excited about it. In those days, the A&R director got a budget from the company and could then spend the money as he wanted to—of course, if you didn't have hits, you didn't work there any more. But if you wanted to sign a new act, you had to get the approval of the top executives at Decca. At the time, Milton Rachmil was the president and Leonard Schneider the vice-president. When Murray kept on to me about the song, I went to the executives and told them I wanted to buy this master and put it out. Well, they turned me down. They felt the record was junk—they thought it was a joke. At the time, Coral was having success with artists like Lawrence Welk, the McGuire Sisters, Teresa Brewer and Steve Lawrence. Rachmil and Schneider thought 'That'll Be The Day' was so bad that it would hurt the image of Coral.

"To this day, when I believe in something and I get turned down, I fight even more. So I kept after them. Now, at the time, I had been putting out jazz on the old Brunswick label. Brunswick was the label for the people I wanted that the company *didn't* want. So I finally convinced them to let me put out 'That'll Be The Day' on Brunswick, where it wouldn't hurt Coral's image, as they saw it. I really believe they did it just to amuse me—sort of, 'Let Bob have his kicks,' you know."

On balance, the Crickets give Deutch primary credit for getting them their record contract. Niki Sullivan says, "If anybody was responsible for getting us placed, it would have to have been Murray Deutch. To us, the man was a genius." Joe Mauldin comments, "I've always felt like Murray Deutch was the one who was responsible for getting us our record deal."

The resulting arrangement left Holly contracted to an autonomous subsidiary of a major record company, with his recording activities in the hands of an independent producer. This gave him the advantages of both worlds. Major companies had advantages over independents in promotion and distribution, but were often so concerned with making records palatable to a broad audience that they diluted the style of rock 'n' roll musicians who came under their control. Independent labels were sometimes run by men closer to the artists and more attentive to new styles; but many such labels, financially weak and apt to lose good artists to the more prestigious majors, had short life-spans, regardless of their artistic success. Holly was now contracted to a major, but only indirectly, through Petty; an arrangement that gave Holly the artistic freedom of artists on independent labels.

It was just a matter of accident, not cleverness or calculation, that Holly signed with a subsidiary of the company that had held his first contract—and which had a right to prevent him from re-recording "That'll Be The Day" for anyone else (even if it had no intention of releasing the song itself). Petty, Deutch and Thiele say they did not know of the prior recording of "That'll Be The Day" at the time the Crickets were signed to Brunswick. Deutch and Thiele knew that a singer named Buddy Holly was the lead singer of the Crickets, but they did not know that Holly had previously had a contract with Decca. In the loosely knit world of Decca, Paul Cohen was not involved in the decision to sign the Crickets for Brunswick, since he was responsible solely for country music on the Decca label. He did not find out about Holly's connection with the Crickets, it seems, until after the Brunswick record was already out. It was fortunate, though, that the Crickets did land with Brunswick, and not with another company, for Decca was hardly likely to sue itself (that is, its subsidiary Brunswick) over the re-recording of "That'll Be The Day". Not that that stopped Decca from *threatening* to sue: before Decca would formally release Holly from the old contract and agree not to enforce the prohibition on re-recording material, Holly had to waive any royalties due him on sales of the version of "That'll Be The Day" which had been recorded for Decca in Nashville.

A more serious legal dispute involved the question of who was entitled to hold the copyright on the song, Nor Va Jak or Cedarwood. When Holly had first recorded the song on Decca, a contract had been prepared by Cedarwood but through an oversight on someone's part, Holly had never signed the contract. Nevertheless, when Jim Denny found out that the song had been issued on Brunswick and published by Nor Va Jak, he threatened a lawsuit. (This might have been of more interest to Paul Cohen than the academic issue of the multiple recording contracts at Decca: Paul Cohen had an unpublicized financial interest in Cedarwood.) To avoid one of the lengthy legal battles so common in the music industry, Petty flew to Nashville and worked out a settlement with Jim Denny. Nor Va Jak got the publishing rights to "That'll Be The Day", while Cedarwood was granted the rights for a future release—which turned out to be "Think It Over". Denny, of course, retained the publishing rights for the other compositions Holly had recorded in Nashville during his year on Decca.

It was always understood that Holly was the leader of the group and its principal figure (the identifying sign on Allison's drum actually read "Buddy Holly and the Crickets"). Even before "That'll Be The Day" became a hit, the decision was made to release records under Holly's own name in addition to the releases bearing the name of the Crickets. Norman Petty may have been responsible for coming up with this idea; Deutch and Thiele would certainly have been agreeable, since both saw Holly as the key figure in the group. In this way, whatever popularity the group gained could be used to the utmost: disc jockeys might not be willing to play two records by the same group at the same time, but they would play one by Buddy Holly, and one by the Crickets, if there was enough variety in the material and the group could come up with a consistent stream of good songs. Thiele got Holly a separate contract on Coral (the earlier Decca contract only affected the re-recording of material: it didn't limit Holly's freedom to sign a new personal recording contract). In the past, singers had sometimes left their own groups to seek a solo career (Thiele, for instance, was about to sign Jackie Wilson of the Dominoes to a solo contract), but this may have been the first time that an artist was to have solo releases while still recording with his group.

● *Buddy, Jerry & Joe B. commissioned these pictures which were taken at June Clark's house*

Holly, therefore, was a forerunner in this, as in so much else; a decade later, Frankie Valli of the Four Seasons successfully followed Holly's example.

Buddy was thus both an individual artist and just one member of a foursome. Even if the first role was more significant than the second, he still insisted on treating the members of his group as more than mere sidemen. He took much less than what might have been considered his fair share of the income.

"Buddy was the most giving person to the people around him that I've ever known," comments Joe Mauldin. "Other stars kept their musicians on salary but Buddy said, 'No, man—share and share alike. You're as much a part of this group as I am. If it wasn't for you guys, I couldn't perform the show that I put on.' When we started out, and it was Buddy, Jerry, Niki Sullivan, and me, Buddy wanted to split everything four ways flat—twenty-five percent for everybody. And Norman said, 'Hey, wait a minute. You're the star, they're sidemen. Put them on salary.' And Buddy said, 'No, I wouldn't do that to a dog.' You know, in so many words."

Sullivan agrees, "We divided everything equal shares, twenty-five percent apiece, the records and the touring. Buddy did insist on that. I can remember Norman saying, 'Buddy is the singer, the leader, and he's entitled to a larger share.' And Buddy at that point said, 'No, I want it equal. I'd rather have it that way.'"

Petty denies that he put things in quite this way, but his own explanation does shed light on how he viewed the contribution of the Crickets: "I suggested the four-way split on the gigs, but not on the records. I said, 'When you're on the gigs, it makes sense, you're participating equally. You're each going through the same amount of discomfort and displeasure on the road, so you should all split it. I didn't say anything about salary, or 'You're the star' but I told Buddy at the time, 'Why have a four-way split on the records, when most artists will go in and hire studio musicians and pay them scale, and that's it—the musicians don't participate in [the income from] the record.' So I said, 'You're being overly generous,' but I added, 'You boys, set up what you want, what you feel is right.'"

When Niki Sullivan left the group at the end of 1957 (by which time the success of "Peggy Sue" had made Holly well-known in his own right), the split on the income from personal appearances was changed to 50/25/25— Buddy got half, Joe and Jerry each got a quarter. On record royalties, Holly got a bigger share, about sixty-five percent. The arrangement held for all records, both the Crickets releases and the records issued under Holly's own name. In fact, Jerry and Joe were entitled to claim this share even on records they did not play on, like "Early In The Morning" and "It Doesn't Matter

Anymore". However, when the contracts were redrawn after Holly's death, they specified which songs they had not played on and refused to collect royalties on them. Mauldin explains, "I had a percentage of them, legally; but if I didn't perform on them or have anything to do with them, why should I be entitled to receive anything?"

None of those involved in the recordings intended the two streams of records, under Holly's name and that of the Crickets, to appeal to different audiences or to differ musically in some way. "When we started to record something," points out Jerry Allison, "we didn't know if it was going to be a Crickets record or a Buddy Holly record." As evidence of this, one pair of early demos tentatively coupled "Peggy Sue" and "Oh Boy!" under the Crickets label, while "Everyday" was paired with "Not Fade Away" under Buddy's name. On the eventual releases, though, "Peggy Sue"/ "Everyday" became the Holly release, and "Oh Boy!"/"Not Fade Away" the Crickets single.

However, the success of "That'll Be The Day", with its distinctive vocal accompaniment, did make it almost mandatory that Crickets releases include such backgrounds. Conversely, it was natural that recordings supposedly by a solo artist should have little or no vocal additions, and so the Buddy Holly records rarely had vocal accompaniment ("Rave On" being a notable exception).

With the exception of Sullivan's background vocals on "That'll Be The Day", "Not Fade Away" and the alternate version of "Maybe Baby", the vocal accompaniments on the Crickets records were by outside vocal groups, not by the Crickets themselves. The background vocals were usually not recorded at the same time (as they had been on "That'll Be The Day"), but were instead dubbed in later. Therefore, Petty and the Crickets could consider what was "in the can", pick the next single, and add vocals if the record was going to be released under the name of the Crickets. They may have considered whether a record would sound better with background vocals added. But Petty confirms that he and Holly were not trying to create two contrasting series. Petty says, "Every time that we would record, there would be some songs that would be conducive to just being a solo, and some that needed backing." Bob Thiele agrees that there was no attempt to appeal to two different audiences.

The vocalists who provided the backgrounds to most of the cuts on the *Chirping Crickets* album were the Picks: brothers Bill and John Pickering and a Texas Tech classmate of John's, Bob Lapham. Bill Pickering had attended high school with Petty in Clovis, and the trio worked steadily at Petty's studio during 1957. Actually, Bill Pickering had already played a role in Holly's career. In 1956, when Pickering was a disc jockey on Lubbock station KLLL, Holly stepped into the studio with a copy of "Blue Days, Black Nights", introduced himself, and asked Pickering if he would play the record on the air. Pickering listened, liked the record, and interviewed Holly on the show before playing the record. It was undoubtedly one of the first times that the record was played anywhere.

In late 1957, Petty began to use another local singing group, the Roses: Bob Linville, Ray Rush and David Bigham. This group sang on "Think It Over"/"Fool's Paradise" and "It's So Easy"/"Lonesome Tears". The Roses also accompanied Holly on some tours in mid-1958. The Picks never performed on any shows with Holly; Holly and Petty had wanted them to sing with the Crickets on Holly's second *Ed Sullivan Show* appearance, for which Holly performed "Oh Boy!", but the union dues and other costs that would have been involved precluded it.

The contracts with Coral and Brunswick called for Holly and the Crickets to receive a royalty of five percent (that is, five percent times ninety percent of the retail price of records sold). This was favourable by the standards of the time: some rock 'n' roll artists were getting just one or two percent (or, too frequently, nothing at all); three percent was considered normal. At the time the contracts arrived, the four Crickets, at Petty's suggestion, made an unusual decision: to take forty percent of their record royalties on "That'll Be The Day"—the difference between the three-percent royalty rate they had expected and the five-percent rate they actually received—and to donate that "extra" amount to their respective churches. Niki Sullivan recalls this decision:

"When the contracts were being brought out to be signed, Norman suggested, in so many words, that since God had seen fit to give us this break in show business, it would only be fitting to donate forty percent of the royalties on our first record to our own churches. We were all Baptists, I believe; Buddy and Norman were the most religious, but we all did attend church at one time or another. Since we were very happy to have what we had, we readily agreed. And it was a very well-meaning thing—there was no phoniness to it. Before we signed the contracts, we held hands in prayer. And it was a very moving moment."

While waiting for "That'll Be The Day" to be released, the Crickets recorded about fifteen songs at Petty's studio—at a time when they did not even know if their first record would have enough success to warrant a second. "Buddy just loved to record," explains Petty. Real costs were minimal. Petty was not so heavily booked that he had to turn down other business to spend so much time with the Crickets. And the Crickets were not being paid as session musicians, nor were they paying Petty for his time.

Besides recording with the Crickets, Holly also played guitar on a number of recordings made by other artists at Petty's studio during the spring of 1957. Among the local performers on whose records Holly played were Buddy Knox, Charlie Phillips, Jim Robinson, Sherry Davis, Fred Crawford and Jack Huddle. (Full details on these recordings are found in the Session file.) In most cases, the background work was fairly routine strumming on acoustic or electric guitar; they are of historic interest to the Holly collector, but don't approach the work he did on his own recordings. One record is an exception to this general statement: "Starlight", by Jack Huddle (a Lubbock TV personality). Holly's guitar work on this recording rates among his finest efforts. He takes two full solo choruses on the moderately paced rockabilly tune. The first chorus contains figures reminiscent of Scotty Moore's guitar playing on Elvis's Sun recordings, and of Donnie Lanier's playing on Buddy Knox's "Party Doll". The second chorus goes one step beyond, into the rapid strumming and syncopated beat of "Oh Boy!" and "Tell Me How", and the effect is stunning. The recording recently became available on the Charly album, *The Clovis Sessions, Volume 1*.

Most of Holly's recordings were made late at night or early in the morning, when Petty could be sure that there would be no interruptions from visitors or telephone calls. Holly himself preferred to record at night. He didn't explain his preference, but one would guess that Holly just felt more relaxed or creative at night—a common enough feeling. The sessions themselves usually had a relaxed and easy feeling to them, even though everyone involved in the recordings was completely professional when it came to the work that had to be done. Adjoining the studio itself were several smaller rooms with kitchen facilities and some beds. And so, if a session was proving difficult or Petty and the musicians were tired, they could take a break for dinner (or breakfast), and then start again. Occasionally, the Crickets would take advantage of the beds and spend two or three days at Petty's studio instead of driving back and forth between Lubbock and Clovis, a two-hundred-mile round trip.

There were three rooms to the studio itself: the control booth, the main studio, and a smaller studio with windows facing on each of the other two rooms. Sometimes, all the musicians were placed in the main studio, but often, Holly performed separately in the small room—so that Allison's loud drumming would not overwhelm Holly's singing or rhythm guitar playing. On one occasion—the recording of "Peggy Sue"—Allison played in the small room instead.

Petty used a live echo chamber to produce the effect on the records. Normally, the sound produced in the studio was fed through a speaker in an empty room above an adjoining garage, picked up by a microphone in the same room, and channelled back to the control room. This gave a much more realistic sound than the tape-delay echo method used on Holly's Nashville recordings. Petty's method of recording the string bass might be considered unusual. He placed a small microphone between the strings and the body of the bass to pick up the percussive effect of the instrument; then, other microphones were used to pick up the tones themselves. (The Fender electric bass was only introduced about 1958. Mauldin played electric bass on one tour in October 1958, but on all the other tours, and on all the records, he played stand-up bass.)

Beyond that, the quality of the recordings depended solely on Petty's equipment, his talent at placing and balancing microphones and instruments—and the talent on hand. Petty himself limits the credit due him for the success of the Crickets recordings. He has said, "Many people give me credit for creating Buddy Holly. I didn't. I exaggerated or captured the various peculiar and natural things he did."

Niki Sullivan credits Norman Petty with establishing an atmosphere at Clovis that contributed to the success of the music the Crickets produced there. He says, "The one thing Norman did for us was just to let us ramble. If there was an idea there and we had it worked out in song form, then we could go into the studio and work on it until we got it the way it sounded good to everybody. Norman just let us keep going; however long it took, it didn't make any difference. There was never any pressure at Petty's studio, and Buddy felt relaxed. Buddy felt he could do what he wanted to; we could experiment. Buddy was able to sing natural. The songs just came natural; ideas came natural. And Norman never stood in the way—he might offer a suggestion here or there, or want to add this or take away that, but he never pressured Buddy to hurry up, or to change what Buddy was trying to present."

Holly only came into his own as a songwriter at the time of these Clovis recordings. Before his association with Petty, Holly had relied on his music partners, Bob Montgomery, Sonny Curtis and Don Guess, for most of his songs. Those which he himself had written were usually heavily blues-inflected and closely related to the rockabilly sound of Elvis Presley and other Sun artists. (For example, compare Holly's "I'm Gonna Set My Foot Down" with Roy Orbison's "Ooby-Dooby".) These early songs lacked the variety of his later compositions; they were imitative, rather than novel and trendsetting, as so many of his Coral/Brunswick recordings were. Holly's new role as a songwriter was not a conscious change in policy, nor was it simply caused by the exit of the earlier songwriters from Holly's group—after all, everyone still remained friends and associated with each other in Lubbock. But as Holly matured as an artist and as a person, he was learning more about music and what went into the making of a good song, and gaining a more experienced vision of life. And he began to have more confidence in his own tastes and intuitions.

On many of Holly's songs, others are listed as co-writers—Jerry Allison sometimes, Norman Petty almost always. So before discussing how much any song reflected Holly's own thinking, the question of just who wrote what must be confronted.

Petty has said, that, usually, Holly wrote the music for a song and brought it to Clovis, where he (Petty) wrote the lyrics. In at least several instances, this is clearly untrue. It's not even necessary to rely on the Crickets' own memories to come up with evidence for this. For example, the hit version of "That'll Be The Day" lists Petty as a co-writer, even though Allison and Holly had written the song and recorded it for Decca before recording it with Petty. (In fact, on the Decca album which included the original Nashville recording, Holly and Allison were listed alone as the writers of the song.) "I'm Looking For Someone To Love" is another case. Although Petty's name is on the song, his contribution to it must have been small, since even before going to Clovis to record the song, Holly had written out the words in a notebook almost exactly as they appear on the recording. On the sheet music for the tune, an extra verse appears which was not used on the recording: "Looking for love, searching for fire, finding true love is my desire. . . ." These lines may be the basis for Petty's credit as co-writer—but the sheet music was only drawn up after Holly had recorded the song. A third instance where Petty's claim to part-authorship is apparently false is the song "Down The Line", a Buddy and Bob recording on the album *Holly In The Hills*—the pair wrote the song and were performing it before Holly had ever met Petty. Likewise, "Last Night" was part of the Four Teens' act before Mauldin joined the Crickets, and yet Petty is listed with Mauldin as co-writer of the song.

As more direct evidence, the Crickets have their own accounts of how things were done. Jerry Allison says, "I wasn't real happy about Norman putting his name on 'That'll Be The Day'. I remember him getting to see us in the control room and saying, 'O.K., now, I'm going to put my name on the record, but it won't be on the contract, or on taking the money. The reason I'm doing this is because I'm popular with the disc jockeys.' 'Almost Paradise' he had had out, and 'Mood Indigo' was a hit record for the Norman Petty Trio; and Norman said, 'We'll get more plays.' And I didn't want to do it at the time. I wasn't really thinking about the money, I was just thinking, Well, that makes it look like I wrote a third of the tune, instead of half. My ego was involved. And Buddy said, 'Man, what difference does it make—forget it.' He just didn't want to hassle him, you know. But of course, as far as money and all this, it made a lot of difference. And the idea of it all still really irritates me."

Joe Mauldin adds, "We all contributed ideas to the arrangements. I can't say any one specific person did the arrangements, but I guess Buddy and Jerry would receive more credit than I would. I didn't contribute all that much, but I did throw in a few ideas that stuck sometimes. Norman would come up with ideas when we went to Clovis; and even on some of the songs that we had written, Norman would come up with lyric changes or chord changes—you know, musical changes. And as to what he changed on which songs, I wouldn't dare try to even say, because I don't think I could remember. But I felt like it was minor. I didn't feel like it warranted equal writer's credits. But that was one of Norman's big ideas. He said, 'I'll just take a manager's fee of ten percent, but let's put my name on the songs, because the jocks know me and they'll see my name, and that'll get you a few plays, and help the records a little bit.' And we said yeah. And then somehow or another, just before it came time for money, there was a little disagreement or argument, and Norman would say, 'Well, we'll just split the money like the contracts read.' And he had an equal share on all the contracts. So, you know, what could we do?"

Niki Sullivan also minimizes Petty's songwriting role. "I really don't mean to put Norman down," he says, "but I honestly do not remember Norman making any serious changes that even stick out in my mind. I cannot remember any songs that Norman definitely had a hand in. Norman did contribute by altering what we had said—you know, the grammar, he might have changed a 'but' to an 'or', or what have you. And he did write out the sheet music on the songs, but that's not co-authoring. There were times when Norman felt he should have a share of the songs, and I think all of us readily agreed. We weren't going to argue. It wasn't important then, because we didn't even have a hit record at that point. We didn't know what the hell we were doing. We didn't care."

Corroborating evidence is furnished by other songwriters whose tunes were published by Nor Va Jak. Bill Tilghman and Sonny West wrote two of Holly's biggest hits, "Oh Boy!" and "Rave On". Tilghman says that he wrote the words and West the music to those songs; they are still writing songs today, in the same fashion. Petty's name is also on both "Oh Boy!" and "Rave On", but Tilghman says flatly that Petty did not have any role in writing the songs.

Petty maintains that he only received credit for those songs to which he actually contributed. He says, "That can be backed up by people who were in here before and afterwards. If I made a major change, my name went on the song; if I didn't, if I just changed a word, I didn't put my name on the song." As for "That'll Be The Day", Petty says he put his name on the song at Murray Deutch's suggestion, as compensation for the legal and personal expenses Petty incurred in settling the dispute with Cedarwood over the copyright to the song. And it was Bob Montgomery's idea, says Petty, that Petty put his name on "Down The Line", "for doing what we were doing—to put the thing out [on *Holly In The Hills*]."

Murray Deutch categorically denies that he suggested that Petty's name be put on "That'll Be The Day". "That is not true at all, whatsoever," he states emphatically. "Never, in thirty years in the business, did I ever suggest anything like that to anybody."

It was a common practice in 1950's rock 'n' roll for songwriting credits to reflect business arrangements as much as artistic reality. Most notably, Elvis Presley was often given co-writer credit in return for agreeing to record a song. From the actual writer's point of view, being left with fifty percent of a million-seller was a lot better than owning one hundred percent of an unrecorded song. For many of the artists who worked at Petty's studio, giving up a portion of the songwriting credits seemed a minor price to pay for the opportunity to record there and gain the benefit of Petty's know-how. It is conceivable (though I personally consider it unlikely) that Petty struck such a deal with Holly privately, with the other members of the group unaware of it. One other artist who recorded with Petty, Jim Robinson, once described to an interviewer the rationale Petty used with him:

"There wasn't that much money available then, there still isn't, but Petty would make a deal. We'd go up there and record and he wouldn't charge us any money for the studio use. He more or less would say, 'O.K., I'm going to put out my time and effort, and we'll split this thing down the middle,' which was a very good situation. He got a lot of boys started that way. I know he did. You know, if I wrote a song, he'd look it over and maybe change a couple of words, and I'd have to put Petty's name on it. Well, that was all right too, it got my name exposed and helped get my foot in the door."

Mr. and Mrs. Holley say that when Buddy wrote a song, he usually worked out the tune first with a conception of the lyrics in mind. Though the lyrics might not yet be fully written, the theme and mood of the words affected the music. This is only observation, since Buddy never explained in that fashion just how he went about writing a song. Mr. Holley has offered this memory of Buddy's manner of songwriting:

"Buddy was a peculiar-type songwriter. He'd leave home in the evening, after we'd have our evening meal, and be gone for an hour, or two or three hours. Then he'd come back, go straight to his room, pick up his guitar, and start to sing it—something he had been thinking about while he was out in the car, by himself."

Though Buddy usually had the original idea for the melody and the themes of the lyrics, the songs were often finished in the company of the other Crickets. Niki remembers, "Buddy was the major contributor or the origin-ator of the idea of the song. We would all contribute, but it was Buddy who was the basic creator. We did pay attention to the lyrics. Rhyme was not our main concern—meaning was. The rhyming would come one way or the other. I think Buddy taught us that, by taking an idea and just writing a story around it."

To add to the confusion over the authorship of the songs, the persons publicly credited with writing a specific song were not always those who had contributed to it. Joe says he helped write "Maybe Baby", and Jerry wrote a lot of "Not Fade Away", but their names aren't on those songs. Allison remembers that he wrote the bridge in "I'm Gonna Love You Too" ("After all, another fella took ya. . . ."), and that the rest of the song was written entirely by Buddy—and yet, the listed writers of the song are Sullivan, Mauldin and Petty.

At the time, it made little difference to the Crickets which of their names went on what. Joe B. explains, "Norman said, 'We'll spread it around, and that way everybody will get a little publicity.' And we were all just having such a good time and never paid much attention. We'd say, 'Well, let's put so-and-so's name on that one.' And I don't think Buddy cared that he might be giving away money this way. I don't think money was that big an interest to him. If it had been, things wouldn't have gotten as screwed up as they did. We didn't have a lawyer—we just did everything on a trust in each other."

From all that has been said, by the Crickets and others, my own conclusion is that Holly was primarily responsible for composing the songs he recorded at Clovis, with the exception of those brought to him by outside writers (such as "Oh Boy!" and "Rave On"). So, I have taken the songs to reflect his personality and outlook, while recognizing that others did make some contributions to the reshaping of the songs.

The next two tunes that the Crickets recorded were "Words of Love" and

"Mailman, Bring Me No More Blues", which became the A and B sides of Holly's first solo single on Coral, released in June 1957.

"Words of Love" did not sell well as a single. It was, perhaps, too unusual and distinctive to have been a commercial success at the time. No one can really say for sure, however, because Holly's rendition of the song never had a full opportunity to find its market. Shortly before Holly's single was issued, the Diamonds, who had just had a national hit with "Little Darling", issued a cover version of "Words of Love" and it became a moderate success for them. The incident demonstrated the vagaries of the recording industry. By copyright law, anyone can record a published song simply by paying the royalties established by law. Hence, the publisher makes money no matter which rendition of the song sells, and it is to his advantage to push the song to numerous artists. Someone at Peer-Southern Music (perhaps without Deutch's knowledge) pushed "Words of Love" to the Diamonds, playing for them a simple demo of the song that Holly had sent to Peer-Southern Music. Before Holly knew what had happened, the Diamonds' version was out. After that, there was nothing to do but to be more careful with demos in the future.

"Words of Love" was Holly's first experience with overdubbing. Although multi-track recording machines were not in use then, it was possible to add voices or instruments to a tape by playing the tape through again while performing new "live" sounds, and recording everything together on a second machine. Fidelity suffered any time this was done, since the final tape was a generation removed from the first recording. Of course, the entire procedure was itself more difficult than it is now with multi-track machines, which permit instruments to be recorded at different times and which allow more leeway in balancing and mixing the sounds. Despite the obstacles, Holly made such dubbed recordings frequently, often first singing and playing rhythm guitar, and then adding lead guitar and occasionally singing in duet with himself through dubbing.

It was Holly's idea to use overdubbing on "Words of Love". Jerry Allison says, "Buddy had two guitar parts worked out, that he wanted to play, before we even started to record that. I don't know just how he got the idea, but he planned to do it that way. It wasn't like he went over to the studio and somebody said, 'Hey, why don't you do this?' Because he had it figured out before." In Norman Petty, Buddy had found a producer who was willing to spend the time on such experiments.

"Words of Love" was recorded one night in April 1957. Holly, Petty and the Crickets spent at least six hours on the tune, working out the overdubbing by a process of trial and error, and trying to achieve just the balance and sound Holly wanted. On the final master, as far as the ear can tell, drums, bass, rhythm guitar (played by Holly) and one vocal were recorded first; Holly then added the lead guitar part and two vocal lines. Though Holly may not have consciously planned it that way, this order took advantage of the loss of fidelity caused by dubbing. By the time the recording was completed, the drumming had receded into the background, providing a distant, rolling rhythm which can be felt and heard but does not obscure the vocal or guitar patterns. Similarly, recording the vocal last gave the song a close, intimate feeling, by placing the vocal in front of the varying guitar patterns.

Petty remembers being quite impressed by Holly's ability to sing along with himself. The technique was experimental then. Les Paul and Mary Ford had worked with multi-track recordings earlier in the decade and the technique had been used sporadically since then, but Holly was probably the first rock 'n' roll artist to use vocal and instrumental overdubbing; Eddie Cochran was another who used overdubbing regularly, primarily to add guitar parts. It was later rock 'n' roll artists such as Neil Sedaka and Jan and Dean who exploited multi-track vocal techniques more fully.

Technique is just a means, though, and Holly never used it at the expense of content. "Words of Love" succeeds because it is a pretty, entrancing and almost hypnotic song. The unusual rhythm and guitar patterns were probably suggested to Holly by Mickey and Sylvia's "Love Is Strange"; Jerry Allison remembers, "Buddy would sit around and listen to that song, over and over, all night long." Holly's voice is subdued and tender, but quietly confident, "soft and true", like the words of love whispered in the song. His sincere and appropriate delivery lends an intensely personal feeling to the simple lyrics.

The recording was not finished until sometime around daybreak. Holly was rather worn out from the close attention demanded by such a recording. Still, the Crickets decided to cut a flip side for the record. The song they chose to do was "Mailman, Bring Me No More Blues", a demo of which had been sent to Petty by Murray Deutch with the suggestion that Holly record it. One of the song's three co-writers was "Stanley Clayton" who, it turns out, was none other than Bob Thiele, though only Deutch knew it at the time. Thiele used the pseudonym for writing songs to avoid any seeming conflict of interest with his job as an A&R director. Thiele wrote the song, he says, specifically with Holly in mind; the melody was based on the rolling bass line in "Blues, Stay Away From Me", a song originally written and recorded by the Delmore Brothers and recorded in 1956 by the Johnny Burnette Trio. Murray Deutch says, "We wanted to see how Buddy would sound on that kind of song. I was thrilled when I heard his version."

Buddy and the Crickets listened to the demo of "Mailman", ran through it once, and then did one take of the song with Vi Petty on piano—and that was it, all in about ten minutes. The lyrics of the tune were not memorable, but Holly gave them an all-out performance—one which, at first hearing, may seem grotesque and overdramatic, but which after more attention comes to be seen as the saving feature of the recording. The vocal is all the more impressive considering the circumstances of the recording and the spontaneity of Holly's performance. All else in the recording, including the piano playing, the drumming and Holly's brief guitar break, is pretty simple and straightforward, since there was no time allowed to work out a more elaborate arrangement.

Through the spring, the Crickets waited for the release of their first single. While they waited, they played some local shows and practised almost constantly. The Crickets were not just a studio band; they were intent on sounding as good in live performances as on records. By the time their first single began to sell and they found themselves in demand across the country for personal appearances, they were a cohesive unit.

Says Mauldin, "We'd rehearse at my house and Jerry's house. Seems like we rehearsed a few times over at Niki's house and a few times at Larry Holley's house, in a garage there. And then we rented a little office out on the south side of Lubbock, and set up our instruments out there. And we'd go out there nearly all the time. Any spare time we had, we were either out there just hanging around, talking about how great it was going to be some day, or rehearsing. I think that's one thing that got us so close together and so tight in our presentations, was the fact that we rehearsed nearly all the time."

Very important to the group's in-person appeal was their ability to match the sound of their records at live shows. Sometimes, when a rock 'n' roll act tried to re-create on stage the sound that had been produced in a studio, fans found the results disappointing. The practice of "lip-syncing" on some television shows was an answer to this gap between recorded and live performances. The Crickets were one group, however, that avoided criticism on this count. Only the vocal accompaniment was lacking at live shows (and Niki Sullivan did sing a bit, to fill in that gap); otherwise, the sound was there. Despite Holly's use of dubbing in the studio, he didn't use any technical trick which would be difficult to reproduce live. Though he did play both lead and rhythm guitars on most recordings, Sullivan could play rhythm in live appearances; though Holly in some cases dubbed on the lead guitar part after the vocal was recorded, he was capable of playing and singing at the same time; and though an echo chamber was used at Petty's studio, it was a live echo which only simulated the sound of a theatre or auditorium anyway.

All this was no accident. Holly was very much aware that fans expected to hear the same overall sound at concerts that they had heard on the records. This was no great problem for Holly in the studio because he deliberately strove for uncomplicated sounds and songs. "He knew that it would help the popularity of his songs if local bands played them at high school dances and the like," explains guitarist Tommy Allsup, who joined Holly in 1958, "and so he rarely did anything that any little ol' band couldn't play." Or at least *try* to play.

The group reached the point where each member could play what he felt and the sound would fit in almost automatically with the styles of the others. Jerry Allison comments:

"To talk about what influenced my drumming—Buddy's guitar playing influenced my drumming more than anything. I haven't played with anyone since that I could play with as well, because I learned to play drums with what Buddy played.

"We played together so much because we used to just sit around and rehearse for no reason, just to be playing. So when a new record would come out—for instance, we were in Wichita Falls for a show when we heard Little Richard's 'Keep-A-Knocking' for the first time on the radio. I think we heard it about three times that afternoon on the radio, and we played it that night on the show. We didn't sit and rehearse it and say, 'Now, it's got to have these breaks in it. . . .'—we just played it. Because however Buddy played, I knew how he was going to play it, and he knew how I was going to play—so we didn't work up 'arrangements'."

And so, the Crickets practised and waited, somehow quite confident that their first release would bring them success. Says Sullivan, "The five of us— Norman and the group—just knew in our minds that we had recorded a hit song. Whether or not 'That'll Be The Day' would be a *hit* was not in our control, but we knew that it was a hit *song*." Money was still tight for the boys; Larry Holley helped keep them going by giving them work in his construction business—one of their assignments being to install ceramic tiles in Norman Petty's echo chamber. By June, Buddy was growing impatient, wondering why Brunswick had failed to release "That'll Be The Day". He called their offices in New York one day, intending to demand the return of the record if they weren't going to release it. He was told that the record had been released that very day; whereupon he asked, "Well—then how about sending an advance?"

On June 10, 1957, *Billboard* covered "That'll Be The Day" in its "Reviews

of New Pop Records". The magazine gave the record a mediocre 72 rating and a moderately favourable review: ". . . Fine vocal by the group on a well-made side that should get play. Tune is a medium beat rockabilly. Performance is better than material."

The record was no overnight success; six weeks passed before anything happened to it. Just what did happen, eventually, is a mixture of fact and legend. The legend is that a disc jockey in Buffalo, New York, locked himself in a control room and played "That'll Be The Day" on the air all day long—and the record took off. The story is based on fact. Tom Clay, who used the name "Guy King" on the air, was a disc jockey on WWOL. He did play the song an unusual number of times a day—more than once an hour and occasionally several times in succession—and undoubtedly that sort of exposure explains why the northern New York State area was one of the first where "That'll Be The Day" began to sell.

The importance of any one particular DJ is hard to determine. Murray Deutch and Bob Thiele actually credit a disc jockey in another city with making the record a success: Georgie Woods, one of the top DJs on WDAS, a popular black station in Philadelphia. "For weeks and weeks," says Deutch, "nothing happened—there were no orders. And then I got a call from Norman Weinstroer, the sales manager for Brunswick. He said, 'Georgie Woods wants to play the record.' And it busted wide open. Woods was the one who broke the record." Thiele adds, "All of a sudden, the record started to sell—the sales department called, and they had one order from Philly alone for 20,000 copies."

In fact, "That'll Be The Day" did follow an unusual pattern on its path to national success. Normally, a new release either moved up the charts quickly and became a hit, or else showed no early movement and was soon forgotten as disc jockeys turned to newer records. However, the record industry at that time was not as nationally homogenous as it is now, and a record could sell in one part of the country while being ignored elsewhere (or two different versions of the same song might sell in different markets). One of *Billboard*'s functions was to monitor key regional markets for tunes which were gaining local success and might have national potential. In the case of "That'll Be The Day", it was several weeks before the record attracted regional attention. The song first appeared on *Billboard*'s "territorial lists" for Boston and northern Ohio (i.e. Cleveland), and a week later, on the one covering northern New York State (including Buffalo). It's hard to say, then, that Tom Clay, Georgie Woods or any one person "made" the record a hit.

While the Crickets were in Clovis early in July for a recording session (the one at which "Everyday" and "Peggy Sue" were recorded), Petty received a telegram from Murray Deutch announcing that the record had sold fifty thousand copies and was beginning to break. Niki Sullivan recalls the big moment:

"We were at Norman's, asleep. It was early in the morning, like 8 or 9 A.M., and we hadn't been to bed but three or four hours because we had been working that night before. Norman came in, and he had a piece of paper in his hand. He said, 'Fellows, I have some news for you, a wire from Murray Deutch,' and it said something like, ' "That'll Be The Day" has reached sales of 50,000 copies, congratulations, prepare the fellows to come to New York.' Norman was ecstatic; but we were so tired, we didn't care. I'm serious—it didn't hit the rest of us that this was any big deal. It hit Buddy—he did get up and look at the telegram. But the rest of us just went back to sleep. I guess we should have started bouncing off the walls, but the timing was just a little off."

It was July 29 before *Billboard* took note of the growing sales for "That'll Be The Day", and listed it as a "best buy": "The record has been out for a while and has suddenly started to move. All of the top markets report that the disc is doing well."

In early August, the single made the Top 100 (the pop listing, called the Hot 100 after August 1958) and within a month it climbed into the top ten in terms of records sold. Simultaneously, the record appeared on the rhythm & blues charts, and was equally popular there. The record hit its national peak on September 23, when it was number one in pop sales and number two in rhythm & blues sales. Its highest position on the Top 100 list, which combined record sales with DJ plays and jukebox activity, was number three. "That'll Be The Day" consistently did better on the sales chart than on the disc jockey performances list—suggesting that, in the case of this record, the disc jockeys followed the tastes of the record buyers, rather than the other way around.

With their first record, the Crickets had a hit—a million-seller. And soon enough, everyone was talking about the "overnight sensation", Buddy Holly—who, like most overnight sensations, had spent several years struggling along before achieving this sudden success. When success came, luck played some part in it; but only Holly's persistence had kept him in a position to take advantage of the luck.

It was sometime in early July that Norman Petty officially became the Crickets' manager. Petty says that when "That'll Be The Day" began to rise on the charts, offers for tours and other promotions began to come in. He felt that, since he himself was not too familiar with the rock 'n' roll markets and booking circuits and had other commitments, someone else would be better qualified to handle the Crickets' tours. "I did not force myself upon them," says Petty. "I didn't say, 'Hey, I'm going to be your manager.' They asked me and, in fact, I tried to convince them that I really wasn't a manager."

Jerry Allison says, "I don't remember if we asked him, or if he just sort of became our manager. I know we all agreed that Norman *ought* to be the manager. I mean, we were all really tight at the time, and Norman really spent a lot of time with us in the studio. And anything we wanted to do, he was willing to try it. Anyway, at the time, all we wanted to do was play rock 'n' roll music. We didn't want to hear about all the trivials, because we thought everything was straight ahead. Norman was always really good about taking care of things so you didn't worry about it. He always seemed to know the right thing to do, so we let him handle all the business."

Niki Sullivan adds, "Norman never pushed it. As I remember, he asked us who we wanted to be our manager, and either Jerry or Buddy said, 'Well Norman, why don't you be?' And it seems like Norman said, 'Well, I've got a business to run here and I can't travel with you,' and things like this. But Buddy took lead of the conversation and said, 'Well, you've brought us this far, you've done this much for us, and we want you to be our manager.' So when it came to actual agreement as to who was to be our manager, the four of us literally pushed ourselves on Norman—we insisted that he do it."

As manager, Petty was concerned with the appearance and life-style of the Crickets. Dress was one issue. Back in early 1956, Holly and his group had been apt to dress as they pleased unless clearly required to do otherwise. Holly was as likely to wear blue jeans or even bermuda shorts (a favourite of Allison's, too) as to wear a sports coat. Even when supposedly "dressed

THE CRICKETS
That'll Be the Day 72
BRUNSWICK 55009—Fine vocal by the group on a well-made side that should get play. Tune is a medium beat rockabilly. Performance is better than material. (Nor-Va-Jak, BMI)
I'm Lookin' for Someone to Love....72
As with the flip, the material is inferior to the rendition. The up-tempo rockabilly gets bright, vigorous treatment, and should do as well as the flip. (Nor-Va-Jak, BMI)

● *Cashbox, June 10, 1957*

up", his tastes were questionable: one early photo shows him wearing a bright green shirt with a brown tweed jacket. Later, Holly began to imitate the loud stage fashions of Elvis Presley. That is how he was dressed when Petty first saw him perform:

"The first time that I saw Buddy on stage, I was quite shocked. I saw him sporting a bright red jacket, bright red shoes, and white trousers. And of course, after I saw that, I decided that it would have to go—because he was playing for some adult audiences, too."

At first, Holly resisted the idea of dressing more conservatively. It was only after travelling with other performers and seeing how they dressed that he went along with Petty's ideas. It was the Everly Brothers who really convinced the Crickets to dress more stylishly. Jerry Allison recalls: "We didn't have it going as far as clothes. Like, we had some suits made, had pants *that* big. So the Everly Brothers finally said, 'Hey, you guys, you got to quit wearing those pleat suits and cuffs, and get you some decent clothes.' So they took us down to a place in New York City and said, get this and this. Helped a lot, too. Because we didn't have a clue as to what was happening."

Soon, the Crickets were dressed in the identical and stylish suits that added to their stage appearance. Off stage, and back at home, Holly was more often dressed in T-shirt, jeans and sneakers. But he did acquire a taste for "good" clothes, wearing them in public out of choice.

At the end of July, the Crickets flew east from the airport at Amarillo to begin their national career as a performing group. Promoters had assumed that the Crickets were a black vocal group, perhaps because the quartet's name resembled those of such groups (in fact, there had previously been an R&B group called the Crickets, and this might have been the direct source of the confusion). No pictures of the Crickets had yet appeared to show otherwise. As a result, the Crickets found themselves scheduled on week-long black package shows booked for the Howard Theater in Washington, the Royal in Baltimore and the Apollo in New York—theatres where the audience was rarely less than one hundred percent black. Among the other acts on the bill were the Cadillacs, Clyde McPhatter, and Lee Andrews and the Hearts. Jerry Allison remembers being delighted by the "mistake":

"It was really great—they were great audiences. And there wasn't any tension at all. I mean, it was really strange to us, coming from Texas where people are really—I don't know just how to phrase this, but . . . there was a definite barrier down there but, man, we loved it all. We didn't get there and say, hey what's this. We were really tickled—because black music was what we were into a lot."

Niki Sullivan recalls, "Just to be doing a *show* was a totally new experience to me, so I was happy just to be there. I didn't think about stepping on to stage before this black audience. I just knew that we were in Washington, D.C., and when we got to the theatre, we saw an awful lot of black people. But everybody made us feel at home."

The Crickets were a hit in Washington from the day they got there; but when they got to the Apollo in New York, the initial reception was frigid, according to Sullivan. "The first time we went on," he says, "it was a weekday matinee. They opened the curtains and Buddy stepped toward the mike, and there was this large black woman in the front row who said, 'It'd better sound like the record!' You could have heard a pin drop. And after we got through, I don't think five people clapped. The same thing on the evening show, and the next day—nothing. The third day, we did our first song, and got no response again. So Buddy turned around and said, 'Let's do "Bo

WESTERN TELEGRAM

A MZA067 NL PD=TDMZ MIAMI BEACH FLO 28=
=BUDDY HOLLY AND THE CRICKETS=
=CARE EDISON HOTEL NYK=
CONGRATULATIONS AND WELCOME TO THE BIG CITY SEE YOU A
LITTLE BIT LATER
=PAPA NORMAN=.

● *The Crickets with Murray Deutch of Southern Music*

● *The Crickets (at the top of the steps) leaving Amarillo airport on their first trip to New York*

Diddley".' And we went into 'Bo Diddley', cutting up and working our butts off. I was dancing around in a big circle, going through a bunch of gyrations, and Buddy was all over the stage, and Joe B. was bouncing that bass back and forth and laying it down, and I've never seen Jerry work harder on those damn drums. And when we finished that song, the people just went bananas. From then on, we were accepted at the Apollo. Funny what it takes to please some people."

The G-Clefs, a black vocal group best remembered for "Ka Ding Dong" (1956) and "I Understand" (1961), had been added to the bill for the Apollo appearances. Ted Scott of the G-Clefs offers another point of view on Holly's reception: "The first show there was at 10.20 in the morning and the people there were saying, 'What is this?' I think that Buddy and his group were shaken by playing in a black theatre in a black territory, and they did get booed when they first appeared on stage. After they did their thing, they got some confidence and they really put on a good show. He was a different kind of white act. He didn't just stand by the microphone and sing as some of the other acts did, he put on a show with his act. He did a lot of jumping around." After the week at the Apollo, the Crickets made appearances on Dick Clark's *American Bandstand* and Alan Freed's local New York City television show, and then performed on Freed's Labor Day holiday show at the Brooklyn Parmount, before joining a package tour organized by Irvin Feld of the General Artists Corporation (GAC), one of the nation's largest booking agencies. The eighty-day cross-country package tour was billed as

RECEIPT

Barracuda Music Inc

At Brooklyn Paramount Theater

From 8/30/57 19** To 7/8/957

NAME: CRICKETS

EARNINGS:
Salary
Scale   1171.71
                          117.17
10% Commission   1288.88

EXPENSES:

DEDUCTIONS:

W. T.

S. S.

N. Y. S. D. B.

BOOKING COMMISSIONS   117.17

AGVA DUES

UNION DUES/TAX   22.13

ADVANCES

                        140.60
TOTAL   1148.28

NET PAYMENT

RECEIVED PAYMENT _____

● *The Crickets first payslip*

● *The Crickets onstage during the August 1957 Paramount show*

"The Biggest Show of Stars for '57". The title wasn't just hyperbole. Back then, touring shows would feature a large number of name artists and Feld's tour included a bunch: Fats Domino, Chuck Berry, Frankie Lymon and the Teenagers, the Drifters, the Everly Brothers, Paul Anka, La Vern Baker, Clyde McPhatter, Jimmy Bowen, Eddie Cochran, and the Crickets. Of course, no one artist performed for very long. On a two-hour show, even the top acts only had time for three or four tunes. But at least a fan could pay two or three dollars for the best seat in a small indoor auditorium or dance hall for a typical package show and see Bill Haley and the Comets, the Everly Brothers and Buddy Holly and the Crickets in one night, all before the intermission. Such all-star touring package shows were possible only because the numerous acts were paid small fractions of what contemporary rock artists now command for solo concerts. Holly and the Crickets earned one thousand dollars a week for the 1957 Show of Stars tour. The most they ever made was about twelve hundred dollars a night for tours a year later that involved fewer acts.

The Show of Stars opened in Pittsburgh on September 6 and then embarked on its long and wearying string of one-nighters. The artists travelled by bus hundreds of miles between shows, two-and-a-half months without a day off. One week went like this: Sunday, Spokane; Monday, Moscow, Idaho; Tuesday, Calgary, Alberta; Wednesday, Edmonton, Alberta; Thursday, Regina, Saskatchewan; Friday, Denver; Saturday, Wichita, Kansas; Sunday, Kansas City; Monday, Omaha.... The performers would sleep on the bus during the night-long drives—if it was quiet enough to sleep—and get to hotels in the next town with time, perhaps, for a few hours rest if the promoters had thought it worth arranging for hotel rooms in that town. Then it was off to the theatre and on stage, usually for two shows, and then back on the bus again for another long ride. Tired from

the grind but often too keyed up to sleep, the young performers would pass the hours with pillow fights, water fights, pulling the pants off someone or another. . . . And in the back of the bus, some of the performers, including Holly, might be singing spirituals, or shooting craps with their night's earnings.

So much for what seemed to outsiders like a glamorous life—fame, wealth, excitement, and so on. Not quite. "It was really a draggy old tour," says Allison. "I think we missed about four states. We'd get on the bus and ride and get off and pick, then get back on and ride."

For Buddy Holly, it was just as wearying, but still exciting, and the success the Crickets were enjoying was a dream come true. Holly was as conscious as anyone of the money to be made in the business, but there was something else that drove him on—he simply loved to perform. Whatever shyness he showed off stage disappeared on stage, and his broad grin, good humour and uninhibited performance made the Crickets as appealing in live shows as they were on record. Guitarist Tommy Allsup recalls how it was when he worked with Holly a bit later:

"He was a different person when he was on stage. You'd never know him. When he was on stage, he worked real hard and got through to the kids. He would tear up an audience. When he was off stage, he was quiet. He just liked to sit around with the guys and talk—mostly about music."

Niki Sullivan makes a similar observation about Holly: "I think the *real* Buddy Holly was there, behind the mike. Away from the mike, he was quiet, reserved, businesslike, shy—introverted, if you will. Behind the microphone, he was just like a bolt of lightning. He had to be happy while he was doing it, that's what he always wanted to do. It was one hundred percent, the real Buddy Holly, the minute he walked on stage."

The other Crickets shared Holly's enthusiasm for performing. Says

● *The Crickets during the Canadian part of the Show of Stars tour*

● *Everything The Crickets earned was split equally—with deductions for on-the-road necessities. (Scotch B referred to a hold-all containing the group's cash)*

● *The Crickets celebrate Ivan's birthday, August 31, 1957*

Mauldin, "When we were on the road for a couple of months, we'd get tired of it and we'd say, 'Let's knock off for two months after we finish this tour, and just hang around at home.' So we'd book two months with nothing to do, and get home, and in just about three days, we'd be ready to get back on the road. So we'd book another tour. The time off was fun, but working was more fun."

Niki Sullivan likewise remembers the weariness, but also the bonds that built up among those on the tour. He says, "My whole life or education seemed to occur, right there on that eighty-day tour. The most outstanding thing to me was the camaraderie—everybody living and working together. Colour just didn't come up. The Drifters treated me as kind of a white sheep of the family. If I had trouble, or worry, or loneliness, they would always sit down and talk to me. After we got back to New York, we had our farewell party, and when they all went out and got on the bus to leave, I cried."

As for non-musical pastimes, whatever the desires, time and opportunities were limited. "I don't recall much drinking," says Niki. "We didn't have time—usually we were too tired. As for dope—zero on dope. I didn't even know what marijuana was until years later. There were girls around, but you know, any time we had to jump on a bus to a show and travel three to five hundred miles, that was out. The musicians on the tour who were veterans, they knew who was waiting for them and where they were going the minute we got in a city; but we weren't veterans, and so for us it could just be a matter of circumstance. To be honest, I don't ever remember seeing Buddy with a girl, or knowing that he slept with one during the tour. I can tell you this, he wasn't looking for guys, either. I think Buddy had enough on his mind, that this was something he could live with."

Mauldin has similar memories of Holly's personal habits. "It was one thing I always wondered about Buddy," he says with a laugh, "he was never hustling girls after the shows. Every once in a while, he'd have some beer, or go have a couple of drinks, but even that was sparingly. And as for drugs—no, absolutely not, for any of us."

Ted Scott of the G-Clefs adds, "I never saw any drugs taken except for a few people smoking marijuana, and that was the older folks, those that had been in the business for a long time. I never saw any of the artists stoned at any time, even from alcohol, because the tour was very strict and you had to perform every night. As for Buddy Holly and his group, I can't even remember him using a cuss word, let alone taking drugs."

The popularity of rock 'n' roll may not have had the effect on racial attitudes for which it has sometimes been credited, but it did at least point out some striking anomalies. The eighty-day tour brought out one clash between law and popular taste. Several cities in the southeast had ordinances forbidding black and white performers from appearing on the same stage in the same show. So, when the primarily black GAC tour went to Chattanooga, Columbus (Georgia), Birmingham, New Orleans and Memphis, the white performers (the Crickets, the Everly Brothers, Jimmy Bowen and Paul Anka—Eddie Cochran had not yet joined the tour) had to be dropped from the show. Ironically, at the time of these performances, "That'll Be The Day" and Paul Anka's "Diana" were at the top of the rhythm & blues charts.

To the Crickets, the situation was ridiculous. Joe says, "Buddy felt like it was a little bit much. Because we had no feeling against associating or performing with coloured people, I don't think Buddy thought that anyone else should feel the way that the Southern states did about it either. But that's the way it was, so we just had to accept it." Niki Sullivan adds, "I don't

The Cash Box

VOL. XIX—No. 1   SEPTEMBER 21, 1957

October 1st, that'll be the day when The Crickets expect to be well over the million mark with their Brunswick recording of — naturally — "That'll Be The Day". Above, the high flying group, flanked on the left by Bob Thiele, A&R head of the Coral-Brunswick diskery, and on the right by Norm Wienstroer, National Sales Manager of the same organization, point to the likely date. The Crickets, in addition to achieving the first big hit for themselves with their waxing, have also delivered the first smash seller for the recently reactivated Brunswick label.

think any of us were raised to be prejudiced. We had never been exposed to racism before—not in that vein. It was simply grotesque about those cities where we couldn't play, because the audiences were white, far and away, even in the deep South." Buddy revealed his own attitude well enough in a comment to his mother when he came home after the first tour. She asked him how he was getting along with Negroes, and he replied, "Oh, we're Negroes, too! We get to feeling like that's what we are."

The Crickets did sometimes find themselves staying in black hotels. Joe Mauldin remembers this happening when they were playing the Apollo. "We were staying at a hotel right across the street from the Apollo, and it was a one hundred percent black hotel. We got a lot of strange looks, and people whispering to each other. We felt a little uncomfortable for a day or two, but everything smoothed out." On the eighty-day tour, says Sullivan, the troupe stayed in integrated hotels north of the Mason-Dixon line, but ran into problems south of the line. "Somebody slipped up, and sometimes the whole tour had been booked into an all-white hotel," he says. "We'd go there, and of course be rejected. So at that point we said, 'Screw it, we'll just go with you guys from now on,' to their own hotels. We didn't ever have trouble getting into a black hotel; we were accepted."

With the success of "That'll Be The Day", Brunswick was anxious to release a Crickets album quickly, but a few more recordings were needed. The five-day vacation from the Show of Stars tour caused by the restrictions on integrated performances gave the Crickets and Petty a chance to rendezvous and cut some additional sides. The group was due to rejoin the GAC tour in Tulsa, Oklahoma; on one of their free nights Petty's Trio had a job in Oklahoma City and so the Crickets arranged to meet him there. Petty brought his recording equipment with him in a truck he used for carrying his Trio's instruments. His gig was at the Officers' Club at Tinker Air Force Base and, after the club closed, he and the Crickets set up the recording equipment in a corner of a room at the club and the Crickets went to work. By morning, they had recorded four tunes: "Maybe Baby", "An Empty Cup", "You've Got Love" and "Rock Me My Baby". The Crickets then went back on the road while Petty took the tapes back to Clovis and overdubbed the background vocals in his own studio.

While the quartet was still on tour, Coral released "Peggy Sue", Holly's second single as a solo artist and by far his biggest under his own name. No other Holly record is so widely remembered or so decisively fixed in the popular mind as embodying the "Holly sound", as "Peggy Sue" is. (In terms of sales, it ran about equally with "That'll Be The Day", each reportedly selling over five million copies.) Strangely enough, like "That'll Be The Day", "Peggy Sue" took a little while to catch on—though released in late September, it was November before it made the Top 100 and late December before it became a top hit.

In terms of long-range effect on rock 'n' roll music, "Peggy Sue" may have been more influential than any other Holly record. The steady and constant rhythm guitar strumming, the rapid, accented drumming of Jerry Allison, the stylized vocal with its full development of the Holly hiccup, the ringing tones of the guitar solo and the rhythmic cadence Holly used so often—all these influenced several musical generations of singers, guitarists and drummers, and found their echoes in records over the next decade and beyond.

Stories differ as to the origin of the song. Petty claims that Holly came to him with the tune early one morning during a session at Clovis, and that he—Petty—wrote the lyrics. Other accounts contradict this. According to the Holleys, Buddy had fairly completed the song in his room at their home when Jerry Allison stopped by to see what he was doing. Holly had written the song as "Cindy Lou", but when Jerry suggested changing the title to name the song after Allison's girl friend, Peggy Sue, Buddy agreed. Petty's only contribution, says Jerry, was the chord alteration in the bridge of the song ("Peggy Sue, Peggy Sue, pretty, pretty, pretty, pretty Peggy Sue"). "I remember when we were cutting it," adds Allison, "I messed it up the first time through and either Buddy or Norman said, 'O.K., if you don't get it right this time, we're going to change it back to "Cindy Lou".' But the second time we got it, and it stayed 'Peggy Sue'."

Niki has his own version of the story. "The song was 'Cindy Lou' originally and it was done with more of a cha-cha beat. Jerry was in the outer office, in a separate room, and we were in the main studio. After a couple of tries, it wasn't working out. A dialogue got started between Jerry and Buddy over the loudspeaker system, saying, you know, 'This isn't it'. So Buddy suggested that they add paradiddles to it—that practice drum roll that drummers use to rehearse their music. And I think that Jerry agreed to do that if Buddy would instead change it from 'Cindy Lou' to 'Peggy Sue'. Then Buddy started that guitar rhythm because now the song was a four-four beat. It couldn't have been more than the second or third cut that the song was finalized."

There was no overdubbing on the record, and just one guitar. Holly strummed rhythm while singing the choruses and played a treble lead in the instrumental break. Initially, Niki Sullivan was accompanying Holly on rhythm guitar, but a problem arose. "Buddy couldn't switch fast enough from playing rhythm on the chorus to playing lead on the bridge," Niki remembers. "He couldn't get his hand to the switch fast enough without breaking rhythm and having it show up on the tape." So Sullivan put down his guitar and the song was recorded with Sullivan pushing the switch on Holly's guitar as Holly went to the bridge and back to the chorus.

Initially, only Allison and Petty were listed as the writers of the song. After

● *The Officers Club, Tinker Air Force Base, where four of the tracks on the 'Chirping Crickets' album were recorded*

● *The real Peggy Sue with her future father-in-law*

Holly's death, Jerry insisted that Holly be given credit and that the royalties on the song be distributed in a more accurate manner. He says, "After Buddy got killed, we all went to New York to straighten things out. So the contract on 'Peggy Sue' said Norman and me, and I said, 'Right, Buddy did write part of "Peggy Sue", and he might be gone and all that, but I'm not gonna set here and say he didn't.' And Norman said, 'Well, you can say what you want to or you can look at the contract.' And he was sort of saying, leave it like it is. And I said, 'Well, the estate can just take my half right now.' And it finally ended up that I got ten percent of it. At that time I had already gotten eight thousand dollars in royalties. And when I signed that agreement I got ten percent instead of fifty, and the eight thousand dollars came out of my account right on the spot. And of course, all the loot that's come in from it since. If I had to do it again, I'd do the same thing. I don't regret that."

Holly, Allison and Petty certainly all deserve credit for the recording's success. Petty's major contribution was in the engineering skill he applied in recording Allison. Allison played only a snare drum, with the snares off. Petty adjusted the volume and switched the echo chamber "on" and "off" to create the unique effect of a rolling, shifting drumbeat. (In live appearances, Allison used a full set of drums to imitate the effect.)

Holly's rhythmic lead guitar playing was equally unprecedented. "I've never seen anyone since who plays it that way," says Allison. "Every other guitar player strums it back and forth with his pick—down-up-down-up down-up-down-up, like that. But Holly did it with just down strokes—down-down-down-down-down-down-down-down." Sixteen to a bar, and singing at the same time, of course. Holly's guitar solo shouldn't go unmentioned, either. Its effect is heightened by the contrast between the solo guitar's vibrant treble sound and the lower-pitched roll of the drums and guitar on the vocal choruses. Like many of Holly's instrumental solos, but with more emphasis on full chords, the solo flashes back and forth between the tonic and sub-dominant chords, and then reaches up to the dominant chord to create a feeling of exaltation that's almost religious in nature. It is all so simple—Holly is only following the blues pattern upon which "Peggy Sue" is loosely based. And yet, it is all so perfectly effective. It is simple, in the most positive sense of the word—it is simple because Holly needs no more to achieve a striking effect.

The flip side to "Peggy Sue" was merely "Everyday", which would certainly have been a major hit for Holly had it been released as a single itself. "Everyday" creates an entirely different mood from "Peggy Sue"—a sweet, quiet and beautiful one. Even on such quieter Holly songs, though, the rhythm remains steady and insistent. The lead instrument is a celesta, a hammer-struck keyboard instrument, played by Vi Petty. The instrument happened to be in the studio that day and, during a break in the recording, Holly began to tinker with it, and Petty said, "You know, that's what this song needs." Holly was always searching for, and willing to try, different sounds—and a celesta was about as different as could be. Now, it is hard to picture the recording without it. (Actually, it was not the first use of a celesta on a rock 'n' roll recording—it had been used on Chuck Willis's "It's Too Late" in 1956.)

Allison's performance on the tune was also a matter of accident. As Holly was playing and singing the song to demonstrate how he thought it should sound, Allison began to slap his hands on his knees in time with Holly's playing. "Hey," said Buddy, "that sounds pretty good." And so the only

"drumming" on the record is the sound of Allison slapping his knees.

To be technical, the melody features a chord pattern found in none of Holly's other songs—the chords in the refrain are built on a new tonic, the flattened seventh of the tonic in the body of the song (i.e. if the song is in C, the chords in the verses are C, F and G, while those in the refrain are Bb, Eb and F). Allison credits the melody and most of the lyrics to Holly, with Petty having some role in rearranging the order of phrases and verses.

Overall, the song has the peculiar uncertainty of so many of Holly's songs. Despite its happy, optimistic tone, it is still about love unfulfilled—a love that is "getting closer" but is not yet there, a love which the singer is a bit shy in expressing directly. But in the end, the song is all the more effective for that. Love is pictured as a feeling that does not emerge spontaneously or full-grown; instead, it slowly but surely builds—and that is a more hopeful and happy message for those in love who would like to believe, too, that love in return will surely come their way.

> *Everyday,*
> *It's a-getting closer,*
> *Going faster than a rollercoaster,*
> *Love like yours will surely come my way—*
>   *hey, a-hey-hey.*
>
> *Everyday,*
> *It's a-going faster,*
> *Everyone said, "Go ahead and ask her,"*
> *Love like yours will surely come my way—*
>   *hey, a-hey-hey.*
>
> *Every day seems a little longer*
> *Every way love's a little stronger,*
> *Come what may, do you ever long for*
> *True love from me?*
>
> *Everyday,*
> *It's a-getting closer,*
> *Going faster than a rollercoaster,*
> *Love like yours will surely come my way*

The vocal is one of Holly's best. The delicate phrasing, gliding tones and variety of vocal effects give the recording a gentle lilt which has defied imitation in later versions of the song.

"Everyday" was the first song to be released bearing the name of "Charles Hardin" as co-writer. The name was, of course, just a pseudonym for Holly, using his given first and middle names. Jerry Allison explains that the pseudonym was used to hide Holly's authorship of his songs from Cedarwood Publishing at a time when matters had not yet been settled with them. Holly did not have a songwriting contract with Cedarwood requiring that he let them publish his songs but he probably wanted to play it safe, lest they claim the songs on some legal technicality that he didn't know about.

How did Holly feel when he had recorded a song—what did he think of it? And what were his own favourites? Jerry Allison answers:

"On those very first sessions in Nashville—it didn't really knock us out, what we had recorded. Because the people in charge weren't all that interested in what we were doing and we thought we could sure do it better if we had more time. I really can't remember what Buddy thought about 'Blue

Days, Black Nights' and those things—at the time, he was pretty tickled just to have a record out and he took it around to the radio stations and said, 'Hey, listen to this.'

"Later, when we were over at Clovis—after we'd cut something—Buddy was pretty enthusiastic about it all. But you know, after we got started and had those records that did some good, there was never much time to sit around and listen to them. I don't think Buddy had any real favourites. He really liked 'Everyday'. And 'Peggy Sue'.—we were all pretty flipped out about that one. We said, 'Man, that's weird. That's different. It sounds good.' My own favourites? 'Everyday' was a good one. 'Not Fade Away.' 'That'll Be The Day' will always be my favourite because that got it all started and it was the first tune I ever wrote part of. And I always liked 'Tell Me How' pretty good—it was the flip side of 'Maybe Baby'."

"That'll Be The Day" stayed in the top thirty for a full three months and the Crickets' second single, "Oh Boy!", was not released until October 27. "Oh Boy!" was written by Bill Tilghman and Sonny West. West was a rockabilly musician in his own right, and had made a record called "Rock-Ola Ruby" at Petty's studio in August 1956; the record had been released on Petty's own label, Nor Va Jak Records. When he and Tilghman wrote "Oh Boy!", they took it to Clovis and made a demo of it. Shortly thereafter, Holly heard the demo and decided to record it in his own style. "Norman called us," remembers Tilghman. "He wanted us to come over to Clovis. He played us Buddy's version of 'Oh Boy!' Needless to say, it was fantastic—kind of put us both on cloud nine."

Holly's recording stands out as the best example of his breathless, frantic, rockabilly style—it's a long way from "Everyday" to "Oh Boy!", but Holly was equally adept at both sounds. Allison's drumming is superb, with his driving beat only increasing in intensity as the song progresses. The dubbed vocal obscures Holly's guitar playing on the solo instrumental chorus, but elsewhere it fills in perfectly. For sheer excitement, "Oh Boy!" is the Crickets at their finest.

The flip side, "Not Fade Away", followed the famed "Bo Diddley Beat" but with a lighter, varied touch and a brighter sound. The vocal shows Holly's sense of variation and control. In spots his voice illustrates the words, pushing forward and retreating on "I try to show it, you keep driving me back", or dying down on the title phrase. Earlier in his career, Holly had studied Elvis's manner of variation, but by now, he was creating his own effects, reflecting the way he himself felt, talked and sang. The overdubbed background vocals were by Holly and Sullivan.

The new single was not the monstrous hit "That'll Be The Day" had been, but it did sell close to a million copies. For sure, it proved that Holly and the Crickets were not one-shot artists, as so many groups proved to be. "America's hottest singing sensation", a trade-paper advertisement called the Crickets; and, for the moment, they were just that.

CHAPTER FIVE

AROUND · THE · WORLD

By December 1957, the Crickets were reaching the height of their popularity in the United States and Canada and plans were already being made for tours of England and Australia.

After the GAC tour ended in late November, the Crickets returned to New York for an appearance on *The Ed Sullivan Show* on December 1. The quartet performed "That'll Be The Day" in the first half of the show, and "Peggy Sue" in the second. The group had been on Dick Clark's *American Bandstand* the previous August to lip-sync "That'll Be The Day", but the Sullivan show was their first appearance on prime-time TV and the first time they had played their songs live on network television.

How did the Crickets feel, playing for a nationwide TV audience? Jerry Allison talks about it:

"I can't speak for everybody, but I was pretty nervous *all* the time. Because it all happened so fast and it seemed like we went straight from setting tile to being on network TV shows. But I was definitely more nervous on TV than I was on regular shows, and I think Buddy was, too. After all, we had picked plenty—we knew we could play it and all that. And in front of people, that wasn't any hang-up. But as far as TV, that was something different—an audience that wasn't there. And also, on the first Ed Sullivan show, they had fixed up a big riser for the drums—it was maybe ten feet tall. So I was sitting way up there and Joe B. was standing on one side of the riser and Niki on the other, and Buddy was out front singing. And of course the amps just went right out front and out the back and I couldn't hear a thing. And when we did the first rehearsal, Buddy said, 'I can't hear the drums good—just take that thing down.' So they struck all that. Because if you can't hear, you can't play together."

"Shock" is the word Niki Sullivan uses to describe his reaction to the Sullivan show. "We were all let down. We expected so many thousands of people in the audience, because that's how it looked when we'd seen the show on TV. But when we walked out there, we just couldn't believe it—it was a very small theatre, with only a couple of hundred people." He too remembers being uncomfortable. "It was the surroundings—the helter-skelter and rush, rush, do everything on time and be here on time. We just weren't used to that immediacy. And then the night of the show, when we stood in the wings, the All-American football team was there and they were giants, every one of them. We felt like ants. Everybody was on pins and needles all the time we were there except for the football players—nobody was gonna press *them*."

After the Crickets performed "Peggy Sue", Ed Sullivan unexpectedly called Holly out front for a few brief questions—the Crickets' ages, where they were from, and if they were going to school in Lubbock ("Well, we did until we got out of high school, finally," Holly replied).

"Were you a big hit right from the start?" asked Sullivan.

"Well, we've had a few rough times, I'd guess you say, but we've been real lucky getting it this quick," answered Holly in a soft Texas drawl.

Holly may have been scared at the start of the evening, but he seemed completely at ease talking with Sullivan. When the interview was over, Holly naturally stuck out his hand for a handshake, and it took a second for the startled Sullivan to respond.

After the show, the Crickets flew back to Lubbock for their first visit home since August. The hopeful young musicians who had left Lubbock then with one record just starting to climb the charts now returned as established stars; but it made little difference in Lubbock. There was nothing triumphant about

● *The Crickets first appearance on the
Ed Sullivan TV show*

the return—no crowds or reporters met them at the airport, and nobody
made any speeches about the home-town success stories. You're never as
big in your home town as you are anywhere else, the show business line
goes—and though their records always sold well locally, the Crickets were
never honoured publicly by their own community. The local newspaper had
printed just one item about the group—a small group photo with a caption
mentioning their appearance on *The Ed Sullivan Show*. Holly never failed to
mention his home town whenever he was given the chance to do so and
it's a pretty good bet that, around the world today, Lubbock is noted more
for Buddy Holly than for its cotton or its university. But the pride Holly
felt for his home town was not reciprocated, at least not by the leading citizens
in it.

The Crickets' families, though, offered them strong support; if their sons
could be successful playing rock 'n' roll, they saw nothing wrong with it.
Joe Mauldin recalls his mother's feelings:

"I quit school before I graduated, to play with Buddy. And I hit Mother
with the same story that Buddy hit me with when he asked me to play regular
with the group. I told her that we were gonna go to New York, and be
stars, and make lots of money. So Mother, against her own better judgement,
agreed to sign me out of school because I was too young to pull it off by
myself. And I remember when we were at the school, she started crying,
and she said, 'I hope you have to work your fingers to the bone the rest
of your life, because you're going to regret this some day.' And, you know,
it hurt me that she felt that way about it, but I felt like I was doing the
right thing. But anyway, after that, Mother just got thoroughly involved.
She kept a scrapbook at home with just about every piece of publicity that
was ever put out on us in the United States, like in *Billboard* and *Cashbox*,
and with all the publicity pictures that we had. And if we played in Oklahoma
City or somewhere in New Mexico or Texas, she and Dad would drive hun-

dreds of miles to wherever we were, just to see us perform."

Shortly after the Crickets returned home, Niki Sullivan quit the group. His decision was sudden and, as he remembers it, unplanned, but it can be seen in retrospect as growing out of tensions and personality conflicts which had built up during the group's four months on the road. It was one thing to rehearse and play around Lubbock; it was another to spend several months, with hardly a break, living with the same people continuously in hotel rooms and on buses. Allison and Holly had been friends for some time before the formation of the Crickets, and Joe Mauldin had fitted right in with them, but Sullivan never achieved the same rapport. Looking back on it now, he is able to describe himself candidly:

"Remember, I was an only child, until I was seventeen. An only child who used to play golf by himself just to entertain himself, do a lot of things by myself—I was a loner. And loners quite often can get in certain moods, you've got to reach out and grab them. And that didn't happen. Now maybe they didn't know to do that, or understand the situation. I'm sure they didn't."

Teasing and horseplay were a way of relieving the tensions that built up during the time on tour, but Niki had less tolerance for it than the others did. Joe Mauldin recollects how the Crickets used to blow off steam while out on the road:

"We teased each other constantly. Buddy, Jerry and I teased hard with each other and then we'd do things to Niki and he'd do things to us. But I guess Niki just didn't dig that kind of humour, or that kind of funning.

"I remember once when Buddy, Jerry and I were on the road, we had the night off and I went to a club, and Buddy and Jerry didn't go. When I got back to the hotel, the lights were out and Buddy and Jerry were asleep, so I thought rather than turn on the lights and wake everybody up, I'd just undress and crawl into bed. Well, I crawled in, and I didn't know what in the world I was putting my feet into. I jumped out of bed and turned the lights on. They'd dumped ashtrays, glasses of ice water—they had had food up in the room and they took the plates and dumped them in there—and so my bed was like a garbage pail. I got so mad I couldn't talk, so I just put my clothes back on and stormed out the door and didn't show up until the next morning. Of course, they were all apologetic then. They said, 'Oh, we were just playing a joke on you, having fun.' And I got over it. We did things to each other constantly, which I think is only normal with any group of people who are together all the time. But I think that was another thing that kept us knit so close, that we learned to cope with each other's personalities."

"We all did pick on each other," Niki says, "but it really grated on me. I had never been around that kind of picking and I took things more personal than the other guys did, and I wasn't prepared for all of that. It wasn't that anyone was trying to drive somebody out of the group or trying to hurt somebody's feelings on purpose. It was mainly for a release. But the bickering and fighting did get to me and I had no way to retaliate, except in doing the same thing, and I didn't enjoy it. But it was constant. Like, we'd go to a restaurant, and I might order a waffle, which I like very much, and the rest of the guys would eat steak, which I didn't particularly care for. And they'd pick on me about it and go on and on and on. And I mean, how long can you pick on a guy for eating a waffle?"

Niki remembers telling Buddy and the others of his decision to leave: "We got back, and I was very tired; we all were. We were over at Clovis, and

I just said, 'Buddy, I want to quit, I'm just not happy.' Buddy didn't understand why, but he didn't pursue it; he just said, 'Well, Niki, if that's what you want to do.' So we had a meeting of everyone in Norman's office and I said, 'Fellas, I enjoyed it and everything, but that's it,' and I walked out and went home."

Sullivan harbours some regret that nobody tried to talk him out of it. "At no time", he says, "did I ever hold any animosity towards Joe B., Jerry or Buddy. But my leaving the group could have been resolved, I think, with a night's sleep—just some rest. And Norman did not make any effort to take something that was broken up for the moment and try to piece it back together. A man who is a manager, in any capacity, knows he has employees who have times they're not proud of, and the best thing you can do is say, 'Let's get some rest, let's talk another day.' But that never happened."

Petty looks at what happened in another way. He recalls that when he was with the group during their first concerts in Washington in August, tension was already building: "The biggest rub was between Jerry and Niki. And Buddy went along with Jerry." According to Petty, when the Crickets returned in December, he had separate conversations in which Niki said that he wanted to quit and the others told Petty that they wanted Niki out of the group. "What was there to patch up?" asks Petty. "I knew that Jerry and Joe B. and Buddy wanted him to leave, and on the other hand that Niki wanted to leave."

That version is disputed by Allison. "We never did really have a fight with Niki or say that we wanted him out of the group. Oh, he and I had a good fight one time when we were playing the Brooklyn Paramount. We got to squirting water at each other, something like that, and we had a fist fight. In fact, my eye was swollen up on the *Chirping Crickets* album cover photo, because he got me good around the eye. But that had nothing to do with him leaving, that was just silly kid stuff. None of us were uptight when he split. He wanted out—it was a mutual thing."

Mauldin, too, remembers that the decision was Niki's own and that it arose from Niki's desire to move out on his own. "After about three months on the road," says Mauldin, "Niki on a few occasions mentioned to me that this kind of life was not for him and that he was going to try to get out and make a record deal on his own. And my response was, 'Hey man, do whatever you think you need to do.' When Buddy and Jerry and I would discuss it, they'd say, 'If he wants out, all he has to do is walk.' Buddy and Jerry never forced or pushed him out."

Sullivan remembers being in two minds about the idea of becoming an individual artist. "I didn't have any desire to be number one. I had joined strictly by chance and I was happy to be where I was—it was like fulfilling a dream," he says, while also admitting, "I really kind of did think about stepping out on my own. I did harbour a few feelings like that when we were on tour." Playing rhythm guitar behind Holly was, as others had previously discovered, a role of limited significance. On stage, Niki saw his role as especially a visual one, "moving around and cutting up" (though for a couple of days, during the week at the Howard in Washington, Holly lost his voice and Sullivan had to do the singing). On recordings, Sullivan sometimes played without being miked, and he recognizes the implication: "Buddy's lead style of guitar was rhythm. By my not being miked, that's one microphone less that Norman has to worry about. Because it's all on one track and if I make a mistake, then we blow the whole thing. So it wasn't necessary. But we went there together and I think that might have been

important to Buddy, to have me sitting there playing, even if I wasn't being miked; Buddy did have a need for people. And anyway," Sullivan adds with a grin, "what else can you do in Clovis, New Mexico at 2 o'clock in the morning?"

Not long after leaving the Crickets, Sullivan did in fact get a contract with Dot Records and had a regional hit with "It's All Over"/"Three Steps to Heaven". (Although Petty has said that this record was made in Clovis and that it was he who sold it to Dot, Sullivan denies this. According to Niki, the recording was made at a Lubbock studio and given by Sullivan to Murray Deutch, who arranged the Dot contract.) Later, Sullivan moved to the West Coast and headed a Los Angeles band, Soul Incorporated, for several years.

When Niki left the group, the remaining trio considered asking Sonny Curtis to join them in Niki's place; but Sonny had other jobs then and was himself about to get a record contract, and so the trio decided to go it alone for a while and see how it worked out. A trio of bass, drums and one guitar was then unprecedented in rock 'n' roll. But, just like a year earlier when Holly and Allison had performed as a duo, Buddy's ability to play as hard as he sang and Jerry's varied and full drumming filled in the gap at rhythm guitar. The Crickets performed with this three-man line-up for several months and were never faulted for their instrumental performance; fans and reviewers were instead amazed by the Crickets' ability to match the sound of larger combos.

At Christmas, the trio returned to New York for a television appearance on *The Arthur Murray Dance Party*, and then played on the celebrated Alan Freed holiday shows at the Paramount Theater—twelve days of live rock 'n' roll that attracted thousands of teenagers and created waiting lines stretching several blocks. To accommodate the crowds, shows were held about every two hours, six or seven times a day. Like the GAC tours, Freed's shows included many top names; heading the bill on this one were Jerry Lee Lewis, Fats Domino, the Everly Brothers and the Crickets. Jerry Allison remembers that the Crickets were a bit big-headed over their success—at the time, "Peggy Sue" and "Oh Boy!" were both high in the charts and "That'll Be The Day" was still in the top fifty—and the Paramount shows furnished

● *The Crickets on stage at the Paramount, this time without Niki Sullivan*

more proof of their popularity.

"That was the high point for me—the New York Paramount show," says Allison. "There were all kinds of people on the show, like maybe twenty acts, and we did better than anyone else as far as getting encores and all that—like nobody else would get an encore and maybe we'd get two or three sometimes. That'd get anybody's head—I'm sure I was proud as hell, just sitting there and thinking, well, I'm with a hot group. And Buddy's ego would show a little bit in those days, too."

Just how did success change Buddy Holly? Allison replies, "Of all the people I've ever known, like before they were successful and after, this changes everybody I've ever seen. No matter what—show biz or whatever. And Buddy definitely changed a bit—he got more moody and big-headed or whatever you want to call it. He sort of got into that—and then he got back out of it. But I remember one trip we were on where he was the star or the biggest thing on the show, and we were with Danny and the Juniors and Dickie Doo and the Don'ts. And we were all kids and fighting all the time; like, I nearly knocked his glasses off one time. And Buddy would say, 'Hey, stop it.' 'Quiet.' 'Quit that pillow fight.' I mean, he wasn't ever really like, 'I'm too big a deal,' but he was a little bit. Oh, as a general rule, he was likeable and all that; and like I say, that sort of passed anyway. But it seemed he didn't want to fool around anymore—it was like he was there to work."

Murray Deutch and Bob Thiele likewise recall Holly becoming more sophisticated and more conscious of his work but not being changed otherwise by success. Deutch says, "The first time I met Buddy and the Crickets in New York, they were real kids, straight off the farm. They were dressed in T-shirts and jeans and everything was 'Mister Deutch', not 'Murray'. Buddy was a very quiet kid who said little until he got to know you. He kept things inside. He never talked too much but he was a very bright guy; he listened, and it sunk in. He did get more worldly—I mean business-wise, about the record business. But he stayed the same person."

Bob Thiele remembers, "Holly seemed to me to be an extremely sensitive individual. He *looked* fragile—like you could blow him over. And somehow

● *Buddy and Jerry with Don and Phil Everly*

I found myself being aware of his sensitivity and trying to be careful of how I said things to him. Even with his country talk, he sounded like a gentleman. And he *was* a gentleman."

It was around this time that Buddy adopted a physical appearance that set styles just as his music had. He changed from the thin plastic and metal eyeglass frames he had previously worn to distinctive all-black curved frames. Allison had something to do with Holly's new glasses: "I said to him, 'If you're going to wear glasses, then really make it obvious that you're wearing your glasses.' I think Phil Everly had something to do with that, too. I remember that Buddy, Phil and I went down to a place and rounded up the pair he's wearing on the *Showcase* album." (In late 1958, Holly began wearing a thicker, squared frame, which had been purchased for him in Mexico by his Lubbock optician.) Don Everly recalls that television host Steve Allen, who wore solid black frames, was in their minds as an example of someone who could wear glasses and still look "cool" by emphasizing the fact.

This was the time, too, when Holly tried to improve the appearance of his smile—already one of his best assets. The mineral-heavy water in Lubbock had left Holly's teeth with a brown stain; now that he could afford it, he decided to have his teeth capped. New glasses, new teeth, new clothes—all this must seem rather vain. But after all, Holly was a performer and his physical appearance was important to his career. Besides, he had to be concerned not only with how he looked to his audiences but also how he appeared to business figures who dealt with him—men who were apt to look down on him for his small-town manners and appearance. Coral producer Dick Jacobs, who admired Holly's talent and worked closely with him, nevertheless unconsciously disclosed the importance of Holly's appearance to more urbanized individuals when he once reminisced: "I first met him when he was appearing in Brooklyn. He had silver-rimmed glasses, gold-rimmed teeth, and looked like a hick from Texas. The next time I saw him, he wore a three-button suit, horned-rimmed glasses, had had his teeth recapped, and looked like a gentleman. He was always a marvellous person . . . a sweet gentle soul."

Remember, too, that despite all the protest which seemed inherent in rock 'n' roll, social expectations were often strangely unchanged. To the audiences, rock 'n' roll singers—both white and black—could look like "gentlemen" and even be more popular for it. It was all right to look neat as long as you didn't seem to be putting on an act about it. "In the 1950's," remembers Don Everly, "how you looked and how you dressed was a mark of success. I mean, I remember when I got my first pinkie ring—you know, just felt like success was there on the end of your finger."

The Crickets never counted on their good looks to win them many fans. "Holly didn't really appeal to girls as far as a teen idol sort of thing," says Jerry Allison. "It wasn't that they didn't dig him; they used to scream just like they did for anybody else. But like if we were doing a show with the Everly Brothers or Eddie Cochran or whoever, and if we were out in the back loading equipment, the fans would come around and get our autographs and then if the Everly Brothers came out, they'd throw it down and hunt for a bigger piece to get the Everly Brothers' autographs. Compared to Frankie Avalon and all those slick dudes, we were just a bunch of ugly pickers who just picked. But really, that made it all seem better—because we felt like everybody that liked us, liked us because of what we *could* pick. They were fans because of the music, not just because of the emotions or the good looks or whatever. And it seemed too like the boys liked us better—you know, with some of the idol-type groups, the boys would be turned off because their chicks would be saying, 'Oh, look at that!'"

Phil Everly noticed Holly's particular appeal to male fans during the New York Paramount shows:

"Young girls would fill the audience in the early shows. As it progressed to the evening, it filled up with men and if you were getting a lot of girl reaction, like screams and things, it would start to wane. You had to really deliver when the men got there, because they weren't so anxious to do any screaming for you. But Buddy Holly was an exception—he would go over more on those evenings when there was a bigger male audience."

Mrs. Holley can also confirm this aspect of the Crickets' appeal: probably ninety percent of the letters she has received since Buddy's death have been from males, even though females make up a large majority of the record-buying audience.

● *A new set of publicity pictures and, encouraged by the Everly Brothers, a new image*

After the Paramount shows, the Crickets made a seventeen-day tour for Irvin Feld and the GAC. They then returned to New York for their second appearance on *The Ed Sullivan Show* (January 26, 1958), which was marred by a run-in between the Crickets and Sullivan the afternoon of the show.

"It was during the dress rehearsal," remembers Allison. "Joe B. and I were wrestling or goofing around somewhere down in the basement. All of a sudden, they struck the act scheduled before us and we were supposed to go on. Sullivan announced us but Buddy just came out alone with his guitar. Ed said, 'Where are the others?' and Buddy said, 'I don't know—no telling!' Finally, we got up there—but Ed Sullivan was turned completely off. I don't remember what all was said—but we were supposed to do two songs that night and two minutes before the show was over, we were still standing there waiting to go on. So we just got time to do one song. And the lighting was bad—you couldn't even see Joe B. and myself, you could just see Buddy—and the sound was terrible, too, and it was like they did that on purpose. It was really a drag—made us look awful."

The one song they did sing was "Oh Boy!", a choice Sullivan had objected to at the rehearsal, perhaps thinking it too wild. Holly, though, insisted on performing the song. "I told my friends down in Lubbock, Texas that I was going to sing that song," he said, "and if I can't sing it—why, I don't want to be on the show." Later, Holly turned down an invitation for a third appearance; he'd apparently had his fill of the Sullivan show. Allison says, "I wasn't there when it happened, but I heard that Buddy was at the booking agency when they called from the Sullivan show and offered a lot more loot, like twice as much as we'd gotten for the second show. And Buddy said, 'Just tell them to forget it, man, they ain't got enough money.' And the agent said, 'Well, I can't tell them that, you tell them.' So I heard that Buddy got on the phone and said, 'Man, you can forget it, we're not gonna do that.' Well, that's not exactly what he told him—I guess it was a little harsher than that."

American rock 'n' roll was by now starting to capture a worldwide audience. The year 1958 saw overseas tours by those artists who had proved

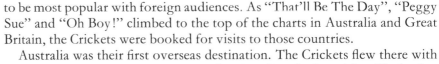

to be most popular with foreign audiences. As "That'll Be The Day", "Peggy Sue" and "Oh Boy!" climbed to the top of the charts in Australia and Great Britain, the Crickets were booked for visits to those countries.

Australia was their first overseas destination. The Crickets flew there with Norman Petty in late January 1958, leaving directly from New York after the Ed Sullivan show. In Honolulu, they caught up with the other artists on the package tour: Jodie Sands, Jerry Lee Lewis and Paul Anka. (Johnny O'Keefe, the leading Australian star of the day, opened the Australian shows.) Top billing on the tour went to Anka, then fifteen years old, who had a few months earlier written and recorded "Diana", the best-selling record of the decade. The billing reflected the current popularity of "Diana" in Australia, but was also a matter of negotiation: according to Petty, Anka agreed to go on the tour for less than his regular price, in return for the top spot on the bill. Holly, says Joe Mauldin, had a different attitude about such questions of prestige:

"Buddy was always one for saying, 'The hell with the billing, man, I want the money.' When we played the New York Paramount on the Alan Freed Christmas show, Fats Domino and Jerry Lee Lewis were both billed above us, but I know for sure that we were making more than Jerry Lee and I think we were making more than Fats. Things like that did go on."

Petty recalls that, whatever Anka's billing, the Australian audiences gave more acclaim to the Crickets and the most of all to Jerry Lee Lewis. Lewis himself, however, once told me, "Buddy was the real star on that one. He just tore them up over there—just drove them wild." What newspaper accounts exist seem to confirm Lewis's impression; the Melbourne *Herald* called Holly "the undoubted star of the show".

The six-day Australian tour consisted of shows in Sydney, Newcastle, Brisbane and Melbourne. Throughout the tour, Holly impressed the Australians with both his music and his demeanor. This was the third Australian tour by American rock 'n' roll groups: a January 1957 tour had featured Bill Haley, while one in October headlined Little Richard, Gene Vincent and Eddie Cochran. Some disturbances had broken out at shows on the earlier tours and the Australians seem to have been relieved by the lack of incidents on Holly's tour. Disc jockeys and other music industry personnel who met Holly were almost surprised by his normality and recall him as being subdued, modest, and perhaps a bit overwhelmed by the attention being given to him. The striking off-stage impression made on the Australian music industry by Holly and the Crickets can be seen in the description of Holly offered years later by Australian record executive Ken Taylor, in his memoir *Rock Generation*:

> ... in the complex world of show business where things are not always what they seem ... a guy called Buddy Holly was favourite and king. Genuine in outlook and unaffected in demeanor, Buddy and his group, the Crickets, were the First Gentlemen of Rock and Roll. ... To meet him Buddy was the perfect representation of a sombre American parson—ascetic, serious, dignified behind the horn-rimmed glasses he perpetually wore. His personality, innate decency—and talent—added up to an American legend.

When Holly and the Crickets returned from Australia, they left behind a legion of devoted fans who have helped keep Holly's popularity alive in Australia to this day.

One unusual by-product of the Australian tour was the recording of Jerry Allison's first single. Australian star Johnny O'Keefe had written and

● *During rehearsals the Crickets found time to jam with Jerry Lee Lewis*

● *Buddy on stage in Australia*

recorded a tune called "Wild One". The Crickets decided that Jerry should record the song when the group got home and so he did, under the title "Real Wild Child" (the subtitle for O'Keefe's original version).

"I was going to try to do it like James Cagney," says Allison, "but that didn't work. So we tried to—well, I forget what I was trying to sound like. Anyway, O'Keefe had done it seriously, and we did it like a joke. But we did one tour, in October of 1958, where we played some places where that record was in the charts and I sang it on the show sometimes. Buddy didn't like it very much—he thought it was kind of a farce, I think."

"At the time," Norman Petty remembers, "the Crickets were so hot that Coral was ready to release *anything* we gave them." Allison's middle name is Ivan (his friends rarely call him Jerry, but instead call him by his initials, "J-I"), and before Petty took the record to New York, Allison decided to put just his middle name down on the disc as the artist. He explains, "I didn't want my name on it. I said I didn't want anybody to know who it was because I thought it was really atrocious."

The flip side was a rock 'n' roll version of "Oh, You Beautiful Doll", in which Allison demolished the lyrics with a comic mumbling doubletalk he had picked up from Sam Hirt, a trombonist in the Paul Williams Orchestra, the stage band on the Show of Stars tour. There was even a bit of a takeoff, in the instrumental break, on the delicate celesta sound of "Everyday": here, says Allison, Petty tinkled wine glasses. The overall result was hilarious, regardless of musical quality. (On both cuts, Petty's studio musician Bo Clarke played drums in place of Allison.)

"Real Wild Child" was in fact a moderate success in some areas and eventually rose to number 68 on *Billboard*'s Hot 100 in October 1958. Allison didn't really have cause for embarrassment. Besides the humour inherent in a novelty record, the song had a danceable beat and several instrumental choruses with memorable lead guitar picking by Holly. Allison's flat, nasal, mocking vocal gave the song that ambivalent mixture of identification and self-parody which marked the first-person narratives of Chuck Berry, Eddie Cochran and Bo Diddley. At the least, the recording showed that the fatigue and tension

● There were few chances to meet fans but Joe McCue, who travelled 300 miles to see the stars at Newcastle, was lucky

● The Crickets with Norman Petty during a short break from touring

● Shortly after arriving at London Airport

● Facing page: High jinks at The Crickets' UK press reception, held at the Whisky-A-Go-Go club in Soho, London. With the Crickets in the final picture are England cricketers Godfrey Evans and Denis Compton.

involved in their performing career had not deprived the Crickets of their sense of humour or perspective.

After a short vacation in Lubbock and a brief swing through Florida with Jerry Lee Lewis, Bill Haley and the Everly Brothers, the Crickets took off at the end of February for a four-week tour of Great Britain. There the Crickets' records had been even more successful than in the United States—a fact emphasized still more in the months after the tour when Holly's group and solo singles remained top-sellers in Great Britain, even when they failed to rise high on the American charts.

The reviews in music papers at the time and Holly's influence on British music in succeeding years show that the tour had a terrific impact. Actually, it opened on an inauspicious note. On the second day of the tour, the Crickets appeared on the *Sunday Night at the London Palladium* television show and were not at their best. Although the Crickets were somewhat nervous when they faced television audiences anyway, the major problem on this performance was technical. Microphone volume and balance were poor—the fault not of the Crickets, but of the show's own technicians. This, and the uncertainty of how a British audience would react to their music, increased the group's nervousness. Also, viewers who had thought that the Crickets themselves sang vocal backgrounds on the records were surprised to find that only Holly sang. The British devotion to authenticity provoked some criticism of the Crickets on this count.

After that show, however, the Crickets met with little but approval during the rest of their stay. On tour, where Petty had more control over sound levels and the Crickets felt more at ease and less inhibited in their stage performances, the group won hosts of new fans. Instead of commenting on the lack of vocal background, reviewers remarked how close the group came in live performances to reproducing their recorded sound. As in Australia, critics were struck by the trio's full sound and contagious excitement. Keith Goodwin of the *New Musical Express* wrote:

If enthusiasm, drive, and down-to-earth abandon are the ingredients necessary for success in the rock 'n' roll field, then Buddy Holly and the Crickets are all set

for a long and eventful run of popularity! They rocked their way through a tremendous, belting 25-minute act without letting up for one moment . . . and the audience showed their approval in no uncertain terms, via handclaps, whistles, shouts, and long bursts of sustained applause.

Much of the trio's success can be attributed to the fact that their "in person" sound is almost identical to the sound that they produce on record. . . . But how these boys manage to make such a big sound with their limited instrumentation baffles me! . . . Take my word for it—this is rock 'n' roll like we've never heard it before in Britain!

Of course, the praise wasn't unanimous; and it's almost as revealing to read an opposite opinion. For example, Peter Holdsworth of the Bradford *Telegraph and Argus* had this to say:

Artistry has been kicked out of the stage door and performers who can provide ephemeral thrills are taking its place. Audiences are in search of the momentary gimmick, of which they tire whenever a new novelty is introduced. At least it would seem so from the fanatical reception given to a screeching guitar player and his two colleagues when they headed the bill at the Gaumont Theatre, Bradford, last night. They were Americans Buddy Holly and the Crickets. Unless they had previously read the lyrics or heard them sung by an articulate vocalist, I would have defied anyone in the audience to tell me what seventy per cent of the words were which issued from the lips of this foot-stamping, knee-falling musician. Where on earth is show business heading? The tragedy often is that many of the performers, like the trio last night, have a basic talent which they distort in order to win an audience's favour.

The Crickets toured on a package show which was quite different from American rock 'n' roll shows. In Britain, true variety shows were more common—a rock 'n' roll group might appear with pop singers, jazz bands, comedians and the like. The arrangement raised rock 'n' roll to the same status level as more established forms of music and entertainment. At the same time, it demanded from rock 'n' roll performers the professional showmanship that the variety show audiences expected. The Crickets had top billing on the tour and most of those who came to see the show had come to see the Crickets in particular. But because they were the only rock 'n' roll act on the show, the Crickets had to convey the whole spirit of their music to an audience of mixed ages and interests.

It was a challenge, but the Crickets liked the change from the routine and enjoyed the tour. The tour was not as tiring as American outings because distances between stops were so much less in Britain. Even so, the trip was no vacation—the Crickets had no days off during their twenty-five days in Britain. Only one feature of the trip really displeased the Texans: the dark, cold, wet weather of late winter that greeted them more often than they cared for.

Ironically enough, the triumphant tour ended badly, thanks to some misfiring backstage antics before the group's last appearance.

"Jerry, Buddy and I were in the dressing room after the first of the two shows that night," remembers Joe Mauldin, "and we were really looking forward to getting back to the States. We had been in England a month and it was cold and it seemed like we'd been away from home forever. I had a great big cigar and I said, 'I'm gonna celebrate, man, I'm gonna smoke this cigar.' Well, it was cold, and all the windows were closed in this small dressing room, and Jerry and Buddy said, 'You're not smoking that cigar

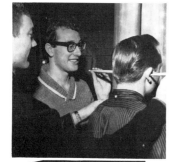

in here.' So we started scuffling around a little and I had the cigar in my mouth, puffing on it and blowing smoke everywhere, and Jerry grabbed my right arm and Buddy grabbed my left arm—they were going to stretch me out and reach up and pull the cigar out of my mouth. I swung around to hit Buddy in the stomach with my head to knock the breath out of him, hopefully, so he'd turn me loose and I could take care of J-I. But when I swung around, Buddy bent down to get the cigar, and instead of hitting him in the stomach, I hit him in the mouth with my head and knocked off two of the caps on his teeth.

"Well, you know how it is when you get your teeth knocked out—and Buddy had two big old holes there where he didn't have any teeth. And Buddy said, 'Just bring it to a halt, I'm not performing—I'm not going on again. We'll forfeit the pay or whatever, but we're not going to do the show.' So Norman called us over and soft-talked us, and said this and that. So what Buddy did was, he chewed some gum and then mashed the gum out and smoothed it over his teeth, and I guess from the audience you couldn't tell the difference. I don't know how he sang with a wad of chewing gum up over his lip; but he did it, and we did the complete show. But Buddy was in such a state of mind after this accident had happened that I'm sure the show we put on was hideous. In fact, Norman told us, 'That's the worst show I've ever seen you guys do.'"

The Crickets flew back to the United States on March 25, immediately after this last show. A segment they had taped for the BBC's *Off The Record* TV show was aired two days later and was a more successful effort than their first TV appearance had been. The tour had helped to increase the Crickets' record sales in Britain—during one week, Holly and the Crickets had four records ("Peggy Sue", "Oh Boy!", "Maybe Baby" and "Listen To Me") in the top thirty. And it was probably no coincidence that guitar sales boomed in the wake of Holly's visit.

● *Just before the first show—with Ronnie Keene and Gary Miller (2nd from top) and The Tanner Sisters (centre)*

● *On BBC-TV's 'Off The Record'*

When the Crickets arrived back in the United States, they immediately set out on another lengthy tour—this one a six-week show under the aegis of Alan Freed which featured the Crickets, Chuck Berry, Jerry Lee Lewis, Larry Williams and Frankie Lymon. (This was the tour that led to the famous indictment of Freed on charges of inciting a riot after violence broke out following the troupe's appearance in Boston on May 3. The charge was dropped a year later.) With such a schedule as the Crickets had been following for the preceding six months, it was fortunate that they had recorded so many tunes in Clovis the year before and at the unusual session in Oklahoma City the preceding autumn. These recordings provided the Crickets with their next singles and with the material for two albums.

"Maybe Baby" was released in the United States in early February and was almost as big a hit for the Crickets as "Oh Boy!" had been. Holly's mother is credited with the original idea for the lyrics of the song. "I had tried to write songs for Buddy before," she says, "but when he'd read them, he'd say, 'Mother, we can't use your songs, they're all too serious—they've got to be more fun.'" However, when Mrs. Holley wrote a couple of lines for "Maybe Baby", Buddy read them and decided to finish the lyrics and write a tune for the song—"But don't put *my* name on it," his mother warned him, and so he didn't. The other Crickets also had a hand in the writing of the tune. In the end, the song had the characteristic ambivalence of many of Holly's songs. The singer has little more than just hope to rely on: *maybe*, baby, you'll be true; and when someday, you do finally want me, I'll be there. But as in "I'm Looking For Someone To Love", the bright melody and happy delivery cast the uncertain lyrics in a new light.

Both "Maybe Baby" and its flip side, "Tell Me How" (in my opinion, a better record), featured the driving beat and jangling guitar sound of "Oh Boy!" The specific drum beat for "Maybe Baby" was, says Jerry Allison, suggested to the Crickets by Little Richard's "Lucille". The vocal backgrounds copied those on "Oh Boy!" and "That'll Be The Day"; the arrangement on "Tell Me How" is especially well done, supporting the vocal without ever obscuring the dramatic rendition of the tune.

At the same time as that single was released, another was issued under Holly's own name: "Listen To Me"/"I'm Gonna Love You Too". This release was a commercial failure in the United States; in Britain, it was Holly's only recording before "Early In The Morning" which failed to make the top ten. The timing of the release may have contributed to its lack of success. "Peggy Sue" was still number three on *Billboard*'s Top 100 and "Oh Boy!" was not far behind when the new singles were released. "Listen To Me" was less obviously commercial than "Maybe Baby", and perhaps there was resistance from programmers to the idea of playing four singles by the same group at the same time.

But so much for history. No matter what the sales figures were at the time, "Listen To Me" and "I'm Gonna Love You Too" today rate among Holly's finest songs—"Listen To Me", especially, has endured in popularity.

Like "Words of Love", "Listen To Me" was recorded with some thought to the example of "Love Is Strange"; and like Holly's first solo single, "Listen To Me" made inspired use of overdubbing to create strange, even eerie effects. Throughout the song, the lead guitar sounds hypnotically in the background as Allison plays a rolling, syncopated rhythm. Holly's double-tracked vocal rises and falls in volume, swaying with its own rhythm, until in the instrumental break it whispers softly, "Listen . . . listen . . . listen to me", followed by the captivating guitar variation running beyond the expected end.

NOT MAYBE
BUT POSITIVELY
A SMASH HIT!

MAYBE, BABY

The Crickets

9-55053

● *Bob Theile (centre) travelled to Clovis to present Buddy and Norman with a gold disc for 'Peggy Sue'*

"Listen To Me" provides another example of the mixed atmosphere of Holly's songs. (Though Petty is listed as a co-writer, Allison remarks: "I think 'Listen To Me' was all Buddy's—I think he had that written in Lubbock, before we ever got to hanging around Clovis.") As in "Everyday", there is an ambiguity to the singer's tale, an unsettled character to the love affair. Though the singer proclaims his love absolutely, he must still convince the one he loves by a direct appeal. The tone alternates between faith in the future and pleas for what is still just a possibility—between what will be and what can be:

Listen to me,
Hear what I say,
Our hearts can be,
Nearer each day,
Hold me, darling—
Listen closely to me.

Your eyes will see
What love can do,
Reveal to me
Your love so true,
Hold me, darling—
Listen closely to me.

I've told the stars
You're my only love,
I want to love you tenderly.
Those same bright stars
In heaven above
Know now how sweet,
Sweethearts can be.

Listen to me,
Hear what I say,
Our hearts can be
Nearer each day,
Hold me, darling—
Listen closely to me.

As always, the lyrics cannot be separated from the musical setting. It is Holly's vocal, especially, that breathes life into the words, varying and moulding the tone of the lyrics and lending them a tense, urgent emotion.

Holly's vocal on "I'm Gonna Love You Too" is even more graphic, with key words emphasized in unexpected ways—for example, the word "heart" is sighed more than sung. Throughout the song, Holly's vocal habits add to the impact of the lyrics. Although he is singing, he is able to produce the controlled variations in mood, tone and attitude that colour everyday speech. His techniques cannot be better explained in print; they must instead be heard to be appreciated.

As with "Maybe Baby", all the good humour in "I'm Gonna Love You Too" is spent on a song whose lyrics describe a troublesome situation. Since quite a few of Holly's songs follow this pattern, some might argue that the lyrics don't mean anything—or else, how could they be sung in this manner? But the situation is not so paradoxical as it seems. It is precisely this characteristic that makes such songs so appealing (and their lyrics so hard to discuss, isolated from the music and Holly's individual performance). Holly's fans, confused by their own hopes and doubts, could find consolation and encouragement in his songs. In his role as a singer, Holly rarely speaks as an outsider merely offering advice to the listener. Instead, he is himself confronted with the problem—hence, it is not so easy for him to provide an answer or retain an optimistic attitude. When he does remain cheerful and, illogically, hopeful in the face of unpleasant reality, he offers a hopeful example to others. If the songs were instead totally cheerful, they would have less impact—because those listeners who needed the encouragement most would be unable to identify with the singer in the first place. Even when Holly cannot see the way out himself, as in songs such as "What To Do" and "Learning the Game", he at least offers the consolation of tragedy: he provides the listener with a friend who has shared his experience and can express it in a general but quite realistic fashion. Holly's songs are uplifting—but not necessarily because they deal with happy situations. So it is with "I'm Gonna Love You Too":

You're gonna say you've missed me,
You're gonna say you'll kiss me,
Yes, you're gonna say you'll love me,
'Cause I'm gonna love you too.

I don't care what you told me,
You're gonna say you'll hold me,
Yes, you're gonna say you'll love me,
'Cause I'm gonna love you too.

After all, another fella took you,
But I still can't overlook you,
I'm a-gonna do my best to hook you,
After all is said and done,

It's a-gonna happen, someday,
You're gonna see things my way,
Yes, you're gonna say you'll love me,
'Cause I'm a-gonna love you too.

You're gonna tell me sweet things,
You're gonna make my heart sing,
Yes, you're gonna hear those bells ring,
'Cause I'm gonna love you too.

(Repeat chorus)

You're gonna say you've missed me,
You're gonna say you'll kiss me,
Yes, you're gonna say you'll love me,
'Cause I'm a-gonna love you too.

The Crickets' Brunswick album, the *Chirping Crickets*, was released in November 1957 in America and three months later in Britain and Australia. It included the tunes that had appeared on the Crickets' first two singles—

"That'll Be The Day", "I'm Looking For Someone To Love", "Oh Boy!" and "Not Fade Away"—as well as "Maybe Baby" and "Tell Me How", which appeared on this album and on an EP before being released as the Crickets' third single. The album added three songs cut the previous spring in Clovis—"Last Night", "Send Me Some Lovin'", and "It's Too Late"— and three songs which, with "Maybe Baby", had been recorded in Oklahoma City—"An Empty Cup", "You've Got Love" and "Rock Me My Baby".

Two of these six songs were rock 'n' roll ballads made famous by other artists: Chuck Willis's "It's Too Late" and Little Richard's "Send Me Some Lovin'". These songs were favourites of Larry Holley's and Buddy recorded them at his brother's suggestion. Holly himself was a fan of both Willis and Little Richard; he frequently performed such Little Richard tunes as "Rip It Up" and "The Girl Can't Help It" in his own live performances. "It's Too Late" is an excellent recording, though the background vocals sometimes seem too "pop" by comparison with Holly's own performance (a problem on several of the slower tunes on this album). "Send Me Some Lovin'" is slightly less successful as the ballad was more suited to Little Richard's vocal style than Holly's. A comparison of the original version with Holly's does reveal, though, just how near Holly tried to come to Little Richard's vocal—and how closely he had studied the original version of the song and Little Richard's vocal idiosyncrasies on that recording. Jerry Coleman, then a disc jockey on Lubbock's KSEL, remembers that Buddy used to come over to the station, pick out records by Little Richard, Fats Domino, Ray Charles and others, and listen to them in an unused studio with the speakers turned way up. Apparently, he was studying, as well as enjoying the records.

Two other tunes were also ballads: "Last Night", which had been cut without background vocals in March 1957, and "An Empty Cup", originally written and recorded by Roy Orbison. (Orbison had made his first recordings at Petty's studio, before moving on to Sun Records.) "You've Got Love" was co-written by Petty, Orbison and Johnny "Peanuts" Wilson, who had played guitar with Orbison and who recorded this song himself as the flip side to his release on Brunswick, "Cast Iron Arm". Holly's rendition is faster paced than Wilson's, with an enthusiastic vocal and a guitar break along the lines of those in "Oh Boy!" and "Maybe Baby".

The last of the cuts on the album was "Rock Me My Baby", a novelty tune by songwriters Shorty Long and Susan Heather based on, of all things, "Hickory Dickory Dock". Allison provides a syncopated Latin rhythm to accent the Crickets' typically strong beat. Holly's guitar solo is varied, skilful and pleasing, and is generally considered one of his finest. The overdubbed vocals are effective, supporting Holly's vocal and instrumental performances in a fashion similar to the blend on "Tell Me How" or "Oh Boy!".

Though the quality of these six songs cannot match the strength of the six cuts that were on the first three Crickets singles, none of the songs in the *Chirping Crickets* album could be considered as merely filler material. By contrast, most rock 'n' roll albums at the time, and for years afterwards, consisted of eleven indifferent tunes and one hit single—the title of which would be prominently displayed on the album cover. Holly's albums by no means followed this pattern. The popularity of his early albums long after his death and the continued demand for packages of his "greatest hits", many of which were never released as singles in his lifetime, reflect the overall quality of his work and not just the success of a few songs.

Holly's solo Coral album, titled simply *Buddy Holly*, appeared in March 1958. It included the "A" and "B" sides of his three solo singles already mentioned, plus six songs not previously released.

Three of the songs on the album had been first recorded by important rock 'n' roll artists. "Baby I Don't Care" was performed by Elvis Presley in the movie *Jailhouse Rock*; it was written by Jerry Leiber and Mike Stoller, the team responsible for so many of the Coasters' biggest hits. The attraction of Holly's version lies in the interplay between Holly's rapidly strummed lead guitar and Allison's irregular rhythms. (On this recording, and also on "Not Fade Away", Allison played only on a cardboard box.) "Valley of Tears", written and recorded by Fats Domino, is another tune which Holly recorded at the suggestion of his older brother. It has a much cleaner sound than the Domino recording, with Holly's vocal and Petty's organ playing unencumbered by other voices or a lush arrangement. "Ready Teddy", one of Little Richard's greatest rockers, was a tune that the Crickets were fond of performing themselves. On Holly's recording the beat is modified—from the New Orleans beat of Little Richard's records to the Texas rockabilly sound of Holly's—and the instrumentation is changed, reflecting the use of guitar rather than saxophone on rockabilly recordings; but despite the differences, the versions are comparable in excitement.

Holly was a co-writer of two other songs on the album: "Look At Me", written with Allison and Petty, and "Little Baby", written with Petty and C. W. Kendall Jr., the pianist in a Dallas band called the Big Beats (a group headed by Trini Lopez) which was also beginning to cut records at Clovis. The former tune has a sweet and playful air to it, with the lyrics and Holly's voice patterns mixing quiet pleading and audacious confidence. Vi Petty played piano on the cut. "Little Baby", at heart a blues song, is dominated by Kendall's heavy rhythmic piano playing and Holly's expressive country-blues vocal.

The one other cut on the album was chosen for Holly's next single, released in late April. To many people, "Rave On" is the most exciting recording the Crickets ever made; the title has become a byword for Holly's frenetic style. Inexplicably, the single was just a minor success in the United States where it only reached number 39 on *Billboard*'s Top 100 (though it was a top ten record in scattered regional markets). In Britain, by contrast, the disc made the top five on the national charts.

A joyful and driving performance, "Rave On" epitomizes the good feeling of rock 'n' roll. As if to prove this, one "good music" station, in a specially prepared LP attacking rock 'n' roll, chose "Rave On" as one of its "examples" and called it "mood music for stealing hubcaps". The song offers the most perfect introduction to Holly's vocal gimmickry—for who else but Buddy Holly could make a rising six-syllable word out of "well", as he does at the very opening of the song?

The song was written by Sonny West and Bill Tilghman, the same team which had composed "Oh Boy!". Tilghman remembers getting the idea for the song after hearing the expression "rave on!" in another record (probably, Carl Perkins's "Dixie Fried"):

"We were driving up and down the street in my home town, Sonny and I," says Tilghman, "and we grabbed onto that title and said, 'Let's do something with it.' First we wrote it as a domestic problem, a disagreement between two people, but Norman turned it down—he told us to bring it back, he wanted us to write a love song out of it. So we worked on it a couple of weeks, to the way it is now, and took it back over." West recorded the song himself at Petty's studio, and the record resulted in a contract for West with Atlantic Records, which released "Rave On" in February 1958.

BUDDY HOLLY (1-12") **Coral CRL 57210** Most of the selections have been released as singles. Holly's hit "Peggy Sue" and his current contender, "I'm Gonna Love You Too," are also included. Holly exercises his vocal gimmick well on the rockabilly tunes. Strongest appeal will be to teen buyers. Good cover shot of the artist.

● Buddy on stage at the Hippodrome, Waterloo, Iowa, April 28, 1958

West's version, which never made the charts, had been out for two months when Holly's rendition of the tune was released in mid-April as a single, a month after the release of the *Buddy Holly* album. Holly's version of "Rave On" was recorded at the Bell Sound Studios in New York City on January 25, the day before their second *Ed Sullivan Show* appearance that preceded the Australian tour. Mauldin remembers that the reason given for making the record in New York was the need for one more song to complete the *Buddy Holly* album and the lack of time to return to New Mexico because of the tight tour schedule; but Bob Thiele says that the New York session came about at his own prodding and that he in fact produced the record.

"I suggested to Buddy that he record in New York," says Thiele. "I wanted to inject my own ideas, or talent—that was my job. I had pushed for a few months on this. Buddy was for it, Norman was against it. There was some tension at the session because of Petty's feelings—he was always afraid that he'd blow his hold on Holly. To be honest, though, I think Buddy was more comfortable at Clovis. I don't think any of us really felt this was a great or successful move, to record in New York."

One other song was recorded at the Bell Sound Studios session: "That's My Desire", a song that had been a hit for Frankie Laine in 1947 and had been recorded by the R & B group the Channels in 1957. Holly's recording of this song was not released at the time and only became available years later on compilation albums. Actually, Holly himself did not want the song issued at the time. "We weren't happy with that song," says Jerry Allison. "I mean, we didn't consider it a record. We sort of said, 'O.K., we'll try that later.'"

The flip side of "Rave On", "Take Your Time", follows the same chordal pattern as "Look At Me" and features Norman Petty on organ. Holly's vocal, his strummed acoustic guitar, Allison's varied effects and Petty's more conventional organ playing provide rhythms that mix and clash to create unexpected patterns. "Take Your Time" was one tune on which Holly, Allison and Petty did actually collaborate. "We wrote it in the back of Norman's studio," says Allison. "I know Norman had a hand in it because I remember Buddy not liking the line Norman came up with about 'Heartstrings will sing like a string of twine.'" The lyrics have the patience and confidence in love found in "Everyday", and, in the refrain, mix humour and seriousness:

Take your time,	*Take your time,*
I can wait,	*And take mine, too—*
For all of the love	*I have time to spend;*
I know will be mine,	*Take your time,*
If you take your time.	*Go with me through*
	Times till all times end.
Take your time,	*Take your time,*
Though it's late,	*I can wait,*
Heartstrings will sing	*For all of the love*
Like a string of twine,	*I know will be mine,*
If you take your time.	*If you take your time.*

The *Buddy Holly* album and the succeeding single showed that Holly was not committed to a guitar sound on all his releases; Petty, his wife and Kendall played organ or piano on several of these recordings. The use of organ, though, was not Holly's idea, but Petty's. Jerry Allison states, "Buddy didn't like organ at all, on anything. I never heard him say he liked it and I always heard him say he didn't like it. Sometimes he'd argue about it; sometimes he'd just save the hassle and let it ride." And Petty himself says, "Buddy was very set in his ways as far as having some of his ideas, and we would argue about ideas sometimes. I think that there was one thing that Buddy didn't particularly agree with me on—we used Hammond organ on 'Take Your Time', sort of against his better judgement, because he felt that organ was to be reserved for church or something or other at the time, but he conceded in the end."

Piano was used on both sides of the Crickets' fourth single, issued in May 1958, one year to the day after the release of "That'll Be The Day". "Think It Over" and "Fool's Paradise" were recorded during the Crickets' visit home in February after the Australian tour. "Think It Over" features one of the better-integrated vocal arrangements among the Crickets' records, the background voices functioning here as both answering chorus and imitation instruments—horns, perhaps. The piano is the lead instrument in the break but instead of standing out as prominently as on some of the recordings on the *Buddy Holly* album, it is blended with the sounds provided by Allison and Holly. The happy, blues-derived melody is matched with words showing the brand of humour that characterized the songs on which Holly and Allison collaborated. Not that the songs were deliberately modelled on any pattern; their style and tone simply reflected Holly's and Allison's own personalities. Jerry comments:

"I never did set and think about it; but a lot of Buddy's songs had a certain attitude—like, 'That'll be the day when *you* say goodbye,' sort of 'I don't need you'. Or 'Think It Over'—you know, 'think it over in your pretty little head—are you sure I'm not the one?' That was his attitude about everything. Because he was really a self-confident, smart-aleck sort of guy, you know. He'd say anything he wanted to—he wasn't ever trying to be really nice to people, he'd just say what he thought. And the same way with chicks—like on the road, a chick would say something like, 'Why do you wear those big glasses?' or whatever, and he'd say, 'Hey, forget you, you get out of here,' and he'd chase the chick off in a minute."

The swinging rhythm of "Think It Over" was close to that of "That'll Be The Day", even though the Crickets' two intervening singles had successfully featured a steadier, driving beat. The more conservative practice in popular music has been to follow a hit record with a near-copy, hoping for similar success with the second record. The Crickets, though, were never so regimented. "When we were making those records," says Allison, "Buddy was never on a trip about 'What's going to be commercial now?' or 'What will everybody like?' We just played what we could play. I remember on 'Think It Over'—we had used that 'straight eight' beat on several songs, and we started to record 'Think It Over' the same way; and then we thought, 'Hey, that might sound better more like "That'll Be The Day".' The other sound was what was happening, but we thought the song was more fun to play with a swing beat. So we cut it like that. We just did what we wanted to do."

The choice of which songs were to be released as singles was actually the responsibility of the A & R director; in practice, Thiele conferred with Murray Deutch about it, and the preferences of Holly and Petty had a strong influence. "I would talk to Buddy on the phone," says Deutch, "and find out which ones he liked. There were no fights about it." Holly and Allison's

● *Buddy recording at Bell Sound Studios, New York*

disregard for the practice of following a commercial success with a close imitation was, fortunately, shared by Thiele, whose lifelong devotion to the recording of jazz makes him an anomaly in the pop music business. His words, in fact, mirror those of Allison. Thiele says, "This is how I've always operated. I sign artists I like and issue records I like, based on my own personal preference. I've never believed in surveys—I've never tried to be 'commercial'. I just do what I feel like doing."

Besides recording with the Crickets, Holly branched out in other directions during this first year of success. In June 1958, he cut "Early In The Morning"/ "Now We're One", the first of Holly's Coral recordings which did not include the Crickets in the instrumental accompaniment. Both tunes had been written by Bobby Darin; Holly's versions were cut in the wake of some complicated manoeuvring involving Darin's record contract.

At the time, Darin was under contract to Atco. His contract had only a few weeks left to run before Atco would have to exercise its annual option or release him. Since he had had no hits on the label, he expected that he would be released. He therefore cut the two tunes for Brunswick, in order to have a record ready to sell on a new label when his old contract expired. (The record was produced by Dick Jacobs, who had been music director for Coral under Thiele but had succeeded Thiele as A & R director when Thiele left to go to work for Dot Records in March 1958.) Brunswick prepared to release the single under the group title of the Ding Dongs. Then, the unexpected happened. Atco decided to release one more single by Darin to see if he was worth keeping under contract. They chose "Splish Splash"— which promptly zoomed to the top of the charts, became a million-seller, and made Darin a star. Atco renewed Darin's contract and, when they found out who the lead singer of the Ding Dongs was, they forced Brunswick to pull back its record.

Petty and Holly were in New York at the time. When Petty heard of Brunswick's problem, he suggested that Holly record the two Darin songs for Coral. When asked, Holly quickly agreed to cut the tunes. The session, produced by Dick Jacobs, was held within forty-eight hours and the record was pressed and released as quickly as possible. Meanwhile, Atco released Darin's recording, labelling his group as "The Rinky Dinks". The two competing singles both made the charts, with Darin's version selling just a bit better in the United States while Holly's recording, as usual, did well overseas.

On Holly's version of "Early In The Morning", Jacobs followed the exact same arrangement he had used in cutting Darin's original recording. Holly was accompanied by the Helen Way Singers (a black gospel chorus), and by the noted saxophonist Sam "The Man" Taylor and drummer Panama Francis. "Early In The Morning" proved convincingly that Holly could be just as believable singing songs written by others—he was a stylist, as well as a creator of his own material. And he made it all seem very easy. According to Jacobs, Holly listened to the song a couple of times and quickly cut three takes—any one of which would have been suitable for release. The flip side, "Now We're One", is best forgotten. The vocal arrangement is sickeningly sweet, and the lyrics are simply awful; Holly does the best he can with it.

"Early In The Morning" was certainly one of Holly's favourites among his own recordings. He had for a long time admired the mixed gospel-and-rhythm & blues sound promoted on the Atlantic label and this was his first chance to cut such a record himself. Though his own wild vocal and Taylor's fine saxophone break really made the record, Holly was especially happy over the chance to use an Atlantic-type vocal accompaniment. "He really thought that was an excellent record," Allison recalls. "He liked having the black chorus singing on it. When I heard the record, I thought at the time, 'This is the best record so far.' My feelings weren't hurt by not playing on it—after all, I wasn't even in New York when he cut it."

Around this same time, Holly moved in another new direction and made his first attempt to write songs intended for artists other than himself. Holly had toured with the Everly Brothers on the Feld show in the autumn of 1957 and on several later tours, and had become close friends with them. During a visit home in the early summer of 1958, he got together with his old friend Bob Montgomery and wrote "Love's Made A Fool Of You" and "Wishing", hoping to have the Everly Brothers record the songs on a single.

Instead of making a simple, unaccompanied home tape of the tunes to play for the Everlys and their manager, Holly went into Petty's studio and recorded the songs with a full band—providing not just his own versions of the songs but also his conception of how the Everly Brothers might sound singing them. He then brought the tunes to Nashville and played them for Wesley Rose, the Everlys' manager. Supposedly, Rose told Holly that the Everlys would be crazy to record the songs since Holly's own recordings, if released, would top any other version. Actually, Rose's response was probably based on other considerations. Besides being the Everlys' manager, he was the head of Acuff-Rose Publishing, for whom Boudleaux and Felice Bryant were then writing their songs. Since the Bryants had written the Everly Brothers' first hits, "Bye Bye Love" and "Wake Up Little Susie", Rose was not in the market for songs by other writers, especially those not writing for Acuff-Rose. (Holly didn't follow a reciprocal course, though: a few months later, he recorded the Bryants' "Raining In My Heart".) Fortunately, Holly's tapes were preserved and were released on record several years later.

Holly did not play lead guitar on these two demos, but turned instead to a guitarist whom he had met at Petty's studio. Tommy Allsup, a native of Tulsa, had come to Clovis a few months before to back up a group on a session, and had been invited by Petty to stay on permanently as a studio musician. Allsup's career had centred on western swing and country music; he had spent several years playing lead guitar in the band headed by Johnnie Lee Wills, Bob Wills's brother. Soon after meeting Allsup and hearing him play, Holly asked Tommy to play with the Crickets. Once again, the Crickets were a quartet—at least on stage, since Allsup was not mentioned on records or in publicity. Buddy and Tommy alternated playing lead in live shows, depending on the song, while on recordings, Allsup played lead and Holly rhythm on the rest of the Crickets' recordings. Obviously, Buddy didn't feel that he was losing face by sharing the limelight with another. Joe Mauldin explains: "Buddy was a star and he knew it, and he didn't mind anybody else sharing the stardom with him. He loved the way Tommy played; he thought he was a fantastic guitar player. Tommy knew a lot about music, too. And he was a very likeable, enjoyable person. It was just one of those things, where you meet somebody and you really hit it off—it seemed like we all hit it off good with Tommy."

Since "Love's Made A Fool Of You" and "Wishing" were just meant to be demos, Holly also used Petty's other studio musicians on the session; neither Allison nor Mauldin played on these recordings. The drummer was Bo Clarke who had come to Clovis with the Roses, Petty's studio vocal group at the time. The bass player was George Atwood, a professional musician

● *Tommy Allsup in 1978*

about twelve years Buddy's senior and a veteran of several jazz groups, including the Gene Krupa band. In the wake of Holly's success, Petty's studio was attracting enough business from hopeful area musicians to warrant a full-time studio band, and Atwood and Allsup helped fill the need.

Holly's version of "Love's Made A Fool Of You" is memorable for its emphatic Latin-flavoured rhythm, folkish sound and striking lead guitar line. The song is masterfully constructed; Holly's vocal, Clarke's accented rhythms, Allsup's picking and Holly's own evenly paced rhythm guitar are mixed with perfect timing. The lyrics, with their bemused acceptance of love's pitfalls, are equally memorable:

Love can make a fool of you,
You do anything that it wants you to.

Love can make you feel so good,
When it goes like you think it should,
Or it can make you cry at night,
When your baby don't treat you right,

When you're feeling sad and blue,
You know love's made a fool of you.

You know love makes fools of men,
But you don't care, you're gonna try it again.

Time goes by, it's a-passing fast,
You think true love has come at last,
But by and by, you're gonna find,
Crazy love has made you blind,

When you're feeling sad and blue,
You know love's made a fool of you.

"Wishing" isn't as strong as "Love's Made A Fool Of You", but it too is well constructed. It features fine guitar work by Allsup, both in the instrumental break and in the background during the vocal refrain where his guitar playing is along the lines of country fiddle music.

By the summer of 1958, Holly had achieved the stature of an established artist—a star, and not just a one-record sensation. Even he, with his determination to "make it", might never have dreamed of the scale of success he and the Crickets had enjoyed over the previous year. Everyone wanted to "make it", but no one knew just what that meant.

Well, not quite—everyone knew it meant money. And for poor boys in Lubbock, Memphis or elsewhere, just escaping poverty was the best reward the music world could offer. Actually, Holly, Allison and Mauldin hadn't yet seen too much of the money; most of what was coming to them was delayed on record company books or in a bank account under the watchful eye of Norman Petty. But there was enough for a few long-desired items. For instance, there was the time the Crickets were returning from a tour by plane; they got off a flight at Dallas and, instead of boarding another plane for the last leg to Lubbock, they decided to go out and buy motorcycles and ride them home.

'We had always dreamed of having motorcycles,'' remembers Allison. "In fact, Buddy had had a Triumph before because we went and saw *The Wild Ones* with Marlon Brando in it, and no time after that Buddy somehow had a motorcycle. Anyway, Buddy was carrying all kinds of cash from the tour we had been on—like, about five thousand dollars. We went first to a Harley Davidson store, but the guy there wouldn't even discuss it with us—we'd say, 'How much is that?' and he'd say, 'Aw, it's too much for you guys.' He was really hateful. So we finally just went out and got a cab and we went to a Triumph place, and the guy there was really nice. Like, we were gonna buy three motorcycles that day, regardless of what happened, but we didn't tell him that. But he said, 'Any one you like the looks of, just get on and ride it around.' He was really a good dude. So Buddy bought an Ariel Cyclone

(650 cc), Joe bought a Triumph Thunderbird, and I bought a Trophy model. And it was a cash deal. Sure was fun."

After Holly's death, his parents kept his bike for over a decade before selling it. Later, it was purchased by a Holly fan from Austin. In 1979, Allison, Mauldin and Sonny Curtis bought the bike and gave it to Waylon Jennings as a birthday present.

Automobiles were also of interest to Buddy. When the money began to come in, in the autumn of 1957, he bought a Chevrolet Impala for his parents—though when he was home, he used it more often than they did. In 1958, he was able to buy a better car; at the suggestion of his father, he bought a pale blue Lincoln. Within a few weeks, Buddy had become dissatisfied with the car. There were some mechanical problems and—well, he just didn't like the car, and he didn't feel like putting up with it. So he traded it in (at a twelve-hundred-dollar loss) for a taupe Cadillac Fleetwood. "Buddy always said he'd have himself a Cadillac by the time he was twenty-one," recalls Bob Montgomery. "So he did."

So the Crickets and Buddy Holly had made it to the top—but now the problem was how to stay there. Holly had learned a lot about the entertainment world in the previous year—about recording techniques, stage presentation and the business aspects of the life of a rock 'n' roll star. He was now beginning to think more actively and creatively about the opportunities open to him and the means of staying in the popular limelight by keeping ahead of the market.

The year had brought other changes, too. When the summer of 1958 rolled around, Buddy was about to be married.

Maria Elena Santiago was born in Puerto Rico. When Maria was eight, her mother died and Maria was sent by her father to New York City to live with her aunt Provi, the head of Peer-Southern Music's important Latin American music division. Despite the family tie, Maria worked at other jobs in New York before joining Peer-Southern Music as a receptionist. The Crickets remember that she was there when they first came to New York in 1957, but Maria doesn't recall having any real contact with Holly until June 1958. She tells the story of their engagement in this way:

"One morning the Crickets came into the office to see Murray Deutch. He was tied up just then, so they sat in the outer office to wait. I had never met them before; at least, I don't think I had seen them, and I know I had never been introduced to them. They were joking around, imitating a Spanish accent and changing English words so they'd sound Spanish, and they introduced each other to me that way.

"When Deutch was free, they went in to see him; and when they came out, Buddy asked me when I'd be free for lunch. Well, when you're a receptionist, you're supposed to greet people and be pleasant to them and not take everything they say too seriously. So I told him I wouldn't be free for a couple of hours. 'O.K.,' he said, 'We'll be waiting for you.' And I thought that was just part of their joking around.

"At lunchtime, Jo Harper, who was in charge of Nor Va Jak business at Peer-Southern, asked me where I was going to eat. I told her I was just going to go downstairs and she said, 'No, come out with me—let's go over to the Howard Johnson's.' 'Why there?' I asked. And Jo said, 'I've got to bring some papers over to Norman Petty and he's waiting for me there.'

"So I said O.K. When we went, Norman was there all right, but that wasn't why Jo had insisted on eating there. You see, the Crickets were there too—Buddy had called Jo Harper and set the whole thing up, telling her to get me down there somehow.

"There were two empty seats and the Crickets were arguing about where I was going to sit. I wound up next to Buddy, on his right. The others were fooling around, playing footsie and grabbing for my hands, while Norman was looking under the table, trying to figure out what was going on. Finally, Buddy grabbed my hand and said, 'O.K. you guys, just cut it out, because I've got her now.' 'But I'll need two hands to eat with,' I said, and he replied, 'Oh, that's all right, I'll help feed you.' And a little while later he said, 'You see this girl? I'm going to marry her. And I'm going to get her to agree in the next two days, before we leave New York.'

"When he took me back to the office, he asked me to go out with him that night—the Crickets were going to record a jingle and we could go out alone afterwards. Well, I wanted to—I really liked him, I knew that already—but I couldn't say 'yes' right then because I had to get my aunt's permission first. Being Spanish, my aunt was very strict. I never went anywhere without her approval. I hadn't even dated anyone before Buddy. So I told Buddy to call me back later in the afternoon because I'd have to ask my aunt first.

"When I asked my aunt if I could go out with Buddy, she said no. The last people she wanted me to be around were entertainers. She thought they were—you know, unreliable and immoral and all that. So when I told her who had asked me out and just who he was, and she heard words like 'singer' and 'musician', she was dead set against it. I said, ask Jo Harper, ask Murray Deutch, ask Mr. Peer—the president of Peer-Southern—they'll tell you he's all right. But she wouldn't agree. When Buddy called back in the middle of the afternoon, I had to tell him that I was still working on my aunt and

● *Maria Elena Santiago*

I didn't know yet if I could go. So he said that if I could make it, I should meet him at his hotel before 6.30.

"It was after 5.30 when I finally convinced my aunt that it was all right. There wasn't time for me to go home and change. So I went to a store right next to our office building and bought some new clothes on the spot, and changed back in the office where we had a shower. And I hopped in a taxi and headed for Buddy's hotel. The Crickets' limousine had just pulled away as my taxi arrived — but Buddy happened to look back down the street and saw me get out, and he had the limousine circle back to pick me up.

"After the recording session, we went out to eat at P. J. Clarke's. And that was where he proposed to me. I didn't take him seriously at first — I thought he was joking. And he got really upset with me and said, 'No, listen to me — I really mean it.' And so I said yes.

"I guess it sounds crazy that he should propose and I should accept the very day we met. But that's really what happened — we just each felt that way, that quickly. The next day I told him, 'Why don't you think about it for a while?' I was sure, but I wanted him to be sure too — everything had happened so fast. But he said, 'I don't have to think it over — I know I want to marry you.'"

Buddy now had to face the task of telling his family about his bride-to-be. He knew there would be problems with that, if only because of the suddenness of the decision. Besides that, his parents might oppose the marriage on the basis of religious doctrine — racial and (especially) religious intermarriage was opposed by many of the Holleys' fundamentalist Baptist brethren for reasons that mixed prejudice and principle. Unsure about approaching his parents directly, Buddy first called his brother Larry; Larry was not opposed, once convinced that Buddy was really sure about his choice. Buddy then told his parents, inviting them to come to New York to meet Maria Elena. In the end, Mr. Holley wholeheartedly approved the marriage; he and Maria became very close, treating each other as father and daughter. Mrs. Holley was less happy. The racial-religious question was an issue; but one suspects that, having been so close to Buddy when he was younger, Mrs. Holley would not really have welcomed anyone he chose to marry. The change that had come when Buddy left home to tour with the Crickets was now to be finalized and it must have been hard to accept. In any case, there was a coolness there and Buddy was aware of it though he did not make an issue of it if he did not have to. Buddy and Maria had decided to be married once the next round of touring was out of the way. In August, Buddy came home for a visit and told his mother, "My girl's going to come down here and visit about a week. And then we're going to get married." Before Mrs. Holley could say much more than "Oh, no", Buddy stated firmly, "Now, Mother, you might as well not say anything because I've made up my mind, and I'm going to marry her."

Buddy and Maria decided not to publicize their marriage. (Not until Holly's death did the marriage become general knowledge.) The tenor of the times may have influenced their decision; by keeping the marriage unpublicized, they avoided the possibility of an ugly controversy over a "mixed marriage". It was an era when editors, ministers and psychologists were alert to any "proof" of rock 'n' roll's bad influence upon public moral standards. Just before Holly's marriage, Jerry Lee Lewis's successful career had been brought to an abrupt halt by the uproar over his marriage to a fourteen-year-old distant cousin — a marriage that was not extraordinary by the standards of the rural South. Under the circumstances, it seemed wise for a rock 'n' roll singer

● *On honeymoon in Acapulco, Maria, Buddy, Jerry and Peggy Sue*

to keep his private life private. Anyway, it was commonly assumed that marriage would lessen a rock 'n' roll performer's popularity. Whatever the influence of these considerations, Buddy and Maria had simply decided that they wanted to keep the news to themselves for a while. However, the marriage was not secret—it just wasn't publicized. "When we travelled on tour," says Maria, "I was supposed to be the Crickets' 'secretary'. But everybody on the tour knew we were married and Buddy always introduced me to everyone as his wife. So it isn't true to say that our marriage was secret. We just didn't feel like broadcasting the news, not for a little while anyway."

On August 15, Holly's pastor, Ben Johnson, married Buddy and Maria in a simple private ceremony in the Holleys' house attended by Buddy's close friends. When the ceremony was over, Jerry Allison slipped into the next room where the phonograph was and put on the flip side of Buddy's latest single—"Now We're One". Then, it was off to Acapulco for a week's honeymoon—a trip which Buddy and Maria made in the company of fellow newlyweds Jerry and Peggy Sue Allison, who had married a few weeks before but had decided to wait for their honeymoon until the time of Buddy and Maria's wedding.

The autumn of 1957 had been completely taken up by the eighty-day tour with the Show of Stars. This year, there were shorter tours and more breaks in the schedule, with more time off for visiting friends in Lubbock and thinking about the future.

In early 1958, radio station KLLL in Lubbock had been acquired by three brothers, Larry, Sky and Ray "Slim" Corbin, and reorganized as an all-country station. Hipockets Duncan had returned from Amarillo to join the Corbins, and Waylon Jennings, a young disc jockey from Littlefield (forty miles up the road to Clovis), had also been added to complete the staff. Like KDAV, KLLL played a mixture of rockabilly and older country styles, including western swing and honky-tonk. Duncan had a morning show and often did "remotes", broadcasting live from local businesses. Jennings sometimes joined Duncan on the remotes and sang on them, and also had a regular afternoon show.

Whenever Buddy was home, he would drop in at KLLL and visit his

● *Time off in Lubbock. Jerry with his father, J.D. 'Buddy' Allison*

● *Waylon and Buddy*

friends there. Hipockets was an old friend and Buddy had known the Corbins for a few years as well. Buddy had first met Waylon Jennings at the time of the KDAV Sunday Party shows; Jennings would drive down to attend them, though he apparently did not perform himself then. In the unused rooms at the KLLL studios, Holly and whichever DJs were not on the air, would talk about Buddy's latest tour, or the happenings in Lubbock, or the music scene there or nationwide. And, naturally enough, they would play music—as often old country or bluegrass tunes as the songs Buddy had himself recorded. On one occasion, Holly taped some promos for the station, strumming his guitar and singing new lyrics to the tunes of his most popular songs, such as "Peggy Sue":

> *If you knew, what I do,*
> *You'd tune our way the whole day through,*
> *To music,*
> *K-Triple-L-uh-L,*
> *Well, it's "Country Style",*
> *On K-L-Double-L.*

As Holly's associations with KDAV and KLLL indicate, artists such as Holly, Presley, Jerry Lee Lewis and the Everly Brothers were always thought of as country artists in the west Texas area, and their records were played as heavily on the country stations as on pop stations. There's a common assumption that the arrival of rock 'n' roll caused a "depression" in the country music field in the late 1950's—but some country DJs in Holly's home area disagree. KDAV owner Dave Stone remembers, "We thought of rockabilly as just being another kind of country music, so we always played it. And I know *I* did well in the 1950's—I bought some other stations in this area and the size of their audiences kept going up during those years. It seems to me like our decline came in the early 1960's when there weren't so many country musicians involved in rock 'n' roll." Tommy Allsup remembers frequently seeing Holly's records, and those of similar artists, on jukeboxes in country & western nightclubs. Perhaps rock 'n' roll's appeal to adult country music fans has been underestimated.

Hipockets Duncan was still promoting concerts and helping rising young artists. Now, his eye was on Waylon Jennings who, besides working as a DJ, was also performing around the Lubbock area, sometimes in a band that included "Slim" Corbin and George Atwood. (Duncan recalls setting up a show in the small town of Spur, Texas [population 1,500] for the town's golden anniversary. The performers included Jennings, Ray Price, June Carter, Sonny Curtis and Holly and the Crickets.) Holly agreed with Duncan's view of Waylon's potential and so set out to launch Waylon's career.

What he did was to arrange for Waylon's first record. It grew out of a session Holly had already set up for himself with King Curtis, the famed rhythm & blues saxophonist featured on the Coasters' records. Holly had become friends with Curtis when the two had appeared on an Alan Freed Paramount show a year earlier. Now, the pair decided to cut a record with Curtis accompanying Holly. (They also planned to record some instrumentals together later on, but this was just one more project left unfulfilled at Holly's death.) Holly paid Curtis's expenses to fly down from New York to Clovis for a session. Buddy decided to record a single with Waylon at the same time; Holly paid the expenses of Waylon's session, produced it himself and played rhythm guitar on the recordings. Studio musicians George Atwood and Bo Clarke played on the cuts made with Jennings, while Allison and

Mauldin backed Holly on the songs he himself recorded.

The song that Jennings and Holly chose for Waylon's first single was the Cajun classic, "Jole Blon". (The flip side was a country tune written by a local songwriter, Bob Venable "When Sin Stops".) The song had come to be a popular country dance tune and maybe Holly and Jennings found appealing the idea of taking a song like that and giving it a rockabilly treatment. Apparently, the idea had been brewing in Holly's mind for some time; it is said that he had considered recording the song himself.

Before Jennings could sing the song, though, he had to learn the words. Buddy and Waylon spent several days listening to a recording of "Jole Blon" by Harry Choates and trying as best they could to figure out the Cajun lyrics—which, of course, they couldn't understand. And so, on the chosen day, a rhythm & blues saxophonist, a national rock 'n' roll star and an aspiring country & western singer combined forces to record a Cajun waltz with a west Texas rockabilly beat and lyrics which were now meaningless in any language. Holly got Brunswick to release the record. Unfortunately, this novel and promising conception in hybrid musical forms was a commercial flop. As Waylon himself once said, "A lot of people who heard the results got a lot of laughs out of it."

The two songs which Holly recorded himself that day were "Reminiscing", written by King Curtis, and "Come Back Baby", co-written by Norman Petty and a New York songwriter named Fred Neil; the two cuts were not released until several years after Holly's death. Holly's voice and Curtis's tenor sax make for an unusual combination that works out well on "Reminiscing". Influenced by Curtis's playing, Holly mixes into his more usual vocal style some new effects to match the saxophone sound; the two are performing together, but playfully trying to top each other. An air of ease and simplicity marks the recording but, in fact, it is Holly and Curtis's careful art that gives the tune such a casual sound.

"Come Back Baby" is a less successful effort and has to be considered mediocre when measured against the standard set by Holly's other performances. There is little fervour or drive in Holly's singing and even Curtis's sax playing can't spark the recording to life. Jerry Allison remarks, "I don't think he was into that tune at all. Norman was probably pushing him to cut it and he probably just said, 'O.K., I'll cut it,' just to save a hassle."

Around the same time that Holly was making these recordings with a top rhythm & blues instrumentalist, he was moving as well in a quite different direction—towards the recording of ballads with traditional pop orchestrations.

Ever since Holly and the Crickets had scored their initial successes, Norman Petty had been urging Buddy to move towards the pop music field in his recordings. Petty pointed out to Buddy that the popularity of teenage singing stars was usually of short duration: two years at the most. When his popularity as a rock 'n' roll star waned, Holly would have to find another style and another audience. Indeed, rock 'n' roll itself might become less important, Petty thought, in which case Buddy should be ready to branch into nightclubs as a solo artist and move into the stabler world of pop music.

At first, Holly didn't think much of the suggestion. "Naw, I don't dig it—I don't like it at all," he told Petty firmly. There was no pressing reason to follow this course. Holly's recordings were successful, and there was no visible decline in the popularity of rock 'n' roll; indeed, the arrival of Holly, Jerry Lee Lewis and the Everly Brothers had marked a resurgence of rock 'n' roll after a period when adult ballads had become more noticeable. (In

July 1957, *Billboard*'s top ten records had included only three catering for the primarily teenage rock 'n' roll audience: Presley's "Teddy Bear", the Everly Brothers' "Bye, Bye, Love" and Marty Robbins's "White Sport Coat".)

By the autumn of 1958, however, Holly had changed his mind about trying some recordings with strings. This does not mean that he had decided to abandon rock 'n' roll, as some have surmised. As the next chapter shows, Holly was considering a wide variety of projects in the last months of his life and did not have the slightest intention of moving on a straight line from his orchestral recordings into the performing and recording world of pop music. When asked if Holly would have gone into nightclub work, producer Dick Jacobs says flatly, "It would never have happened."

Holly was not abandoning his field; instead, he was trying to stay on top of it through constant innovation. This was becoming a more pressing concern in the autumn of 1958 when his last few singles had not reached, in America, the gold-record-rank popularity of his first three or four releases. (In Britain, it was a different story.) Larry Welborn remembers running into Buddy in Lubbock about this time: "I had been trying to get my own recording career started and hadn't gotten anywhere; and I asked Buddy how he managed to come up with one successful record after another. Buddy kind of grinned and shook his head and said, 'It's getting tougher all the time. You have to keep coming up with something new—something they haven't heard before.'"

Phil Everly remembers the uncertainty that many rock 'n' roll artists felt, and how Holly reacted to the challenges they faced:

"Every time you put out a record, your whole career was on the line. It was live and die all the time. After your first hit, you were afraid you'd be a one-record act; after the second, just two records—you were continually worried. It wasn't like, 'Wow, I'm sitting on top of the world.' It was a time of thinking about what you're doing, and why, with nobody around, really, in the industry to advise you because they really didn't understand rock 'n' roll.

"I think Buddy actually understood that this rock 'n' roll wasn't going to fade away, that a career would last many, many years. I never thought much about it but I think Buddy was cognisant of it. I think he had it somewhere in his mind that this thing would keep growing, if you innovated. He was extremely aware, more aware of subtleties than I, and maybe had a little more faith in the music."

Don Everly adds:

"He was a thinking man. He was thinking about progressing and moving on. We were all looking—we knew that you couldn't just follow that one same hit every time, you knew the music was moving along. We both tried strings, looked for outside songs, looked for different sounds. But no one quite knew what was going to happen. First of all, the press and the whole establishment said, 'Well, this isn't going to last anyway,' and they were just waiting for it to die. I mean, your interviews consisted of, 'What are you going to do when this is all over?' It was the first question. And the people directing your career didn't care about the music so much. To them it was a commodity—they didn't have the passion that we had about it."

Like the Beatles years later, Holly was always trying to come up with a novel sound—not just to satisfy his own creative ambitions but also to stay one step ahead of the market. Recording with King Curtis was one innovation; using strings was another. It's easy for music critics to categorize styles and expect artists to respect the boundaries but, in fact, they are the last ones to do so—Holly least of all. If he ever had, Holly no longer rejected ideas just because he hadn't tried them out before. It's true that he was under some pressure from his record company to record ballads. Coral was autonomous, but not completely independent—and executives of the parent company, Decca, were passing suggestions down the chain that it would be good for the company's few rock 'n' roll artists to move in the direction of pop music. (The sentiment was not shared by Dick Jacobs, at the time one of the few producers working for a major label who really *liked* rock 'n' roll.) But the decision was up to Holly and it was one he made on his own. One day in September, while the Crickets and Petty were at the San Francisco airport, Holly startled Petty with the remark, "Well, Norman, what songs are we going to record on my first session with strings?" It was the first time Holly had mentioned the idea since rejecting Petty's suggestion six months before.

The string session was scheduled for mid-October in New York, during an East Coast swing by the Crickets. The four tunes recorded then were "True Love Ways", "Moondreams", "Raining In My Heart" and "It Doesn't Matter Anymore". Dick Jacobs arranged and produced the session, which was held in a studio at the Pythian Temple. (This was Holly's only stereo recording session; although Coral engineers had experimented with their stereo equipment during the "Early In The Morning" sessions a few months earlier, no tapes have been found so far. The stereo versions of these songs, however, have often not been used on album releases.)

"True Love Ways" stands out as the best of the ballads. Holly's vocal perfectly expresses the tenderness and calm of the lyrics, and the accompaniment is complete but not ostentatious—the song is never overwhelmed by orchestral theatrics, always a tempting danger in such recordings. Especially fortunate is the use of tenor saxophone to balance the strings and provide an intimate feeling. Moreover, the recording treads the path Holly intended. Despite the orchestration, the ballad is still close to slow-dance rock 'n' roll tunes and the song adapts itself readily to rock 'n' roll triplets as Tommy Allsup showed on an instrumental version of the song several years later. Holly's recording might be contrasted with Peter and Gordon's 1965 hit version, a faithful but over-dramatic rendition of the song. The beautiful melody was based in part on "I'll Be All Right", a black gospel hymn which had been among Holly's favourite tunes since his high school years when he first heard it on a Nashboro Records recording by the Angelic Gospel Singers. Even the tone of Holly's lyrics—the sense of patience, faith and acceptance—was related to that of the original hymn.

"Moondreams" was composed by Petty and had been recorded sometime earlier by his Trio with Holly accompanying the combo on rhythm guitar. The orchestration of "Moondreams" is heavier and the overall sound is closer to pop than is the case on "True Love Ways"; but on both songs, it is Holly's vocal which defies definition as pop. His distinct Texas accent, high voice and, most of all, country phrasing and sense of pitch (the wavering in tone so distinctive of folk, blues and country performers) mark Holly not so much as an imitator of earlier pop vocalists but as a forerunner of later country and rock artists who used strings effectively. Buddy Holly's records could have gained some airplay and sales from pop audiences on the basis of such recordings but it is difficult to conceive of him having become a strictly pop singer, even if he had wanted to—he just didn't have that type of voice. This is not to say that his voice wasn't good enough—it was just different, following different norms than the usual in pop music.

"True Love Ways" and "Moondreams" were not released during Holly's lifetime; instead "It Doesn't Matter Anymore" and "Raining In My Heart" were the "A" and "B" sides of the single issued in January 1959, just weeks before Holly's death. In the years since then, "It Doesn't Matter Anymore" (written by Paul Anka) has remained one of Holly's most popular recordings, remembered not only for its sheer beauty, but also for the coincidence that a song with such a title and such lyrics should have been Holly's last release. Like Hank Williams's "I'll Never Get Out Of This World Alive" and both sides of Chuck Willis's last record, "Hang Up My Rock 'n' Roll Shoes"/ "What Am I Living For?", Holly's last single appeared in retrospect to have been strangely appropriate.

Like "True Love Ways", "It Doesn't Matter Anymore" should not be considered as marking a total break with Holly's previous recordings. True, electric guitars and background vocal choruses are replaced by violins; but the ballad is performed at a moderate tempo and with a light but persistent beat. The string accompaniment highlights the tune without overwhelming it; Holly's bright, clear vocal dominates the recording throughout. Once again, his country background is obvious. His distinctive hiccups and vocal slides are used again, with more frequency than on most of his songs; here, they are more than a gimmick and also embellish the lyrical melody. His Texas accent is still quite perceptible. In short, Holly's vocal makes few concessions to the standards of pop singing set by the white vocalists who had dominated the pre-rock 'n' roll era. Most of these comments also hold true as well for the slower-paced ballad "Raining In My Heart", which has a more elaborate but still restrained arrangement and a distinctive and sincere vocal.

The simplicity of the string arrangement on "It Doesn't Matter Anymore" resulted in part from the last-minute nature of Holly's decision to record the song. Some time before, Paul Anka had asked Holly, "Would you record a song I'm writing?" "Sure, why not," Buddy replied, "let me see it." "Oh, but it's not finished yet," Anka said. "I'll bring it to you when I'm done with it." Anka finally brought the song to Holly on the very day of the recording session. Holly ran into Jacobs's office with the song just two hours before the evening session was scheduled to begin. (As Jacobs remembers it, Holly had originally planned to record something else, but Jacobs cannot recall what the song was. According to Petty, there wasn't any other song: Holly had simply left the fourth slot open for the song that he knew Anka was writing for him.) While Holly played the tune on a guitar and sang the lyrics, Jacobs worked out a quick arrangement. "We had violins on the date and I had no time to harmonize the violins or write intricate parts," he later told an interviewer, "so we wrote the violins all pizzicato. . . . That was the most unplanned thing I have ever written in my life."

Holly and Anka had first met when they travelled together on the 1957 Show of Stars tour; they apparently had it in mind to collaborate on songs or to write songs for each other, with "It Doesn't Matter Anymore" being the first effort of this sort. Niki Sullivan dates Holly's friendship with Anka to an accident during that first tour.

"Paul was a brat," says Sullivan. "All the time he was getting into trouble, or doing something wrong. He just couldn't sit still—a thousand, billion volts of energy. We were on stage in St. Louis and Paul was horsing around backstage when he kicked the microphone plug out of the floor and all the mikes went dead. We just stood there on stage, helpless. It was just a few minutes but it seemed like three or four days until the microphones got plugged back in and we could start over. At this point, Buddy was boiling up

inside, just ready to explode. When we walked off, the clapping stopped the minute we got off stage into the curtains—it wasn't a very long clap. So it's totally quiet and the MC is walking out on to the stage to introduce the next act, and Buddy yells, 'Who in the hell kicked out the goddamn plug?' It rang throughout the auditorium. He calmed down after a bit and went back to the room, and later Paul Anka came back and apologized. And in fact, from that incident, Buddy and Paul became very close and even rehearsed a few songs together."

The recordings made with King Curtis and with Dick Jacobs's orchestra were held for future release; the Crickets and Holly singles issued in the autumn of 1958 were in more familiar styles, though with innovations. The Crickets' single, "It's So Easy"/"Lonesome Tears", was released in September—and went absolutely nowhere on the national charts. As with other Holly singles of that year, the commercial failure of "It's So Easy" seems inexplicable now for it is an excellent record in many ways. The song follows an unexpected and novel lyric and melodic pattern—there is little in the way of clear division between verse and refrain. This unconventional structure was repeated years later in some of the Beatles' compositions—two early songs, "Tell Me Why" and "When I Get Home", come first to mind—suggesting that the record had an impact out of proportion to its sales figures. The flip side of the single, "Lonesome Tears", was more conventional. Though a good record, it is below the level of Holly's most famous songs and it lacks the sparkle of "It's So Easy".

The single marked Tommy Allsup's first appearance on Holly's releases—"Love's Made A Fool of You", of course, had been just a demo not intended then for release. Allsup's country-based guitar playing at times provides a sound resembling that produced by a country steel guitar; this effect is particularly noticeable on "It's So Easy". Allsup's and Holly's styles are distinct, but congenial   the styles are similar enough that anyone unaware that Holly did not play lead on all his songs might not guess it from the recordings. This is, in fact, the case in the United States at least, where the omission of any mention of Allsup on Holly's albums made his contribution to Holly's recordings practically unknown.

Holly's solo release, "Heartbeat"/"Well . . . All Right", was issued in November. It was not much more successful than "It's So Easy", getting only as far as number 82 on *Billboard*'s charts and barely making the top thirty in Britain. Why "Heartbeat" was not more of a hit is, again, a mystery. It did lack the pounding beat of "Oh Boy!" or "Think It Over"—but so too did many of the top records in late 1958, when *Billboard* articles were noting the resurgence of ballads, instrumentals and Latin-flavoured rhythms, and the decline of the rock 'n' roll beat.

"Heartbeat" incorporated a bit of a Latin beat, while retaining as well the steady rhythm guitar sound of "Peggy Sue". The lyrics swing with the melody and allow much play for Holly's vocal slides and hiccups. Like "Love's Made A Fool Of You", "Heartbeat" alternates vocal lines and answering instrumental passages. (The two songs were written about the same time and, although Petty and Bob Montgomery are listed as the writers of "Heartbeat", Holly's parents remember Buddy and Bob working on both "Heartbeat" and "Love's Made A Fool Of You" at the Holleys' home.) Allsup's brief but perfect guitar solo reaches upwards to build the same sort of emotion created by Holly on "Peggy Sue" and "Listen To Me". Something in the tone of the guitar and the sweep of the pretty melody lends the song a classical air and provides an illusion of strings. Overall, the song is a fine

example of the west Texas rockabilly sound whose roots are difficult to trace, but which has an absolutely distinctive flavour.

The flip side, "Well . . . All Right", has for many years been ranked by Holly's fans as among his best recordings, even though the song has almost never been played on the radio and was for a long time practically unavailable in the United States (the tune was not placed on any of the compilation albums issued between 1960 and 1972). Polls of Buddy Holly Memorial Society members in 1977 and 1978 showed that "Well . . . All Right" was their fourth favourite Holly song, topped only by "That'll Be The Day", "Peggy Sue" and "Rave On".

As with many of Holly's songs, the germ of the tune was just a common saying—here, a simple phrase which the Crickets had picked up from Little Richard and decided to use as the title for a song. So much for their original intentions; by the time they had finished, they had produced one of their most unusual recordings. The song is so unified that just listing some of its distinctive elements hardly does it justice. There is the unusual harmonic pattern with a dominating chord change found nowhere else in Holly's songs: from the tonic major to a major built on the flattened seventh—i.e. if the song is played in C, from C major to B-flat major. The pattern lends the song a modal, folkish air which corresponds to its unelectrified sound and the dominance of the picked-and-strummed country guitar (played by Holly). The song is a polyphony, not of melodies, but of rhythms. The separate rhythms of Holly's guitar and Allison's cymbals (no drums were used) contrast dramatically with the vocal, which defies the underlying rhythms and follows its own sense of emphasis and phrasing.

The repressed tension of the instrumental and vocal performances matches the flavour of the lyrics—lyrics which capture so perfectly and poetically the mixture of hope, pride and uncertainty that is the adolescent experience—if not really the human experience. The lyrics are unified without any air of deliberate construction; they move easily and subtly from the general to the particular, leaving the connection unspoken. Holly sings the words with an unselfconscious sincerity, affirming rather than preaching, and only hinting at the strong emotions veiled by his calm delivery. Rather than addressing a transient concern or narrating just one particular story, the song has a timeless quality and carries a general message valid over and over again to those who turn to it:

Well all right, so I'm being foolish,
Well all right, let people know,
About the dreams and wishes you wish
In the night when lights are low.

Well all right, well all right,
We'll live and love, with all our might,
Well all right, well all right,
Our lifetime love will be all right.

Well all right, so I'm going steady,
It's all right when people say
That those foolish kids can't be ready
For the love that comes their way.

Well all right, well all right,
We will live and love, with all our might,
Well all right, well all right,
Our lifetime love will be all right.

In the early autumn of 1958, Holly made a decision he had been contemplating for some time: to end his association with Norman Petty. In the aftermath of Holly's death, the fact that this split did occur was forgotten or ignored or simply covered up; it was never suggested that Holly's and Petty's relations were anything other than amicable. The truth is quite different.

There is no doubt that Norman Petty played a key role in opening up a national audience for the Crickets. One would like to think that, even if he had never met Petty, Holly would have kept knocking on doors until he found a person or a company willing to record him on his own terms; but there is no way to be sure that he would have succeeded. Petty had the stature and the contacts to get the Crickets a record contract and to ensure for them a large degree of control over their recordings. He was the middle-man that Holly had lacked during his year on Decca. Holly knew all this when Petty began to work on the Crickets' behalf. At the time, it was literally the only game in town, but even then Buddy viewed his association with Petty as a stepping stone to something else, not as a permanent arrangement. Larry Holley says that Buddy knew he would have to go through Petty to get a contract—but that Buddy intended to go off on his own and be his own boss once he had learned enough about the industry and met enough people to make this feasible.

At the start, the Crickets were all young and naive, without experience in handling money or negotiating business arrangements; they were content to let Petty take care of those matters for them. Each member of the group gave Petty power of attorney, and all income from the songs and records was directed to Petty and remained under his control. As mentioned earlier, Petty had assured the Crickets that, regardless of the names on the song con-tracts, the money would eventually be split up according to who had actually written the songs; he also talked about involving the Crickets in his own publishing and recording enterprises. As Joe Mauldin recalls, "Norman kept telling us, 'This is *our* company—we're all in it together, and we're going to all share from it.' Of course, none of us ever saw a nickel of the publishing money. But I saw this beautiful studio and all those nice offices he had, and I was thinking, 'Wow, I own a piece of this—I've got it made.' And I think that's one thing that led us into letting him sign for equal shares on our songs."

In our interview, Mauldin still defended Petty's actions and motives:

"Are you going to put this in print, saying Norman Petty is a big so-and-so, and he steals from people and all that? Because I think that would hardly be fair. You know, I have hostilities against Norman, but I think this is only normal with any group that has a manager—at some time in their career, they get crossways. I still do feel that Norman Petty was very instrumental in our career and our success. Number one, if we hadn't met him and gone through him, we might never have gotten a recording contract. And then two, who's to say that the disc jockeys would have played our records if Norman's name hadn't been on them?"

As Holly's insistence on splitting all the income with the Crickets indicates, Buddy was not dominated by a concern for money—but he was unwilling to be taken advantage of and he came to resent the way in which Petty was collecting a share of the songwriting royalties. "I talked to Buddy once early in 1958," says Hipockets Duncan, "and he was steaming mad. He said, 'Hipockets, I wish a thousand times I had talked with you before I got involved with that man.'" Holly didn't believe that Petty would actually carry out his promise and distribute the money according to the way the songs had really been written. In the end, Holly's suspicions were borne out—Petty did keep the share of the royalties granted him in the official song contracts.

Allison too defends Petty's intentions: "I really believe that if we had all stayed together in Clovis, then it would have all been squared away. We would have sat down and said, 'O.K., I wrote half of that and you wrote

half of this,' and I think Norman would have probably said, 'Right, we'll split the money that way.' But when it all fell apart, then the way the contracts went—the way Norman had fixed the contracts—that was the way it stayed."

The ambivalence Mauldin and Allison feel to this day reflects their awareness of Petty's significance to their success, and also of Petty's sincere emotional attachment to the young musicians. Whether or not he thought about it consciously, he tried, in effect, to act as a father to them. This aspect of their relationship was even a subject for joking—while the Crickets were on their first tour, Petty sent them a congratulatory telegram and signed it "Papa Norman". The Crickets would in turn kid Norman about him "getting old": even though Petty was just eight years older than Holly, it was enough for them to look on him as belonging to an older generation. In interviews years later, Petty and his wife always referred to the Crickets as "the boys", not in the least meaning to be patronizing, but rather to be honestly affectionate.

Particularly in the realm of finances, Petty sought to protect the Crickets from others and, indeed, from themselves. This was bound to lead to trouble eventually. Petty had some reason for setting up financial arrangements as he did—none of the Crickets had had any experience in handling a lot of money and there were enough sad examples of sports and entertainment figures who had run through vast sums too quickly and been left broke. The Crickets appreciated Petty's concern but they began to resent his absolute control over even the smallest expenses. They didn't see why they shouldn't be able to make up their own minds on how to spend their money.

Says Allison, "When we needed some tyres, we had to go to Norman for the money—and he'd say, 'O.K., you can get a good deal on thin white sidewalls at Ward's, so go to Ward's.' And we'd say, 'We don't want Ward's tyres, we want Sears tyres.' Or Firestone, or whatever. And he'd say, 'Nope, you don't want to waste your money like that.' He was trying to do the right thing for us but it just seemed like he had too much control."

Petty's contacts and experience had been crucial when the Crickets were just getting started. However, as the group's first records became hits and they spent almost all their time on the road, Holly himself began to gain the insight and know-how that had been Petty's chief assets as manager. Petty accompanied the group on their first trip to New York and on their foreign tours but the rest of the time the Crickets were usually on their own, and Buddy was responsible for keeping tabs on the group, its equipment and the promoters. As a result, he became more sophisticated in handling problems on his own. Allison recalls a "dance party" tour the Crickets made in the early summer of 1958, where they were accompanied only by a dance band headed by Tommy Allsup. The dance would run from eight P.M. to midnight, with the Crickets (including Allsup) performing two forty-five minute sets and Allsup's band playing the rest of the time. At one such show, the local promoter didn't want the dance band to appear on the show and so the Crickets just did their own sets.

"When it came time to collect the money," says Jerry, "the promoter said, 'O.K., we're only going to pay you half, since the big band didn't play.' Buddy said, 'Man, they were there, out in the audience, playing. Whistling and humming. You didn't want them to play on the stage—but you've still got to pay all of us, the way the contract reads.' And the guy said, 'Well, they didn't play.' And Buddy said, 'O.K., they may not have played, but they're all gonna come over here and beat the hell out of you.' So the guy finally paid up. He was really trying to jive us because he thought we were

Buddy in Australia – and with The Crickets in New York . . .

Buddy with his parents and Jack Neal in 1953

The Crickets in Lubbock with their motorcycles, Summer 1958 . . .

Buddy's guitars – he made the leather cover for his Gibson in 1956

Buddy & Maria's wedding day, August 15th, 1958 . . .

Clockwise from top left: with Peggy Sue & JI; with Pastor Ben Johnson; with Larry &
Travis Holley and J. E. Weir; with J. E Weir; and with Buddy's parents

Clockwise from top left: backstage at the Riverside Ballroom; with Judy & Joan Bender; with Frankie Sardo and Dion DiMucci; on stage with Waylon & Tommy; and with Bob Oestreich

just a bunch of dumb kids. But Buddy didn't let anything get by him—he'd take care of the business fine." "'Taking care of the business'" included protecting the money once it was received. Holly began to carry a pistol in 1958, keeping it in a false bottom of his travel bag.

By mid-1958, Holly had reached the point where Petty could not do much more for him than he could do himself. In addition, Holly was displeased with the way his career was being handled by Petty. Jerry Allison says, "One of the main reasons that I recall for Buddy splitting was that he wanted more publicity. At the time, people like Fabian and Frankie Avalon were getting all kinds of write-ups in magazines, but Norman didn't believe in that sort of publicity. He told Buddy, 'You don't need that—you'll make it on records, you're making it bigger than all that anyway.' We had a couple of offers for movies, too, and Norman turned them right down—they were just rock 'n' roll movies and I guess Norman was waiting for a really big one. But that turned us right off, because we wanted to see ourselves in the movies."

Petty replies that the decision to turn down the movie offers was a joint one. "The only time that movies came up," says Petty, "was when they were going to do this Alan Freed quickie." (Probably, *Go Johnny, Go*.) "They called me and I presented it to the boys. They weren't going to pay them—Jack Hook, who was Freed's personal manager at the time, said, 'The only thing you're going to get out of it is the publicity.' It was Jerry himself who said, 'If they don't want to give us any money, the hell with it—let's don't do it.'" Allison responds with a rhetorical question: "Can you imagine three kids turning down a chance to be in a movie?"

The break would have come sooner or later, once Buddy felt himself fully capable of running his own affairs. But the event which led directly to the split was Buddy's marriage—and Petty's opposition to it.

Allison and Mauldin remember that Petty was against the very idea of any of the Crickets getting married. His reasons appear to have been a mixture of self-interest and paternalism. He feared (correctly) that he would lose dominance over the musicians as they established their own lives and demanded more control over their own affairs. "When you get married," Allison explains, "it's a different thing—because you can't have your wife saying, 'Well, shall I go ask Norman if we can have some money?'" But Allison adds, "I think he thought that we were too young to get married and weren't stable enough—which was probably true. Well, I don't know about for Buddy—but I was definitely too young to know what I was doing." (Allison has since been divorced and has remarried.) Both Holly and Allison were irritated by Petty's objections. "I remember when we were in Hawaii on the way to Australia," says Jerry, "and I had already decided I was going to get married. We were riding along and Norman said, 'Well, Buddy, what are we going to do for another drummer when Jerry gets married?' And Buddy said, 'Well, Jerry, what are we going to do for another manager since Norman's *already* married?' And I was kind of P.O.'d at Norman because of that."

Petty denies that he objected to either of the two marriages. "The only thing I did tell Jerry at the time," says Petty, "was whenever he got married to make sure, because I felt that marriage was a one-time thing. I don't recall that remark about 'what are we going to do for another drummer'. Jerry was prone to exaggerate. I might have said something that Jerry based it on. But I think if I had made a statement that strong, that I would remember it."

Maria Elena, however, charges that Petty actively tried to dissuade Holly from marrying her. She says, "Norman told Buddy that I was a cheap girl who tried to get picked up by practically every entertainer who walked in the office—that I'd run around with a lot of men. Norman said this certain executive at Peer-Southern Music had told him this. Well, Buddy told me about the stories Norman was spreading. So the next time Norman came into the office I called this executive over and brought him face-to-face with Norman and told him what Norman had been saying and asked him if any of this had come from him. And he said no, he had never told Norman any such thing. They never liked Norman up there very much after that."

Petty denies that this incident at Peer-Southern ever happened. He acknowledges that there was no love lost between himself and Maria, but he rejects the notion that this arose out of any fear on his part that Maria posed a threat to his role. "It was very antagonistic, naturally. But it was a two-way street. There probably was jealousy on both sides. To make it look like I feared Maria Elena's entering the picture is just not so. You never fear something when you do the best you know how to do, and I would certainly not fear anybody that really didn't know anything about the business. If I would be prone to, it would be somebody that was in the management field—a Dick Jacobs, you know—who'd make you feel like your position was jeopardized. But I never felt that Maria Elena jeopardized my position whatsoever." Nevertheless, Petty does trace Buddy's decision to break with him back to Maria Elena's urging: "She told him that he didn't need the Crickets—that he didn't need me."

Whether or not Petty perceived it as such, Maria Elena did in fact represent a threat to his control over Holly. With her personal experience and family ties in music publishing, she had know-how that was to aid Buddy in charting his own career—and also, she was able to make clearer to him just what his association with Petty was costing him. Joe Mauldin notes, "I think Maria Elena, right off the bat, wanted Buddy to move to New York and get away from Norman Petty—because I think she knew what was going on with our money. She probably had access to publishing records that we didn't." Maria was apt to be more businesslike than Buddy. She asked a lot of questions, and she insisted on having everything down in writing—she was less willing than Buddy to settle for vague promises, or to trust in the goodwill of others. But a good business sense wasn't all that Maria Elena Santiago gave to Buddy Holly. She gave him what he most needed just then: more confidence in himself.

"You're the best thing that ever happened to Buddy," Mr. Holley told Maria not long after the marriage. "You've cut his umbilical cords. When he was younger, he was tied to his mother, then he was tied to Norman Petty, but now he's come into his own—he's finally a *man*." It wasn't so much that marriage changed Buddy Holly; rather, it unleashed him, freeing him to put his desires into action—to make realities of his hopes. Holly's personality was always full of contradictions. On stage, he was uninhibited, always trying to reach out and touch an audience and never holding anything back; off stage, he was quiet, shy and cautious towards strangers, sometimes moody and withdrawn even with friends. The tension in his music between the willingness to put absolute faith in high hopes and the knowledge that fulfilment of those hopes was always uncertain, mirrored a conflict in Holly's own soul. He was outwardly self-confident, often aggressive; but fear of failure, as much as any deep ambition, was what spurred him on. Never quite satisfied with his success, never sure it would last, he sought something permanent—something that would indeed last "through times till all times

end". Love gave him that sense of permanence and encouraged him to cut loose from his old moorings and chart his own course with new confidence.

Maria was no silent or passive support. Her spirit had much in common with Buddy's. She was strong-willed and high-tempered, outspoken and independent. Contrary to what Petty may have thought, she did not make Buddy's decisions for him; but she was a perceptive judge of people and situations and Buddy put great weight in her judgement. And like Buddy, she looked to the future. She says, "Buddy always seemed to me to be very old for his age—he was more mature than the others around him." (Maria herself was four years older than Buddy.) "He could be happy fooling around for a while—but when he had to be, he was all business. He cared about what happened, he thought about what he was doing. He was always trying to think of ways to improve himself, to improve his performances and his music. Backstage at a show, he'd be thinking all the time about what he was going to do and whether he should do it differently. Really, everything he did on stage, he had thought it out ahead of time or planned it out with Jerry and Joe. His mind was constantly working."

It was a trait Hipockets Duncan noticed too: "When we'd talk, he'd be listening to what I was saying and he'd respond, but you could just feel that his mind was somewhere else at the same time. He was always in a hurry, trying to do so much, and his mind would be working on more than one thing at once."

The conflict between Petty and Maria Elena flared more intensely after the marriage. "We went to Clovis for a recording session in September," Maria recalls, "and Norman and his wife and his secretary started to make fun of the way I spoke English. Well, I didn't have to take that. I had grown up in New York City—I knew how to eat and dress and act—they thought they were so sophisticated, but I knew more than they ever would. So I said to his wife, 'I want you to talk to me in Spanish.' And of course she couldn't. And I said, 'You see, I can speak your language—but you don't know a word of mine.' But that's how it stood. Norman knew I couldn't stand him—and he knew what he had done, and why he couldn't hold Buddy any longer."

Petty remembers this incident differently. "We had very little contact after the marriage. I don't recall ever having been abusive to Maria Elena. The only thing I can recall is that she said something about the funny way we talk, about our drawl; and if anything was said, Norma Jean [Petty's secretary] or Vi said something, just jokingly, about 'Well, you talk funny, too.' That was the gist of it. But as to making fun of her because she was Puerto Rican or Spanish, that's just not so."

In October, the Crickets appeared on the Alan Freed television show in New York City and then set out on a seventeen-day GAC package tour with Eddie Cochran, Bobby Darin, Frankie Avalon, Clyde McPhatter and the Coasters. Buddy and Maria travelled in their Cadillac, while Allison, Mauldin, Allsup and the Roses (accompanying the Crickets on tour for the first time) rode in a yellow DeSoto station wagon purchased at the time of the summer dance party tour. The tour showed that strains were developing not just between Holly and Petty but within the group as well.

"On that tour," explains Joe Mauldin, "we weren't as close as we had been before. Of course, now I can understand why—Buddy was a married man and had his wife with him, and he had to devote more time to her than he did to Jerry and I. But at the time, I felt like Buddy didn't want to be a part of the group anymore, he wanted to be a bigshot star himself. And I was jealous of Maria Elena because it seemed that she was taking Buddy away from Jerry and I. Buddy had been like a brother for so long, and suddenly Buddy was no longer a brother."

It was probably not wholly coincidental that Allison and Mauldin seemed to show less interest in their work than before. Drinking became an issue between them and Holly—what had only been a sidelight in the past was now starting to affect the trio's performances. Jerry Allison gives his memories of that last tour:

"We really didn't see each other that much except at the shows. And Buddy got kind of put out with us—things got sort of tense. Because we were really shucking it. Sometimes we'd get drunk in the morning and stay drunk all day. And Buddy wasn't out-and-out opposed to drinking but he didn't like us at it all the time, the way we were doing. Anyway, after that tour was over, he talked to Joe B. and me and said, 'O.K., you guys, I can't take all this—if we're going to do this thing, let's do it right. We're getting older and we got to take this more seriously. You guys drink too much—it's obnoxious, and I hate it. If you want to stay with me, great—but you've got to be more interested in what you're doing.' So we finally said, 'Yeah, O.K., we understand, we'll tighten up a little bit.'"

Holly's desire to break with Petty was discussed during the tour. Joe Mauldin says, "There were a few conversations where Buddy mentioned, 'Hey, guys, we're gonna have to move to New York, to get away from Petty.' And I was somewhat confused because I didn't think that was the right thing to do. Norman had hyped us so much on the people in New York, and how we'd never see any of our money. Norman would say, 'Look at all those groups that have had a bunch of hit records and they've never made a nickel—they're stone broke. They'll take it all away from you, and you'll wind up the same way.'"

Jerry Allison remembers that Holly's decision was definite, and that he and Mauldin agreed at first to follow Holly. "Buddy said, 'I'm going to move

to New York, and I'm going to go out from Norman. There's a lot of stuff I want to do.' We agreed that we'd all move to New York and start our own publishing company, and we had it all worked out. We even called Norman and told him that we were hanging it up and moving to New York." Mauldin doesn't remember being very settled about it one way or the other, in his own mind, during the tour.

After the tour itself, the Crickets had two television appearances to make for Dick Clark—one on the Saturday night stage show, on October 25, and the second on the afternoon *American Bandstand*, on Tuesday, October 28. After the last show, Allison and Mauldin flew back to Lubbock, while Buddy and Maria decided to make the long drive back in their car. When Joe B. and Jerry got back, they decided to go over to Clovis to drop in on the Roses and to pick up some personal belongings.

"We went over to Clovis, and Norman talked us out of splitting, that's what happened," says Jerry. "He said, 'You know, you guys better hang down here—when you get to New York, you're gonna see, you'll be cheated out of everything.' All that kind of stuff. So we said, O.K."

Mauldin gives his account of how the conversation went:

"The feelings that I had had on the tour could have been one of the reasons that Norman influenced me as much as he did when we got back to Clovis. But it's not that Maria broke the group up—I felt like Petty's the one who broke the group up. Norman said, 'Look, let's stay down here where we have control of everything.' And he had us built up, saying, 'You guys are the Crickets, you will be the Crickets and you'll keep the Crickets name. And we'll get another lead singer and a guitar player'—so forth and so on. He told us that the Crickets were the ones that had had all the hits—Buddy Holly had only had 'Peggy Sue', and he couldn't make a living on the name Buddy Holly. So if we stayed down in Clovis with Norman, we could keep the name of the Crickets, and Norman had—quote—'all his money in the bank, and we'll starve him to death'—end quote."

Petty objects to this account of what happened. "I didn't talk anybody into anything. I didn't brainchild the whole thing, or engineer it. As for that statement about starving him to death—that's awful strong, for somebody that really thought of all the kids as his sons. I know I never said it."

When Buddy got back to Lubbock, he called Allison's house and discovered that Jerry and Joe had gone ahead to Petty's studio, instead of waiting for him to arrive. Still not knowing what had happened in Clovis, Buddy drove up there to make his own settlement with Petty.

"Maria Elena and Buddy were both in the office," says Petty, "but Maria Elena did all the talking. She said, 'Buddy and I have decided that Buddy can do better—that you're not fit for Buddy's manager.' And I said, 'What's this—is it something I've done?' She said, 'It's what you haven't done—you haven't done near enough for him.'"

Maria remembers, "Norman asked Buddy, 'Are you sure that's what you want? You know, I can't give you any money until we get settled who gets what money, and just how much money each of you has coming. I'll need time.' And Buddy said, 'I don't *have* the time. Just give me the money and I'll give it to them—we can split it ourselves.' And that's when Norman told him—he said, 'Uh uh—they're staying with me.'"

Jerry Allison remembers that Buddy was disappointed but not angry: "We sat in the car and went through it all and Buddy was agreeable to the whole thing. He said, 'I wish you guys would go with me, you're gonna be sorry you didn't. But I can understand, if you don't want to, you don't want to.'

We weren't uptight, or anything like that. And he said, 'O.K., you guys can have the name of the Crickets, and I'll just work as Buddy Holly.'"

In fact, Buddy was hiding his feelings from Mauldin and Allison. He was deeply disappointed and hurt by what had happened. "He felt sort of betrayed," says Maria. "'I thought I had treated them fair,' he said, 'I don't see why they should have done that to me.' He felt like they had put a knife in his back; but if that was how they felt, he wasn't going to beg them. But he cried that night." Holly's parents remember him being so discouraged that he talked of quitting; they say Maria Elena talked him out of it. But she doesn't recall him suggesting anything like that: "He was hurt by what had happened, but it didn't change his mind about what he wanted to do—he knew he could still be a star."

The moment of discouragement passed, and Buddy and Maria returned to New York. "There's a lot of stuff I want to do," he had told Allison. New York was the place to start.

CHAPTER SEVEN

PLANS FOR THE FUTURE

"What would have happened to Buddy Holly if he had not died? What would he be doing today?"

Those are common subjects for debate, both among his fans and among those interested in the history of rock music. The intriguing questions can be argued endlessly because they cannot be answered with any certainty. What Buddy Holly would have done would have depended in part on the state of the industry and the directions of popular taste; but conversely, the industry and popular tastes would have been shaped in part by Holly's music. This much can be said: the scope of Holly's plans in the last months of his life indicates that with his death, rock 'n' roll lost more than a talented performer—more importantly, it lost a creative figure whose innovations could have profoundly affected the development of all American popular music.

For many years after Holly's death, rock music critics and historians commonly assumed that the use of full orchestral arrangements on Holly's last studio recordings indicated Holly's intention to abandon rock 'n' roll in favour of adult pop music. This assumption was based on a lack of information about Holly's unrealized projects and on the example furnished by other teenage rock 'n' roll stars who sought to broaden their appeal by moving to a more adult sound and into the field of nightclub work. (Often overlooked were those who continued to play rock 'n' roll, at the risk of obscurity, or who found loyal audiences among the country music and rhythm & blues fans who had contributed to the rise of rock 'n' roll in the first place.) Actually, Buddy Holly's musical horizons were expanding in unexpected and unpublicized directions.

"Buddy was always open to ideas," Maria remembers. "He looked into every type of music. We'd sit at home and listen to records—and he wouldn't just be entertaining himself—he'd be analysing the sound, noting what he liked, and getting ideas. He'd comment on the records and talk about how some sound or effect compared with something in a whole different field of music. He'd always listen to suggestions, and be willing to try something out and see if he could do it—see if it sounded good. His attitude was, 'You don't lose anything by trying.' And he wasn't one to just talk and do nothing—when he got something in his head, he wanted to carry it out. There was nothing new he saw that he didn't want to do immediately."

Marriage had brought Holly in contact with Latin American and Spanish music. Spanish guitar styles attracted his attention. Maria recalls, "We went out to eat almost every night and often we'd go to Spanish restaurants where there were flamenco guitarists performing. Buddy really liked that music. He was attracted by Spanish classical guitar playing, too. He wanted to learn how to play in those styles. So he bought albums by Andres Segovia and by several flamenco guitarists and he started to take lessons from a neighbour of ours." With Maria's help, Buddy was also learning Latin American songs, with the idea of recording them himself. The first one he wanted to learn was, naturally, "Maria Elena"; others were suggested by Maria's aunt Provi who hoped that Buddy would record songs from Peer-Southern's large Latin American catalogue. "I'd sing songs in Spanish for him to learn," says Maria, "and he'd try to pick up the words that way. We had tapes of us doing this together but somehow they got lost—it's too bad, because it was pretty funny sometimes. But Buddy was really interested—he told me that he wanted to learn how to speak Spanish, so I was going to teach him when he had time."

Others also helped Holly expand his musical interests. Tommy Allsup's wide background included a knowledge of jazz and he got Holly interested in it; the record collection Holly left behind includes a single by Louis Armstrong and an EP from Miles Davis's "Miles Ahead" album. As shown by the recording of "Jole Blon" made with Waylon Jennings, Holly was also attracted to Cajun music. Holly's brother Larry had a collection of Cajun recordings and that seems to be how Buddy first heard the style. Tommy Allsup remembers also that Holly liked the records he had heard by the young Cajun-country act, Rusty & Doug (the latter, of course, now performs under his full name, Doug Kershaw). It was just one more interest that Buddy was eager to follow up on—according to Larry Holley, Buddy was planning to spend some time in southern Louisiana, meeting Cajun musicians there and learning their style and techniques.

Rhythm & blues and gospel were streams of music with which Buddy was long familiar, and now he had projects in mind involving those fields, too. Since the early 1950's, Holly had been a great fan of Ray Charles. Indeed, while everyone talks of Elvis Presley's influence on Holly, Buddy's rock 'n' roll vocal style owed at least as much to the example of Ray Charles, and the use of vocal background on the Crickets records was likewise related to Charles's gospel-blues recordings. Now, Holly wanted to do an album with the "Ray Charles sound". What he had in mind, says Maria, was an album of Charles's material, with arrangements similar to those Charles used. "When we were in California in the fall," she says, "we managed to find out where Ray Charles lived and we went over to his house, but he was out on tour. Buddy was hoping to talk with Charles and see if he'd be willing to work with Buddy on this—help with the arrangements and maybe play on it. Buddy really loved Charles's style and he wanted to meet him and talk with him about it."

Another album that Buddy was planning to record was an album of gospel music. As the album was meant to be a sort of gift for his parents, it would seem that white gospel music would have provided the songs; but Holly liked black gospel singers too, especially Mahalia Jackson, and talked of recording black gospel himself, so it is likely that some material from that tradition would also have been on the album. Holly's desire to please his parents was, of course, not his only reason for planning such an album; his own religious faith had remained a strong force in his life. In truth, it is by no means stretching matters to see a strong Christian strain in the attitudes of faith and patience that colour Holly's songs. Like others in his church, he followed the Biblical practice of tithing and gave ten percent of his earnings to his Baptist congregation. And, hard as it may be to believe, he sometimes had doubts about the propriety of his vocation. He never expressed his doubts to anyone outside his own family; but to them, and especially to his brother Larry, he talked about these qualms. Music was Buddy's life, and he neither wanted to nor would have been able to break away from it; but he wanted to feel that he was doing "God's work" too, even while remaining a secular entertainer. The planned gospel album would therefore have been an expression of his own conscience.

Holly was becoming involved in other aspects of the music business besides performing. He wanted to make a role for himself on "the other side of the glass", as a producer—he particularly wanted to work with young artists and help them realize their potential. He planned, too, to devote some of his songwriting talents to producing material for these and other artists.

Maria recalls: "Buddy didn't have in mind just writing songs that fit his own style and then finding someone else to record them. Instead, he wanted to try writing songs meant deliberately for somebody else in particular, and meant to suit that singer's style and potential audience. And that's how Buddy was going to record people, too—not just work with rock 'n' roll singers, but also help anyone who had potential at what he was doing. Like with Waylon Jennings—maybe Buddy thought Waylon could become a rock 'n' roll star, I don't know, but he felt sure that Waylon could be popular in country music, so that's the way he meant to record him. 'Let's start with *something*' was his attitude.

"Buddy meant to be really close to the artists he chose to work with. He actually wanted Waylon to come and move in with us—because Buddy felt like that way he could really come to know Waylon and his feelings, and write songs that matched them. And with other artists too, he wanted to write songs that really expressed how *they* felt."

Besides producing Jennings's first record, Holly also produced a record for a singer named Lou Giordano. Giordano was a close friend of Joey Villa, lead singer of the Royal Teens (best remembered for "Short Shorts"), and it was Villa who introduced Giordano to Holly. Holly and Phil Everly collaborated on Giordano's debut single: Holly wrote a new song for one side called "Stay Close To Me", while Everly wrote the flip side, "Don't Cha Know". (Holly never recorded his composition himself.) The recording was made in New York on September 30, with Holly and Everly playing rhythm guitars on "Stay Close To Me" and singing falsetto background vocals with Joey Villa on "Don't Cha Know".

Holly took the record to Coral, who signed Giordano to a contract in November. The record was released on Brunswick in late January 1959. Despite good trade reviews, the record was not a commercial success. Giordano later cut a few records for other labels under his own name and as Lou Jordan, but none sold well; he also wrote songs for other artists, including Al Martino. (Giordano died in 1969.)

"Stay Close To Me" is a pretty composition, and it is a great shame that Holly himself never recorded it: Giordano's straightforward vocal style failed to convey the emotion that Holly expressed through his own recordings. That sort of miscalculation might have troubled any later efforts by Holly to write songs for other artists. "Buddy never realized how much of an impact he had on his audience," says Maria. "He didn't have time. He knew they liked his style, but he didn't know just why."

Jennings's and Giordano's first singles were Holly's initial efforts as an independent producer; he had made an agreement with Brunswick to produce a certain number of masters for them annually. The first masters were to be made in New York—but Holly intended to build his own full-time recording studio in Lubbock. Buddy discussed his plans with Tommy Allsup and George Atwood. Holly also thought of asking two others to join him: his old friend Bob Montgomery, and Snuff Garrett. In the 1960's, Garrett became one of the most successful producers on the West Coast; but before that, he was a disc jockey in Lubbock and Wichita Falls and had been a friend of Holly's for several years.

Maria explains what lay behind Holly's plans: "Buddy wanted to build a studio in Lubbock so kids growing up the way he had could have a chance to get started. The studio would have been built as part of the house he was going to build for his parents—the plans were all drawn up. He was going to start his own publishing company, too, to help promote their songs and his own."

But the studio wasn't meant just to help out local talent; it was to serve as a base for recordings by Holly himself. Tommy Allsup remembers that

LOU GIORDANO
★★★ **Don't Cha Know**
BRUNSWICK 55115—Lou Giordano comes thru with a swinging reading of this rocker, which was penned by Phil Everly of the Everly Brothers. Gals behind him lend a wild sound. A good side. (Acuff-Rose, BMI)

★★★ **Stay Close to Me**
On this side the new chanter sells a ballad penned by Buddy Holly very smoothly over clever combo support. Both sides have a chance. (Maria, ASCAP)

● *From Billboard, February 9, 1959*

Buddy had in mind assembling a group of Lubbock area country and rockabilly musicians to serve as a studio band. The group would have been used to back up Waylon Jennings; but Holly also meant for them to play on his own recordings. "He wanted to try out fiddles, steel guitars and all that on his own releases," says Tommy.

Of course, no one can tell just how all this would have sounded. It seems clear that Holly did not intend just to record country songs in traditional country styles—he was thinking, rather, of adding a novel country flavour to his own brand of rock 'n' roll. One remembers his remark to Larry Welborn: "You have to keep coming up with something new—something they haven't heard before." Fiddles and steel guitars were not new sounds, but they would have been new to the rock 'n' roll audience—rock 'n' roll had been on the scene now for several years and many fans were too young to remember what had existed before it, or too far removed socially to have ever been familiar with the varied sources of the music. In line with this change in the character of the audience, the trend in rock 'n' roll was to Dick Clark's "Philadelphia sound"; but instead of just following this trend or even copying the most successful of his own releases, Holly was both moving in new directions and reaching back to his own roots—seeking to create his own trends.

In this and so much else, Holly was at least a decade ahead of his time. He had won a freedom to manage his own career that few artists were to have before the Beatles paved the way. As his varied plans show, he wasn't obsessed by the need for a hit single—they were nice to have, of course, but Holly was already thinking in terms of "theme" albums that could stand on their own. And in his specific ideas for integrating rock 'n' roll and country music, Holly was proposing something which was hardly attempted before the "country-rock" movement of the late 1960's and 1970's.

There is no way to be sure that Holly's efforts would have been commercial successes. The time might not have been right for such a movement. A check of *Billboard* charts shows that although a number of country-flavoured records did make the pop charts in 1959, country music as a whole was returning to the isolation from pop music it had had in the pre-rock 'n' roll era. The rock 'n' roll audience might have ignored Buddy Holly, and rock 'n' roll might have still suffered through the "pretty boy era" that preceded the British invasion. But if Holly had managed to overcome the trends, the subsequent course of American popular music could have been radically altered. When asked once if Holly would have changed back to country music, Waylon Jennings replied, "No—actually, I think country music would have caught up with *him*." At the very least, Holly's studio might have become a recording centre with a distinctive regional flavour, as studios in Detroit, Memphis, Muscle Shoals and elsewhere did in succeeding years. But Buddy Holly did not get the chance; since then, ambitious and talented West Texas musicians have had to travel to Los Angeles or Nashville to get anywhere in the business, with a consequent loss in the regional distinctiveness of the music.

The wide-ranging nature of Holly's musical plans and tastes suggests the sense of freedom and opportunity he felt in the last months of 1958. He was occasionally troubled by the failure of his most recent records; but Jerry Allison says that, during the time he and Buddy were together, Holly was never too concerned about it: "He didn't care if he had a number one record, or a record at all, as long as he could play and somebody would like it." Little more than a year before, Holly and his comrades had been poor boys in West Texas with dreams of being rich. Now, Holly no longer felt compelled to make a tour or produce a hit record for the sake of money alone—his circumstances had changed and so had his attitudes. He wanted to make fewer tours, picking and choosing among them. Jerry says, "It would depend on who was going to be on the tour and if the tour looked like it would be fun to do—if it paid a million dollars and it didn't sound like any fun, he'd pass." Allison remembers one particular discussion with Holly right after the return from their honeymoons in Acapulco:

"We got home and we were sitting around, and we had some offers for tours. And I said, 'Man, let's take those tours and make that money. Because one day we may not be able to—it may cool off and we won't be able to make it that way.' And Buddy said, 'Man, what do you want money for? Are you going to buy a Cadillac? If you want one, you go get it, I'll pay for it. Everybody wants to work for work. Why do we want to go out on the road and work all the time? What if you get killed tomorrow? Let's have some fun—let's ride our motorcycles and just do what we want to do. We've got enough money—let's enjoy it.' And I said, 'O.K., you're right,' and we knocked off for a while after that. Maybe it was a month we goofed off, maybe two weeks; but whatever that time was, it was just what he wanted. Everything that happened afterwards—it really made me think about what he'd said. I was really glad that we had taken that break, and glad that he had had that attitude."

Holly's recording and producing plans were just that—only plans—when he died; but not all that went on in the last months of his life was so indefinite. It was in this period that Holly wrote some of his finest songs, tunes which show that he was only beginning to reach his potential as a songwriter and as a performer.

In December 1958, Holly recorded six original songs on his tape recorder in his New York apartment: "That's What They Say", "What To Do", "Peggy Sue Got Married", "That Makes It Tough", "Crying, Waiting, Hoping" and "Learning The Game". Holly only taped the songs as a way of taking down the tunes and lyrics and establishing models for eventual studio sessions. Fortunately, his sense of perfection resulted in recordings which were outstanding in their own right.

Remembering how Buddy went about writing his songs, Maria says: "He often worked on his songs over at my aunt's apartment because she had a piano and he liked to work the tunes out on that. I can't say that the words or the music came first. He did them together—he'd get the tune down first, but he'd be writing the words at the same time. Then he'd play the song on his guitar to see how it sounded that way—he'd go back and forth between the piano and his guitar. (He had just gotten a new Guild, custom-made, and that's the one he played when he taped these songs.) But he didn't just write down the words and forget about it. The first set of words would come quickly enough—but then, he'd change it, over and over. Even the way he had it down on the tapes he left behind, I know he wasn't finished with them—he would have changed them some more, or added to them. He really cared about the way the songs sounded and the words he chose—he'd keep asking, 'Do you think this sounds good? It doesn't sound like I want it to.' Or, 'That's not what I want to say—it isn't what I had in mind.' I remember once he was sitting and working on some song and I did something that was distracting—maybe I made some noise. And he suddenly got up and exploded, 'I'll be back directly!' and stomped out and took a walk to cool off. Then he came back and went to work again."

● From Cashbox

● KLLL studios were on the top floor of the Great Plains Life Building in Lubbock

Five of these last songs deal with the disappointments of love in striking and sometimes ambivalent fashion. "That's What They Say" is particularly complex. The singer would like to believe the conventional wisdom but he has not yet found true love himself, and so wonders if what "they" say is true. This doubt is never outrightly expressed, only implied, in the ironic lyrics, the tone of Holly's singing and the music (the use of minor chords in the refrain). The matter is left unsettled—making the song realistic, since no one in such a position can state the answer.

> *"There comes a time for everybody,*
> *When true love will come your way.*
> *There comes a time for everybody—"*
> *That's what they tell me,*
> *That's what they say.*
>
> *I didn't hear them say a word*
> *Of when that time would be;*
> *I only know that what they say*
> *Has not come true for me.*
>
> *"You just keep waiting,*
> *And love will come your way—"*
> *That's what they tell me,*
> *That's what they say.*

The other four songs about love deal more specifically with the end of a love affair. They may be autobiographical to some extent, drawing on Buddy's high school romance. Holly's experience made it possible for him to express the varied feelings one might have in such a situation. Like a novelist whose fictional characters are based on the reality of human life even if they are not completely modelled on the lives of specific individuals, so a songwriter or a poet can create a situation which is no less real for being fictional. He can write about such matters in terms based on his own experience but in such a way that the lyrics have general application. The best of the rock 'n' roll songwriters were able to create this sort of poetic reality in their songs. The devotion of Holly's fans both before and after his death was based in part on the lasting validity of his lyrics and their continued significance to the lives of the listeners.

The title of "What To Do" expresses the singer's dilemma. Although his love no longer wants him, he must admit to himself that he still wants only her and he cannot escape reminders of the times and places they had shared: the record hops, the soda shops, the walks to school. "That Makes It Tough" has a similar theme. The melody itself and the manner of Holly's performance mark the song as his closest approach during his rock 'n' roll years to the sound of country & western. Holly shows Hank Williams's influence upon his vocal style, while the guitar accompaniment on Holly's original, solo tape—picked bass notes and strummed chords—is reminiscent of Jimmie Rodgers's song style. However, some of Holly's friends say that this was one of the songs he intended to record with a Ray Charles-style blues arrangement. Of course, they may be mistaken; but this shows the impossibility of determining with any precision just what these songs would have sounded like had Buddy lived to record them with a full band or orchestra. Even Maria doesn't know what sort of arrangement Buddy had in mind. In the original undubbed version, "That Makes It Tough" is one of Holly's most compelling performances. There are many who feel that, given the right arrangement, it would have been a sizeable hit for Holly in all three record markets (popular, country and R & B):

● *Buddy's Ampex tape-recorder*

> *. . . Memories will follow me forever,*
> *Though I know our dreams cannot come true,*
> *All those precious things we shared together—*
> *Time goes by, I'll still remember you—and*
>
> *That makes it tough*
> *Oh, so tough,*
> *When you tell me,*
> *You don't love me.*
> *That makes it tough,*
> *Oh, so tough—*
> *When you say you don't care for me no more.*

"Crying, Waiting, Hoping" expresses the mixture of discouragement and hope that coloured some of Holly's earlier songs; in the space of a few lines, the singer first tells himself that his hopes are useless, and then hopes yet again that the past can be restored:

> *Crying, waiting, hoping,*
> *You'll come back,*
> *I just can't seem*
> *To get you off my mind.*
> *Crying, waiting, hoping,*
> *You'll come back,*
> *You're the one I love,*
> *And I think about you all the time.*

> *Crying,*
> *My tears keep a-falling,*
> *All night long.*
> *Waiting,*
> *It feels so useless,*
> *I know it's wrong, to keep*
>
> *Crying, waiting, hoping,*
> *You'll come back,*
> *Maybe some day soon,*
> *Things will change and you'll be mine.*

"Learning the Game" does not offer even this limited hope, but it does put the loss in a slightly different light—by treating it as something which is to be accepted as only natural: life and love are games, with victories and defeats—perhaps more of the latter. So the song is in one sense highly pessimistic; and yet, like "Love's Made A Fool Of You", it offers a sort of consolation by suggesting that the situation is universal.

Hearts that are broken
And love that's untrue,
These go with learning the game.

When you love her
And she doesn't love you,
You're only learning the game.

When she says
That you're the only one she'll ever love,
Then you find
That you are not the one she's thinking of,

Feeling so sad,
And you're all alone and blue,
That's when you're learning the game.

The last of the six songs was the playful "Peggy Sue Got Married". Buddy's father had suggested the title as a possible subject for a sequel to "Peggy Sue"—something along the lines of the thematic sequels of Hank Ballard's "Annie" songs. Like Annie and a few other "names" in rock 'n' roll songs, Peggy Sue had become a figure who could be mentioned in a song to attract the attention of listeners and to gain their identification with the song—rock 'n' roll fans could feel like part of an "in" group by being familiar with the names and tunes referred to in the new song. Thus, Peggy Sue made an appearance at the living room party in "Splish Splash", and was mentioned in Bobby Darin's "Queen of the Hop" and Ritchie Valens's "Ooh My Head".

Peggy Sue had indeed married Jerry Allison, and Holly's song sets out to reveal the event to the uninformed public. Holly ironically places himself in the position of the audience—he cautions the listener that all he's heard is just "a rumour from a friend" which may or may not be true—and only at the end of the lyrics does he reveal his information about "the girl that's been in nearly every song". Although the song's melodic lines follow the AABA pattern of verses and choruses that Holly used frequently, the structure of the lyrics is without precedent in his songs—rather than making up verses and refrains, the lyrics comprise a continuous whole without breaks or repeats:

Please don't tell—no, no, no—
Don't say that I told you so,
I just heard a rumour from a friend.

I don't say that it's true,
I'll just leave that up to you,
If you don't believe, I'll understand.

You recall a girl that's been
In nearly every song,
This is what I've heard—of course,
The story could be wrong—

She's the one, I've been told,
Now she's wearing a band of gold,
Peggy Sue got married not long ago.

The music itself was a bit of a sequel to "Peggy Sue". Holly hints at the chordal pattern of the twelve-bar original in his thirty-two bar sequel and, in his own rhythm guitar playing, mixes in quotations from the earlier song—for example, the rhythmic I-IV-I-V chord pattern in the opening bars of "Peggy Sue" is repeated on "Peggy Sue Got Married". Unfortunately, the

musical joke is totally lost on the version of the song released in 1959: the overdubbed vocal and instrumental accompaniments that were added to Holly's original tape by Coral obscure Holly's acoustic guitar. The other five songs discussed above also suffered from the arrangements added to Holly's tapes after his death in hopes of making the songs commercial. (The circumstances of the posthumous releases are discussed in Chapter 9.) The songs are at their best on the original undubbed tapes; Holly's acoustic guitar style and sense of rhythm and timing are then audible, as they are not in the dubbed versions.

Holly's last six songs all rank high when compared to his earlier efforts. As in his earlier songs, Holly uses simple melodies which follow patterns long established in American popular and folk music; he apparently felt no cause to lay those traditional forms aside. Although Holly's songs have a distinctive sound, they rarely follow identical chord patterns—each song uses a few chords, but the bar-by-bar chord pattern varies from song to song. In the lyrics to these last songs, Holly demonstrates a growing ability to balance personal directness and laconic generalization. As a result, the songs are notable both for immediacy and timelessness.

When Holly came home to Lubbock for a visit at Christmas, he spent some time with his friends at KLLL, playing some of his new songs for them on guitar and piano. These get-togethers led by chance to the composing and recording of "You're The One". While Holly was visiting one morning, he, Waylon Jennings and Slim Corbin decided to write a song. In ten or fifteen minutes, it was finished, and someone decided that it should be taped. Holly sang the song and accompanied himself on a borrowed guitar, while Jennings and Corbin tried (sometimes unsuccessfully) to match Holly's driving rhythm with hand clapping.

Fortunately, the tape (less than ninety seconds long) was preserved, and over five years later, was released on an album, just as is. Considering the speed with which the song was composed, it is not really surprising that some of the lines are filled out with pop clichés; and yet, the sum total of the song is something else, going beyond the clichés to create a striking mixture of emotions that is both contradictory and coherent—and quite typical of a Buddy Holly song. Mrs. Holley admits, "I always liked his music; but I couldn't see much sense in his songs then—one line said one thing, and the next said the exact opposite. Like in 'Maybe Baby'—you're the one that makes me glad, and you're the one that makes me sad—that didn't make much sense to me. But now, when I listen to those songs—and think of what the fans have written—I understand the songs better." More than one fan wrote the Holleys to say how directly the lyrics spoke to them; the simple beauty of the lyrics, the melody and the solo guitar accompaniment made the song a favourite:

You're the one that's a-causing my blues,	*Sometimes you make me feel so bad,*
You're the one I don't wanna lose,	*You make me cry deep in my heart.*
You're the one that I'd always choose,	*I feel like an actor in a play,*
You're the one that's a-meant for me.	*Who doesn't fit the part.*
You're the one that I'm thinking of,	*You're the one, and I want you to know,*
You're the one that I'll always love,	*You're the one that thrills me so,*
You're the one sent from heaven above,	*You're the one—I can't let you go,*
You're the one that's a-meant for me.	*You're the one that's meant for me.*

Mr. Holley recalls, "When Buddy came home at Christmas, it seemed like it was one of the happiest times in his life. He was free, and he had it pretty well made—he could do just about what he wanted to do." Buddy didn't even have to worry about his career being interrupted by the draft—he had flunked a physical the preceding July because of a stomach ulcer.) Holly could spend his time and energy as he wished. On one occasion, the star who had played the Palladium in London and the Paramount in New York performed live on a KLLL remote broadcast from the Morris Fruit and Vegetable Store. It was Holly's first "appearance" in Lubbock since the Crickets had become national stars. Buddy may have actually avoided opportunities to perform in Lubbock—not out of conceit or arrogance, but from a real timidity. "He said he'd rather make a flop anywhere in the world than in his home town," says Mr. Holley. Now, though, as another indication of his growing ease and confidence, Buddy told Slim Corbin to go ahead and book him for a "homecoming" appearance in Lubbock in the summer of 1959.

On New Year's Eve, Buddy and Maria flew back to New York, where Buddy made arrangements for his first tour since the break-up of the Crickets two months before.

In explaining Holly's continued popularity in the years since his death, it has often been said that he died "at the peak", before revealing any decline in the quality of his output. One wonders whether, if the Beatles had died in 1964, the same evaluation would have been made of them? Probably, because what they did afterwards was unforeseeable. Likewise there is no way of telling where or how far Buddy Holly's expanding ambitions and interests would have taken him. When he died, Buddy Holly had not yet reached his peak—his career had only just begun.

CHAPTER EIGHT

THE LAST TOUR

Not all of Holly's activities in the last part of 1958 involved music directly. He and Maria were also deep in the promotional and business aspects of Holly's career which had come under his control following the break with Petty.

As mentioned, publicity had been an issue in the break. Maria says, "Nobody was trying to arrange magazine articles or any other kind of publicity, and nobody was going around to the talent agencies or booking organizations or the disc jockeys to promote Buddy—Norman wasn't doing anything and neither was the record company. Other artists had fan clubs and newsletters but nothing like that had been set up for Buddy. And he felt like that was why his records weren't getting played while these artists with Dick Clark were having big hits—Buddy would never criticize other artists or their music but he knew that publicity was making a big difference.

"So those were the things we started working on. We worked at answering the fan mail and organizing fan clubs—we didn't have any secretaries or anything, we just went ahead and did it ourselves. We started going around to the agencies; and of course they wanted pictures for publicity work so we went to a studio and had a series of photographs taken." The photos included the one which appeared on the cover of *The Buddy Holly Story*—the one which people say "makes him look like a concert pianist". It was what the agencies wanted to see—a quiet, thoughtful artist without a hair out of place—the very image of decorum. Later, such shots helped fuel the myth that Holly had ended his rock 'n' roll phase; and it didn't help that his record company never used the few available shots of Holly performing, with his curly hair tumbling over his forehead and his mouth in a wide, happy grin.

Buddy and his wife were also spending time just getting settled in New York and enjoying their new life together. They had rented an apartment in Greenwich Village and were in the process of furnishing it—a task in which Buddy took an active role. "Buddy was head-to-toe music," recalls Maria, "and he didn't really have any other interests. But he did like to draw and design. In fact, he said once that if he couldn't be a success in music, he'd like to be an engineer or a draftsman—you know, it wasn't that he was worried about that, it's just something every artist thinks of at some time or another. So Buddy designed all the cabinets for our apartment and a bar that was going to open up onto the balcony. Did Buddy drink himself? No— he told me he couldn't understand why people had to drink to be happy; he said listening to or playing music was all he needed to feel happy. Anyway, he couldn't drink even if he wanted to because of the stomach ulcer he had. I remember on the night of my birthday in December I got him to drink a couple of glasses of champagne to celebrate—and he was sick the whole next day. I told him I'd never push him like that again." (Maria's comments on this point are a bit too absolute: Holly's friends do remember him drinking beer occasionally, though rarely to excess.)

"There was one thing we did," continued Maria, "that didn't involve music, but it did have to do with Buddy's career, so I guess it was the same thing. I wanted Buddy to take dance lessons and go to an acting school too. He didn't like to dance—said he had two left feet. But I told him he should do this because he could use the training for his work on stage. And acting school was for when Buddy got to make some movies, as he wanted to do. So we started to go to the Lee Strasberg Acting School—that was something we were doing together."

Living in New York gave Holly a chance to enjoy the city's night life and to visit with such friends as the Everly Brothers and Eddie Cochran when they came into town. Phil Everly has a favourite memory of those times:

"We were in a place down in the Village, Maria Elena was there and I had a date with me. We had dinner and we went down to hear some Spanish music. We all had a round of drinks—in those days, it cost about eight dollars. Buddy was going to the men's room and the check was coming, so he said, 'Here, take this, take care of it,' and gave me a bill. Well, when he came back, he said, 'Did you get the change?' I said, 'No, I tipped the waiter.' And Buddy started laughing. I thought he'd given me a ten-dollar bill, but it was a hundred-dollar bill. And he just laughed about it."

The move to New York was not intended to be permanent—at least, not yet. Buddy and Maria expected to be travelling, going wherever Buddy's plans took him. New York was, of course, the place to be when business and promotion were involved or when large orchestras (whether of the pop or rhythm & blues variety) were required. But stays in California might have been made for movies or recordings there and Holly's studio in Lubbock would have required his presence some of the time, so the pair had decided to rent apartments and not buy any home. They had decided for certain not to live in the large house Buddy had planned as a gift for his parents. (After Buddy's death, the Holleys dropped the plans and bought a smaller house instead.)

The racial prejudices in Lubbock were a consideration. Maria explains: "I would never have stayed in Lubbock. The way they felt about blacks and Mexicans—it didn't intimidate me at all, but after growing up in New York City and being with everybody, I couldn't have stood that sort of thinking. Somehow, Buddy had been brought up there, but he didn't have any of those prejudices. I remember that when we were on tour, there was nothing that made him madder than the blacks having to go to one hotel and the whites to another—'We're all part of one show,' he said, 'why shouldn't we be together all the time?' He didn't just 'accept' blacks, that wasn't the way he acted—and the black performers knew that. As for Lubbock, he said to me once, 'This is one of the things I don't like here—but as much as I hate it, that's how these people are.' But he just couldn't see how people who read the Bible could feel like that."

Although he had received offers for new tours, Buddy had been holding off on accepting any. One-nighters were especially unappealing. Being able to travel by car instead of by bus was a little more comfortable but the schedules were still exhausting. Maria remembers, "I liked show business and I took better to the touring than some others—I wanted to be part of what Buddy did, I wanted to be active, doing things myself. But the tours were no fun. It was all travelling and performing, with no free time. Those kids didn't even have time to do their laundry, so I used to do it for them. Buddy didn't use make-up on stage, but the others did, and it'd be all over the collars; and they'd be wearing these clothes for days because there was never time to get their things cleaned. And everyone thought it was such a glamorous life—if only they could have seen me doing the laundry!

"It's true that we had the Cadillac—but I didn't have a licence so Buddy still had to do all the driving. A couple of times he was just so tired he was falling asleep at the wheel and so I took over and drove, licence or no licence. And of course you were trying to go as fast as you could and get to the next city so you could rest up, and a couple of times we got stopped for speeding. Once in New Jersey, Buddy was stopped and he started arguing, so they took him to the station—he had me stay with the car, he thought

it'd be safer. When he got to the station and they found out who he was, they said they'd let him go if he'd give them all his autograph! Well, he did, but he told me he was so mad about being held up like that for nothing that his signature was probably unreadable, the way he dashed it off."

Besides his reluctance to go on a series of one-nighters, Buddy had another reason for delaying new appearances. If he went on tour, he would have to form a new group; and he was still hoping that, given time, the Crickets would change their minds and rejoin him. "He wanted to give them time to think it over," says Maria. "He was hoping the situation would clear up. Buddy was the kind of person who didn't like arguments—they depressed him. He'd stick to what he thought was right but he worried about hurting others. He felt very bad about what had happened with the Crickets and with Norman Petty. He always wanted everything to come out right for everybody." (Mrs. Holley offers a sidelight to this: "Buddy never really told us why he had broken with Norman. Once when he was home and some of his friends were over, somebody started to make some remark about Norman and Buddy cut it right off—'I don't want anyone bad-mouthing Norman,' he said, 'I don't want to hear anything about it.'")

Holly preferred to put off touring and instead start carrying out his recording and producing plans. But that required money—and, for reasons which are still subject to angry dispute, the money wasn't there.

The tale of what happened to the money earned by Holly and the Crickets is a tangled one and the truth is difficult to discern. Maria Elena and all of the Crickets charge that much of the money which was rightfully due to the musicians was instead retained by Norman Petty; Petty denies this and says that all of the money owed to the members of the group was fairly paid out to them. I have talked to each party, but I have not seen the accounts. No solution to the question is presented here but only an outline of the arguments.

The money earned by the Crickets fell into three categories: income from personal appearances, songwriter royalties and artist royalties on record sales. Each of these three sources was handled differently.

Money from personal appearances and performances was generally paid directly to the Crickets by the tour promoter (such as GAC) or the individual concert promoter. On the first long tour in 1957, the Crickets were paid $1,000 per week; each of the four kept $100 apiece for expenses, and the remaining $600 was sent back to Petty and placed, Petty says, in a special bank account under the Crickets name. Only Petty had access to this account. He says, "That wasn't at my insistence—it was at theirs. Joe B., in fact, said something about, 'Well, suppose J.I. decides he wants to write himself a cheque?' So they all agreed that they would not even be co-signers of a cheque or have access to it. The account wasn't for control of the money; it was for control of paying the bills."

Sometime during 1958, the Crickets began to keep more of this tour income for themselves, rather than sending it home. Petty says, "They got ticked off at me because they said, 'Well, we're making all this money, why should we just be on salary?' And that's when they stopped sending anything to the Crickets account." Joe Mauldin says, however, that some money was still being sent back to Clovis: "We started taking more for expenses—we were making more, so we felt that it was justifiable to hold back more and spend a little more. But I don't remember any tours where we kept *all* of the money. Like, when we bought those motorcycles, we were still sending money home, because I remember we called Norman and said, 'We want to buy some motorcycles—we're going to go through Dallas and pay for them. So we're not going to send any money home for a few weeks.' And Buddy hung onto the money until we had enough."

Just how much was left over after payment of all expenses for these tours may be hard to figure. Touring was then primarily a vehicle for promoting records and not always all that financially rewarding in itself. Those musicians who were on salary, such as Allsup and (on one tour) the Roses, considered themselves to be well paid. Allsup recalls, "I was paid $250 a week by Holly, plus my expenses, and that was good pay in those days. Before I worked with Holly, I had been getting $80 a week playing in a western swing band."

Songwriter royalties were disbursed by Peer-Southern. The songwriter royalties would have been about one cent per record sold (another cent, the publisher's share, would have been split between Peer-Southern and Nor Va Jak); additional songwriter royalties came from Broadcast Music, Inc. (BMI), which collects fees from radio and television stations for record airplays. These royalties would have been split according to whose names were on the songs: one-third each for Petty, Holly and Allison on "That'll Be The Day", for example. Thus, if "That'll Be The Day" had sold five million copies, songwriter royalties should have been $50,000, to be split three ways. According to Petty, the disbursements for songwriter royalties were sent directly to the individual songwriters and did not pass through his hands. Mauldin disagrees with this; he says, "I don't think I ever received any money directly from the music publishers until after we split with Petty, after Buddy's death. All the money, even the BMI cheques, went to Petty." Allison agrees with Mauldin that all songwriting royalties were paid to Petty and were not transmitted to the Crickets.

The most significant earnings were those derived from record sales. Niki Sullivan says that the first cheque received from Coral/Brunswick at the end of 1957, reflecting much of the sales of "That'll Be The Day" and part of the sales of "Peggy Sue", was for $192,000. Ten percent of this income would have gone to Norman Petty as his manager's share; of the rest, the Crickets understood that forty percent would go to their churches and the rest would be divided among them. The contracts with the record company called for the payments to be made to Petty, on the Crickets' behalf, so there is no disputing who first handled the money; but what happened to it thereafter is much disputed. While Petty will not give any numbers, he maintains that "a great deal" of these record royalties had indeed been paid out to the Crickets by late 1958. He says, "The only thing we were holding up was some of the 'Crickets' money" (the tour income that had been deposited in the special Crickets account) and, according to Petty, that was done at the request of Allison and Mauldin. Everyone else, though, tells another story.

Take Niki Sullivan's account. Even before his decision to leave the group, Sullivan and his parents had begun to have questions about what was happening to the money earned by the Crickets. Sullivan says, "My father had been to Clovis quite a few times, just to talk to Norman about seeing the books, and never once did he ever get to see them. They were always at the accountant's or somewhere being worked on." Though he will not say so outright, Sullivan implies that this inquisitiveness may have been a reason why Petty did not try to keep Sullivan in the group. "It could have been salvaged, with a little effort, but I don't think it wanted to be salvaged on certain people's parts. That effort never occurred; whether by design or not, that's not for me to question."

After Sullivan had made his exit from the Crickets, something had to be worked out as to what share he would receive of the group's earnings. Since he would no longer be touring and helping to promote the records, it was arguable whether he was entitled to a full share in the royalties, and Sullivan was willing to accept less. He says, "I went back to Norman's when the fellows weren't there. Norman had arranged for me to take ten percent of the income from 'That'll Be The Day', and I would forfeit everything on anything else that I'd played on. And I said, 'Well, that'll be fine.'"

However, the money was never paid. "To this day," says Sullivan, "I have never gotten any money—not a dime." The only income that Sullivan earned from his association with the Crickets was the $100 a week he retained from the income on the GAC tour and a thousand-dollar cheque which the Crickets gave him early in 1958, after their first tour without Sullivan. (Allison explains, "It wasn't part of any settlement because we didn't know what the deal was that Norman had worked out with him. It was just a gesture, a way of saying, 'Hey, Niki, we don't dislike you.'") Since then, all that Sullivan has received are the songwriting royalties paid to him for his share in "I'm Gonna Love You Too".

Sullivan's church never saw its share of the royalties on "That'll Be The Day", either. In fact, according to Allison, Mauldin and Mrs. Holley, none of the other churches ever received the funds, either.

When I queried him about Sullivan's story, Petty said, "Niki was to share in everything that he had been on, if I remember right. And then from that day on, anything he wasn't on, he wouldn't share in. To the best of my recollection. But he was paid on whatever he was on, the best I remember. It was reduced to writing, whatever the agreement was. He signed a release." Sullivan denies that he ever signed any agreement on the payments.

What may seem puzzling is why Sullivan never did anything about this. He explains, "I wasn't about to go back to Norman and ask for it. I figured that I had checked out, and that's the way I wanted it. I didn't want the money, it wasn't worth the hassle. Money is just a means to an end. If I've got a lot of it, great; if I don't, what the hell. I still have to watch the sun get up in the morning and go down at night."

Both Allison and Mauldin were unaware, until I told them, that Sullivan had not received the share that was agreed upon. They say they did not fare all that much better: after their own split with Petty following Holly's death, they settled for what they believed to be a lot less than what was due them, just to put the past behind and to straighten out matters for the future. Mauldin says, "As best I remember, Petty had received all the record and songwriting royalties and it was all being held—I never saw any royalties until we split with Petty. When we split, Petty said, 'Well, here's all that's in the account, this is all you have coming because you spent the rest of it,' and we didn't agree with him but there wasn't any way we could prove otherwise. Our lawyer said, 'Take what he gives you and run, and forget it—mark it up as a good lesson learned.'" Allison and Mauldin do now receive songwriting and record royalties directly from the companies involved.

Petty maintains that he dealt fairly with the Crickets and has continued to do the same with all the other artists he has had since. "Any time I have an artist, to this day, they get a Xerox copy of the royalty statements and the cheque itself. This has been a thing that we established years ago." He also says, "They kept huge sums—it used to worry me because Buddy would keep six thousand dollars, he had as much as ten thousand dollars in cash. And he would sit in the middle of a bed and he and Jerry would play with it like they were playing Monopoly." His secretary and assistant, Norma Jean Berry, adds, "I think some of the difficulty came after Buddy was dead when there was so much speculation about how much money had been made, not based on fact. People thought it must be tremendous, and it really wasn't that great, at that point. And the boys themselves forgot how much money they simply wasted. I mean, they'd get several thousand dollars from their engagements and they didn't remember that they had spent a lot of money. They had wasted a lot of money. And because they didn't have it, they thought, 'Well, Norman's got it.' Except it wasn't true."

Allison and Mauldin also differ with Petty on whose idea it was to hold back whatever money was due to Holly. Mauldin says, "Neither one of us ever insinuated in any way that Petty should hold it. In fact, Jerry and I felt it was unfair that Petty hold it because Buddy needed it—we knew he needed it." Allison takes a similar line: "I only found out after Buddy's death that Norman had been telling Buddy and Buddy's lawyer that Buddy owed us a bunch of money from tours and that we'd have to get that all straight before Buddy got his money. I hope to this day that Buddy knew better than that—because we weren't telling Norman to hold the money. Buddy might have owed us money because when we were touring we used to get the loot in cash and we'd say, 'Look at that!' and Buddy'd say, 'How much you want? Five hundred dollars? A thousand?', whatever, you know. We kept receipts but none of us cared. And sure, there might have been sometimes when we didn't get our part and some when we might have gotten more than our part. But Joe B. and I didn't ever at one time say, 'O.K., we want to be sure that we get our part of that.' Buddy would never have cheated us out of a thing."

Holly and Maria Elena clearly believed that there was money owing to them for they undertook legal action in the months after the split with Petty to recover the disputed funds. Despite Petty's position that there was not much money involved, Holly obviously thought otherwise. Tommy Allsup remembers that the day before Holly's death, Holly was infuriated to learn that an audit of one account had found less than $5,000 in it—Holly, according to Allsup, believed that there should have been over $50,000 there. One friend of Holly's says that the total amount in dispute was about $80,000.

There is no doubt that, in the year after the success of "That'll Be The Day", Holly received enough money to pay for some major items, including his Ariel motorcycle, his Cadillac and the Impala he bought for his parents. On the other hand, Holly had apparently not yet received much of what was due him from all sources. Between his death and the time when his will was probated, some $70,000 was paid to his estate. At the time that he decided to go back on tour in early 1959, Holly was definitely short of cash. Tommy Allsup remembers that Holly had to borrow money from GAC, drawing an advance on his income from the tour in order to pay for his anticipated expenses.

I am neither an accountant nor a lawyer, and I am not sure that I would be any more able to make sense of all this even if I were. After talking with each of the Crickets, with Petty, with the Holleys and Maria Elena and with others who were close to the situation, it is my own judgement that Holly and the Crickets never received much of what was rightfully theirs— although they may well have been paid all that was *legally* due to them. In the entertainment industry, even more than in other businesses, what is fair and what is legal are often worlds apart. This is just my opinion, and others may conclude differently.

The fate of Holly's earnings is an issue that is part of his story and can hardly be avoided; but in truth, it is one which none of the parties enjoys discussing. The principal people involved have willingly laid out their recollections for me, and each wants to give his or her side of it, but it brings them no pleasure to do so. Having to talk about this aspect of the past brings to the surface bitter memories and feelings of antagonism and these are only aroused further, not eased, by the recollection. For the sake of peace of mind, they wish it could all be put far in the past; no one any longer seeks revenge or recompense. It is, as more than one of them says, "Not worth the hassle."

I have found myself, therefore, regretting that I had to ask the questions I did, wishing not to reopen the wounds, and wanting not to seem so preoccupied with this part of Holly's life. Maybe the best way to react to all this is not to concentrate on how much the conflicts affected the course of Holly's life, but rather on how little they altered Holly's spirit and his music. I find it something to marvel at that in the midst of all these personality conflicts and financial disputes, and in the face of the enormous emotional and commercial pressures of the pop music business, Holly and the Crickets survived to create and perform music of lasting grace, vitality and good spirit. The more one learns about the distractions and the obstacles, the more remarkable becomes Holly's legacy, the transcending joy that is released whenever his records are played.

Early in the new year, Holly was asked to head a package tour which GAC was organizing. Influenced by both finances and friendship, Buddy reluctantly agreed. Maria explains:

"More than anything, Buddy went on the tour as a favour to GAC. They had put this show together but they felt that they needed a bigger attraction on the bill than the acts they already had. So they really urged Buddy to help them out. Of course, the money was a reason for going—my aunt had been lending us money to fix up our apartment and all. But I think he went more because he had gone on so many GAC tours before and he had friends there, and he didn't feel like he could turn them down if they said they needed him."

As Jerry Allison said, Buddy didn't want to go on tours if they didn't sound like they would be fun—and a wintertime tour did not sound like fun to a Texas native. Billed as "The Winter Dance Party", this package was booked for a three-week tour through the heart of the Midwest, with most of the appearances scheduled in Minnesota, Wisconsin and Iowa. The acts on the show were not so numerous or so impressive as on Holly's previous tours. Due to a national economic recession and to changes in rock 'n' roll music itself, the big package shows had declined in size and strength over the previous year and were becoming much more segregated. The Winter Dance Party had just five acts: Holly, Ritchie Valens, the Big Bopper, Dion and the Belmonts and Frankie Sardo.

Holly now had to form a new band for the tour. For a guitarist, he turned naturally to Tommy Allsup, who readily agreed to go on the tour. On Holly's behalf, Allsup contacted a drummer named Carl Bunch who had recorded in Clovis with a group from Odessa, Texas called Ronnie Smith and the Poor Boys. For a bass player, Holly turned to Waylon Jennings, who jumped at the offer and obtained a "leave of absence" from KLLL. Jennings was used to playing a regular six-string guitar, but had to learn the electric bass guitar almost from scratch for the tour. He remembers Holly's instructions: "Here's the bass—you learn it. Now, here are my albums—you learn 'em. You've

● *Onstage during the last tour, Waylon, Buddy and Tommy*

got a week and a half to do it." Tommy Allsup helped to teach him.

Despite Holly's agreement with Allison and Mauldin giving them title to the Crickets name, Holly's new group was billed as the Crickets. Allison believes that GAC did this without Holly's approval, but it is possible that Holly, as part of the legal manoeuvring over the group's earnings, found it necessary to use the Crickets' name as a way of maintaining his claim to the disputed funds. A spectator at Holly's last show remembers that the singer never referred to his band as the Crickets.

Fans wonder how Holly would have responded had the original Crickets asked to rejoin him, now that he had this new band. "Buddy still hoped to patch things up with the Crickets," says Maria. "He tried to call them once, in fact, from New York, but they weren't home, they were over in Clovis. He felt that if he could just talk to them, they could get back together. Of course, Tommy Allsup would have stayed in the band, and Buddy was going to promote Waylon as an individual artist, anyway, so it wasn't a case of having to choose some people over others. When he went on the tour, Buddy really missed the Crickets—he felt like they added something special to his act. Once when he talked with me on the phone, he said, 'If you get a call from Jerry and Joe B., tell them I'll be back in two weeks, and I want to talk to them—alone.'" Carl Bunch agrees that Holly wanted Allison and Mauldin to rejoin him: "Buddy fully intended to get back with those guys. I'd like to say that he intended to keep me forever, but I know that was not his intention."

Buddy and Maria decided that, for reasons of health, Maria should skip this tour—she was pregnant and had been having spells of nausea and so it seemed best for her to avoid the rigours of a series of one-nighters. (She suffered a miscarriage a few weeks after Holly's death.) Since he was going to be travelling alone, Buddy decided to leave his Cadillac with Maria in New York and go by bus with the rest of the troupe.

Allsup, Jennings and Bunch flew to New York to join Holly in mid-January, which allowed for about a week of rehearsals before setting out on the tour. At breakfast on their last day in New York, Allsup remembers, Holly told his friends of strange dreams Maria and he had had the night before. Maria tells the details:

"I had always had a fear of small planes and Buddy knew it. But his brother Larry had a plane and Buddy wanted to fly, too—he was taking lessons behind my back, and when I found out, I got mad. I told him that he shouldn't fly small planes—that it scared me, and that should be reason enough not to do it.

"The night before Buddy left, I had this dream. I dreamed I was with Buddy, and then there was a lot of commotion—people were scared and running every which way, and then I found myself alone in a big, empty prairie or desert. Then I heard shouts and screams, and saw hundreds of people running towards me shouting, 'Look out, it's coming!' They all passed by me and I turned to watch them go; and when I turned back, I saw this big ball of fire coming through the air. It passed by me and fell a few feet from where I was and made a deep hole in the ground. Then I woke up, and I must have screamed because I woke Buddy up, too. And then he told me about the dream he had been having.

"He had been dreaming that he was in a small plane with Larry and me. Larry didn't want me to be there but Buddy told him, 'Anywhere I go, Maria comes with me.' They kept arguing about it and Larry kept landing the plane because he wanted me to get off, and Buddy wouldn't agree, so they'd take off again. Finally, Larry won the argument, and they landed on the roof of a tall building and left me there. And Buddy said, 'Don't worry, just stay put—I'll come back and get you.' And then he flew off. And that was when he woke up. So I guess our dreams meant something, if you put them together. . . ."

The Midwest, for some reason, was prime territory for rock 'n' roll stage shows. There were few real metropolises in the upper Midwest, but even the small cities of 25,000 to 100,000 people had large ballrooms which, for such a touring show as this, were usually filled by crowds wholly out of proportion to the size of the local population.

The performances before enthusiastic audiences were enjoyable—but the travelling conditions were dreadful. It was the worst possible season and locale for such a tour: the heart of winter, in a region where winter is most severe. The tour opened in Milwaukee, where the thermometer read twenty-five degrees below zero. Allsup remembers being astonished, upon arriving at the ballroom in a taxicab, to see long lines of teenagers standing outside, waiting for the doors to open.

Bus travel, never comfortable, was now positively hazardous. Travelling through the cold darkness, up to five hundred miles between successive dates, the performers rode on poorly heated buses that were prone to breakdowns. The troupe had to switch buses several times during the first week of the tour as mechanical problems beset the vehicles. En route from Duluth, Minnesota to Green Bay, Wisconsin in the early morning hours of February 1, the tour bus simply died while ascending a hill on a lonely highway. The musicians burned newspapers inside the bus, trying to keep warm. Finally, a truck came along and took several people to a nearby town, where the local police were notified and came to the rescue of the other performers still on the bus. By this time, Carl Bunch had suffered frostbite on his feet. He stayed behind in a local hospital, while the rest of the troupe continued on to Green Bay (making the last leg by train).

The original itinerary for the Winter Dance Party did not show any appearance scheduled for the day after the Green Bay show but, in a late booking, an appearance in Clear Lake, Iowa was scheduled to fill the open date. Clear Lake is an important resort centre, thanks to the large lake from which it takes its name. It is located ten miles west of Mason City, a small city of thirty thousand people in north-central Iowa. Close by the shore of Clear Lake lies a large dance hall called the Surf Ballroom. Here, the Winter Dance Party performers were to appear on Monday evening, February 2.

In the years since then, the ballroom has expanded in function and has been renamed the Surf Civic and Convention Centre. It still retains the raised stage, the beautiful, polished dance floor and the rows of green leather-covered padded booths lining the side and rear of the dance floor that were there in 1959.

On the way from Green Bay to Clear Lake, a distance of about 350 miles, the troupe again had trouble with the bus they were riding, and it was 6.00 P.M. before they arrived in Clear Lake. The show that night was scheduled to run from eight to midnight; immediately after the dance, the performers would pile back onto the bus and ride all night to Moorhead, Minnesota, where they were booked for two shows the next night. It would be a ride of 430 miles north and west from Clear Lake. In Moorhead, they would hopefully have a few hours to rest in a hotel before the evening shows.

By the time the tour reached Clear Lake, Holly was as tired as the rest of the performers were. He was worried that his weariness might detract

Joanie Svenson took these pictures on
January 26, 1959

● *Buddy and Tommy Allsup*

● *The Big Bopper*

● *Ritchie Valens*

from his group's performance. He was also concerned with their stage appearance. The group had been performing every night and then riding in the buses fully dressed to fight off the sub-zero weather, and their stage clothes were now pretty well rumpled and soiled—it had been at least several days since the group had been in one town long enough to get their clothes cleaned.

At Clear Lake, Buddy decided to charter a small plane so that he and his sidemen could fly on ahead to Moorhead. That way, the group could get a decent night's sleep and have a chance to do the laundry before the shows the next night. The idea met with the approval of the tour's road manager, Rod Lucier; by going to Moorhead ahead of the troupe, Holly could still take care of necessary last-minute arrangements for the shows there, even if the bus were delayed by more mechanical problems.

Buddy explained his plan to Waylon Jennings and Tommy Allsup, and the two agreed to go with Holly and share the cost of renting the plane. Upon arriving at the Surf Ballroom, Holly spoke to the manager of the dance hall, Carroll Anderson, and asked Anderson to try to arrange such a flight. Anderson attempted to reach Jerry Dwyer, owner of Dwyer's Flying Service, the charter company based at the Mason City Airport. Dwyer was at a Junior Chamber of Commerce meeting in Mason City; Anderson next called Roger Peterson, a young pilot who worked for Dwyer, and asked if Peterson could make the flight. Although the next day was supposed to be his day off, the pilot agreed to fly the group to the airport at Fargo, North Dakota, just across the Red River from Moorhead. The flight was scheduled to leave the Mason City Airport about 12.30 A.M.

When the other performers on the tour heard of Buddy's arrangement, Jennings and Allsup got separate requests to give up their seats on the plane. J. P. Richardson, the "Big Bopper", approached Jennings. Richardson pointed out that the long bus rides were particularly rough on large men like himself who could not sleep comfortably on the bus; "Those bus seats bug me," he said. Besides, J. P. had caught a cold, and his condition certainly wasn't going to be improved by a night-long ride on a cold bus. Waylon actually wasn't minding the bus rides as much as the others were—for him, the tour was a novelty, and he was finding it fun to be with the other performers on the tour. Jennings agreed to let Richardson make the flight instead.

When Ritchie Valens learned of the planned flight, he tried to convince Tommy Allsup to give up the final seat. Valens had never flown on a small plane before and was excited by the idea. Valens pestered Allsup about it through the evening but Allsup refused to give up his seat. Ritchie persisted after the show, even as the troupe's gear was being loaded on the tour bus.

"Let's flip a coin for it," Valens proposed. Allsup finally agreed to this, provided that he could use a sleeping bag that the Big Bopper had bought in Green Bay, if he lost the coin toss. The Big Bopper agreed. Allsup flipped Ritchie's coin, a new half-dollar, and Ritchie called "heads". "Heads" it was.

Somewhere between eleven and fifteen hundred teenagers paid the $1.25 admission charge to see the Dance Party that night; Anderson says that it was the best crowd ever for a rock 'n' roll show at the ballroom. A few adults were there, too, since it was Anderson's policy to admit parents free as his "guests".

Bob Hale, a local DJ, was master of ceremonies that night. He agrees with Anderson: "It was the biggest crowd that Carroll Anderson had ever had in the Surf—it was the biggest thing I had ever seen. We had people that had driven in from St. Paul, others that had driven in from Illinois and Minnesota. The place was filled to the rafters."

According to Fred Milano, a member of Dion and the Belmonts, the show was opened by Frankie Sardo, who was followed by Ritchie Valens, the Big Bopper, the Belmonts and Holly. But both Milano and Bob Hale remember that Holly was on stage earlier in the evening—playing drums! Holly's band had been backing up the other groups on the tour and with Bunch out with frostbite, Holly filled in on drums. During Holly's own set, the bass singer for the Belmonts, Carlo Mastrangelo, played drums. According to Hale, each act played two sets, and there was also about fifteen minutes of "goofing off", with Holly, Valens and the Big Bopper singing together as a trio.

The tour had dispelled any fears anyone might have had that Holly's popularity was on the wane. The crowds that turned out for the shows were greeting him as warmly as they had before, and listening to his music and his singing just as closely. At the time, Ritchie Valens had the second best-selling single in the country with his two-sided hit, "Donna"/"La Bamba", while the Big Bopper's "Chantilly Lace" had been on the charts for six months; even so, eyewitness accounts and newspaper reports of the show in Clear Lake agree that Holly was the best-received act on the bill. Holly and Carroll Anderson chatted backstage in the manager's office before the show; when Anderson asked the singer how far he expected to go in the music business, Holly replied with a grin, "Well, I'm either going to go to the top—or else I'm going to fall. But I think you're going to see me in the bigtime."

Touring with Jennings and Allsup, both of whom were well acquainted with country music, Holly had occasionally mixed in country songs with his more familiar hits and the reaction had been good. Waylon Jennings once told an interviewer, "We did country songs on stage—we did 'Salty Dog Blues', and that's as country as you can get—and the kids really thought, 'Man, that's it, that's what's happening.'" This night in Clear Lake, Buddy opened his act by coming on stage ahead of his band, strumming his electric guitar and singing a country tune that had crossed over onto the pop charts to become a top ten hit for Billy Grammer:

> I've laid around, and played around,
> This old town too long,
> Summer's almost gone,
> And winter's coming on.
> I've laid around, and played around,
> This old town too long,
> And I feel like I've gotta travel on . . . .

Daniel Dougherty, a resident of a small farming village south of Mason City, was at the show. He writes: "The hall was pretty well packed full that night. There wasn't much dancing while Buddy sang—they all wanted to just listen to him sing. He didn't dance around the stage much, but stayed in one place most of the time; he moved his neck a lot when he sang. He wore a suit with a bow tie and those big black glasses that made him stand out on the stage. After each song he sang, he got right into another one—he never said hardly a word but 'thank you'."

Holly sang most of his single releases—"Peggy Sue", "That'll Be The Day", "Maybe Baby", "Heartbeat", "Rave On" and "Everyday" were among the tunes he sang that night. "One thing for sure," writes Dougherty, "Buddy never sang 'It Doesn't Matter Anymore'"—even though it was his current release.

Sometime during the evening, Buddy called Maria in New York. She remembers: "He told me what an awful tour it had been. The buses were dirty and cold, and things just weren't as had been promised. He said everybody on the tour was really disgusted with the whole thing. Then he said that the tour was behind schedule and he had to go on ahead of the others to the next stop to make arrangements for the show. He didn't tell me that he was going to fly. I said, 'Why should *you* go?' And he said, 'There's nobody else to do it.'"

When the Dance Party show was over in Clear Lake, Carroll Anderson drove Holly, Valens and the Big Bopper to the Mason City Airport. They arrived there about 12.40 A.M. and were met by Roger Peterson and by Jerry Dwyer, who had been informed about the flight during the evening and had come to the airport to help Peterson get the plane ready. Dwyer later expressed his surprise upon meeting the three musicians—"I thought all entertainers got drunk. But they hadn't been drinking; they were just real nice kids."

Peterson had checked the weather forecasts several times during the evening. Conditions were acceptable; all stations en route were reporting visibility of ten miles or greater, although snow showers were forecast for Fargo sometime after midnight. At Mason City itself, the temperature was eighteen degrees, the wind was gusting to thirty-five miles per hour, and light snow was falling by the time the plane was ready to take off—not the best of conditions, but still adequate. The air traffic communicators at the airport did not inform Peterson of two special weather bureau advisories, one predicting lowered visibility in snow and fog over an area including Iowa, and the other reporting a band of snow moving southeastward through Minnesota and North Dakota.

Since he did not see the special advisories, Peterson may not have realized that he might have to fly by instruments. The twenty-one-year-old pilot had been flying for four years, but had not yet been certified for instrument flying. He had failed his first instrument flight check a year before when he had had difficulty holding at the required altitude. That did not mean that he was prohibited from flying by instruments; he had had many lessons on them, and was familiar, though inexperienced, with the equipment involved. However, the Dwyer Flying Service was certificated for visual flights only and its pilots were not supposed to fly under conditions requiring navigation by instruments.

Anderson and the performers went into Dwyer's office, where the three passengers paid their thirty-six-dollar fares individually. They spent a few minutes chatting with Dwyer, who later remembered Holly discussing his own interest in flying small planes. Then, they walked out to the aircraft, a red Beechcraft Bonanza four-seater, and Anderson helped the three load their baggage on the plane. Valens and Richardson climbed into the back seats, while Holly got in front with Peterson. Anderson left for his home and Dwyer went to the control tower to watch the plane's departure.

It was a little before 1.00 A.M. when the single-engine aircraft moved down the airport's north–south runway and took off. Levelling off south of the field, it made a 180-degree left turn and headed north, and then took up a northwest bearing, in the direction of Fargo.

Now, the lights of Mason City and Clear Lake were left behind. The moon and stars were obscured by the snow and the overcast sky; and the thinly populated countryside below, with its scattered farmhouses and snow-covered cornfields, offered no lights or landmarks or visible horizon to the night-time travellers. Peterson was immediately forced to depend upon his instruments. The gusty winds caused most of the instruments to fluctuate,

making them difficult to interpret. Peterson had to rely on the plane's Sperry attitude gyroscope, which displayed the plane's pitch attitude in exactly the opposite manner from the way it was shown on the conventional gyroscopes Peterson had encountered during his instrument flight training. Under such conditions of stress and inexperience, Peterson probably became confused in reading the unfamiliar gyroscope. He may never have realized that while executing what he thought was a climbing turn, the plane was actually descending.

From the airport tower, Jerry Dwyer watched the plane's white tail light recede in the distance. When the plane was about four miles from the airport, Dwyer saw the plane descend slowly, until it was out of sight. He later stated, "I thought at the time that probably it was an optical illusion due to the plane going away from us at an angle." Dwyer was disturbed, though, by Peterson's failure to file a flight plan immediately after take-off. Attempts were made to contact the plane by radio, but there was no answer.

That same night, Joe Mauldin, Jerry Allison and Sonny Curtis were at Jerry's house in Lubbock, talking things over. Jerry and Joe felt that they had parted with Buddy as friends; but although they had not seen him or talked to him since the break they could tell now that some sort of tension had built up, and they did not know quite why. They wondered too why the name of the Crickets was being used for the group touring with Holly. For Mauldin and Allison, the situation had not turned out the way Norman Petty had pictured it—in the three months since Holly's departure from the group, the original Crickets (augmented by Curtis and vocalist Earl Sinks) had not got any engagements and had cut just one single, "Love's Made A Fool Of You", which had not yet been released. Jerry and Joe decided to call Buddy to talk things out and get matters straight—with the idea that the call might lead to the reunion of the group, perhaps with Sonny Curtis likewise rejoining Holly.

Joe Mauldin explains: "During that tour, Jerry and I broke with Norman. And then we started trying to get in touch with Buddy because Buddy had said, 'You ever want to get back with me, all you have to do is call.' So we were trying to call Buddy to say, 'We want to put the group back together.'"

They called Maria a couple of hours after her conversation with Buddy; she told the pair where Buddy was playing that night, and where he would be the next day. When Mauldin and Allison called the ballroom in Clear Lake, they found that Holly had already left. Then, says Joe, "We called the next place he was going to play and left a message, and we were expecting a call that night or the next day when he got there. But we never got to talk to him."

Through the night, Jerry Dwyer checked with the Mason City Airport several times to learn if anything had been heard from Peterson, but there was no news. Airports in Minnesota and the one at Fargo were contacted, and they too had heard nothing from the plane. Shortly before dawn, an alert was issued for the missing aircraft. Dwyer went to the airport in the morning, but found that there was still no news. "I decided I just couldn't sit there," he told Civil Aeronautics Board investigators, "and decided I would go fly and try to follow the same course that I thought Roger would have taken. I was only approximately eight miles northwest of the field when I spotted the wreckage. I believe the time was approximately 9.35 A.M."

Guided by Dwyer's radioed directions, police arrived at the crash site shortly afterwards. The wreckage lay in a cornfield several hundred yards

from the nearest farmhouse; no one had seen or heard the crash. The right wing of the plane had struck the ground first and been ripped off as the plane hit the ground, bounced fifty feet on and then ploughed five hundred feet through the snow and stubble before piling into a wire fence at the north end of the field. The body of J. P. Richardson had been thrown forty feet beyond the fence, while those of Holly and Valens lay twenty feet south of the wreck; Peterson's body was still in the ball of wreckage which was all that was left of the plane. All had surely died at the moment of impact.

Carroll Anderson was called from Clear Lake to make a positive identification of the bodies; there was some confusion at first since an extra billfold had been found at the crash site, one belonging to Tommy Allsup. (Allsup recalls that he had given his wallet to Holly so that Holly could pick up a registered letter waiting for Allsup in Moorhead.) Meanwhile, a radio station in Mason City was listening to the radio conversations between search planes, the airport control tower and the police. The station soon discovered who had been on the plane and the story went out over the national newswires, even before the wreckage was discovered and the bodies positively identified.

Just after noon, the bus carrying the other members of the tour reached Moorhead. As Tommy Allsup walked into the hotel lobby, he could see a nearby television. A photograph of the Big Bopper was on the screen but Allsup could not hear the announcer's words. He walked up to the desk to check in and it was the desk clerk who told him what had happened. Allsup brought the word back to the others still on the bus. "Boys," he said, "they didn't make it."

Maria Elena had been feeling ill and was still in bed when she got a telephone call from Lou Giordano. "He asked me if I had seen the television or listened to the radio yet," she says, "and when I told him I hadn't, he said, 'Don't turn them on—I'm on my way over.' But I turned on the radio. And my aunt came in just as I heard the news . . . ."

The Holleys learned of the crash in much the same, sudden way. Sometime during the morning, a friend of Mrs. Holley's called her and mentioned that a radio station was playing many of Buddy's songs. "Well, I didn't think much of that," Mrs. Holley says, "they were always doing that. Then the woman asked, 'By the way, how was Buddy travelling?' 'By bus,' I told her. She said, 'Oh,' and said goodbye." Not long afterward, another woman called and said with little tact, "Have you heard the news? There's some news about Buddy on the radio; turn it on." Mrs. Holley told her husband to do so; the station was indeed playing Buddy's songs, and before long the news story was repeated: "A light plane has crashed in Iowa . . . ." "I don't remember hearing any more," says Mrs. Holley. "I put it all together, and I knew what had happened. And I knew that the plane flight must have been all Buddy's idea."

In Moorhead, the surviving performers at first didn't want to go through with their engagement, but finally agreed to carry on with the performance. The two scheduled shows were combined into one, and an audience of over two thousand tried to forget their loss with the sound of rock 'n' roll; but when Holly's band appeared on stage, minus its star, and sang his songs, many in the audience could not hold back their tears. "After the show," Waylon Jennings remembers, "the promoters tried to dock us for how much Buddy and the Big Bopper and Ritchie Valens had made. This, after begging us to play. Real nice people."

To fill out the shortened bill that night, the Moorhead promoters had held auditions that afternoon for local talent. A newly formed band of students from Central High School in Fargo, who had been eagerly awaiting Holly's forthcoming appearance, was chosen to be on the show. Too new to have stage clothes or a name, the band members bought themselves identical angora sweaters, like the one worn by Holly in his new publicity photos, and named themselves "The Shadows". Seventeen-year-old Bobby Velline was chosen to be the vocalist, since he knew more lyrics than anyone else in the band. Over the next few years, Bobby Vee used a voice which bore some resemblance to that of Buddy Holly to gain his own degree of success as a recording artist.

The next night, in Sioux City, Iowa, the troupe was joined by Jimmy Clanton and Frankie Avalon, who had dropped other commitments to take the place of the dead stars. Carl Bunch rejoined the tour here, and Ronnie Smith (the singer for whom Bunch had been playing in Texas when contacted by Holly) was flown in by GAC to play with Holly's group. Jennings and Allsup had wanted to quit the tour, but GAC promised to pay them a share of what Holly would have earned and to fly them to Lubbock for Holly's funeral. The band members then agreed to complete the tour, but neither promise was fulfilled.

On Wednesday, the 4th, a plane was sent from Texas to bring Holly's body home; delayed by a storm, it returned on Thursday. The funeral was held on Saturday afternoon at the Tabernacle Baptist Church and was attended by one thousand people, many of them Buddy's young local fans and friends. The pallbearers were the contemporaries with whom Buddy had played and performed since he had picked up a guitar: Bob Montgomery, Jerry Allison, Joe Mauldin, Niki Sullivan, Sonny Curtis and Phil Everly. Bill Pickering of the Picks sang a hymn, "Beyond the Sunset". Another reminder of Buddy's musical life was included in the service. Someone, remembering Holly's long-time enthusiasm for the Angelic Gospel Singers' "I'll Be All Right", had found a copy of the record and the black gospel tune was played during the funeral.

IN LOVING MEMORY
OF OUR OWN
BUDDY HOLLEY
SEPTEMBER 7, 1936
FEBRUARY 3, 1959

● *Lubbock City Cemetery—Holly's grave is in the foreground*

The body was buried in the Lubbock City Cemetery, on the eastern edge of town, where the land is as flat and open as on almost all of the bare but imposing West Texas plains. The grave lies one hundred yards up the road which leads north from the office at the cemetery entrance. The site is but a few feet from the road, as if to be all the more accessible to the many fans who have come there from up to ten thousand miles away in the years since Buddy Holly's death. The inscription on the headstone reads simply, "In Loving Memory of Our Own Buddy Holley—September 7, 1936–February 3, 1959." On the stone, to the right of the inscription, is one last gesture of silent affirmation to a city which hardly accepted his music in his lifetime and has only grudgingly acknowledged him since his death: a raised carving of Buddy's electric guitar.

"The day the music died"—so Don McLean termed that cold February day in his number one song "American Pie" almost thirteen years later. He was not the first to see Holly's death as a decisive event in the history of rock 'n' roll. At the time, no one could sense fully just what the fatal accident meant for the development of the music; and yet, on three continents, the news brought an indescribable feeling of something lost—something which could never be regained. Holly was memorialized in song and several albums were issued after his death.

Within weeks of Holly's death, "It Doesn't Matter Anymore" climbed to number thirteen on the Hot 100 ("Raining In My Heart" also made the list). Coral then issued a new album, *The Buddy Holly Story*, which included hits from the two earlier albums as well as some singles not previously available on an LP. This release climbed high on the album chart and was in and out of *Billboard*'s list of top one hundred albums for some three-and-a-half years, eventually earning a gold record. These successes led Coral to look for other recordings by Holly which could be issued to meet the continued demand.

Few studio masters still remained unissued; and so, almost immediately, Coral turned to unmastered material which might somehow be made to sound "commercial". A pattern was set which was followed on almost all future Holly releases: Holly's demos and tapes were not released untampered, but were instead given a bigger or fuller sound through overdubbing. The results were rarely satisfactory—at least, not to the ears of Holly's fans.

The first songs subjected to this "sweetening" were the six original songs that Holly had written just before his death. Coral got the tapes of these from Maria Elena and put them in the hands of in-house producer Jack Hansen, who was Dick Jacobs's assistant. "Peggy Sue Got Married" and "Crying, Waiting, Hoping" were issued on a single in July 1959; all of the songs were released on *The Buddy Holly Story, Volume 2* (April 1960), along with the unreleased masters "True Love Ways" and "Moondreams"; "Little Baby", from Holly's first album; and three songs which had been flip sides on singles: "Well . . . All Right", "Now We're One" and "Take Your Time".

Though it could not be known how Buddy himself would have arranged the material, there was a general feeling that the Coral recordings were not even close to Buddy's intentions. Vocal backgrounds (by the white pop group, the Ray Charles singers) were added to all the songs, probably with the thought of matching the vocal and instrumental blend of the Crickets recordings; however, at times Holly's own vocal is barely audible through the "background" instrumentation. All of the songs were "stretched" to some extent by repeating the instrumental break or the closing verses. All this made it necessary to obscure Holly's own guitar playing. Even so, the accompanists sometimes failed audibly in trying to follow Holly's shifting, accented rhythm.

Of the six songs, "Crying, Waiting, Hoping" suffered the least, "That Makes It Tough" and "That's What They Say" suffered the most, and "What To Do", "Learning the Game" and "Peggy Sue Got Married" fell somewhere in between. Overall, the songs came out sounding more "pop" than anything Holly had done up to that point; and ironically enough, with the passage of years and the ignorance among newer fans about the posthumous nature of these arrangements, the songs strengthened the impression that Holly had been turning decisively away from rock 'n' roll or rockabilly and toward pop music.

The new album's sales were nowhere near those of *The Buddy Holly Story*,

CHAPTER NINE

THE MAKING
· OF A ·
LEGEND

One day soon the reservoir of Holly's songs will be drained. I give the cult five years.
Adrian Mitchell,
London *Daily Mail*,
July 13, 1962

By MIKE GROSS

Immortality comes easy in the record business. If there are enough masters in the morgue or tapes in the vault, the "death rattle" goes on perpetuating the performer, and, very often, filling the record company coffers.

The necrophiles-on-parade pass through the disk scene touching all areas — pop, country & western, jazz, longhair—for a posthumous payoff. Sometimes it doesn't work, as with 20th Fox Records' album compilation of song tracks made by Marilyn Monroe shortly after the screen star's death last summer, but that was the exception to the rule. For some reason disk "tributes" and "salutes" continue to be hot properties.

This disk-after-death activity came into the spotlight again this week with release of a "new" LP by Buddy Holly, called "Reminiscing," on the Coral label. Holly, who died in an airplane crash in February, 1959, at age 22, has been a consistent seller since his death. Five LPs have been put into the market since '59, including two volumes of "The Buddy Holly Story," and according to rough figures given out by Decca-Coral sales execs, the albums have sold more than 1,-000,000 copies.

The current package, which was mastered for stereo from previously unreleased tapes by Holly's manager Norman Petty, has been blueprinted for a prime merchandising push. In the works now are special disk jockey shows to commemorate the fourth anniversary of the singer's death. The new package, as well as Holly's other LP and single releases, will be getting hefty programming time on a nationwide scale as part of the deejay "salutes."

Holly, who had about three hot disking years before his death with such single clicks as "Peggy Sue," "Every Day" and "That'll Be The Day," continues to build new teenage fans. Some wonder if he would be as popular today if he hadn't died, while others say that the Holly image has remained constant and will continue to attract the juvenile disk buyer because his "young sound" stays the same.

At any rate, the Coral boys are pegging their merchandising and promotion techniques on Holly as though he were a "living act." Lenny Salidor, Decca-Coral publicity-promotion chief, reports that material on Holly is kept in the active file to handle the flood of requests for photos and bio information that continually pour in.

Another effort by Coral to perpetuate the Holly name was its recent purchase of a master made in Australia by young singer Mike Berry. The disk, titled "Tribute To Buddy Holly," has been stirring up some noise for Coral in the singles field. Meantime, royalties on Holly's disks continue to amass. The beneficiaries are his widow, his parents and his manager.

but there was still a clear demand for more Holly recordings. At first, Holly's family was reluctant to allow new releases. Neither Maria nor the Holleys wanted Buddy's name exploited, and they felt it would be wrong to allow Coral to issue material which would have been below Holly's own professional standards. However, the flood of letters from Holly's fans asking that all such material be issued convinced his widow and parents to allow the release of these additional recordings. The continued flow of new albums during the 1960's reflected the willingness of the fans to accept the technical limitations of the previously unissued material.

Legal complications prevented any new releases for a couple of years. At the time of Buddy's death, his recordings were scattered along the course of his musical career. Demos made in the days of the Buddy and Bob Show were in the hands of the Holleys, Bob Montgomery, Hipockets Duncan and others in Lubbock; sides cut during the period of Holly's Decca contract were in Decca's Nashville office or in the possession of Jim Denny's Cedarwood Publishing firm; Norman Petty had masters Holly had recorded before the break between them; and Coral had a claim to anything Holly had recorded during his period on the label. (Maria had turned all her tapes over to the Holleys shortly after Buddy's death, feeling that the tapes could have only sentimental value. She had also, it should be added, assigned half of Holly's estate to his parents, even though his death without a will had left her sole heir.) The legal tangle involved in determining rights to these recordings is apparent at a glance, and would be beyond a layman's powers of explanation even if all the facts in the matter were readily available.

As part of the settlement finally reached in 1962, Norman Petty regained control of Holly's recordings. Petty's leverage in the negotiations had been that he still possessed some of Holly's material and was not obligated to give it up or allow it to be issued; but Mrs. Holley denies that this was a factor in Petty's return to authority. The main reason, she says, was simply that Norman was the person who could do the best job of producing the remaining material, since he presumably had the most familiarity with Holly's style and taste in arrangements. Also, the Holleys knew they would need someone to handle the complicated business arrangements involved, and so they turned to Norman for that aid. Under the agreement worked out, Coral remained Holly's label (and took over as well the recordings he had made on Brunswick with the Crickets), and Maria Elena, the Holleys and Petty split Holly's future royalties.

Jerry Allison comments: "I think Buddy would have been terrifically unhappy with the fact that his folks went back to Norman. I can understand why they did it—when you're in Lubbock, Texas, you don't have much choice. They didn't have any choice if they wanted to keep Buddy's name alive and keep records coming out for the fans. They couldn't go flying to New York to keep it going—if they had, they would have just gotten mixed up with some straight biz cat who just wanted to put more records out. Like, what those people had done with Buddy's last songs—that was awful, Buddy would have hated that stuff. But Norman kept it straight for the Holleys, as good as possible, and he was more into Buddy's style than those biz cats in New York. Plus the fact that he had all the tapes. So Norman got back in charge. But I think that's the last thing Buddy would have wanted."

Petty's studio band was the Fireballs, a Texas-New Mexico group most famous for their hit recordings of "Sugar Shack" and "Bottle of Wine". They were undoubtedly more capable of providing suitable backgrounds for Holly's recordings than were the musicians associated with the Decca com-

plex in New York. Still, there were instances where there was really no reason to use any overdubbing at all.

The first album released under the new contract was *Reminiscing*, issued in early 1963 (a single of the title song had been released the previous summer). Besides the title song, the album included two songs recorded by Holly on his own tape recorder in the months before his death: "Slippin' and Slidin'" and "Wait 'Til the Sun Shines, Nellie", and eight others recorded in 1956 before the formation of the Crickets: "Baby, Won't You Come Out Tonight", "Because I Love You", "I'm Gonna Set My Foot Down", "Rock-A-Bye Rock" and "I'm Changin' All Those Changes", all written by Holly; "It's Not My Fault", written by Ben Hall and fellow country musician Weldon Myrick; and the rock 'n' roll classics "Bo Diddley" and "Brown-Eyed Handsome Man".

The Fireballs' best contribution on the album was to Holly's rendition of "Slippin' and Slidin'", a recording that leaves few Holly fans indifferent. The song had been recorded originally by Little Richard in his usual wild and swinging fashion. By contrast, Holly's version is slow, quiet and rather eerie. Many fans wondered why Holly would have chosen to make a tape of this song at a pace so much slower than the original version. In 1984, MCA producer Steve Hoffman, who had become responsible for the Holly catalogue, solved the mystery. Hoffman noticed that this song had been recorded on Holly's tape recorder at $7\frac{1}{2}$ inches per second (IPS) while all other songs were recorded at the higher speed of 15 IPS, a speed which offers better recording quality. Hoffman also discovered some dialogue on the tape, in which Holly can be heard to say, "Play it back fast and see how funny we sound." When played back at 15 IPS, the tape sounds like the novelty records of Alvin and the Chipmunks (who had a hit in December 1958 with "The Chipmunk Song"). Apparently, Holly taped his "slow" version of "Slippin' and Slidin'" as a musical joke to entertain himself, Maria and his friends. (Personally, I always liked the slow version; and now I know that it was meant as a joke, I can only say that I *still* like it.)

Overdubbing was less restrained on "Wait 'Til The Sun Shines, Nellie", an old favourite of Mrs. Holley's which Buddy had promised to record for her. Holly's practice tape, just seventy seconds long, was subjected to splicing and rearranging; the added instruments and vocals which hide these alterations obscure Holly's own performance. The whole feel of the recording is too heavy for the low-keyed and reflective mood of Holly's rendition.

"Bo Diddley" and "Brown-Eyed Handsome Man" were two demos which Holly had cut in Clovis sometime during 1956 at the suggestion of his brother Larry. Though the tunes had been recorded with a full band, the Fireballs were still used when the cuts were prepared for the *Reminiscing* album. Most of the lead guitar playing on the released version of "Bo Diddley" was, in fact, not on the original demo. All Buddy had played on his recording was a lower-pitched tremolo effect similar to Diddley's own playing on the hit version of the song; but on the overdubbed release, a whole new guitar part was added and the other instruments on Holly's original recording were also "reinforced". The changes made on Holly's recording of Chuck Berry's "Brown-Eyed Handsome Man" were less significant; the lead guitar work is entirely Holly's.

The six remaining recordings on the *Reminiscing* album illustrate the variety of Holly's style at the time of his first Decca contract. The version of "I'm Changin' All Those Changes" included here is simply a shorter, alternative version of the song previously released on the Decca album of Holly's Nashville recordings. The other five, it is believed, were recorded as demo tapes for Jim Denny's Cedarwood Publishing; they were not published then, and were filed and forgotten until a search was made for unissued Holly material in the early 1960's. "It's Not My Fault" is a tune closer to country music than "Blue Days, Black Nights", Ben Hall's other effort for Holly, but the lilting beat and accented vocal effects produced by Holly give a different flavour to the country melody. "Because I Love You", a slow, emotional ballad, is one of the first songs that Holly wrote himself and he gives it a beautiful and moving performance.

By sharp contrast, the three remaining tunes on the album are driving rock 'n' roll dance numbers. "Rock-A-Bye Rock", "I'm Gonna Set My Foot Down" and "Baby, Won't You Come Out Tonight" demonstrate vividly Decca's failure to appreciate the talent it had on hand. These recordings *are* Buddy Holly in 1956, not as he sounded in a recording studio under the direction of older country musicians, but as he sounded with Allison, Curtis and Don Guess on the bandstand at a teenage rock 'n' roll dance. The numbers are as furious and exciting as any contemporaneous rockabilly, and lack only the polish and finesse of later recordings such as "Rave On" and "Oh Boy!"

Although the five tracks just discussed were not cut as masters, the sound quality is good, and they are still complete performances with a full band; so it is hard to understand why extra background was added to these recordings. The additions only annoy the fan who is intent on listening closely to the original performances by Holly and his group. Allison is still irked by this procedure: "The Fireballs were good boys and I really like them, and the way they played is fine for the Fireballs—but not for Buddy Holly records. I really hated that things got all mixed up—because if somebody was gonna play some drums on those things, I would have liked to play on them. I mean, I was back in Texas and back in Clovis, and Norman could have called me and said, 'Hey, you want to overdub some stuff?' And I would have loved it. But he had all these hang-ups. The Fireballs were his boys at the time. He had them play on some stuff that didn't even need it, like 'Brown-Eyed Handsome Man' and 'Bo Diddley'; and when he did it, it was like a slam at Joe B. and me, if nothing else—like 'O.K., we'll put the Fireballs in and cover them up.' Even now, it kind of bugs me to pull all those records out and listen to them and hear all that bad overdubbing."

The next album of previously unissued material was *Showcase*, released in early 1964. On this album, more of the original recordings were left intact. Two of the cuts, "Rock Around With Ollie Vee" and "Girl On My Mind", were from the recordings Holly had made with Decca in 1956; the others (including "Come Back Baby", "Love's Made A Fool Of You" and "You're The One") appeared publicly for the first time on this album.

"I Guess I Was Just A Fool" was recorded as a demo for Decca in 1956. The song, written by Holly, is closely modelled on Elvis Presley's Sun recording of "I Forgot To Remember To Forget", which was a special favourite of Holly's. (Buddy in fact once made a demo of the Presley tune for KDAV, but the demo was destroyed when it seemed that playing it might violate Holly's Decca contract.) Holly's vocal owes something to both Presley and Hank Williams. The lead guitar on the recording was probably played by Sonny Curtis. Holly's one-minute recording of "Gone" apparently dates from about the same time—Allison guesses that it was made sometime in late 1956. This would have been, then, a couple of years before Ferlin Husky recorded the hit version of the song; the tune had in fact been written by Smokey Rogers in 1952, and a lesser known version recorded by Husky (as Terry Preston) the same year.

Four cuts on the album were versions of the early rock 'n' roll hits "Shake, Rattle and Roll", "Blue Suede Shoes", "Rip It Up" and "Honky Tonk". All of the tunes appear to have been Holly-Allison duets, recorded in late 1956 when the two were playing without a bass player or second guitarist; the original performances are, once again, obscured by overdubbing. The tapes were made on a primitive tape recorder, but regardless of the technical limitations, the recordings offer good performances. Particularly interesting is Holly's guitar playing, both on the three vocal cuts where he must accompany himself and also on the instrumental "Honky Tonk". The original recording of that tune by Bill Doggett and his combo was in two parts, issued on both sides of a 45 r.p.m. single record; Holly used figures from both parts of the Doggett original and adapted the tenor sax and guitar solos on that recording to his own style of guitar playing. On the other three cuts, Holly is clearly aware of preceding recordings of the tunes, but his guitar solos follow his own ideas on how the songs should sound.

One revealing feature of Holly's version of "Shake, Rattle and Roll" is the set of lyrics he uses. Holly would have been aware of three recordings of the song: the original version by Joe Turner; the cover of that by Bill Haley; and a version by Elvis which was first released in 1956 on an RCA single. In making his cover version, Haley changed or omitted some of Turner's original lyrics, believing them to be too suggestive for airing on pop stations, however normal they might be as rhythm & blues lyrics went. As was mentioned earlier, the national pattern did not hold in Lubbock— white teenagers there listened to the original Turner recording as much as they did to Haley's cover version. Presley and Holly each use just one of Haley's verses, choosing to follow the tougher Turner wording most of the way. Their choices reflect the tastes of their peers and audiences and reveal the familiarity with Turner's recording in that part of the country.

The remaining cut on the *Showcase* album was drawn from the solo tapes Buddy had made on his own tape recorder shortly before his death. "Ummm, Oh Yeah"—or "Dearest", as it was correctly called on a later album—had been recorded by Mickey and Sylvia, the duo whose "Love Is Strange" had been such a favourite of Holly's. Buddy apparently intended to record both Mickey and Sylvia tunes himself, giving them a quiet, folkish flavour. The overdubbing obscures Holly's rhythm guitar playing, but the soft, restrained mood of Holly's vocal comes through clearly enough.

The following album, released in early 1965, offered a valuable glimpse of the origins of Holly's music and certainly surprised many of his fans unfamiliar with the roots of his career. *Holly In The Hills* (a catchy and suggestive title, to be sure, though obviously coined without much regard to the topography of the Lubbock area!) reached farther back into the past than previous albums had done, back to recordings made by Holly and Bob Montgomery in country & western and rockabilly styles. Eight of these early sides were included. The album was filled out with "Lonesome Tears" and "Fool's Paradise", the only two Crickets recordings which had not previously appeared on albums; "Wishing", one of the songs Buddy had hoped to have the Everly Brothers record; and a new version of "What To Do", substituting a more adequate backing by the Fireballs for the unsatisfactory New York arrangement. In Britain, three additional Buddy and Bob tracks ("Queen of the Ballroom", "Baby It's Love" and "Memories") were used in place of "What To Do" and the Crickets recordings—apparently these were discovered by Hipockets Duncan after the American album had been mastered.

Exact information is lacking as to where and when the early demos were made and who played on them. Apparently, most of them were made at the Nesman Studios in Wichita Falls, while others were recorded at the Jim Beck Studio in Dallas and at KDAV's studios. The demos seem to date from 1954 to 1955, although it is possible that some were made even earlier than that. Most of the vocals on the country tunes are duets, with Montgomery handling solo choruses and Holly providing instrumental breaks—along with Sonny Curtis, who plays the fiddle on some of these recordings. Don Guess is believed to have played steel guitar on those records where it is present; Guess and Larry Welborn shared the bass playing. Holly's guitar playing is most notable on "Gotta Get You Near Me Blues", an example of his picking ability which shows why Lubbock area musicians and disc jockeys remember Buddy today as much for his fine country guitar playing as for his singing style. The two rock 'n' roll-oriented cuts, "I Wanna Play House With You" (called "Baby, Let's Play House" when Presley recorded it for Sun) and "Down The Line", demonstrate how quickly and surely Holly and his friends had moved into rockabilly in the wake of Presley's original recordings. Whatever their inexperience and amateur status, the entire group performs with a drive and energy that could make later rock 'n' roll groups envious.

Regrettably, the *Holly In The Hills* cuts are not totally accurate presentations of what Holly and his fellow musicians were playing in those years since, as on the earlier albums, overdubbing distorts the original sound. Most significant is the addition of drums which were not present originally on the six country-style recordings—made at a time when drums were rarely used in small country groups. Jerry Allison probably did play on "I Wanna Play House With You" and "Down The Line", even though most of the drumming heard on the finished release was provided by the Fireballs—as was some of the guitar playing.

After several years' delay (caused in part by the new popularity of older Holly records in the mid-1960's), an additional collection of Holly's home-type recordings was released in 1969 under the title *Giant*. The advent of multi-track recording equipment enabled Norman Petty to experiment more freely with the recordings; several include unusual orchestral effects, and those with backings by studio musicians have a brighter sound in which the dubbing is a bit less obvious. As with the earlier posthumous releases, though, opinions differ as to the propriety of the backings.

On "Love Is Strange", "You're The One" and "Dearest", Petty added a string effect, actually played on an Ondeoline, a keyboard instrument, to give the songs a lush, full sound more in line with "the sound of the times". Of the three, "Love Is Strange" has perhaps the most successful arrangement; at least, it is not out of line with Holly's rendition. Still, one wonders if Holly ever would have chosen to record the piece that way. Holly gives the 1957 "chalypso"-flavoured hit a surprisingly quiet, reflective treatment—the mood presented is quite different from that found in Mickey and Sylvia's original version. As for "You're The One" and "Dearest"—the original, simpler versions released on the *Showcase* album five years before were, to many fans, preferable to the new dubbed versions.

Three songs on *Giant* were early rock 'n' roll hits recorded in late 1956 under the same circumstances as the similar cuts on the *Showcase* album. They are Fats Domino's "Blue Monday", Clarence "Frogman" Henry's "Ain't Got No Home" and "Good Rockin' Tonight", which dates back to Roy Brown's 1948 rhythm & blues recording of it—Holly may have heard that at some time, but he was undoubtedly thinking of Elvis Presley's Sun version when he made his own recording. As on the *Showcase* tunes, Holly and Allison were probably the sole performers on the original tapes.

Holly recorded "Smokey Joe's Cafe" and "Slippin' and Slidin'" in late 1958 or early 1959 on the tape recorder in his apartment, accompanying himself on electric guitar (the strange guitar break after each verse on "Smokey Joe's Cafe" is Holly's own). The dubbed backing on these matches the style of Holly more closely than had the backings on earlier albums. The version of "Slippin' and Slidin'" on this album is up-tempo, unlike the "slow" version on the *Reminiscing* album.

"Have You Ever Been Lonely" was recorded at Buddy's home one day in 1956 when he and his band were practising there. As the album liner notes explain, Holly recorded it for his mother, who liked the song. Left on the tape is Holly's call, "Mother!" at the song's conclusion. It is really quite fitting that the recording was left as it is, for the tone of his voice, and the fact that he made such recordings, is testimony to the close family ties Holly had and to the encouragement he received from them in pursuing his ambitions.

The last cut on the album was an instrumental, "Holly Hop", a brief introduction to Holly's individual guitar style and some of the figures he commonly used. One Lubbock resident remembers that Holly used this instrumental as an intro to the KDAV Sunday Party show; it does sound like the sort of instrumental rock 'n' roll dance bands would use to open and close sets, so Holly might likewise have used it for his appearances at teenage dances in Lubbock. The acclaim for Holly's singing should not cause anyone to overlook his instrumental talent, though it is heard less often and is more difficult to appreciate immediately or fully.

In coming down as harshly as I have on the use of overdubbing on Holly's posthumous albums, I have not meant to imply that the job could have been done any better. The sound on the tapes and demos was of poor quality to begin with, so the clearer, "live" sound of the overdubbing was likely to obscure the original performance, no matter what. The question which remains is, how much dubbing was really necessary? What was the intention in providing such backings—and what *should* have been the intention?

A clue to the attitude is to be found in one remark in the liner notes written by Norman Petty for *Giant*. In speaking of guitarist George Tomsco's added accompaniment to Holly's performance on "Holly Hop", Petty writes: "What a combination Buddy and George, together, would have been for the music fans!" Maybe so—but should these releases have been used to make that point? Originally, the creators of the posthumous albums wanted to ensure that the record buyer did not feel cheated by being presented with home-type recordings of limited instrumentation and/or fidelity. As a solution, the records were overdubbed, with the hope of making them sound like studio recordings—thus bringing them up to contemporary standards, one might say. (Not that there was any attempt at deception—except for *The Buddy Holly Story, Volume 2*, each album's liner notes made clear the limitations of the recordings and the use of dubbing.) But too often, the original Holly recordings wound up being used as a base for something else—"Play Along With Buddy Holly" became the appearance, if not the intent, of such releases.

In attempting to create "contemporary" albums, the producers of the posthumous releases both failed to reach their own objective and lost sight of the original purpose of the series. Primarily, these albums served fans already acquainted with the recordings released during Holly's lifetime. The fans wanted the recordings never intended for release made available, regardless of the technical limitations—for they knew that Holly was an artist even when recording under casual conditions with limited intentions. Such buyers never expected the new releases to have the full sound of "That'll Be The Day" or "It Doesn't Matter Anymore"; it was enough that Buddy's performances not be discarded simply because they had not been recorded in a modern studio. Overdubbing just obscured Buddy's vocal or (especially) instrumental performance without adding much to the total recording, and the final product always *sounded* dubbed.

The object of the releases should have been to present the recordings in their original form, doing all possible to eliminate technical flaws (such as scratches on demos) without harming the sound. Where the original pieces were unfinished, they should have been left that way. As a parallel, consider the various modern LP releases of early jazz and blues recordings dating from the 1920's. Though the fidelity on these is poor by modern standards, no one suggests that new trumpet parts should be added to Louis Armstrong's recordings, or that a vocal chorus should be assigned to sing along with Bessie Smith. The buyers of these albums know what they are getting but they want the original material anyway. It is my guess that Holly's fans would have reacted in a similar fashion. It was not until twenty years after Holly's death that his record company began to approach his recordings with these considerations in mind. Recent album releases (see the next chapter) have shown greater concern for the integrity of Holly's work, and have paid more attention to the tastes of the record buyers.

After the initial nationally carried newspaper reports on the fatal plane crash, the deaths of Holly, Richardson and Valens went largely unnoticed in the adult media. It was, appropriately, through popular music that they were eulogized, and then honoured by imitation.

Tommy Dee was a disc jockey on KFXM in San Bernardino, California. He was on the air on February 3 when the story of the plane crash came in over the wire services. "I read it on the air," he remembers, "and so many people called up—kids calling, girls crying, everyone upset. It made such an impression on me that when I got off the air, I wrote a song about it, as I was driving home in my car."

The song was "Three Stars", a slow narrative ballad in which the narrator described in turn the "three new stars" in the heavens and expressed the most striking traits of each singer. The physical description of Holly—hair out of place, a shy grin on his face—was followed by an acknowledgment that Holly had been a complicated and distant figure. "Not many people actually knew you, or understood how you felt," said the song, though they all could respond to the warmth of Holly's songs. Dee recalls, "A lot of people thought I had a feel for Buddy Holly in the record, which was strange, because I had never met him. I felt, just from looking at his picture, that he was a shy and bashful type of guy. It seems that I hit the nail on the head."

The next day, Dee brought a tape of the song to a music publisher (American Music), and the following Monday he recorded the song for Crest, backed on the vocals by Carol Kay and the Teenairs. Dee's record eventually reached number eleven on the *Billboard* Hot 100, despite competition from a cover version on King by Ruby Wright.

"Three Stars" has been criticized for being maudlin or corny. In response to the criticism, it should be pointed out that in its topicality, eulogistic tone, and acceptance of the afterlife, the song followed older traditions of folk, gospel and country music; the religious view expressed was one shared, after all, by Holly and his family.

The honest emotions in the song were best expressed in the recording of it by Holly's friend and fellow rock 'n' roll star Eddie Cochran. According to Tommy Dee, the idea of having Cochran record the song came up the day Dee brought it to American Music. Cochran came to the office to hear the song and recorded it himself that night. Overcome by his own sense of loss, Cochran's choked voice broke as he sang and spoke the lyrics about Holly. (Cochran had originally been scheduled to go on the Winter Dance Party tour himself.) Cochran's recording of "Three Stars" was not released until several years later. He had wanted to donate the royalties on it to the families of the dead singers, but problems arose in working out the details with his record company and the proposed single was never issued. Just fourteen months after Holly's death, Cochran was killed in an automobile accident in England.

"Three Stars" was by no means the only tribute song: over the years there have been about a dozen tunes written about Holly (or about the three singers collectively), and another dozen more which mention Holly in the longer roster of now-dead rock 'n' roll stars. Waylon Jennings recorded two: "The Stage" and "Old Friend". The best-known tribute song from England was "Tribute to Buddy Holly" by Mike Berry. Several of the other tribute records were in the country-music tradition of ballads written to commemorate tragic events; examples of these include "Gold Records in the Snow" by Bennie Barnes and "The Great Tragedy" by Hershel Almond.

Imitation of Holly's vocal style and melodic patterns began during his own lifetime—Robin Luke's "Susie Darling" (1958) is a notable example. In the years after Holly's death, several new figures built careers around their ability to copy his performances. (The popular image of the Holly hiccup may owe more to its use by his imitators than to his own use of the device, which wasn't nearly so frequent.) Bobby Vee's voice and style resembled Holly's so closely that many people are still under the delusion that "Rubber Ball" was recorded by Holly, not by Vee. Vee did have a sincere respect for Holly's

● The Crickets in 1959—Joe B. Mauldin, Tommy Allsop, Jerry Allison and Earl Sinks. This combination of Crickets never toured or recorded as a unit

talent and never disguised the origin of his style; he recorded one album with the revived Crickets and toured with them for a time, and also made an album of Holly's songs titled *I Remember Buddy Holly*. The overall sound of Holly's records also became a subject for imitation. The best-remembered attempt to duplicate the instrumental feel of Holly's recordings was Tommy Roe's "Sheila", which copied the rolling drumbeat and background guitar arrangement of "Peggy Sue".

The Crickets—or at least one set of them—attempted to carry on after Holly's death and enjoyed some success, especially in Britain. However, personal plans and military obligations prevented the group from establishing a stable line-up—and anyway, without the drive Holly had lent the group, the Crickets were never quite the same. They were always willing to play rock 'n' roll as long as anyone wanted to hear them—but they knew themselves why the band had been a success in the first place. Jerry Allison says with a smile, "We've pretty well proved in the years since 1958 that the Crickets without Buddy Holly aren't too hot an item." Only Allison remained a constant member of the group; others at times included Joe Mauldin, Sonny Curtis and several other West Texas natives—Glen Hardin, Earl Sinks and Jerry Naylor—who had never actually played with Holly. (One vocalist, David Box, was with the group just a short time before he was killed in a plane crash in Texas.) Allison also worked independently as a road and session musician for other artists; he was the drummer on Vee's "Rubber Ball", and provided the distinctive drumming on the Everly Brothers' "Till I Kissed You". Neither Tommy Allsup nor Waylon Jennings ever belonged to the re-created Crickets. Allsup went to the West Coast and worked on country and pop recordings for Liberty Records before becoming a Nashville session musician. Jennings, stunned by Holly's death, returned to radio broadcasting in Texas and Arizona before resuming a musical career that eventually placed him among the top stars in the country field.

In Britain, Holly's popularity actually increased in the decade after his death. Recordings which had not been released prior to Holly's death or had been available only on albums were issued as singles in a steady stream through the early 1960's and continued to rise high in the charts. "It Doesn't Matter Anymore" was number one for three weeks in 1959, "Midnight Shift" was a hit later the same year, "True Love Ways" was a success in 1960, and in 1963 Holly's recording of "Bo Diddley" reached the top five of the singles chart, while *The Buddy Holly Story* was still among the top twenty LPs. Even as late as 1967, Holly came in seventeenth in a music weekly's popularity poll—rather remarkable when one considers how many of the paper's readers were too young to have heard Holly's music before his death.

The early recordings of Holly and the Crickets made a profound impact upon young rock 'n' roll musicians in Britain. Their notions of what a rock 'n' roll band should be were derived from the example set by the Crickets: that of a self-contained band dominated by guitar and drums, one which wrote and sang much of its own material and in which the musicians shared the spotlight. (Obviously, Holly was the leader, but it is revealing how much attention Allison and Mauldin got as well from the British fans and press during the 1958 tour.)

Today, this notion seems obvious and basic but it was not always so; Holly and the Crickets deserve much of the credit for introducing the concept and demonstrating that it could be successful. Don Everly sees this as Holly's legacy:

"His was the first musically enclosed group in which the band played and sang and did the whole thing. No one had ever really done that. I think that young kids sitting out there could say, 'Well, you play the drums, I'll be the singer, and you be the guitar player and you be the bass player, and we'll be like Buddy Holly and the Crickets.'"

The example of Holly and the Crickets served as a direct inspiration to John Lennon and Paul McCartney. McCartney has said, "At least the first forty songs we wrote were Buddy Holly-influenced." And Lennon drew a personal lesson from Holly: in a letter to a Holly fan, Lennon wrote, "He made it O.K. to wear glasses. I was Buddy Holly." The first recording Lennon and McCartney ever made, in their pre-Beatles days as the Quarrymen, was a version of "That'll Be The Day". The name of the Beatles was coined by John Lennon in 1959—the example of the Crickets had brought other insect names to mind.

Actually, the musical style of the Beatles derived at least as much from the hard rock 'n' roll sound of Larry Williams, Chuck Berry and Little Richard, the female choral groups such as the Shirelles and the Crystals, and the duet style of the Everly Brothers. But the Beatles were influenced by the unique vocal texture of the best Crickets recordings and, most of all, by the melodic and chord patterns of Holly's songs. The latter is most noticeable in songs the Beatles wrote for other artists: "Nobody I Know" and "World Without Love", Peter and Gordon's earliest hits, and "Bad To Me" and "From A Window", recorded by Billy J. Kramer and the Dakotas. Among the Beatles' own songs, "Every Little Thing" (on the *Beatles VI* album) was very reminiscent of Holly's material, as was, strangely enough, one of their last recordings: "Here Comes The Sun"—which in rhythm and melody was not far removed from "What To Do", "That's What They Say", "Words of Love" or similar Holly songs.

For other British groups, the clear tenor vocals and quick driving beat of Holly's recordings were important influences. Peter and Gordon owed their early style to the duet example of the Everly Brothers and the less nasal, lower-pitched sound of Holly's singing—a combination which Holly had himself produced five years before by double-tracking his own voice on "Wishing". The Searchers, one of the finest early English groups, recorded Holly's "Listen To Me" and "Learning The Game" (which they sang as "Led In The Game") on an early "live" album, and showed his influence on such songs as "Don't Throw Your Love Away" and "Every Time That You Walk In The Room". Freddie and the Dreamers, a curious, short-lived phenomenon, featured a lead singer who not only sounded like Holly and sang some of his songs, but who even *looked* like him. The list could be carried much further. But this is not to claim that Buddy Holly was the father of all British rock 'n' roll—this would be too much of a generalization. It could be said, though, that British fans and performers had the good fortune, or good taste, to be influenced by the best of the early American rock 'n' roll performers, with Holly, Chuck Berry, Little Richard, Eddie Cochran and Elvis Presley as the most influential.

The rock 'n' roll renaissance brought to the United States by the British groups in 1964 sparked new interest in the recordings of rock 'n' roll pioneers—especially when the new groups not only imitated the sound but also recorded songs made famous by the preceding generation of performers. Many younger fans learned for the first time who Chuck Berry was after hearing the Beatles sing "Roll Over Beethoven" and "Rock and Roll Music"; Buddy Holly also benefited from this sort of recognition. In 1964, "Not Fade Away" was the Rolling Stones' first American release, while Peter and

Gordon recorded "Tell Me How". In 1965, "Words of Love" appeared on the *Beatles VI* album, "It Doesn't Matter Anymore" was recorded by Freddie and the Dreamers, "Heartbeat" was sung by Herman's Hermits and, most notably, "True Love Ways" became a top ten hit for Peter and Gordon.

The Beatles' recording of "Words of Love" was particularly important in making Holly's name familiar again. Their version was a fairly close imitation of Holly's original recording and was released at a time when every song on a new Beatles album attracted close and constant attention and a great deal of airplay. The Beatles' frequent mention of Holly as one of their early favourites likewise brought new attention to Holly's recordings. When "True Love Ways" became a hit later in the year, some disc jockeys presented special features on Holly's recordings, or periodically juxtaposed the original and new versions of the revived Holly songs.

In the United States, the influence of Holly's work in the mid- and late 1960's was reflected most genuinely in occasional outbreaks of individual performers and groups whose debt to Holly sometimes went unrecognized. The career of one such group, the Bobby Fuller Four, involved close personal and stylistic ties to early rock 'n' roll. Bobby Fuller was from El Paso and grew up listening to and admiring the recordings of Buddy Holly. Fuller corresponded with Holly's parents and, after making some local recordings on minor labels, got a contract in Los Angeles with Bob Keene, who had been Ritchie Valens's manager.

In early 1966, the Bobby Fuller Four had one of the best-selling records of the year with "I Fought The Law"—a song which had been written by Sonny Curtis and recorded by the Crickets not long after Holly's death. The song had the "Buddy Holly sound"—the rhythm, the pounding drumbeat, the tenor vocal, the chordal guitar solo, the shifting chords and triadic effects of the melody. Still, it was not an "imitation" of Holly's style—the song came from a major songwriter who composed what came naturally to him, and was played by artists in the way that was natural for them. Though the term "Tex-Mex sound" was really a promotional creation, there was still a Texas brand of rock 'n' roll, though not even the performers themselves could explain just what it was or where it came from.

Fuller's first album was one of the most danceable rock 'n' roll albums in some time. Most of the album cuts were written by Fuller, and were obviously modelled on Holly and Cochran tunes. And yet, something was lacking—the songs had the drive and feel of Holly's recordings, but lacked the lyrical content and emotional depth of those songs. Maybe Fuller would have developed as a songwriter later; but in the summer of 1966, he was found dead of asphyxiation in his car. (His death was officially ruled a suicide, despite strong evidence that he was murdered.)

The limited artistic success of the Bobby Fuller Four brings up a quite troubling and controversial element in the inheritance left by Buddy Holly to later popular performers. A line of influence can be traced from the music of Buddy Holly through that of Bobby Fuller to the much shallower sounds of Gary Lewis and the Playboys, and on to the simplistic "Bubblegum" sound of the late 1960's, typified by the Archies' "Sugar, Sugar". Some critics have therefore suggested that Holly was partially responsible for the deterioration of rock music in the decade after his death. (For an extreme and rather grotesque statement of this argument, see Nik Cohn's *Rock From the Beginning*.)

This view of Holly ignores the balanced nature of Holly's sound, and of early rock 'n' roll in general, compared to the products of the late 1960's and 1970's. Early rock 'n' roll (on through the early years of the British invasion) was able to balance the use of loud, amplified sound with the use of forms and lyric themes that had their roots deep in preceding musical styles: a heavy beat and a pretty melody were not incompatible. In the late 1960's, the unity broke down, and the disparate elements split apart. Bubblegum music was one offshoot; another was the overpowering sound of the "heavy metal" groups. While a line can be traced from Holly to the bubblegum sound, it is equally valid to see Holly's stress on a full guitar sound and heavy drumming as the basis for heavy-metal rock. (The same might be said of Eddie Cochran.) A creative artist in any field, whether it be music, literature or the fine arts, ought not to be blamed for the mediocrity or banality of those who later imitate just one element of his work, while losing the sense of balance that held it together.

Here and there in the late 1960's, a few American performers began to acknowledge the true value of Holly's music (and that of other early rock 'n' roll performers). Tom Rush's album *Take A Little Walk With Me* included his quite individualistic interpretations of several rock 'n' roll songs, including Holly's "Love's Made A Fool Of You"—which Rush also made a standard in his concert performances. Rush's quiet and reflective rendition of the song fully captured the spirit of the lyrics, and his instrumental accompaniment was at one and the same time quite distinct from that of the original Holly version, and yet totally appropriate to the song. Hundreds of artists have recorded Holly's songs at one time or another, but few have been as successful as Rush in producing a recording which, while the artist's own creation, fully captures the spirit of Buddy Holly's music.

In the years that followed, several other rock and folk performers acknowledged their debt to Holly or showed his influence in their songs. Bob Dylan grew up on rock 'n' roll and has said that Holly was an influence upon his style. In 1974, a *Newsweek* feature article on Dylan's national concert tour contained the following:

> *Musically, he says, he doesn't consider his taste a part of the nostalgia so fashionable today in pop. "I just carry that other time around with me," he says. "The music of the late fifties and early sixties when music was at that root level—that for me is meaningful music. The singers and musicians I grew up with transcend nostalgia—Buddy Holly and Johnny Ace are just as valid to me today as then."*

Bob Dylan wasn't the only singer to antagonize his folk-music following by revealing his rock 'n' roll roots. In 1970, Phil Ochs stepped out on the stage of Carnegie Hall wearing an Elvis-style gold-lamé suit and carrying an electric guitar, and played medleys of songs by Presley and Holly to a mixture of boos and cheers. (A live album of the concert was later released under the title *Gunfight At Carnegie Hall*.) In introducing his favourite Holly tunes, Ochs tried to offer an explanation to those who had come to hear him play the protest songs for which he was best known:

> *I'd like to sing some songs that are just as much Phil Ochs as anything else. These songs were first recorded by somebody I hold very dear to my heart, from the 1950's—[boos and groans]—Could this be a generation gap?... He formed that part of my musical mind which wrote anything like "I Ain't Marching Anymore", "Changes"—that thought process came from certain people, and this is one of them: Buddy Holly. [applause and jeers] These are a collection of his songs I memorized as a kid....*

Another performer with roots in Holly's music was John Denver (a graduate of Texas Tech, for whatever significance that might have). Denver recorded "Everyday" and released it on a single in 1972; some of his most successful compositions, like "Leaving on a Jet Plane" and "Country Roads", bear the mark of Holly's influence. The Nitty Gritty Dirt Band paid their respects to Holly with a recording of "Rave On". When they appeared in Lubbock in late 1971, they were amazed to find that most of their young audience didn't know who Buddy Holly was, and so they tried to enlighten the crowd by playing a medley of Holly's songs.

Critics, too, began to praise Holly and the brand of rock 'n' roll he had fashioned. Holly was the subject of articles in *Rolling Stone*; and in *Rock Encyclopedia*, Lillian Roxon had this to say about Holly:

> *He was one of the giants of early rock, a figure so important in the history of popular music that it is impossible to hear a song on the charts today that does not owe something to the tall, slim bespectacled boy from Lubbock, Texas. . . . More than any other singer of that era, he brings back a time when music was fun. . . . Adults put him down with the rest of the Presley era as shock rock. Kids just remembered it was impossible not to dance, not to groove, while he sang. Most of the giants of ten years later, of the booming rock scene of the late sixties, were teenagers when Holly was king and their music reflects it. Looking back from the twin peaks of psychedelia and electronic gadgetry, he comes through fresher than ever.*

No tribute to the legacy of Buddy Holly had more impact than Don McLean's "American Pie", which won gold records and spent weeks in the number one positions on the *Billboard* pop singles and LP charts in late 1971 and early 1972. Some of the symbolic lyrics could be given many (or no) explanations and, although the album was openly dedicated to Holly, the song never mentioned him by name. However, anyone familiar with the story of Buddy Holly had little trouble understanding the first verse:

> *A long, long time ago,*
> *I can still remember, how that music used to make me smile.*
> *And I knew if I had the chance,*
> *That I could make those people dance,*
> *And maybe they'd be happy for a while.*
> *But February made me shiver,*
> *With every paper I'd deliver,*
> *Bad news on the doorstep—*
> *I couldn't take one more step.*
> *And I can't remember if I cried,*
> *When I read about his widowed bride,*
> *But something touched me deep inside,*
> *The day the music died.*

In a matter of weeks, Holly received more publicity and recognition than he had ever received in his own lifetime. And by 1973, McLean's view of rock history had been expressed so widely and become so standard that it rated inclusion in the much-acclaimed movie, *American Graffiti*. "I can't stand that surfing shit," says hot-rodder John Milner as he turns the radio off in disgust—"rock 'n' roll's been going downhill ever since Buddy Holly died."

The resurgence of interest created by McLean's song led after some delay to Decca's release of a new collection of Holly's recordings. (By 1972, the separate Coral label had been dropped and its roster absorbed by Decca.)

The new double album showed all the flaws in thinking that had affected the presentation of the posthumous releases and the selection of cuts on two previous "greatest hits" albums. What is most regrettable is that an opportunity to do better was lost. Decca originally had an independent producer, John Boylan, working on the project; plans were for a low-priced three-album boxed set containing a booklet with photographs, biographical information and a discography. All songs were to be presented in their original, undubbed forms, and the choice of songs reflected the consensus of most fans as to the best of Holly's recordings.

Then, Decca got cold feet. The plans were scrapped, and a two-album set which had been released in Germany a year before was issued instead under the title *Buddy Holly: A Rock 'n' Roll Collection*. There were no liner notes of any sort—this at a time when other companies, notably United Artists and Atlantic, were re-releasing recordings by their own rock 'n' roll artists in attractive packages with informative commentaries. The choice of selections was irrational—among the cuts not included in the new album were "Everyday", "Early In The Morning", "Think It Over", "True Love Ways", "I'm Gonna Love You Too" and "It's So Easy". The original tapes of the posthumous releases were once more passed over in favour of the dubbed versions made with the Jack Hansen combo and the Fireballs. And, as the most astonishing boner of all, the recording of "Love's Made A Fool Of You" included on the new set was not Buddy Holly's own recording of it, but instead the recording cut by the Crickets shortly after Holly's departure from the group. A lot of strange things had been done to Holly's recordings over the previous thirteen years, but never before had a Buddy Holly album included a cut that Holly himself did not play on.

The new seed of interest in Holly which was planted in the early 1970's took several years to come to fruition. When the rock 'n' roll nostalgia craze had come and gone, musicians, fans and critics began to look more closely at those few artists whose impact had been truly lasting. It was Buddy Holly as much as anyone who benefited from that attention. The late 1970's were to demonstrate the breadth of the new interest in and respect for Holly.

CHAPTER TEN

"BUDDY HOLLY LIVES"

THE HOLLY RENAISSANCE

As the second decade after Holly's death came to a close, interest in his music surged upwards, and a whole new musical generation was introduced to him. Many people played their role in this "Holly Renaissance": musicians, filmmakers and Holly's own fans helped to bring Buddy Holly back into the spotlight.

The level of general public interest in Holly has varied through the 1970's and 1980's, but his strong influence on knowledgeable musicians has been continuous. The range of Holly's material has been a key to his continued popularity: he has provided inspiration for performers whose styles cover a broad spectrum. Such disparate recording artists as the late Phil Ochs, John Denver, Waylon Jennings, Linda Ronstadt, Elvis Costello, Marshall Crenshaw and Bruce Springsteen have recorded Holly's songs, performed those songs in their own concerts, or pointed to Holly as an influence. In a period when it has been hard to discern any decisive trends in pop music, Buddy Holly's sound has remained a common reference point for musicians of all kinds.

Of all the performers who have recorded Holly's songs in the two decades since his death, Linda Ronstadt has scored the biggest commercial successes with her recordings of "That'll Be The Day" (1976) and "It's So Easy" (1977). These were the first Holly compositions to make the top ten on pop charts since Peter and Gordon's version of "True Love Ways" in 1965 (fittingly enough, the man who produced the two Ronstadt records was Peter Asher, late of Peter and Gordon). Ronstadt's versions were imbued with the spirit of Holly's original recordings, but were anything but slavish imitations and were all the better for the difference. Once more, Holly's name was before the public, and the timing could hardly have been better. Ronstadt's hits served to prime interest in the film biography of Holly which, coincidentally, was about to begin production.

Proposals for films on Holly's life first arose in the early 1960's, but it was 1973 before studios began to show serious interest in the idea. In 1973, the American Broadcasting Corporation (ABC) gave Universal Studios the go-ahead to make a television *Movie-of-the-Week* dramatization of Holly's life. A preliminary script was prepared, but the project was shelved in 1974 when the studio was unable to obtain authorizations from all of the people (including Allison, Mauldin, Petty, Maria Elena and the Holleys) who were to be portrayed in the television film. It seemed to be impossible to arrive at a financial agreement (and, perhaps, a script) that satisfied all parties.

It was not long before two other proposals surfaced for films on Holly. Both were intended to be for general theatrical release, in contrast to the ABC-TV project.

One of the proposals was initiated by a small Philadelphia-based firm called Innovisions, whose principals—Steve Rash and Freddy Bauer—had experience in producing TV rock concert productions, but had never made a full-length motion picture. Working with the pair was Ed Cohen who specialized in packaging TV and movie production proposals and seeking independent investors as backers. In late 1974, Rash and Bauer travelled to Florida to meet Maria Elena and present their proposal for a movie biography of Holly. In 1975, Maria Elena and the Holleys signed contracts with Innovisions granting the rights for a Holly movie, in return for a percentage of the profits (an arrangement ABC-TV and Universal Studios had been unwilling to offer on the *Movie-of-the-Week* proposal). Also, Innovisions signed an agreement for the right to base the movie on the original edition of this book.

In the same time period, Jerry Allison was working on a different project.

Allison's idea was for a Holly movie that would be a fictionalized account of the Crickets' first tour in 1957, when they played on shows where they were the only (or one of just a few) white performers. Such a movie would not be a complete biography of Holly but would instead take the approach of showing his character by focusing on just a month in his life. The movie would have a broader purpose, too: to comment on race relations in early rock 'n' roll and the music's role in breaking down racial barriers.

Allison worked on this idea with a screenwriter named Tom Drake, and the pair sold the rights to the film (eventually titled *Not Fade Away*) to Twentieth Century-Fox. The limited scope of the film seemed to simplify the problem of securing permissions: with only Allison, Mauldin and Holly portrayed in the movie, any need to obtain portrayal rights from Petty, the Holleys or Maria Elena appeared to have been eliminated. The Holleys and Maria Elena were in fact contacted about becoming involved in the film, but they did not endorse it. The Holleys were unhappy with the subject matter of the script and its frequent use of vulgar language. Maria Elena also insisted, as she had in the case of the proposed ABC-TV movie, that she and the Holleys were entitled to more than the small portrayal fee that Twentieth Century-Fox was offering.

The filming of *Not Fade Away* began in Mississippi in September, 1975. Steve Davies was cast as Holly, Gary Busey as Jerry Allison and Bruce Kirby as Joe B. Mauldin. Allison himself was cast in a bit role as the owner of a music store, and Bob Montgomery was cast in a major role as the white promoter of the all-black tour. MCA agreed to allow the use of Holly's original recordings in the film.

Three weeks after filming began, when the movie was one-third complete, Twentieth Century-Fox halted the shooting and announced that the film had been cancelled. The reason was "differences in artistic interpretation" between the studio and the director, Jerry Friedman. It was the view of the studio that the film was dwelling too heavily on the fictionalized conflicts between the Crickets and the black acts on the tour and was too serious in tone; although the language had been toned down from early versions of the script to ensure a PG rating, the film still had a roughness that the studio feared would make it commercially unacceptable. Friedman was told to lighten up the story and make it more comic—like the highly successful *American Graffiti*—but Friedman resisted. It appears that an expensive game of "chicken" was played. Friedman, knowing the amount of money already spent on the project, thought he could successfully insist on doing the film his own way, and Twentieth Century-Fox, with its bluff called, felt compelled to show who was in charge. In the end, nobody won; another Holly film was shelved, and Twentieth Century-Fox, it can be estimated, lost a million dollars by shutting down the half-completed film.

Some attempts were made by the film's production team to interest another studio in the project, but Twentieth Century-Fox put a high price on the rights to the story and the completed footage (perhaps to prevent anyone from testing its judgement about the film). Any lingering hopes for the project were probably finished off when Innovisions, having signed its agreements with the Holleys and Maria Elena, placed a full-page ad in *Variety* on October 28, 1975. The ad announced that the exclusive rights to Holly's life story had been granted by his estate to Freddy Bauer and Steve Rash, and warned that "No other person or entity may use the name, represent the person, or interpret the life of Buddy Holly in film, TV, or any other performance media." The threat of legal action was enough to ward off any lingering inter-

est in *Not Fade Away*. (Actually, the claim of exclusive rights over dramatic portrayal of a deceased person's life was of dubious legal validity; Innovisions itself ultimately portrayed deceased performers Sam Cooke, Eddie Cochran, Ritchie Valens, the Big Bopper and King Curtis in its film, without obtaining releases from the survivors of those individuals. In any event, no one tested the Innovisions claim.)

Two years passed before Innovisions could begin to film *The Buddy Holly Story*. The trio of Bauer, Rash and Cohen sought independent financing rather than involvement with a major studio, and it took time to find interested investors. After the financing was obtained, the decision was reached to make the film in the Los Angeles area, beginning in late 1977.

Innovisions never did secure portrayal permissions from any of the Crickets or from Norman Petty. Bauer did speak to Allison in early 1975, before the filming of *Not Fade Away* began, but Allison (and Mauldin) were already committed to that project. According to Allison, he was never contacted again, even after the demise of *Not Fade Away*. "I just kept waiting for Innovisions to contact me," he says, "because I just assumed that they couldn't make a movie portraying me without talking to me first." Mauldin was never contacted at all. In the end, Innovisions decided to portray Allison and Mauldin in the film, but altered their names to "Jesse" and "Ray Bob": no knowledgeable Holly fan who saw the film, however, had any doubts that the two film characters represented Allison and Mauldin.

Niki Sullivan and Norman Petty never made it into the film at all, even under fictional names. Sullivan had not been included either in the scripts to the aborted ABC *Movie-of-the-Week* and *Not Fade Away*. One reason for this exclusion was that Sullivan's time with Holly had been shorter and his role less publicized than that of Allison and Mauldin, who had continued to perform as the Crickets after Holly's death. Scriptwriters seeking to condense Holly's story found it too easy to omit Sullivan for the sake of simplicity. (Similarly, the musicians that Holly played with before the formation of the Crickets, including Bob Montgomery and Sonny Curtis, were not included in the scripts.) Also, unlike Allison and Mauldin, Sullivan was not living in Los Angeles, where the scripts for the two ill-fated projects were written, and that, too, made it easy to overlook him. Therefore, Sullivan's absence as well from the Innovisions script was not surprising, although regrettable.

The situation with Petty was more complicated, and the reasons for his absence are unclear. After the release of the movie in 1978, Innovisions stated that Petty had not been portrayed because he had sought control over the script as a condition for granting the portrayal release. Petty says that he merely asked to *see* the script—and that not until late 1977, just a few months before filming began, when Innovisions last contacted him. In truth, Innovisions does not seem to have cared one way or the other whether Petty was involved in the movie. Disagreements over money or script content might ultimately have blocked Petty's participation, but it does not appear that any negotiation ever took place on these issues.

One of the most crucial choices faced by Innovisions concerned the music for the film. One option was to have the actors lip-sync to Holly's original recordings; a second was to have a new vocalist and band re-record the songs (as was done, for example, in *Lady Sings The Blues*, where Diana Ross sang the Billie Holiday numbers herself). An argument in favour of using the original recordings was that Holly's own music was what people would most want to hear; but on the other side of the coin, it was argued that lip-syncing usually looks as unnatural as it truly is, so that re-recording the songs would make the film more believable. Also, scenes showing songs being composed or practised were only possible if the songs were to be re-recorded.

After considering these arguments, Innovisions decided to re-record the songs, and to have the actual actors in the film make the new recordings. Innovisions gambled that the right actors would make the movie believable, and that the music could be made close enough to the spirit of Holly's original recordings to win acceptance, or at least avoid strong criticism. It was a decision which was to prove to be a correct one.

The actor chosen to play Holly was Gary Busey, who was to have played Jerry Allison in the defunct *Not Fade Away*. Busey, who was born in Texas and grew up in Oklahoma, had several years of experience as a rock drummer under the name Teddy Jack Eddy, and had performed regularly with Leon Russell; he also knew how to play the guitar. Busey's acting credits included the role of Jeff Bridges's brother in *The Last American Hero* and Kris Kristofferson's road manager in *A Star Is Born*. The other lead roles went to Don Stroud, cast as the drummer "Jesse", and Charles Martin-Smith, chosen as the bass player "Ray Bob". Stroud's most recent film appearance had been in *The Choirboys*; unlike Busey, he did not have a professional musical background. Smith had gained fame for his performance as "Terry the Toad" in *American Graffiti*. Though he had not played string bass before, he had played piano and guitar, and had performed in a rock band in high school.

The filming of *The Buddy Holly Story* began in November 1977 and was completed in January 1978. Shortly thereafter, Columbia Pictures purchased the distribution rights to the movie from Innovisions. (Like Holly's records, then, the movie was produced independently and then distributed by a major company.) At first, the premiere was scheduled for Lubbock; however, it was later decided to open the movie on the same night in several Texas and Oklahoma cities, including Lubbock, and to hold the major festivities in Dallas, where Maria Elena now lives.

On May 18, 1978, the world premiere was held at Dallas's Medallion Theater, and was followed by a private party at the Longhorn Ballroom, a famous country music showplace originally opened by Bob Wills in the early 1950's. Busey, Stroud and Smith were at the premiere, as were Niki Sullivan, Jerry Allison, Joe Mauldin and Sonny Curtis, who had been invited by Columbia at the suggestion of Steve Bonner, a Dallas resident and long-time Holly fan. Sullivan had not seen the other original Crickets in over a decade, and none of them had seen Maria Elena since shortly after Holly's death.

The early reviews of the movie in the Dallas newspapers and in *Variety* were highly favourable, and the stream of good notices continued as the movie opened on the West Coast in mid-June, in New York a month later, and in New England late in August. The film was on *Variety*'s list of the fifty top-grossing films for fifteen weeks, reaching as high as number ten.

It was a summer when a wave of movies featuring rock music swamped American theatres. Rather than suffering from the competition offered by other rock movies (*Thank God It's Friday*, *FM*, *American Hot Wax*, *Grease*, *Sergeant Pepper*, and so on), *The Buddy Holly Story* benefited by the comparison. The Holly movie was one of the few which was more than a mere device for publicizing a soundtrack album or furthering the careers of leading rock musicians, and it was praised for the difference.

In almost every review, Gary Busey's performance was singled out for special praise, as the major factor contributing to the movie's success. (Busey

● *Gary Busey played Holly in 'The Buddy Holly Story'*

gained an Academy Award ["Oscar"] nomination for Best Actor for his performance.) Since film clips of Holly are rare and relatively few people can remember seeing him perform live, Busey did not have to match any widely held preconceived image of how Holly looked when performing. Instead, Busey was free to play the role as he felt it—and he did exactly that, becoming so caught up in the spirit of the music that he actually became a rock 'n' roll performer himself, and not just an actor playing one. The movie's music was, in most spots, acceptable rock 'n' roll and a reasonable attempt was made to match the essence of Holly's style; only the movie's closing medley, in which Busey was backed by a large orchestra, strayed far from the Holly sound. The vibrancy of Busey's visual performance obscured his vocal limitations, which were more obvious if one played the soundtrack album separately. (The music was performed and recorded live, without overdubbing; some of the more difficult lead guitar parts were played not by Busey but by an off-camera guitarist.)

Although most Holly fans and the public at large found the movie enjoyable, there was some adverse reaction to the liberties taken with the facts of Holly's career. The basic features of Holly's character did shine through in Busey's performance but the story itself contained many inaccuracies, some of which seriously distorted the nature of Holly's relationships with his family and fellow musicians, as well as the direction in which his career was headed. To cite just a few of the most obvious and most important changes:

—Holly's parents never tried to dissuade him from a musical career, as the movie indicates; rather, they wholeheartedly supported him.

—Holly's first hits were recorded in Clovis at Norman Petty's studio, not in New York City. Though Holly did have the most say as to how the music was to be arranged and performed, it was Petty who produced the records and provided the careful technical expertise that made Holly's recordings sound so bright and unaffected.

—Dick Jacobs, not Holly, arranged and produced the string session. Holly did not read music.

—Holly went on his last tour for financial reasons and as a favour to GAC, not to boost sagging record sales.

—Holly had neither turned his back on Lubbock nor made a decisive move in the direction of pop orchestral music, as the movie implies. At the time of his death, he was planning to establish his own recording studio in Lubbock and experiment on his own recordings with everything from country fiddles to big-band jazz musicians.

The inaccuracies in the movie reflected Innovision's desire to film what it considered to be the "legend" of Buddy Holly. "We're not out to make a true-to-life movie," Bauer had told me at one point, "we're out to make a movie that's *bigger* than life." Facts were consequently adapted, altered, overlooked and re-arranged, as suited the production team's idea of what would be most "commercial". The movie was about a man who broke new ground and trusted his own instincts rather than the existing formulas for pop music stardom; and yet, the movie itself clung to clichés about rock 'n' roll history and followed standard Hollywood plot formulas.

I was not directly involved in the film's production. I did not see a preliminary script until a few months before filming began; my reaction at that time was that the truth of Holly's life would make for a more interesting and more successful movie than the version presented in the script. When I saw the completed movie, I enjoyed it and was able to applaud it for what it was, but I also felt twinges of regret for what it could have been and was not. The movie certainly did publicize Holly and lead to increased sales of his records, but it missed an opportunity to depict accurately the early years of rock 'n' roll. I worried how the movie would ultimately affect our memories of Holly. History is not what really happened, but what we *think* really happened, and a movie that does not distinguish between fact and fancy threatens to create confusion rather than comprehension.

The film drew mixed reactions from those who had known Holly best. The person who displayed the most enthusiasm for the film was Maria Elena. Although she had had her own objections to some items in the script (particularly the fictional scene in which Maria's aunt is portrayed as an antique Spanish *señora* whose permission Holly must win before he can court Maria), she was emotionally overwhelmed by the completed film upon seeing it for the first time at its Dallas premiere, and was unable to sit through to its completion. "Gary Busey came through so vividly," she said later. "It seemed like Buddy was inside him. All of Buddy's characteristics, his forcefulness and determination, came through."

Although he was left out of the movie, Niki Sullivan was nevertheless happy with it. "That was just the way Buddy was," Sullivan said. "Busey picked up a lot of Buddy's mannerisms—how, I don't know." Dick Jacobs, who was likewise absent from the script, also enjoyed the movie and took a relaxed attitude to the movie's liberties with the truth, including the scenes in which Holly is shown creating his own string arrangements. Jacobs says, "People ask me if it bothers me that I don't get mentioned, and I say, 'No, why should it? It's just a movie.'"

Others, however, were unhappy with the movie. Norman Petty was angered by his absence from the film. "I felt like a nonentity," he told Chet Flippo of *Rolling Stone*, "like some very important years of my life had just been wiped out." Jerry Allison said something similar to me not long before the movie was released: "The years I spent with Holly are really precious to me and it's like they are trying to steal those times away." Allison was particularly angered by the racist remark ("you can get all the dark meat you want") attributed to him in the film. He and Mauldin were bitter that they were portrayed without their permission and that the name Crickets (which they long ago trademarked) was used in the movie and on the soundtrack album. They were also irked that the movie's script, in places, borrowed from the story line for *Not Fade Away*, and also from chats Allison had had with Gary Busey on the set of that ill-fated film.

The Holley family was upset with several aspects of the film, especially its skimpy treatment of Holly's youth. "We were disappointed that they didn't have more about the Holley family and about Buddy's life in and around Lubbock," Mrs. Holley told me. "We felt like we played a big part in his career, but there isn't very much about that in the film." Larry Holley said, "I didn't feel like I was watching my brother on the screen." Mrs. Holley was also bothered by the occasional swear words (which, to be sure, were few and mild compared to most contemporary movies), and by the fictional church scene. Innovisions had not involved the Holleys at all in the film's production. "We never did see a script," Mrs. Holley told a reporter after the premiere. "We just took their word for it that we were going to like it. I guess we were kind of stupid, huh?" When asked how much of the movie differed from the truth, Mrs. Holley answered, "Almost all of it."

Some months after the film, Mrs. Holley reflected further on it: "Now that we have had time to think about it, we realize that the movie did show some of Buddy's ways and his characteristics, and Gary Busey did portray

Buddy real well. We do hope the movie does well, so people will be more interested in Buddy. We're not mad, then—just disappointed." But both she and Larry Holley express the wish that there could be another movie about the Buddy Holly *they* knew.

Like Holly's fans and rock music critics, the family recognized the dilemma. The movie gave a tremendous boost to Holly's popularity, but it also threatened to misguide forever the public's perception of Holly. The September 21, 1978 issue of *Rolling Stone* highlighted the growing controversy with two articles, printed side by side: "The Gary Busey Story" and "The Buddy Holly Story". The latter article, written by Chet Flippo, was subtitled "Friends Say Movie's Not Cricket". It explored the film's dramatic liberties and Innovision's's excuses for the deliberate inaccuracies. "There's no way to refute the reality that is invented by a movie," wrote Flippo. "*The Buddy Holly Story* now stands as the official version of his life, but the movie does not seem to be about the real Buddy Holly."

The very appearance of the *Rolling Stone* article itself highlighted the dilemma: if the film had not been made, would Buddy Holly ever have become the subject of a three-page, profusely illustrated article in *Rolling Stone*? Though the film may not have given a satisfactory or truthful answer to the question, "Who was Buddy Holly?", it at least provoked a lot of people into asking the question for the first time.

Throughout the 1970's, for anyone who wanted to learn more about Holly by acquiring his records, it was better to be in Britain. British releases of Holly records continued to outdistance by far the quality and scope of MCA's American efforts. (MCA, the parent company of Decca, Coral and Brunswick, eliminated the old label names in 1972.)

Beginning in 1974, the British branch of MCA began a series of Holly reissues and packages with the assistance of John Beecher, president of the Buddy Holly Appreciation Society through the 1960's. First came *Legend*, a well-compiled and sensibly ordered two-album set of Holly's best-known recordings. Later, there were reissues of the original *Buddy Holly* and *Chirping Crickets* albums, with the original front covers and new liner notes; an album entitled *The Nashville Sessions* containing most of the 1956 Decca recordings; and one called *Western and Bop* containing material from the *Holly In The Hills* and *Reminiscing* albums. The albums were all marked by accurate liner notes, complete discographical information and careful production. Another package of outstanding technical quality and physical attractiveness was prepared by Malcolm Jones who produced a five-record box set titled *The Buddy Holly Story* for World Records under a licence from MCA. The World Records set, which was sold only by mail, included nearly all Holly material except for the Buddy and Bob recordings.

In 1979, the British division of MCA issued a definitive six-album box set, prepared by Jones and Beecher, called *The Complete Buddy Holly*. (The set was released in the United States in 1981.) This set contained a total of 122 cuts, including some interviews, a recording of the first Ed Sullivan Show appearance, the records Holly produced for Waylon Jennings and Lou Giordano, and—the best treat of all—the original, undubbed versions of "Peggy Sue Got Married", "That Makes It Tough" and "Learning the Game". At long last, Holly fans had an opportunity to hear these songs as Holly had himself recorded them.

The almost inexhaustible market for Holly records overseas was shown by the unprecedented success of an album titled *Twenty Golden Greats*, issued

by the British branch of MCA in the spring of 1978. The album contained the songs which had been hit singles for Holly in Britain, and featured a graffiti-style front cover with the slogan "Buddy Holly Lives". Well promoted on British radio and TV, the record soared to the top of the British charts, establishing itself as the best-selling album in Britain for some five weeks and earning gold and platinum records. A similar package (with a different selection of cuts) also went to the top of record charts in Germany and Switzerland. Nineteen years after his death, Holly had his first number one album and his first overseas gold record.

Some of these British albums could be found in the import sections of large American record shops. Most American record buyers, though, had to settle for *A Rock and Roll Collection*, the 1972 two-record album. MCA continued to maintain that the *Collection* package was sufficient to meet the demand for Holly records in the United States.

Only with the success of Ronstadt's cover versions of "That'll Be The Day" and "It's So Easy" did MCA begin to consider any new Holly releases. Company executives authorized the planning of a two-record set which would include most of Holly's hits plus some of the original undubbed tapes never released before, and would be accompanied by adequate liner notes. Then, as had happened six years before, an ambitious and innovative project was shelved in favour of the tried and true. Noting the success of the British *Twenty Golden Greats* album, MCA issued the same record in America to coincide with the release of the Holly film biography, and postponed indefinitely any plans for new albums. MCA did not bother to change the wording on the back of the *Twenty Golden Greats* album which read, "In just eighteen months, Buddy Holly recorded 9 Top Ten smash hits"—a statement which was true for Great Britain but not for the United States. Nor did MCA alter the selection of songs which had been chosen according to their success as singles in Britain, not their popularity in the United States. More importantly, the sound quality of the American pressing was simply atrocious: the brilliant ring of the guitar solo in "Peggy Sue" on the original *Buddy Holly* album of twenty years before became a muffled tinkling on the brand new *Twenty Golden Greats*. MCA attributed this loss in fidelity to the number of cuts—ten—on each side of the album, and yet the sound of the identical British album was far superior.

It was, all the same, a compact collection of Holly's best-known songs, and the album soon rose into the Top 100 on the *Billboard* charts; it was the first Holly album to reach that high since *The Buddy Holly Story* in 1959. (It eventually earned gold and platinum records.) The album did make Holly's music more widely available and it received some favourable reviews. *Time* advised its readers, "You will not hear better rock 'n' roll this summer." But knowledgeable rock critics, such as Ken Emerson writing for *High Fidelity*, laced into MCA:

> *MCA has done it again. The company cannot have spent more than $100 of its money and ten minutes of its time packaging "20 Golden Greats" . . . . there are no liner notes, no indication that at least three of the tracks were overdubbed after the artist's death, and within twenty-seven words, the blurb on the jacket's back makes two factual errors. . . . In short, MCA has accorded one of rock 'n' roll's most brilliant artists less respect than it does the least talented of the many mediocre contemporary artists on its roster.*

In fact, the American division of MCA had not released any Holly album

● *Buddy's parents, Lawrence and Ella Holley in 1983*

of its own creation since *Giant* in 1969, and had not produced a greatest hits package of its own since *The Best of Buddy Holly* in 1966. The only two packages issued in the 1970's (excepting Vocalion budget-line assortments) were *A Rock and Roll Collection*, originally assembled by a German subsidiary, and the British-derived *Twenty Golden Greats*. As the executor and trustee, figuratively, of Buddy Holly's musical estate, MCA had shown incompetence.

The situation began to improve in the 1980's. Producer Steve Hoffman was put in charge of the Holly catalogue, and in early 1983, MCA issued its first truly new album in fourteen years. Called *Buddy Holly: For The First Time Anywhere*, the album contained the original, undubbed recordings of ten songs which had previously only been available in overdubbed versions. Eight songs were studio demos made in 1956, whose overdubbed versions had been released on the *Reminiscing* album: "Rock-A-Bye Rock", "Because I Love You", "I'm Gonna Set My Foot Down", "Changin' All Those Changes", "Baby, Won't You Come Out Tonight", "It's Not My Fault", "Brown-Eyed Handsome Man" and "Bo Diddley". The other two were the alternative version of "Maybe Baby" (that is, the recording made several months before the version used on the hit single), and "That's My Desire", the rejected master from the session that produced "Rave On". Even the photographs used on the front and back of the cover were previously unseen shots of Holly and the Crickets. The record sold well and offered hope of a new era in the handling of Holly's material by his record company.

"Are there any more recordings still unreleased?" In an earlier edition of this book, I gave the answer as a "conditional 'no'". There are some early demos of Holly solo and with Bob Montgomery which have never been released, primarily because of poor sound quality, or because they are duplicate versions of titles already released (in some cases, these have appeared on bootleg albums). One persistent rumour about unreleased songs concerned a tune called "I Tried to Forget", but MCA's files confirm that no such record existed: it was just an alternate title for "I Guess I Was Just A Fool".

With these exceptions (and recognizing the many recordings that have been released only in overdubbed versions), the Holleys and Norman Petty long believed that all of Holly's work had been made available. Then, in 1983, Norman Petty found a tape box in his "tape vault" in Clovis which contained material by Holly that had not previously been released. He immediately informed Steve Hoffman at MCA of the find. Before arrangements could be finalized for the release of this material by MCA, Petty became seriously ill with leukaemia; he passed away in August 1984. MCA hopes to release this newly found material, once legal complications can be ironed out.

In the absence of much support from Holly's American record company, the "Holly Renaissance" of the mid- and late-1970's was spurred on by others. In Britain, the fortieth anniversary of Holly's birth became the occasion for a "Buddy Holly Week" celebration in September 1976. The promotion was the brainchild of Paul McCartney, whose company, MPL Communications, had purchased from Norman Petty the Nor Va Jak publishing rights to Holly's songs. For this first Buddy Holly Week, Petty was invited to Britain to be the guest of honour at a luncheon attended by leading rock stars. Later in the week, a rock 'n' roll dance attended by thousands was held in a London theatre. When Buddy Holly Week was repeated in September 1977, the main event was a free concert by Jerry Allison, Joe Mauldin and Sonny Curtis at the Gaumont Theatre in London's Kilburn district where Holly and the Crickets had played in 1958. For 1978, Buddy Holly Week began with a

special midnight showing of *The Buddy Holly Story*, which had not yet been released in Britain. In originating the annual celebrations, McCartney was acting both as a fan and as a smart businessman, since it was to MPL's interest to promote the songs it owned. The publicity given to Holly through these promotional efforts certainly helped lay the basis for the enormous success of the *Twenty Golden Greats* album in 1978.

In 1979 MPL's 'Buddy Holly Week' reunited The Crickets on stage with Bob Montgomery, Maria Elena and Don Everly

The same month that the first Buddy Holly Week was held in Great Britain, a new organization of Holly fans came into existence. Bill Griggs, a Holly fan and record collector from Connecticut, was bothered that Holly fans lacked any way to communicate with each other, buy and sell records, exchange photos and new information, and work cooperatively to promote Holly. (The British-based Buddy Holly Appreciation Society had been inactive for a number of years.) At his own initiative and expense, Griggs began the Buddy Holly Memorial Society (BHMS) and issued its first newsletter in September 1976. The BHMS soon attracted thousands of members from all fifty United States and about twenty foreign countries. The organization kept fans up-to-date on new releases and the progress of the forthcoming movie, provided definitive lists of recordings associated with Holly (including cover records and tribute songs), and provided access to photos and otherwise-unavailable records, including imports.

While the respect for Holly's work increased around the world in these years, his home town of Lubbock continued to pay him little heed or honour. When advance men for the Columbia Pictures publicity department arrived in Lubbock in the spring of 1978 to begin planning the premiere of *The Buddy Holly Story*, they were surprised to find nothing in the city memorializing Holly. There were no markers or statues, no parks or schools or streets or public buildings named after him, and no brochures available publicizing his connection with the city.

With some embarrassment, the city scrambled for a way to honour Holly and commemorate the opening of the film. It was decided to name a new park on the city's northern outskirts after Holly. The site, which had once been the location of the city landfill, was still a barren spot, but Lubbock had made plans to develop the site over a period of several years into a well-landscaped park with special facilities for physically and mentally handicapped children. On the morning before the movie's premiere, with city officials, Holly's family and Gary Busey in attendance, a marker was unveiled identifying the site as the "Buddy Holly Recreation Area".

Several days after the park dedication, Bill Griggs, John Beecher and I drove to Lubbock from Dallas where we had attended the premiere of *The Buddy Holly Story*. I had not been to Holly's home town for several years, and I wondered if the advent of the movie had altered the community's previous attitude of indifference towards its native rock 'n' roller. Not much had changed. When we tried to find out the location of the Holly Recreation Area, the information office at Lubbock City Hall, the reception desk at the Chamber of Commerce, and even the city parks department itself were unable to give us exact directions to the site. Neither the city government nor the Chamber of Commerce had any special leaflets available on Holly, and Holly went unmentioned in their historical and promotional brochures.

When we drove down Sixth Street, we received a shock: the site where Holly's birthplace had once stood was now an empty lot. A check with city building department officials showed that the property had been inspected the previous autumn, found to be in unsuitable condition for human habitation and condemned to be demolished—with the demolition date set, ironically enough, for February 3, 1978, the anniversary of Holly's death. Before the destruction could be carried out, a man had bought the house, moved it outside the city limits (and thus beyond the jurisdiction of the city's building code), and begun to fix it up for his family's use. The city officials who had condemned the house for demolition were unaware that the house was Holly's birthplace, as was the man who had, providentially, bought it and saved it for his private use. A city report listing all historically significant sites and buildings in Lubbock, including those connected with the lives of famous persons, did not include Holly's birthplace or any other site associated with him.

In the aftermath of that visit, I wrote the following:

"In the town of Tupelo, Mississippi, a city park has been established at the birthplace of Elvis Presley. In the tiny community of Turkey, Texas, the residents have erected a $15,000 monument to honour the memory of Bob Wills, who grew up there. But in the city of Lubbock, the achievements of Buddy Holly and other West Texas musicians have been given scant recognition."

To their credit, the residents of Lubbock have sought to remedy this situation in recent years. In 1980, a statue of Holly was erected in front of the Lubbock Civic Center and a "Walk of Fame" was inaugurated to honour performers from the West Texas area. There seems to be a recognition at last that Buddy Holly has made the name of Lubbock, Texas famous around the world.

In the 1978 movie *American Hot Wax*, a fictionalized account of Alan Freed's last days as a rock 'n' roll disc jockey in New York, one of the leading characters is a young teenager, identified as the head of a 5,000-member Buddy

Holly Fan Club. A huge yellow button reading "Buddy Holly Lives" decorates the fan's sports jacket. When a slick promo man who is pushing an unknown but sure-to-be-big pop singer (undoubtedly from Philadelphia) tries to switch the youth's allegiance by questioning the logic of promoting a dead singer, the fan replies, "Well . . . sure, he's dead—but his music isn't." He tears up the agent's business card, defiantly saying "Buddy Holly lives, man!" as he flings the pieces down and walks away.

The thoughts expressed by the character are commonplace today, but hardly anyone would have been able to put it that way in 1959. There was at that time no Buddy Holly Fan Club and no "Buddy Holly Lives" buttons; while many mourned Holly, few could appreciate fully the loss that Holly's death represented, or the strength of the dedication to his music. In fact, to be a Buddy Holly fan in America was, for many years, an isolated act. When I began wearing *my* custom-made "Buddy Holly Lives!" button in 1967, strangers would occasionally stop me and ask me for one, but for the most part I (like most other Holly fans in the United States) wondered if I was the only one in the world who felt so strongly about Holly and his music. It took "American Pie", *The Buddy Holly Story* and the Buddy Holly Memorial Society to bring the "Buddy Holly Underground" to the surface and to reveal its extent.

After the years of privacy, the fans wanted a chance to meet each other in person. In August 1978, the BHMS held its first Buddy Holly Convention at the Ramada Inn in Wethersfield, Connecticut. The fans came from as far away as England, Canada, California and Florida. Some had been Holly fans since 1957 and were now in their thirties or forties; others had not even been born when "That'll Be The Day" became a hit, and had not discovered Holly until the 1970's. Some were fully fledged record collectors who owned thousands of singles and LPs; others owned but one or two Holly albums of recent vintage. There were high school graduates and Ph.Ds, truckdrivers, clerks, teachers and engineers.

When asked why they had come, they gave a variety of reasons. Some came simply to learn more about Holly by talking with the other fans, watching rare film clips and listening to tapes, and asking questions of the speakers. "I want to learn all I can about him," was their explanation. Others came as a way to pay tribute to Holly. "I felt I owed it to Buddy to be here," said one fan; another said, "The trip was a pilgrimage—it was the least I could do." Another reason offered by some was to pick up tips on what could be done to publicize Holly and get his records played and displayed more widely—they saw the BHMS as a movement and wanted to become more involved in an active way. And finally, they came just to prove to themselves that it was not so eccentric or unusual, after all, to believe so strongly in the music and message of a long-dead pop singer. "Until this weekend," said one, "I thought I was all alone. Now, I know I'm not." Holly's own song furnished a theme: "Well, all right, so I'm being foolish—well, all right, let people know . . . ."

For all those who came, the highlight of the Convention was the surprise, on stage reunion of the Crickets. For the first time in twenty years, Jerry Allison, Joe Mauldin and Niki Sullivan played together, joined and led by Sonny Curtis who has been lead guitarist and vocalist for the Crickets over most of the period since Holly's death. The Crickets had planned to attend the Convention, but their decision to play came only at the last moment. The day before the Convention, Allison phoned Bill Griggs to ask a question: "Bill," said Allison, "do you need a band?"

● *1980 saw the unveiling of a statue and 'Walk of Fame' area in Lubbock*

The Crickets' presence and performance turned the Convention into an emotional event which those who were present would never forget, and those who could not attend would long regret having missed. They played the old Holly hits—"Oh Boy!", "Peggy Sue", "That'll Be The Day" and others—plus the post-Holly Crickets hit "I Fought The Law", showing all of the drive and exuberance identified with the west Texas rockabilly sound. But the audience's longest and loudest applause came for a new song—one which Sonny Curtis had written just hours before the Crickets got on stage at the end of the Convention's second day. Curtis introduced the song as his reaction to *The Buddy Holly Story*. "I didn't think that they had all of their facts quite straight when I saw the movie," he explained, "so I thought I'd just write my own version, the way I remembered it." In part, it went like this:

> . . . *We had a good country band, and I played the fiddle,*
> *Buddy played the guitar, and he used to play the banjo some,*
> *We harmonized like Bill Monroe and the Bluegrass Boys,*
> *Bob wore my hat and played the flat-top with his thumb.*
>
> *We picked them joints and had a lot of fun with the women,*
> *Swigged on bootleg beer and played licks in the sun,*
> > *We got our picture in the paper with our eyes covered up,*
> > *They said our music made the kids do sinful stuff,*
> *We were crazy back then, but we sure had lots of fun.*
>
> *Then Elvis came along and old Bud' just loved him,*
> *But I couldn't tell where rock'n'roll was coming from,*
> *But I stuck around, 'cause someone had to pick like Scotty,*
> *Joe B. played the bass, and J.I. played the drums.*
>
> *Then I grew up and had to go out and make a living,*
> *I played a Slim Whitman tour, and I wound up on the road,*
> *And them good ol' boys began to make some noise around Texas,*
> *And they got hot as a pistol, picking that rock'n'roll.*
>
> *But "That'll Be The Day" came much too soon for Buddy,*
> *He was a good ol' boy, and he had a good Christian soul,*
> > *He never knocked nobody down in his life—*
> > *He loved us all, and he treated us right.*
> *And you know, the music didn't die—*
> *And the levee ain't dry—*
> *'Cause Buddy Holly lives, every time we play rock'n'roll.*

● *The Crickets in 1986—Jerry Allison, Gordon Payne and Joe B. Mauldin*

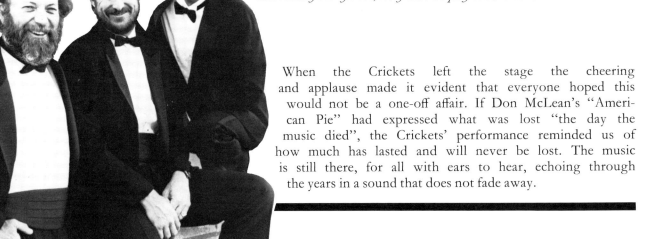

When the Crickets left the stage the cheering and applause made it evident that everyone hoped this would not be a one-off affair. If Don McLean's "American Pie" had expressed what was lost "the day the music died", the Crickets' performance reminded us of how much has lasted and will never be lost. The music is still there, for all with ears to hear, echoing through the years in a sound that does not fade away.

CADENCE

The best rock 'n' roll musicians, though openly attentive to commercial considerations, still created music which honestly reflected their own personalities and the problems and assumptions of their audience. Their songs chronicled the concerns of a musical generation. Whether or not such musicians can be properly labelled "folk artists", it is at least certain that no country but America could have produced them or their music.

Rock 'n' roll was both revolutionary and conservative. For the first time ever, teenagers had their own culture. But for all their proclaimed independence of the standards of their elders, teenagers could still hunger for fast and fancy cars and sharp clothes, boast of steady girl friends or boy friends or else long for the security of one true love, and worry about their esteem (and "reputation") among their peers. Although rock 'n' roll provided a new sound, it was also a reaction against the artificiality and sterility of pop music, and a return to music that was more basic and sincere—music that had an emotion and spontaneity that modern adult life seemed to lack. Teenagers were tugged between old and new customs and rock 'n' roll had the fortune to thrive at that moment of tension.

Buddy Holly was labelled a "giant" on one album, but that was really a bit of a misnomer. He may indeed have been a giant in terms of business and advertising clichés. But giants are curiosities, abnormal, removed from the race of men. Buddy Holly was anything but that; his hold on his fans is to be explained by his very humanity. He did not inspire the awe or ecstatic adoration that Elvis Presley did; nor was he able, like Chuck Berry, to stand above the fray and comment upon it. Holly was always in the struggle himself. And like the others of his generation, he was fresh and new, but still lived by old rules of ambition and achievement, and longed for the accepted standards of success.

Buddy Holly was not a giant, or a god—but he was a sort of hero. Though a star, he still sounded and looked like a friend. He was one with his listeners, with one important difference: he could successfully express through his music the feelings that those listeners could not express for themselves. And since he was unusual only in his ambition, perseverance and musical talents, his concerns were shared by his audience. When he sang his song, his audience could claim it for their song, too.

Buddy Holly's life was an enactment of the American dream, and his music mirrored its spirit. What we long for, we never quite obtain, and yet we keep reaching; and if we have no reason to be sure of the outcome, we cling to our faith that the effort will not go unrewarded. In Holly's music, there is this knowing trust in the very process of life—a willingness to hope for the best, even when it is unrealistic to expect it. The promise may have failed in the past, but there is still hope that this time, or next time, the promise will be fulfilled; and so we all think we see a light, though it be but dim and distant. As we listen to Buddy Holly's songs, they bring us closer to the glow, and the light burns brighter.

SESSION FILE

This listing was initially prepared from record company session, release and copyright files. Those recordings made at record company studios were well documented and included details of session musicians, take numbers and other information which was not generally logged in the smaller non-union studios (which include Norman Petty's, where the majority of tracks were recorded). For those recordings which were not documented at the time, we have had to rely on such information (including acetate labels and tape boxes) as was available, together with aural evidence and the memories of those who were present as musicians or bystanders. Further contributions to the session files over the years were made by Norman & Vi Petty, Ella and Lawrence Holley, Dick Jacobs, Malcolm Jones, Bill Griggs and many other collectors and fans who made suggestions and comments. By far the most valuable information resulted from a study of the Clovis tape archives undertaken by Jerry MacNeish and John Ingman. Although they were unable to listen to all the Holly-related material stored in Clovis, thanks to Vi Petty's kindness it was possible to examine acetates, tape boxes and many of the documents stored there. We are grateful to John Ingman for allowing us access to his detailed and comprehensive files. It is hoped that where the information contained herein is used by others some credit will be given, although this has often been lacking in the past where the only acknowledgement has been the repetition of typographical and other errors by those who have appropriated this material.

All recordings made in Clovis are presumed produced or engineered by Norman Petty unless otherwise stated—producers of other sessions where known are listed by name. Matrix numbers are not generally significant in themselves since they were rarely assigned at the time of a session but were a convenience for the record company in identifying versions of a recording selected for release and were often only assigned when masters were completed or delivered to record company tape libraries. A few recordings made in Nashville also bear a separate Nashville (NA) series but as these tapes arrived at the Coral-Brunswick tape library in New York they were assigned fresh numbers. Take numbers were often not recorded—these are shown where known and listed as version numbers when no actual take numbers were recorded. Unissued recordings are only included where authenticated, that is they have been heard, documented or reliably known to have existed—most of these are presumed to be extant but in some cases may not have survived or may be in the hands of those who would prefer to keep them private.

Many Buddy Holly recordings were overdubbed in order to make simple voice and guitar demos and low quality tape recordings and acetates appear to be of higher quality. This overdubbing has always been a contentious issue among Buddy Holly fans and collectors. These overdub sessions will probably be of secondary interest, and because they too were mostly completed in Clovis, they were not well documented. We have listed such details as are available and, so that the source recording may be more easily identified, these overdub listings in most cases follow the original recording date entries and are printed in italics. Unless stated, all overdubs were added to the undubbed version listed and may be identified in the case of several versions or takes by the master number shown in parentheses. The original undubbed versions of some recordings were not always retained, especially when vocal backings by the Picks and the Roses were added to Crickets recordings during Holly's lifetime. We have shown the undubbed versions as unissued even though they may no longer be available for release.

The Session File details listed below are shown in the following format:
Session number. Location, time and date
Personnel and Producer
Matrix number   Title (take or version number) Writer/s   1st US Release   1st UK Release
'Unissued' indicates that, at the time of writing, the recording has not been released on a commercially available record.

01. Home recording, 3315 36th Street, Lubbock, Texas. c.1949. Buddy Holly, vocal and guitar

	MY TWO TIMIN' WOMAN (C.E. 'Hank' Snow)	HH EP	Unissued

02. Home recording, 3315 36th Street, Lubbock, Texas. c.1952. Buddy Holly, vocal and mandolin; Bob Montgomery, vocal and guitar

	I'LL JUST PRETEND (Jessie Mae Martin)	HH EP	Unissued
	TAKE THESE SHACKLES FROM MY HEART (Unknown)	VIGO 134	Unissued

03. (prob.) Home recording, 3315 36th Street, Lubbock, Texas. c.1953. Buddy Holly, vocal and guitar; Bob Montgomery, vocal and guitar

	FOOTPRINTS IN THE SNOW (Trad. arr Buddy Holly/Bob Montgomery)	VIGO 134	Unissued

04. Radio Station KDAV, 6602 Quirt Ave, Lubbock, Texas. c.1953 (acetate dated November 10, 1953). Jack Neal. vocal and acoustic guitar; Buddy Holly, guitar

	I SAW THE MOON CRY LAST NIGHT (Jack Neal)	Unissued	RCCD 3017
	I HEAR THE LORD CALLIN' FOR ME (Jack Neal)	Unissued	RCCD 3017

05. (prob.) Nesman Recording Studio, 3108 York Avenue, Wichita Falls, Texas. c.1954/55. Buddy Holly, vocal and guitar; Bob Montgomery, vocal and guitar; Sonny Curtis, fiddle; (prob.) Larry Welborn, bass on*, (prob.) Don Guess, steel guitar on*, bass on +

	FLOWER OF MY HEART* (Bob Montgomery/Don Guess)	Unissued	Unissued
	DOOR TO MY HEART* (Bob Montgomery)	Unissued	Unissued
	SOFT PLACE IN MY HEART+ (Bob Montgomery)	Unissued	Unissued
	GOTTA GET YOU NEAR ME BLUES + (Bob Montgomery)	VIGO 134	Unissued
	I GAMBLED MY HEART+ (Buddy Holly/Bob Montgomery)	Unissued	Unissued

***05a. Overdub session: Norman Petty Studios, 1313 W. Seventh Street, Clovis New Mexico.** (Poss.) October 6, 1963. George Tomsco, guitar; Stan Lark, bass; Keith McCormack, rhythm guitar; Lyn Bailey, bass; Doug Roberts, drums*

114930	*FLOWER OF MY HEART* (Bob Montgomery/Don Guess)*	*CRL 7/57463*	*LVA 9227*
114931	*DOOR TO MY HEART* (Bob Montgomery)*	*CRL 7/57463*	*LVA 9227*
114932	*I GAMBLED MY HEART+ (Buddy Holly/Bob Montgomery)*	*CRL 7/57463*	*LVA 9227*
114933	*SOFT PLACE IN MY HEART+ (Bob Montgomery)*	*CRL 7/57463*	*LVA 9227*
114936	*GOTTA GET YOU NEAR ME BLUES + (Bob Montgomery)*	*CRL 7/57463*	*LVA 9227*

06. Radio Station KSEL, Lubbock Texas. c. 1955. Ben Hall, vocal, Buddy Holly, guitar; Sonny Curtis, fiddle; Weldon Myrick, steel guitar; Dena Hall, bass

	ALL FROM LOVING YOU (Ben Hall)	Unissued	RCCD 3004

07. Radio Station KDAV, 6602 Quirt Ave, Lubbock, Texas. c. 1955. Ben Hall, vocal, Buddy Holly, guitar; Sonny Curtis, fiddle; Weldon Myrick, steel guitar; Dena Hall, bass

	ROSE OF MONTEREY (Ben Hall)	Unissued	RCCD 3004

08. Radio Station KDAV, 6602 Quirt Ave, Lubbock, Texas. August,1955. Buddy Holly, vocal and lead guitar; Bob Montgomery, vocal, guitar; Sonny Curtis. fiddle; (prob.) lead guitar on*; (prob.) Don Guess, bass

	YOU AND I ARE THROUGH* (Bob Montgomery)	VIGO 134	Unissued
	BABY IT'S LOVE (Bob Montgomery/Ella Holley)	Unissued	Unissued
	MEMORIES (Bob Montgomery)	VIGO 134	Unissued
	QUEEN OF THE BALLROOM (Don Guess)	Unissued	Unissued
	SOFT PLACE IN MY HEART 2nd version) (Bob Montgomery)	Unissued	Unissued
	MEMORIES (2nd version) (Bob Montgomery)	Unissued	Unissued

***08a. Overdub session: Norman Petty Studios, 1313 West Seventh Street, Clovis, New Mexico.** Unknown dates between October 1963 and December 1964. George Tomsco, guitar; Keith McCormack, rhythm guitar; Stan Lark or Lyn Bailey, bass; Doug Roberts or Eric Budd, drums*

114935	*YOU AND I ARE THROUGH* (Bob Montgomery)*	*CRL 7/57463*	*LVA 9227*
115917	*BABY IT'S LOVE (Bob Montgomery/Ella Holley)*	*Cr 002000*	*LVA 9227*
115918	*MEMORIES (Bob Montgomery)*	*PR 100*	*LVA 9227*
115919	*QUEEN OF THE BALLROOM (Don Guess)*	*Cr 002000*	*LVA 9227*

09. Nesman Recording Studio, 3108 York Avenue, Wichita Falls, Texas. June 7, 1955. Buddy Holly, vocal and guitar; Bob Montgomery, vocal and guitar; unknown, bass; Jerry Allison, drums

	DOWN THE LINE (Buddy Holly/Bob Montgomery/Norman Petty)	Unissued	Unissued
	YOU AND ! ARE THROUGH (Bob Montgomery)	Unissued	Unissued

NB: These two recordings may in fact have been made at Jim Beck's Studio, Dallas, Texas or recordings of the same songs made there may not have survived. Date may be date of acetate cutting.

10. Nesman Recording Studio, 3108 York Avenue, Wichita Falls, Texas. Mid-1955. Buddy Holly, vocal and guitar; Bob Montgomery, vocal and guitar on *; Larry Welborn, bass; Jerry Allison, drums

	BABY LET'S PLAY HOUSE (Arthur Gunter)	VIGO 134	Unissued
	DOWN THE LINE* (Buddy Holly/Bob Montgomery/Norman Petty)	VIGO 134	Unissued

10a. Overdub session: Norman Petty Studios, 1313 West Seventh Street, Clovis, New Mexico. *Between May 1962 and December 1964. George Tomsco, guitar and rhythm guitar; Stan Lark, bass; Keith McCormack, rhythm guitar; Doug Roberts or Eric Budd, drums*

114937	*BABY LET'S PLAY HOUSE (Arthur Gunter)*	C 7/57463	LVA 9227
114934	*DOWN THE LINE* (Buddy Holly/Bob Montgomery/Norman Petty)*	C 7/57463	LVA 9227

11. (Prob.) Nesman Recording Studio, 3108 York Avenue, Wichita Falls, Texas. Date unknown, c. 1955. Sonny Curtis, vocal & guitar; Buddy Holly, guitar; (poss) Don Guess or Larry Welborn, bass; Jerry Allison, drums

	BECAUSE YOU LOVE ME (Sonny Curtis)	VIGO 137	Unissued
	I'LL MISS MY HEART (Sonny Curtis)	VIGO 137	Unissued

(Poss.) recorded during the same session:

	QUEEN OF THE BALLROOM (Don Guess)	Unissued	Unissued
	THIS BOTTLE (Sonny Curtis)	Unissued	Unissued

12. Nesman Recording Studio, 3108 York Avenue, Wichita Falls, Texas. Late 1955. Buddy Holly, vocal and guitar; Sonny Curtis, guitar; Don Guess, bass, Jerry Allison, drums

	MOONLIGHT BABY (aka BABY WON'T YOU COME OUT TONIGHT) (Don Guess)	Unissued	Unissued
	DON'T COME BACK KNOCKIN' (Sue Parrish/Buddy Holly)	Unissued	Unissued
111001	I GUESS I WAS JUST A FOOL (aka I TRIED TO FORGET) (Buddy Holly)	Unissued	Unissued
	(poss.) CHANGIN' ALL THOSE CHANGES (Buddy Holly)	Unissued	Unissued

13. Nesman Recording Studio, 3108 York Avenue, Wichita Falls, Texas. December 7, 1955. Buddy Holly, vocal and guitar; Sonny Curtis, guitar; Don Guess, bass; Jerry Allison, drums

	MOONLIGHT BABY (aka BABY WON'T YOU COME OUT TONIGHT) (Don Guess)	VIGO 134	Unissued
	I GUESS I WAS JUST A FOOL (Buddy Holly)	VIGO 134	Unissued
	DON'T COME BACK KNOCKIN' (Sue Parrish/Buddy Holly)	HH EP	Unissued
	LOVE ME (Sue Parrish/Buddy Holly)	Cr 002000	Unissued

NB These were the four recordings submitted on acetates to US Decca in response to a telegram from Eddie Crandall to Dave Stone. Date may refer to date of acetate cuttting at KDAV.

14. Bradley's Barn Studio, 804 16th Avenue South, Nashville, Tennessee. Between 7.15 and 10.15 p.m., January 26, 1956. Buddy Holly, vocal; Sonny Curtis, lead guitar; Grady Martin, rhythm guitar; Don Guess, bass; Doug Kirkham, percussion. Producer: Owen Bradley

89280 (NA 9280)	LOVE ME (take 10) (Sue Parrish/Buddy Holly)	D 29854	O 5581
89281 (NA 9281)	DON'T COME BACK KNOCKIN' (Sue Parrish/Buddy Holly)	DL 8707	OE 9457
89282 (NA 9282)	MIDNIGHT SHIFT (Earl Lee/Jimmie Ainsworth)	DL 8707	O 5800
89283 (NA 9283)	BLUE DAYS. BLACK NIGHTS (Ben Hall)	D 29854	O 5581

14a. Overdub session: Sound Masters Recording Studio, 9717 Jensen Drive, Houston, Texas. *February 19, 1984. The Picks (John Pickering, Bill Pickering, Bob Lapham), backing vocals*

[89280/NA 9280]	*LOVE ME (take 10) (Sue Parrish/Buddy Holly)*	Pi 1111	CDMF 088
[89281/NA 9280]	*DON'T COME BACK KNOCKIN' (Sue Parrish/Buddy Holly)*	Pi 1111	CDMF 088
[89282 NA 9282]	*MIDNIGHT SHIFT (Earl Lee/Jimmie Ainsworth)*	Pi 1111	CDMF 088
[89283 NA 9283]	*BLUE DAYS. BLACK NIGHTS (Ben Hall)*	Pi 1111	CDMF 088

15. Norman Petty Studios, 1313 West Seventh Street, Clovis, New Mexico. Date unknown between February and April 1956. Buddy Holly, vocal and guitar; Sonny Curtis, guitar (lead on*); Don Guess, bass; Jerry Allison, drums on +

110997	BABY WON'T YOU COME OUT TONIGHT+ (Don Guess)	MCA 27059	MCM 1002
110999	I GUESS I WAS JUST A FOOL+ (Buddy Holly)	C 7/57450	LVA 9222
111000	IT'S NOT MY FAULT (Ben Hall/Weldon Myrick)	MCA 27059	MCM 1002
111002	I'M GONNA SET MY FOOT DOWN*+ (Buddy Holly)	MCA 27059	MCM 1002
111003	CHANGIN' ALL THOSE CHANGES*+ (Buddy Holly)	MCA 27059	MCM 1002
111004	ROCK-A-BYE ROCK+ (Buddy Holly)	MCA 27059	MCM 1002
111006	BECAUSE I LOVE YOU+ (Buddy Holly)	MCA 27059	MCM 1002

15a. Overdub session: Norman Petty Studios 1313 W. Seventh Street, Clovis, New Mexico. *Date unknown between May 1962 and January 1963. George Tomsco, guitar; Stan Lark, bass; Keith McCormack, rhythm guitar; Doug Roberts or Eric Budd, drums*

112766 [110997]	*BABY WON'T YOU COME OUT TONIGHT (Don Guess)*	C 7/57426	LVA 9212
112768 [111006]	*BECAUSE I LOVE YOU (Buddy Holly)*	C 7/57426	LVA 9212
112771 [111003]	*CHANGIN' ALL THOSE CHANGES* (Buddy Holly)*	C 7/57426	LVA 9212
112770 [111002]	*I'M GONNA SET MY FOOT DOWN* (Buddy Holly)*	C 7/57426	LVA 9212
112769 [111000]	*IT'S NOT MY FAULT (Ben Hall/Weldon Myrick)*	C 7/57426	LVA 9212
112772 [111004]	*ROCK-A-BYE ROCK (Buddy Holly)*	C 7/57426	LVA 9212

15b. Overdub session: Sound Masters Recording Studio, 9717 Jensen Drive, Houston, Texas. *June 28, 1984. The Picks (John Pickering, Bill Pickering, Bob Lapham), backing vocals*

[111004]	*ROCK-A-BYE ROCK (Buddy Holly)*	Pi 2221	CDMF 088

15c. Overdub session: Sound Masters Recording Studio, 9717 Jensen Drive, Houston, Texas. *June 29, 1984. The Picks (John Pickering, Bill Pickering, Bob Lapham), backing vocals*

[111006]	*BECAUSE I LOVE YOU (Buddy Holly)*	Pi 2221	CDMF 088
[111000]	*IT'S NOT MY FAULT (Ben Hall/Weldon Myrick)*	Pi 2221	CDMF 088
[111002]	*I'M GONNA SET MY FOOT DOWN (Buddy Holly)*	Pi 2221	CDMF 088

16. Radio Station KLLL, Suite 2001, Great Plains Life Building, Lubbock, Texas. c.1956. Buddy Holly, vocal and guitar; other personnel unknown

	I FORGOT TO REMEMBER TO FORGET (Stan Kesler/Charlie Feathers)	Unissued	Unissued

NB This recording was purposely rendered unplayable by scratching the surface of the only acetate copy at KDAV at Buddy Holly's request during 1956 when he sought to prevent broadcast of it instead of his current Decca release.

17. Bradley's Barn, 804 16th Avenue South, Nashville, Tennessee. Between 10.30 a.m. and 1.30 p.m., July 22, 1956. Buddy Holly, vocal and guitar; Sonny Curtis, guitar (lead on*); Don Guess, bass; Jerry Allison, drums

	ROCK AROUND WITH OLLIE VEE (fragment) (Sonny Curtis)	VIGO 134	Unissued
100440 (NA 9453)	ROCK AROUND WITH OLLIE VEE (Take 8) (Sonny Curtis)	DL 8707	O 5800
	I'M CHANGIN' ALL THOSE CHANGES (Prob. Take 3)*+ (Buddy Holly)	Unissued	Unissued
100441 (NA 9454)	I'M CHANGIN' ALL THOSE CHANGES (Take 4)* (Buddy Holly)	DL 8707	OE 9457
100442 (NA 9455)	THAT'LL BE THE DAY (Take 19) (Buddy Holly/Jerry Allison)	D 30434	AH 3
100443 (NA 9456)	GIRL ON MY MIND (Take 3) (Don Guess)	DL 8707	OE 9457
100444 (NA 9457)	TING-A-LING (Take 7) (Nugetre; aka Ahmet Ertegun)	DL 8707	OE 9456

NB: + This take would probably be unsuitable for release due to a mistake during the guitar solo by Sonny Curtis. All other takes from Nashville sessions not used on released records appear to have been destroyed, although it was recently reported that some out-takes had survived, having been sold to a Decca engineer in the 1950s as re-usable tape .

17a. Overdub session: Sound Masters Recording Studio, 9717 Jensen Drive, Houston, Texas. February 19, 1984. The Picks (John Pickering, Bill Pickering, Bob Lapham), backing vocals

100440 (NA 9453)	ROCK AROUND WITH OLLIE VEE (Take 8) (Sonny Curtis)	Pi 1111	CDMF 088
[100443/NA 9456]	GIRL ON MY MIND (Don Guess)	Pi 1111	CDMF 088
[100444/NA 9457]	TING A LING (Nugetre, aka Ahmet Ertegun)	Pi 1111	CDMF 088

18. Bradley's Barn, 804 16th Avenue South, Nashville, Tennessee. November 15, 1956. Buddy Holly, vocal; Harold Bradley, guitar; Grady Martin, guitar; Don Guess, bass; Floyd Cramer, piano; Farris Coursey, drums; E. R 'Dutch' McMillin, alto saxophone. Producer: Owen Bradley

101033 (NA 9586)	ROCK AROUND WITH OLLIE VEE (Take 12) (Sonny Curtis)	D 30434	CDLM 8038
101034 (NA 9587)	MODERN DON JUAN (Take 76)+ (Don Guess/Jack Neal)	D 30166	OE 9456
	YOU ARE MY ONE DESIRE (false start) (Don Guess)	VIGO 134	Unissued
101035 (NA 9588)	YOU ARE MY ONE DESIRE (Take 2) (Don Guess)	D 30166	OE 9456

+ This take number seems hardly credible, but the engineer's voice on the master tape 'slate' would appear to confirm it. It may be an error.

18a. Overdub session: Sound Masters Recording Studio, 9717 Jensen Drive, Houston, Texas. February 19, 1984. The Picks (John Pickering, Bill Pickering, Bob Lapham), backing vocals

[101034/NA 9587]	MODERN DON JUAN (Don Guess/Jack Neal)	Pi 1111	CDMF 088
[101035/NA 9588]	YOU ARE MY ONE DESIRE (Don Guess)	Pi 1111	CDMF 088

19. Venture Studio, 1926 19th Street, Lubbock, Texas. Date unknown, late November or early December 1956. Buddy Holly, vocal and guitar; Jerry Allison, drums (& vocal accompaniment on #); unknown rhythm guitar on +; unknown bass on*

	GONE (incomplete version 1)* (Smokey Rogers)	VIGO 134	ROLL 2013
	GONE (version 2)* (Smokey Rogers)	VIGO 134	ROLL 2013
	GONE (Version 3) (Smokey Rogers)	Unissued	Unissued
	HAVE YOU EVER BEEN LONELY (Version 1)* (Peter De Rose/George Brown)	VIGO 134	ROLL 2013
	HAVE YOU EVER BEEN LONELY (Incomplete Version 2) (Peter De Rose/George Brown)*	VIGO 134	ROLL 2013
	HAVE YOU EVER BEEN LONELY (Incomplete Version 3) (Peter De Rose/George Brown)*	VIGO 134	ROLL 2013
	BROWN-EYED HANDSOME MAN* (Chuck Berry)	HH EP	ROLL 2013
	GOOD ROCKIN' TONIGHT (Roy Brown)	Cr 002000	ROLL 2013
	RIP IT UP# (Robert Blackwell/John Marascalco)	VIGO 134	ROLL 2013
	BLUE MONDAY (Dave Bartholomew/Fats Domino)	VIGO 134	ROLL 2013
	HONKY TONK+ (Bill Doggett/Clifford Scott/Beresford Shepherd/Billy Butler)	VIGO 134	ROLL 2013
	BLUE SUEDE SHOES (Carl Perkins)	VIGO 135	ROLL 2013
	SHAKE RATTLE AND ROLL (incomplete)# (Charles Calhoun)	VIGO 135	ROLL 2013
	BO DIDDLEY* (Ellas McDaniels)	VIGO 135	ROLL 2013
	AIN'T GOT NO HOME* (Clarence 'Frogman' Henry)	VIGO 135	ROLL 2013
	HOLLY HOP+ (Ella Holley)	VIGO 135	ROLL 2013

NB Portions of this recording (which were only preserved on a 3 3/4 ips copy tape) may have been made earlier at Holly's home nearby at 1906 19th Street and copied at Venture Studios.

19a. Overdub sessions: Norman Petty Studios, 1313 W. Seventh Street, Clovis New Mexico. Prob. October 6 1963. George Tomsco, guitar; Stan Lark, bass; Keith McCormack, rhythm guitar; Doug Roberts, drums, Vi Petty, piano

114095	GONE (Version 3) (Smokey Rogers)	CRL 7/57450	LVA 9222
114087	RIP IT UP (Robert Blackwell/John Marascalco)	CRL 7/57450	LVA 9222
114091	HONKY TONK + (Bill Doggett/Clifford Scott/Beresford Shepherd/Billy Butler)	CRL 7/57450	LVA 9222
114089	BLUE SUEDE SHOES (Carl Perkins)	CRL 7/57450	LVA 9222
114097	SHAKE RATTLE AND ROLL (incomplete) (Charles Calhoun)	CRL 7/57450	LVA 9222

19b. Overdub sessions: Norman Petty Studios, 1313 W. Seventh Street, Clovis New Mexico. Dates unknown prob. between January and August 1968. George Tomsco, guitar; Lyn Bailey or Stan Lark, bass; Keith McCormack, rhythm guitar; Doug Roberts, drums

120717	HAVE YOU EVER BEEN LONELY (Version 1)* (Peter De Rose/George Brown)	CRL 757504	MUPS 371
120715	GOOD ROCKIN' TONIGHT (Roy Brown)	CRL 757504	MUPS 371
120716	BLUE MONDAY (Dave Bartholomew/Fats Domino)	CRL 757504	MUPS 371
120722	AIN'T GOT NO HOME* (Clarence 'Frogman' Henry)	CRL 757504	MUPS 371
120723	HOLLY HOP (Ella Holley)	CRL 757504	MUPS 371

20. Norman Petty Studios, 1313 W. Seventh Street, Clovis, New Mexico. Date unknown between December 1956 and January 1957. Buddy Holly, vocal and guitar; unknown second guitar; Larry Welborn, bass; Jerry Allison, drums.

111005	BROWN-EYED HANDSOME MAN (Chuck Berry)	MCA 27059	MCM 1002
110998	BO DIDDLEY (Ellas McDaniels)	MCA 27059	MCM 1002

20a. Overdub session: Norman Petty Studios, Clovis New Mexico. Dates unknown between May 1962 and February 1963. George Tomsco, guitar; Stan Lark, bass; Keith McCormack, rhythm guitar; Doug Roberts or Eric Budd, drums

112767 [111005]	BROWN-EYED HANDSOME MAN (Chuck Berry)	CRL 7/57426	LVA 9212
112764 [110998]	BO DIDDLEY (Ellas McDaniels)	CRL 7/57426	LVA 9212

21. KDAV Studio, 6602 Quirt Avenue, Lubbock, Texas. February 21, 1957. Garry Dale (aka Gary Tollett), vocal; Buddy Holly, guitar, Jerry Allison, drums; Ramona Tollett, June Clark and Niki Sullivan, backing vocals

	GO BOY GO (Floyd Wilson)	Unissued	Unissued
	GONE (Smokey Rogers)	Unissued	Unissued

22. Norman Petty Studios, 1313 W. Seventh Street, Clovis, New Mexico. February 24 and 25,1957. Buddy Holly, vocal and guitar; Larry Welborn, bass; Jerry Allison, drums; Niki Sullivan, Gary Tollett and Ramona Tollett, backing vocals

102021	I'M LOOKING FOR SOMEONE TO LOVE (Buddy Holly/Norman Petty)	B 55009	Q 72279
102022	THAT'LL BE THE DAY (Buddy Holly/Jerry Allison/Norman Petty)	B 55009	Q 72279

23. Norman Petty Studios, 1313 W. Seventh Street, Clovis, New Mexico. March 1,1957. Gary Dale (Tollett). vocal; Buddy Holly, guitar; Jerry Allison, drums; Ramona Tollett, June Clark and Niki Sullivan, backing vocals

	GO BOY GO (Floyd Wilson)	VIGO 137	Unissued
	GONE (Smokey Rogers)	VIGO 137	Unissued
	THE GOLDEN ROCKET (C.E. 'Hank' Snow)	VIGO 137	Unissued
	I OVERLOOKED AN ORCHID (Carl Story/S. Lyn/Arthur Q. Smith)	VIGO 137	Unissued

24. Norman Petty Studios, 1313 W. Seventh Street, Clovis, New Mexico. March 12, 1957. Buddy Holly, vocal and guitar; Joe B. Mauldin, bass; Jerry Allison, drums; Niki Sullivan, 2nd vocal on*

	LAST NIGHT (Joe B Mauldin/Buddy Holly/Norman Petty)	VIGO 135	Unissued
	MAYBE BABY* (Buddy Holly/Norman Petty)	MCA 27059	MCM 1002

Possibly recorded during same session: Buddy Holly, vocal and guitar

	WORDS OF LOVE (Buddy Holly)	VIGO 135	Unissued

Buddy Holly, double-tracked vocal and guitar; Norman Petty, organ

	WORDS OF LOVE (Buddy Holly)	Unissued	Unissued

Billy Walker, vocal and guitar; (prob.) Buddy Holly, guitar; (prob.) Joe B. Mauldin, bass; unknown drums; Jerry Allison and The Bowman Brothers, (Lowell Bowman, Jay Bowman, Dee Bowman), backing vocals

41304	ON MY MIND AGAIN (Dean Beard/Slim Willett/Ray Doggett)	Col 40920	Unissued
41305	VIVA LA MATADOR (Billy Walker)	Col 40920	Unissued

NB: Billy Walker has both confirmed and denied in different interviews that Buddy Holly and the Crickets played on this session

24a. Overdub session: Norman Petty Studios, 1313 W. Seventh Street, Clovis, New Mexico. Between October 12 and 14 1957. The Picks (Bill Pickering, John Pickering, Bob Lapham), backing vocals

103532	LAST NIGHT (Joe B Mauldin/Buddy Holly/Norman Petty)	BL 54038	LVA 9081

24b. Overdub session: Norman Petty Studios, 1313 W. Seventh Street, Clovis New Mexico. Prob. February 3 1966. George Tomsco, guitar; Stan Lark, bass; Keith McCormack, rhythm guitar; Doug Roberts, drums

117146	MAYBE BABY (version 1) (Buddy Holly/Norman Petty)	C 001000	Q 72483
	MAYBE BABY (version 2) (Buddy Holly/Norman Petty)	Unissued	Unissued

25. Norman Petty Studios, 1313 W. Seventh Street, Clovis, New Mexico. March or April 1957. Jim Robinson, vocal; Buddy Holly, guitar; Jerry Allison, cardboard box percussion (drums on*); Vi Petty, piano on*; unknown bass; The Bowman Brothers backing vocals on*; The Roses (Robert Linville, Ray Rush, David Bigham), overdubbed backing) vocals on +

	A WHOLE LOTTA LOVIN' (Version 1) (Jim Robinson/Jack Huddle/Norman Petty)	VIGO 137	Unissued
	WHOLE LOTTA LOVIN' (Version 2) (Jim Robinson/Jack Huddle/Norman Petty)	VIGO 137	Unissued
JZSP 42150	WHOLE LOTTA LOVIN' (Version 3)+ (Jim Robinson/Jack Huddle/Norman Petty)	Ep 9234	Unissued
JZSP 42149	IT'S A WONDERFUL FEELING* (Jim Robinson/Norman Petty/Jack Huddle)	Ep 9234	Unissued

Jack Huddle, vocal; Buddy Holly, guitar; Jerry Allison, drums; unknown, bass; The Bowman Brothers backing vocals on*

HO8W 0164	STARLIGHT (Jack Huddle/Jim Robinson/Norman Petty)	Pe 1002	CR 30236
HO8W 0165	BELIEVE ME* (Jim Robinson/Norman Petty)	Pe 1002	CR 30236

26. Norman Petty Studios, 1313 W. Seventh Street, Clovis, New Mexico. April 8, 1957. Buddy Holly, double-tracked vocal, double-tracked guitar; Jerry Allison, drums; Joe B. Mauldin, bass

102255	WORDS OF LOVE (Buddy Holly)	C 61852	LVA 9085

Buddy Holly, vocal and guitar; Jerry Allison, drums; Joe B. Mauldin, bass; Vi Petty, piano

102256	MAILMAN BRING ME NO MORE BLUES (Ruth Roberts/Bill Katz/Stanley Clayton)	C 61852	LVA 9085

26a. Overdub session: Decca Record Co. Ltd., 254 Belsize Road, London NW6. October 1961. Echo added during mastering of single release

[102256]	MAILMAN BRING ME NO MORE BLUES (Ruth Roberts/Bill Katz/Stanley Clayton)	Unissued	Q 72445

27. Norman Petty Studios, 1313 W. Seventh Street, Clovis, New Mexico. Date unknown between April and May 1957. Fred Crawford, vocal; Buddy Holly, guitar; Jerry Allison, drums; (poss.) Joe B. Mauldin, bass; (poss.) The Bowman Brothers, backing vocals

ST 2613	BY THE MISSION WALL (Ken Cline)	St 314	Unissued

28. Norman Petty Studios, 1313 W. Seventh Street, Clovis, New Mexico. May 29, 1957. Buddy Holly, vocal and guitar; Jerry Allison, cardboard box percussion; Joe B. Mauldin, bass; Buddy Holly, Jerry Allison and Niki Sullivan, overdubbed backing vocals (on Version 2 and part of Version 1 only)

	NOT FADE AWAY (incomplete version 1)* (Charles Hardin/Norman Petty)	VIGO 135	Unissued
103104	NOT FADE AWAY (version 2) (Charles Hardin/Norman Petty)	B55035	Q 72298

NB: The incomplete version 1 was spliced with the opening part of version 2 by Steve Hoffman at MCA in order to make a complete master; thus the opening part has backing vocals and the remainder does not.

Buddy Holly, vocal and acoustic guitar; Jerry Allison, knee slapping; Joe B. Mauldin, bass; Vi Petty, celeste

103105	EVERYDAY (Charles Hardin/Norman Petty)	C 61885	Q 72293

28a. Overdub session: Sound Masters Recording Studio, 9717 Jensen Drive, Houston, Texas. June 29, 1984. The Picks (John Pickering, Bill Pickering, Bob Lapham), backing vocals

[103105]	EVERYDAY (Charles Hardin/Norman Petty)	Pi 2221	CDMF 088

29. Norman Petty Studios, 1313 W. Seventh Street, Clovis, New Mexico. Dates unknown between May and July 1957. Buddy Holly, vocal and lead guitar; Niki Sullivan, rhythm guitar; Joe B. Mauldin, bass; Jerry Allison, drums; Vi Petty, piano

104199	READY TEDDY (Robert Blackwell/John Marascalco)	CRL 57210	LVA 9085

Buddy Holly, vocal and guitar; Joe B. Mauldin, bass; Jerry Allison, drums; Norman Petty. organ; Vi Petty, piano

104201	VALLEY OF TEARS (Fats Domino/Dave Bartholomew)	CRL 57210	LVA 9085

Buddy Holly, vocal and lead guitar; Niki Sullivan, rhythm guitar; Joe B. Mauldin, bass; Jerry Allison, drums.

	TELL ME HOW (Charles Hardin/Jerry Allison/Norman Petty)	Unissued	Unissued

30. Norman Petty Studios, 1313 W. Seventh Street, Clovis, New Mexico. June 24, 1957. Jim Robinson, vocal; Buddy Holly, guitar; (poss.) George Atwood, bass; unknown drums; Vi Petty, piano; The Picks (John Pickering, Bill Pickering, Bob Lapham), backing vocals

K80W 2764	A MAN FROM TEXAS (M. Russell/Norman Petty/S. Dougherty)	Bri 2	Unissued

31. Norman Petty Studios, 1313 W. Seventh Street, Clovis, New Mexico. Between June 29 and July 1, 1957. Buddy Holly, vocal and guitar (double-tracked vocal and guitar on *); Joe B. Mauldin, bass; Jerry Allison, drums

	PEGGY SUE (Version 1) (Buddy Holly/Jerry Allison/Norman Petty)	VIGO 135	Unissued
103180	PEGGY SUE (Version 2) (Buddy Holly/Jerry Allison/Norman Petty)	C 61885	Q 72293
103258	LISTEN TO ME* (Charles Hardin/Norman Petty)	C 61947	Q 72288

Probably recorded during this session:

	THAT'LL BE THE DAY JINGLE FOR BOB THEILE (Buddy Holly/Jerry Allison)	VIGO 135	Unissued
	THAT'LL BE THE DAY JINGLE FOR MURRAY DEUTCH (Buddy Holly/Jerry Allison)	VIGO 135	Unissued
	THAT'LL BE THE DAY JINGLE FOR BILL RANDALL (Buddy Holly/Jerry Allison)	Unissued	Unissued

NB: The Crickets also recorded promotional announcements for Bill Randall

Buddy Holly, vocal and guitar; Joe B. Mauldin, bass, Jerry Allison, drums

	OH BOY! (Sonny West/Bill Tilghman/Norman Petty)	VIGO 135	Unissued

31a. Overdub session: Norman Petty Studios, 1313 W. Seventh Street, Clovis, New Mexico. August 19, 1957. The Picks (John Pickering, Bill Pickering, Bob Lapham), backing vocals

[103179]	OH BOY! (Sonny West/Bill Tilghman/Norman Petty)	B 55035	Q 72298

31b. Overdub session: Sound Masters Recording Studio, 9717 Jensen Drive, Houston, Texas. June 29, 1984. The Picks (John Pickering, Bill Pickering, Bob Lapham), backing vocals

[103180]	PEGGY SUE (Version 2) (Buddy Holly/Jerry Allison/Norman Petty)	Pi 2221	CDMF 088

32. Norman Petty Studios, 1313 W. Seventh Street, Clovis, New Mexico. July 1, 1957. Buddy Holly, double-tracked vocal and guitar; Joe B. Mauldin, bass; Jerry Allison, drums; unknown cricket, chirping

103257	I'M GONNA LOVE YOU TOO (Joe B. Mauldin/Norman Petty /Niki Sullivan)	C 61947	Q 72288

NB: This recording comprised two versions which were spliced together by Norman Petty in order to include the sound of a cricket chirping in the studio echo chamber at the end of one version.

33. Norman Petty Studios, 1313 W. Seventh Street, Clovis, New Mexico. July 14, 1957. Gary Dale (Tollett), vocal; Buddy Holly, guitar; Jerry Allison, drums; unknown bass; Ramona Tollett and The Picks (John Pickering, Bill Pickering, Bob Lapham), backing vocals

	LOOK TO THE FUTURE (Norman Petty/Niki Sullivan)	VIGO 137	Unissued
	HONEY HONEY (Gary Tollett)	VIGO 137	Unissued

NB: The unusual (for 1957) guitar sound on Look To The Future was achieved by plugging Holly's guitar into Norman Petty's 'Leslietone' organ amplifier

34. Norman Petty Studios, 1313 W. Seventh Street, Clovis, New Mexico. (Prob.) during July 1957. Sherry Davis, vocal; Buddy Holly, lead guitar; Jack Vaughn, rhythm guitar; Jerry Allison, drums; unknown bass; The Picks (John Pickering, Bill Pickering, Bob Lapham), backing vocals; Gene Medley, backing vocal on+

F80W 7200	BROKEN PROMISES (Ray Winkler/Ralph Newton)	Fa 1001	Unissued
F80W 7199	HUMBLE HEART+ (John Loftus)	Fa 1001	Unissued

35. Norman Petty Studios, 1313 W. Seventh Street, Clovis, New Mexico. (Prob.) during July 1957. Charlie Phillips, vocal; Buddy Holly, lead guitar, harmony vocal on + ; Jack Vaughn, rhythm guitar; Jerry Allison, drums; Vi Petty, piano; Norman Petty, organ; Jimmy Blakely, steel guitar; unknown bass; The Roses (Robert Linville, Ray Rush, David Bigham), backing vocals

	SUGARTIME (Version 1) (Charlie Phillips/Otis Echoles)	Unissued	Unissued
103260	SUGARTIME (Version 2) (Charlie Phillips/Otis Echoles)	C 61908	Unissued
103259	ONE FADED ROSE+ (Otis Echoles/Nina Baggett/Charlie Phillips)	C 61908	Unissued

36. Norman Petty Studios, 1313 W. Seventh Street, Clovis, New Mexico. July 20, 1957. Buddy Holly, vocal (guitar on*); Niki Sullivan, guitar on +; Joe B. Mauldin, bass; Jerry Allison, drums

	SEND ME SOME LOVIN' (version 1)+ (John Marascalco/Lloyd Price)	VIGO 135	Unissued
	SEND ME SOME LOVIN' (version 2)+ (John Marascalco/Lloyd Price)	Unissued	Unissued
	IT'S TOO LATE* (version 1) (Chuck Willis)	VIGO 135	Unissued
	IT'S TOO LATE* (version 2) (Chuck Willis)	Unissued	Unissued

36a. Overdub session: Norman Petty Studios, 1313 W. Seventh Street, Clovis, New Mexico. Between October 12 and 14 1957. The Picks (John Pickering, Bill Pickering, Bob Lapham) backing vocals

103531	SEND ME SOME LOVIN' (version 2) (John Marascalco/Lloyd Price)	BL 54038	LVA 9081
103528	IT'S TOO LATE* (version 2) (Chuck Willis)	BL 54038	LVA 9081
103529	TELL ME HOW (Charles Hardin/Jerry Allison/Norman Petty)	B 54038	Q 72307

37. Norman Petty Studios, 1313 W. Seventh Street, Clovis, New Mexico. Between July 20 and 22, 1957. Norman Petty, organ; Vi Petty, piano; Buddy Holly, guitar, Mike Mitchell, percussion.

	MOONDREAMS (Version 1) (Norman Petty)	Col 41039	Unissued

As above, plus The Picks (John Pickering, Bill Pickering, Bob Lapham), harmony vocals

	MOONDREAMS (Version 2) (Norman Petty)	Unissued	Unissued

38. The Officers Club Lounge, Tinker US Airforce Base, Oklahoma City. (Prob) September 30, 1957. Buddy Holly, vocal and guitar; Niki Sullivan, rhythm guitar (2nd lead guitar on *); Joe B. Mauldin, bass; Jerry Allison, drums.

	AN EMPTY CUP (And A Broken Date) (Roy Orbison/Norman Petty)	Unissued	Unissued
	ROCK ME MY BABY (Shorty Long/Susan Heather)	Unissued	Unissued
	YOU'VE GOT LOVE (Johnny Wilson/Roy Orbison/Norman Petty)	Unissued	Unissued
	MAYBE BABY* (Buddy Holly/Norman Petty)	Unissued	Unissued

38a. Overdub session: Norman Petty Studios, 1313 W. Seventh Street, Clovis New Mexico. Between October 12 and 14, 1957. The Picks (John Pickering, Bill Pickering, Bob Lapham), backing vocals

103530	AN EMPTY CUP (And A Broken Date) (Roy Orbison/Norman Petty)	BL 54038	LVA 9081
103533	ROCK ME MY BABY (Shorty Long/Susan Heather)	BL 54038	LVA 9081
103526	YOU'VE GOT LOVE (Johnny Wilson/Roy Orbison/Norman Petty)	BL 54038	LVA 9081
103527	MAYBE BABY* (Buddy Holly/Norman Petty)	BL 54038	Q 72307

39. Georgia Auditorium, Vancouver, Canada. October 23, 1957. Buddy Holly; Red Robinson

	INTERVIEW WITH RED ROBINSON	S 10003	RSR-LP 1005

40. Albany Hotel, Denver, Colorado. November 2, 1957. Buddy Holly, Jerry Allison, Eddie Cochran, Guybo Smith, Freeman Hover

	INTERVIEW WITH FREEMAN HOVER	LG 60006	RSRCD 008

NB: Recorded for Radio KCSR, Chadron, Nebraska

41. Municipal Auditorium, Topeka, Kansas. November 5, 1957. Buddy Holly, Dale Lowery

	INTERVIEW WITH DALE LOWERY (short version)	Cr 00100	UPLP 004
	INTERVIEW WITH DALE LOWERY (long version)	VIGO 136	Unissued

NB: Recorded for KTOP Radio, Topeka, Kansas

42. Ed Sullivan Theatre, 1697 Broadway, New York, NY. December 1, 1957. Buddy Holly, vocal and guitar; Joe B. Mauldin. bass; Jerry Allison, drums

| | THAT'LL BE THE DAY (Buddy Holly/Jerry Allison) | Cr 002000 | CDSP 807 |
| | PEGGY SUE (Buddy Holly/Jerry Allison/Norman Petty) | Cr 002000 | CDSP 807 |

Buddy Holly, Ed Sullivan:

| | INTERVIEW WITH ED SULLIVAN | Cr 002000 | CDSP 807 |

Broadcast live on The Ed Sullivan TV Show (Toast of the Town). NB Although Niki Sullivan appeared on screen his guitar was not audible.

43. Norman Petty Studios, 1313 W. Seventh Street, Clovis, New Mexico. December 19, 1957.
Buddy Holly. vocal and guitar; Joe B. Mauldin, bass; Jerry Allison, drums, cardboard box percussion on *; C. W. Kendall jr., piano.

104204	LITTLE BABY (Buddy Holly/Norman Petty/C.W. Kendall, jr)	CRL 57210	LVA 9085
104200	(You're So Square) BABY I DON'T CARE* (Jerry Leiber/Mike Stoller)	CRL 57210	LVA 9085
104203	LOOK AT ME* (Buddy Holly/Jerry Allison/Norman Petty)	CRL 57210	LVA 9085

43a. Overdub session: Decca Record Co. Ltd., 254 Belsize Road, London NW6. October 1961. Echo added during mastering of single release
| *104203* | *LOOK AT ME (Buddy Holly/Jerry Allison/Norman Petty)* | *Unissued* | *Q 72445* |

43b. Overdub session: Sound Masters Recording Studio, 9717 Jensen Drive, Houston, Texas. June 29, 1984. The Picks (John Pickering, Bill Pickering, Bob Lapham), backing vocals
| *[104200]* | *(You're So Square) BABY I DON'T CARE* (Jerry Leiber/Mike Stoller)* | *LG 6006* | *CDMF 088* |

44. Norman Petty Studios, 1313 W. Seventh Street, Clovis, New Mexico. Unknown date (prob.) December 1957 or April 1957. Buddy Holly, vocal and acoustic guitar; Jerry Allison, drums (and acoustic guitar at beginning of version 1)

	MONA (Version 1) (Ellas McDaniel)	VIGO 135	Unissued
	MONA (Version 2) (Ellas McDaniel)	VIGO 135	Unissued
	MONA (Version 3) (Ellas McDaniel)	VIGO 135	Unissued

NB: Rehearsal session only, remainder of tape reel may have been erased by Norman Petty when re-using tape for a session with the Big Beats during 1957 or 1958

45. CBS-TV Studio, New York, NY. December 28, 1957. Buddy Holly, vocal and guitar; Joe B. Mauldin, bass,; Jerry Allison, drums

| | PEGGY SUE (Buddy Holly/Jerry Allison/Norman Petty) | Unissued | Unissued |

Broadcast live on the CBS Arthur Murray Party TV Show

46. Bell Sound Studios, 237 W. 54th Street, New York, NY. From 8 p.m. January 25, 1958 to 2 a.m. January 26, 1958.
Buddy Holly, vocal; Al Caiola, guitar; Donald Arnone, rhythm guitar; Joe B. Mauldin. bass; Jerry Allison, drums; Norman Petty, piano; William Marine, Robert Bollinger, Robert Harter, Merril Ostrus and Abby Hoffer, backing vocals. Produced by Milton De Lugg; A& R: Sonny Lester

	RAVE ON (Take 1) (Sonny West/Bill Tilghman/Norman Petty)	Unissued	Unissued
	RAVE ON (Take 2) (Sonny West/Bill Tilghman/Norman Petty)	Unissued	Unissued
104202	RAVE ON (Take 3) (Sonny West/Bill Tilghman/Norman Petty)	CRL 57210	Q 72325
	THAT'S MY DESIRE (false start take 1) (Helmy Kresa/Carroll Loveday)	VIGO 135	Unissued
	THAT'S MY DESIRE (incomplete take 2) (Helmy Kresa/Carroll Loveday)	VIGO 135	Unissued
104215	THAT'S MY DESIRE (take 3) (Helmy Kresa/Carroll Loveday)	MCA 27059	MCM 1002

NB Although tapes of takes 1 & 2 of Rave On were sent to Norman Petty in 1962 they have not yet been traced and may not have survived.

46a. Overdub session: Norman Petty Studios, 1313 W. Seventh Street, Clovis New Mexico. Poss. February 3 1966. George Tomsco, guitar; Stan Lark, bass; Keith McCormack, rhythm guitar; Doug Roberts, drums
| *117145 [104215]* | *THAT'S MY DESIRE (Helmy Kresa/Carroll Loveday)* | *MCA-6 80000* | *Q 72483* |
| | *THAT'S MY DESIRE (Helmy Kresa/Carroll Loveday)* | *Unissued* | *Unissued* |

47. Ed Sullivan Theatre, 1697 Broadway, New York, NY. January 26. 1958. Buddy Holly, vocal and guitar; Joe B, Mauldin. bass; Jerry Allison, drums

| | OH BOY! (Sonny West/Bill Tilghman/Norman Petty) | VIGO 136 | Unissued |

Broadcast live on The Ed Sullivan TV Show (Toast of the Town)

48. Newcastle Stadium, Newcastle, Australia. January 31, 1958. Buddy Holly, Norman Petty, Pat Barton,

| | INTERVIEW WITH PAT BARTON (Short version) | S 10003 | Unissued |
| | INTERVIEW WITH PAT BARTON (Long version) | VIGO 136 | Unissued |

NB: Portions broadcast on Radio 2KO, Newcastle, Australia

49. Nurses Memorial Centre, St. Kilda's Road, Melbourne, Australia. February 5, 1958. Live recording with Jerry Lee Lewis, Paul Anka, Jodie Sands, Johnny O'Keefe and the Colgate Palmolive Showcase Band for Radio 3AW, Melbourne. Broadcast in two parts on February 17 and 24, 1958 by 3AW and other Macquarie Network radio stations; Compere: Geoff Manion
Buddy Holly, vocal and guitar; Joe B. Mauldin, bass; Jerry Allison, drums.

| | TITLES UNKNOWN | Unissued | Unissued |

NB The songs recorded were probably those performed by the Crickets during their Australian tour. It is possible this recording has survived in the Canberra, Australia, National Sound Archives, where it was sent by 3AW. The archive, which is still not yet fully catalogued, includes many similar recordings made over thirty or more years.

50. Norman Petty Studios, 1313 W. Seventh Street, Clovis, New Mexico. February 12, 1958. Buddy Holly, vocal and guitar; Joe B. Mauldin, bass; Jerry Allison, cymbals

| 104739 | WELL...ALL RIGHT (Buddy Holly/Jerry Allison/Norman Petty/Joe B Mauldin) | C 62051 | Q 72346 |

50a. Overdub session: Sound Masters Recording Studio, 9717 Jensen Drive, Houston, Texas. June 28, 1984. The Picks (John Pickering, Bill Pickering, Bob Lapham), backing vocals
| *[104739]* | *WELL...ALL RIGHT (Buddy Holly/Jerry Allison/Norman Petty/Joe B Mauldin)* | *LG 6006* | *CDMF 088* |

51. Norman Petty Studios, 1313 W. Seventh Street, Clovis, New Mexico. (Prob.) February 14, 1958. Buddy Holly, vocal and guitar; Joe B. Mauldin, bass; Jerry Allison, drums (cardboard box on *); Norman Petty, organ on *

	TAKE YOUR TIME (incomplete version 1)* (Buddy Holly/Norman Petty)	VIGO 135	Unissued
	TAKE YOUR TIME (incomplete version 2)* (Buddy Holly/Norman Petty)	VIGO 135	Unissued
	TAKE YOUR TIME (version 3)* (Buddy Holly/Norman Petty)	VIGO 135	Unissued
104738	TAKE YOUR TIME (version 4)* (Buddy Holly/Norman Petty)	C 61985	Q 72325
	FOOL'S PARADISE (Version 1) (Sonny Leglaire/Horace Linsley)	VIGO 135	Unissued
	FOOL'S PARADISE (Version 2) (Sonny Leglaire/Horace Linsley)	VIGO 135	Unissued
	FOOL'S PARADISE (Version 3) (Sonny Leglaire/Horace Linsley)	VIGO 135	Unissued
	THINK IT OVER (false start version 1) (Buddy Holly/Norman Petty/Jerry Allison)	VIGO 135	Unissued
	THINK IT OVER (false start version 2) (Buddy Holly/Norman Petty/Jerry Allison)	VIGO 135	Unissued
	THINK IT OVER (version 3) (Buddy Holly/Norman Petty/Jerry Allison)	VIGO 135	Unissued
	THINK IT OVER (version 4) (Buddy Holly/Norman Petty/Jerry Allison)	VIGO 135	Unissued
	THINK IT OVER (version 5) (Buddy Holly/Norman Petty/Jerry Allison)	VIGO 135	Unissued

51a. Overdub session: Norman Petty Studios, 1313 W. Seventh Street, Clovis, New Mexico. *February 19, 1958. Vi Petty, piano; The Roses (Robert Linville, Ray Rush, David Bigham), backing vocals*

104994	FOOL'S PARADISE (Version 3) (Sonny Leglaire/Horace Linsley)	B 55072	Q 72329
104993	THINK IT OVER (Version 5) (Buddy Holly/Norman Pelly/Jerry Allison)	B 55072	Q 72329

Probably recorded at this session:
Jerry Allison. vocal; Buddy Holly, rhythm guitar and backing vocal; overdubbed lead guitar and backing vocal on *; Joe B. Mauldin, bass; Bo Clarke. drums; unknown (prob. Jerry Allison, Joe B. Mauldin & Bo Clarke), handclaps on *; (prob) Jerry Allison, overdubbed drumsticks on+; Norman Petty, overdubbed water-filled wine glasses on +

	REAL WILD CHILD (Version 1) (J O'Keefe/D. Owens/J. Greenan)	VIGO 137	Unissued
105286	REAL WILD CHILD (Version 2)* (J O'Keefe/D. Owens/J. Greenan)	C 62017	Q 72341
	OH YOU BEAUTIFUL DOLL (Version 1) (A.S. Brown/N.D. Ayer)	VIGO 137	Unissued
	OH YOU BEAUTIFUL DOLL (Version 2) (A.S. Brown/N.D. Ayer)	VIGO 137	Unissued
105287	OH YOU BEAUTIFUL DOLL (Version 2)+ (A.S. Brown/N.D. Ayer)	C 62017	Q 72341

NB: C 62017 and Q 72341 credited to 'Ivan'

52. Unknown location, prob. backstage Fort Hesterley Amory, Tampa, Florida. (Prob.) February 21, 1958. Buddy Holly, guitar and vocal, Jerry Lee Lewis, piano and vocal; Bob Chesney

INTERVIEW WITH BOB CHESNEY	Unissued	Unissued
DROWN IN MY OWN TEARS (Henry Glover)	Unissued	Unissued
HALLELUJAH I LOVE HER SO (Ray Charles)	Unissued	Unissued

53. Unknown location, prob. Fort Hesterley Amory, Tampa, Florida. (Prob.) February 21, 1958. Buddy Holly, vocal and guitar; Joe B. Mauldin, bass; Jerry Allison, drums

EVERYDAY (fragment) (Charles Hardin/Norman Petty)	Unissued	Unissued
THAT'LL BE THE DAY (fragment) (Buddy Holly/Jerry Allison/Norman Petty)	Unissued	Unissued

54. The London Palladium, Argyle Street, London W1, England. March 2, 1958. Buddy Holly, vocal and guitar; Joe B. Mauldin, bass; Jerry Allison, drums

THAT'LL BE THE DAY (Buddy Holly/Jerry Allison/Norman Petty)	Cr 001000	Unissued
PEGGY SUE (Buddy Holly/Jerry Allison/Norman Petty)	Cr 001000	Unissued
OH BOY! (Sonny West/Bill Tilghman/Norman Petty)	Cr 001000	Unissued

NB: Broadcast live by Associated TeleVision and sound recording off-air preserved by Jack and Vic Chinn

55. Studio 2, BBC Riverside TV Studios, Crisp Road, Hammersmith, London, W6, England. March 14 1958. Buddy Holly, vocal and guitar; Joe B. Mauldin, bass, Jerry Allison, drums

MAYBE BABY (Buddy Holly/Norman Petty)	Unissued	Unissued

NB: transmitted March 27th 1958 by BBC Television and sound only recorded off-air by Fred Porter
(Prob.) Buddy Holly

SPOKEN TRAILER FOR OFF THE RECORD	Unissued	Unissued

NB: transmitted March 26th 1958 by BBC Television. The film and soundtrack to these tele-recordings were, according to their records, destroyed by the BBC in March, 1960

56. Norman Petty Studios, 1313 W. Seventh Street, Clovis, New Mexico. May 25,1958. Buddy Holly, vocal and rhythm guitar; Tommy Allsup, lead guitar; Joe B. Mauldin, bass; Jerry Allison, drums

	LONESOME TEARS (Buddy Holly)	Unissued	Unissued
	IT'S SO EASY (Buddy Holly/Norman Petty)	Unissued	Unissued

Buddy Holly, vocal and rhythm guitar; Tommy Allsup. lead guitar; George Atwood, bass; Jerry Allison. drums

105511	HEARTBEAT (Bob Montgomery/Norman Petty)	C 60251	Q72346

56a. Overdub session: Norman Petty Studios, 1313 W. Seventh Street, Clovis, New Mexico. *May 27,1958. The Roses (Robert Linville, Ray Rush, David Bigham), backing vocals*

105563	LONESOME TEARS (Buddy Holly)	B 55094	Q 72343
105562	IT'S SO EASY (Buddy Holly/Norman Petty)	B 55094	Q 72343

56b. Overdub session: Sound Masters Recording Studio, 9717 Jensen Drive, Houston, Texas. *June 29, 1984. The Picks (John Pickering, Bill Pickering, Bob Lapham), backing vocals*

[105511]	HEARTBEAT (Bob Montgomery/Norman Petty)	LG 6006	CDMF 088

57. Norman Petty Studios, 1313 W. Seventh Street, Clovis, New Mexico. June 2, 1958. Buddy Holly. double-tracked vocal and rhythm guitar; Tommy Allsup. lead guitar; George Atwood, bass; Bo Clarke. drums

	LOVE'S MADE A FOOL OF YOU (Buddy Holly/Bob Montgomery)	VIGO 135	Unissued
113149	WISHING (Buddy Holly/Bob Montgomery)	C 62369	Q 72466

57a. Overdub session: Norman Petty Studios, 1313 W. Seventh Street, Clovis, New Mexico. *January 7, 1964. Unknown, handclaps*

114368	LOVE'S MADE A FOOL OF YOU (Buddy Holly/Bob Montgomery)	CRL 57450	LVA 9222

57b. Overdub session: Norman Petty Studios, 1313 W. Seventh Street, Clovis, New Mexico. *Unknown date between January and December 1964. Unknown, rhythm guitar*

114085	WISHING (Buddy Holly/Bob Montgomery)	CRL 57463	LVA 9227

58. Norman Petty Studios, 1313 W. Seventh Street, Clovis, New Mexico. June 6 and 7, 1958. Carolyn Hester, vocal and guitar; Buddy Holly, guitar; George Atwood, bass; (poss.) Jerry Allison, drums or percussion

TAKE YOUR TIME (Buddy Holly/Norman Petty)	Unissued	Unissued
A LITTLE WHILE AGO (Carolyn Hester)	Unissued	Unissued
HURRY SANTA HURRY (Gordon Hester/Norman Petty)	Unissued	Unissued
CHRISTMAS IN KILLARNEY (Trad arr. Carolyn Hester)	Unissued	Unissued

59. Norman Petty Studios, 1313 W. Seventh Street, Clovis, New Mexico. (Prob) June 1958. Buddy Holly, guitar; George Atwood, bass; Jerry Allison, drums; Vi Petty, piano; Lloyd Call, overdubbed vocal on *;

JO8W 0247	IF I HAD KNOWN* (Lloyd Call/Norman Petty)	NVJ 1321	Unissued

Ken James (akaHomer Tankersley) & The Roses (Robert Linville, Ray Rush, David Bigham), overdubbed vocals on + using same backing track

LITTLE COWBOY+ (Lloyd Call/Norman Petty)	Unissued	Unissued

60. KPIX TV Studios, San Francisco, California. June 11 1958. Buddy Holly, Joe B Mauldin, Ted Randal

INTERVIEW WITH TED RANDAL	Unissued	Unissued

Broadcast live on KPIX-TV, San Francisco

61. Coral Records Studios, The Pythian Temple, 135 W. 70th Street, New York, NY. Between 8 pm and 10 pm June 19, 1958. Buddy Holly, vocal; Al Chernet, guitar; George Barnes. lead guitar; Sanford Bloch, bass; Ernest Hayes, piano; David "Panama" Francis, drums; Philip Kraus, drums; Sam Taylor. alto saxophone; Helen Way. Harriet Young, Maeretha Stewart and Theresa Merritt, backing vocals. Produced by Dick Jacobs; Musicians contractor, C. John "Jack" Hansen

105182	EARLY IN THE MORNING (Bobby Darin/Woody Harris)	C 62006	Q 72333
	NOW WE'RE ONE (fragment) (Bobby Darin)	VIGO 135	Unissued
105183	NOW WE'RE ONE (Bobby Darin)	C 62006	Q 72333

NB This session was recorded experimentally in stereo (according to Coral files and Norman Petty) but these recordings have probably not survived.

62. Radio Station KLLL, Great Plains Building, Lubbock, Texas. September 1, 1958. Buddy Holly. vocal and guitar

	PROMOTIONAL JINGLE (to tune of EVERYDAY) (Buddy Holly)	Pr 102	Unissued
	PROMOTIONAL JINGLE (to tune of PEGGY SUE) (Buddy Holly/Jerry Allison)	Pr 102	Unissued

63. Norman Petty Studios, 1313 W. Seventh Street, Clovis, New Mexico. September 7, 1958. Jerry Engler, vocal; Buddy Holly, guitar and overdubbed chimes on +; unknown, bass; unknown, drums

	I SENT YOU ROSES (Jerry Engler)	Unissued	RCCD 3017
	WHAT A YOU GONNA DO? (Jerry Engler)	Cl 55037	RCCD 3017

64. Norman Petty Studios, 1313 W. Seventh Street, Clovis, New Mexico. September 10, 1958. Buddy Holly, vocal and guitar; Joe B. Mauldin; bass; Jerry Allison, drums; Curtis Ousley (aka King Curtis), tenor saxophone

	COME BACK BABY (version 1) (Fred Neil/Norman Petty)	Unissued	Unissued
	COME BACK BABY (version 2) (Fred Neil/Norman Petty)	C 7/57450	LVA9222
	REMINISCING (King Curtis)	Unissued	Unissued

Waylon Jennings, vocal on *; Buddy Holly, guitar; George Atwood, bass; Bo Clarke, drums; Curtis Ousley (aka King Curtis), tenor saxophone; The Roses (Robert Linville, Ray Rush, David Bigham), overdubbed backing vocals on +. Producer: Buddy Holly for Prism Recording Company

	WHEN SIN STOPS (Take 1) (Bob Venable)	Unissued	Unissued
	WHEN SIN STOPS (Take 2) (Bob Venable)	Unissued	Unissued
	WHEN SIN STOPS (Take 3) (Bob Venable)	VIGO 137	Unissued
	WHEN SIN STOPS (Take 4)* (Bob Venable)	Unissued	Unissued
	WHEN SIN STOPS (Take 5)* (Bob Venable)	VIGO 137	Unissued
107120	WHEN SIN STOPS (Take 6)*+ (Bob Venable)	B 55130	CDSP 807
107121	JOLE BLON* (Harry Choates)	B 55130	CDSP 807

64a. Overdub session: Norman Petty Studios, 1313 W. Seventh Street, Clovis, New Mexico. c. 1962. George Tomsco, guitar; Keith McCormack, rhythm guitar

112352	*REMINISCING (King Curtis)*	C 62329	Q 72455

64b. Overdub session: Norman Petty Studios, 1313 W. Seventh Street, Clovis, New Mexico. (prob.) October 29, 1962. George Tomsco, guitar; Stan Lark, bass; Keith McCormack, rhythm guitar; Eric Budd, drums

112762	*REMINISCING (King Curtis)*	CRL 757426	LVA 9212

64c. Overdub session: Sound Masters Recording Studio, 9717 Jensen Drive, Houston, Texas. June 29, 1984. The Picks (John Pickering, Bill Pickering, Bob Lapham), backing vocals

[112352]	*REMINISCING (King Curtis)*	Pi 2221	CDMF 088

65. WNEW-TV Studios, 205, E. 67th Street, New York. NY. Recorded September 23, 1958. Buddy Holly; Alan Freed

	INTERVIEW WITH ALAN FREED	C 001000	CDSP 807

Broadcast by WNEW-TV on October 2,1958 and (sound only) recorded off-air by Val Warren.

66. Beltone Recording Studio, 4 W. 31st Street, New York. NY. September 30, 1958 Lou Giordano, vocal; Buddy Holly, guitar; Phil Everly. guitar; unknown bass; unknown drums; Buddy Holly, Phil Everly and Joey Villa, falsetto vocals on *; Produced by Buddy Holly and Phil Everly

	STAY CLOSE TO ME (7 false starts) (Buddy Holly)	Unissued	Unissued
	STAY CLOSE TO ME (Take 1) (Buddy Holly)	Unissued	Unissued
	STAY CLOSE TO ME (Take 2) (Buddy Holly)	Unissued	Unissued
	STAY CLOSE TO ME (Take 3) (Buddy Holly)	Unissued	Unissued
106309	STAY CLOSE TO ME (Take 4) (Buddy Holly)	B 55115	CDSP 807
	DON'T CHA KNOW (3 false starts) (Phil Everly)	Unissued	Unissued
	DON'T CHA KNOW (Take 1) (Phil Everly)	Unissued	Unissued
	DON'T CHA KNOW (Take 2) (Phil Everly)	Unissued	Unissued
106310	DON'T CHA KNOW (Take 3)* (Phil Everly)	B 55115	CDSP 807

NB The issued takes only were purchased by Brunswick Records. Remaining takes may not have survived.

67. Coral Records Studios. Pythian Temple, 135 W. 70th Street, New York, NY. Between 7 p.m. and 10.30 p.m. October 21. 1958. Buddy Holly. vocal; Al Caiola, guitar; Sanford Bloch, bass; Ernest Hayes. piano; Doris Johnson. harp; Clifford Leeman, drums; Abraham "Boomie" Richman, tenor saxophone; Sylvan Shulman, Leo Kruczek, Leonard Posner, Irving Spice. Ray Free, Herbert Bourne. Julius Held and Paul Winter, violins; David Schwartz and Howard Kay, violas; Maurice Brown and Maurice Bialkin, cellos. Producer: Dick Jacobs; A & R: C. John "Jack" Hansen

105869	TRUE LOVE WAYS (mono mix) (Buddy Holly/Norman Petty)	CRL 57326	Q 72397
105869	TRUE LOVE WAYS (stereo mix) (Buddy Holly/Norman Petty)	MCA6-80000	CDSP 807
105870	IT DOESN'T MATTER ANYMORE (mono mix) (Paul Anka)	C 62074	Q 72360
105870	IT DOESN'T MATTER ANYMORE (stereo mix) (Paul Anka)	7CXSB-8	CDSP 802
105871	RAINING IN MY HEART (mono mix) (Boudleaux Bryant/Felice Bryant)	C 62074	Q 72360
105871	RAINING IN MY HEART (stereo mix) (Boudleaux Bryant/Felice Bryant)	C 757269	Unissued
105872	MOONDREAMS (mono mix) (Norman Petty)	CRL 57326	Q 72397
105872	MOONDREAMS (stereo mix) (Norman Petty)	MCA6-8000	CDSP 807

NB: This session was recorded on Ampex 4-track recorders and mixed later into stereo versions, although only RAINING IN MY HEART was released in stereo at the time. It was Coral Records practice in 1958 to mix directly from the console into mono for reference but retain the 3 or 4-track tapes for later stereo or mono mixing and re-mixing. The stereo versions on CDSP 807 were re-mixed by Malcolm Jones at Abbey Road Studios, London.

67a. Overdub session: Sound Masters Recording Studio, 9717 Jensen Drive, Houston, Texas. June 28, 1984. The Picks (John Pickering, Bill Pickering, Bob Lapham), backing vocals

[105869]	*TRUE LOVE WAYS (Buddy Holly/Norman Petty)*	Pi 2221	CDMF 088

68. WFIL-TV Studios, 46th & Market Street, Philadelphia, PA. October 28, 1958. Buddy Holly; Joe B. Mauldin; Jerry Allison; Dick Clark

	INTERVIEW WITH DICK CLARK	MCA6-8000	CDSP 807

Broadcast on American Bandstand. (Sound only tape-recorded off-air by Val Warren)

69. Apartment 4H The Brevoort, 11 Fifth Avenue, New York, NY. December 3,1958. Buddy Holly, vocal and acoustic guitar

THAT'S WHAT THEY SAY (Version 1) (Buddy Holly)	Unissued	Unissued
THAT'S WHAT THEY SAY (Version 2) (Buddy Holly)	VIGO 136	Unissued
WHAT TO DO (Buddy Holly)	VIGO 136	Unissued

70. Apartment 4H The Brevoort, 11 Fifth Avenue, New York, NY. December 5,1958. Buddy Holly, vocal and acoustic guitar

PEGGY SUE GOT MARRIED (Buddy Holly)	MCA6-8000	CDSP 807

71. Apartment 4H, The Brevoort, 11 Fifth Avenue, New York, NY. December 8. 1958. Buddy Holly. vocal and acoustic guitar

THAT MAKES IT TOUGH (Buddy Holly)	MCA6-8000	CDSP 807

72. Apartment 4H, The Brevoort. 11 Fifth Avenue, New York, NY. December 14, 1958. Buddy Holly. vocal and acoustic guitar

CRYING. WAITING. HOPING (Buddy Holly)	VIGO 136	Unissued

73. Apartment 4H, The Brevoort, 11 Fifth Avenue, New York, NY. December 17, 1958. Buddy Holly. vocal and acoustic guitar

LEARNING THE GAME (Buddy Holly)	Cr 001000	CDSP 807

70/72a. Overdub session: Studio A, Coral Records, 48 W. 57th Street, New York, NY. *June 30, 1959. Andrew Ackers, piano; David 'Panama' Francis, drums; Sandford Block, bass; Donald Arnone, guitar; The Ray Charles Singers, backing vocals. Producer C. John "Jack" Hansen*

PEGGY SUE GOT MARRIED (Buddy Holly)	C 62134	Q 72376
CRYING, WAITING, HOPING (Buddy Holly)	C 62134	Q 72376

69/71/73a. Overdub session: Studio A, Coral Records, 48 W. 57th Street, New York, NY. *January 1st, 1960. Andrew Ackers, piano; David 'Panama' Francis, drums; Sandford Block, bass; Donald Arnone, guitar; The Ray Charles Singers, backing vocals. Producer C. John "Jack" Hansen*

108598	THAT'S WHAT THEY SAY (Version 2) (Buddy Holly)	CRL 57326	LVA 9127
108599	WHAT TO DO (Buddy Holly)	CRL 57326	LVA 9127
108600	LEARNING THE GAME (Buddy Holly)	C 57326	Q 72411
108601	THAT MAKES IT TOUGH (Buddy Holly)	CRL 572326	Q 72411

69/70/71/72/73b. Overdub session: Norman Petty Studios, 1313 W. Seventh Street, Clovis, New Mexico. *Dates unknown between June 1962 and December 1963. Prob. George Tomsco, guitar; Stan Lark, bass; Doug Roberts or Eric Budd, drums*

114086	WHAT TO DO (Buddy Holly)	C 62448	Q 72469
114088	PEGGY SUE GOT MARRIED (Buddy Holly)	DXSE 7-207	FEP 2070
114090	CRYING, WAITING, HOPING (Buddy Holly)	Cr 0020000	FEP 2070
114092	THAT MAKES IT TOUGH (Buddy Holly)	Pr 101	FEP 2070
114093	THAT'S WHAT THEY SAY (Buddy Holly)	Cr 0020000	CPS 71
114096	LEARNING THE GAME (Buddy Holly)	Cr 0020000	FEP 2067

69b. Overdub session: Sound Masters Recording Studio, 9717 Jensen Drive, Houston, Texas. *June 28, 1984*
The Picks (John Pickering, Bill Pickering, Bob Lapham), backing vocals

[114093]	THAT'S WHAT THEY SAY (Buddy Holly)	Pi 2221	CDMF 088

70b. Overdub session: Pelican Studios, 15 Stukeley Street, London WC2 and Abbey Road Studios, 3 Abbey Road, London NW8, England. *1995 The Hollies; Tony Hicks, rhythm guitar & lead guitar; Bobby Elliott, drums; Ian Parker, keyboards; Ray Stiles, bass; Alan Coates, percussion.*

PEGGY SUE GOT MARRIED (Buddy Holly)	DRND 11260	MCD 11260

NB: This session is not strictly an overdub of the original vocal and guitar demo, as the instruments on the June 30, 1959 overdub version were removed using computer technology. Further vocal and instrumental overdubs were then added to the resulting vocal only tape, thus the distortion which appeared on the June 30, 1959 overdub remains.

74. Radio Station KLLL, Great Plains Life Building, Lubbock, Texas (Prob.) December 27, 1958. Buddy Holly, vocal and guitar; Waylon Jennings and Ray "Slim" Corbin. handclapping

111007	YOU'RE THE ONE (Buddy Holly/Waylon Jennings/Slim Corbin)	CRL 57450	LVA 9222

(Poss) recorded during the same session: Waylon Jennings, vocal and guitar; Buddy Holly, guitar

MORE AND MORE (Waylon Jennings)	Unissued	Unissued

74a. Overdub session: Norman Petty Studios, Lyceum Theatre, Main Street, Clovis, New Mexico. *Date unknown, (prob.) between December 1967 and December, 1968. George Tomsco, guitar; Jimmy Gilmer, guitar; Stan Lark, bass; Doug Roberts,drums; Norman Petty, Ondeoline*

120719	YOU'RE THE ONE (Buddy Holly/Waylon Jennings/Slim Corbin)	CRL 757504	MU 1059

75. Apartment 4H, The Brevoort, 11 Fifth Avenue, New York, NY. Unknown dates between January 1 and 20, 1959. Buddy Holly, vocal and acoustic guitar. electric guitar on *

WAIT 'TIL THE SUN SHINES NELLIE* (Andrew Sterling/Harry Von Tilzer)	VIGO 136	Unissued
SLIPPIN' AND SLIDIN' (Slow version 1)* (Richard Penniman/Edwin J Bocage/Albert Collins/Floyd Smith)	VIGO 136	Unissued
SLIPPIN' AND SLIDIN' (Slow version 2) (Richard Penniman/Edwin J Bocage/Albert Collins/Floyd Smith)	PR 103	CDSP 807
SLIPPIN' AND SLIDIN' (Fast version) (Richard Penniman/Edwin J Bocage/Albert Collins/Floyd Smith)	VIGO 136	Unissued
DROWN IN MY OWN TEARS (fragment only) (Henry Glover)	VIGO 136	Unissued
DEAREST (incomplete version 1 and false start) (Ellas McDaniel/Prentice Polk/Mickey Baker)	VIGO 136	Unissued
DEAREST (Version 2) (Ellas McDaniel/Prentice Polk/Mickey Baker)	PR 103	CDSP 807
LOVE IS STRANGE (Ethel Smith/Mickey Baker)	Cr 001000	CDSP 807
SMOKEY JOE'S CAFE* (Jerry Leiber/Mike Stoller)	VIGO 136	Unissued
UNTITLED INSTRUMENTAL+ (Buddy Holly)	VIGO 136	Unissued

+(believed to have been based on LEAVE MY WOMAN ALONE and subsequently given the title BUDDY'S GUITAR

75a. Overdub session: Norman Petty Studios, 1313 W. Seventh Street, Clovis, New Mexico. *Date unknown, c. 1962-1963. George Tomsco, guitar; Stan Lark, bass; Keith McCormack, rhythm guitar; Doug Roberts or Eric Budd, drums;*

114094	DEAREST (Version 2) (Ellas McDaniel/Prentice Polk/Mickey Baker)	C 7/57450	Q 72469
112763	SLIPPIN' AND SLIDIN' (Slow version 2) (Richard Penniman/Edwin J Bocage/Albert Collins/Floyd Smith)	CRL 7/57426	Q 72459

75b. Overdub session: Norman Petty Studios, 1313 W. Seventh Street, Clovis, New Mexico. *prob. October 29, 1962. George Tomsco, guitar; Stan Lark, bass; Keith McCormack, rhythm guitar; Eric Budd, drums; poss. Vi Petty, George Tomsco, Homer Tankersley , backing vocals on**

112353	WAIT 'TIL THE SUN SHINES NELLIE* (Andrew Sterling/Harry Von Tilzer)	C 62329	Q 72455
112765	WAIT 'TIL THE SUN SHINES NELLIE* (Andrew Sterling/Harry Von Tilzer)	CRL 757426	LVA 9212

75c. Overdub session: Norman Petty Studios, Lyceum Theatre, Main Street Clovis, New Mexico. *Dates unknown c. 1968. George Tomsco, guitar; Stan Lark, bass; Keith McCormack, rhythm guitar; Doug Roberts, drums; Norman Petty, Ondeoline on +; poss. Vi Petty, Barbara Tomsco, George Tomsco,; Homer Tankersley , backing vocals on**

120714	LOVE IS STRANGE+ (Ethel Smith/Mickey Baker)	C 757504	MU 1059
120718	SLIPPIN' AND SLIDIN' (Fast version) (Richard Penniman/Edwin J Bocage/Albert Collins/Floyd Smith)	MUPS 371	C 757504
120720	DEAREST (Version 1)* (Ellas McDaniel/Prentice Polk/Mickey Baker)	C 757504	MUPS 371
120721	SMOKEY JOE'S CAFE* (Jerry Leiber/Mike Stoller)	CRL 757504	MUPS 371

SESSION FILE INDEX

This list may be used to locate a title and the session during which it was recorded, by referring to the session number in the last column which relates to the numerical entry in the Session File. For example the original 1955 recording of You And I Are Through appears as session 10 and the subsequent overdub 10a. Overdub sessions are shown in italics, as in the Session File. We have listed the catalogue numbers shown in the discography for the first release in the US and UK for each title, which may help to identify different takes, recordings and overdubs. Also included in this listing are those recordings on which Buddy Holly and the Crickets appeared as session musicians; again the details of the artists involved and the session information may be found in the Session Files.

Title	US Release	UK Release	Session No.
LOVE ME	VIGO 134	Unissued	13
LOVE ME (take 10)	D 29854	O 5581	14
LOVE ME (take 10)	*Pi 1111*	*CDMF 088*	*14a*
LOVE'S MADE A FOOL OF YOU	VIGO 135	Unissued	57
MAILMAN BRING ME NO MORE BLUES	C 61852	LVA 9085	26
MAILMAN BRING ME NO MORE BLUES	*Unissued*	*Q 72445*	*26a*
MAYBE BABY	BL 54038	Q 72307	38a
MAYBE BABY	MCA 27059	MCM 1002	24
MAYBE BABY	Unissued	Unissued	55
MAYBE BABY	Unissued	Unissued	38
MAYBE BABY (version 2)	*Unissued*	*Unissued*	*24b*
MAYBE BABY(version 1)	*C 001000*	*Q 72483*	*24b*
MEMORIES	*PR 100*	*LVA 9227*	*08a*
MEMORIES	VIGO 134	Unissued	08
MEMORIES (2nd version)	Unissued	Unissued	08
MIDNIGHT SHIFT	DL 8707	O 5800	14
MIDNIGHT SHIFT	*Pi 1111*	*CDMF 088*	*14a*
MODERN DON JUAN	*Pi 1111*	*CDMF 088*	*18a*
MODERN DON JUAN (Take 76)	D 30166	OE 9456	18
MONA (Version 1)	VIGO 135	Unissued	44
MONA (Version 2)	VIGO 135	Unissued	44
MONA (Version 3)	VIGO 135	Unissued	44
MOONDREAMS (mono mix)	CRL 57326	Q 72397	67
MOONDREAMS (stereo mix)	MCA6-8000	CDMSP 807	67
MOONDREAMS (Version 1)	Col 41039	Unissued	37
MOONDREAMS (Version 2)	Unissued	Unissued	37
MOONLIGHT BABY	Unissued	Unissued	12
MOONLIGHT BABY	VIGO 134	Unissued	13
MORE AND MORE	Unissued	Unissued	74
MY TWO TIMIN' WOMAN	HH EP	Unissued	01
NOT FADE AWAY (incomplete version 1)	VIGO 135	Unissued	28
NOT FADE AWAY (version 2)	B55035	Q 72298	28
NOW WE'RE ONE	C 62006	Q 72333	61
NOW WE'RE ONE (fragment)	VIGO 135	Unissued	61
OH BOY!	*B 55035*	*Q 72298*	*31a*
OH BOY!	VIGO 135	Unissued	31
OH BOY!	Cr 001000	Unissued	54
OH BOY!	VIGO 136	Unissued	47
OH YOU BEAUTIFUL DOLL (Version 1)	VIGO 137	Unissued	51a
OH YOU BEAUTIFUL DOLL (Version 2)	C 62017	Q 72341	51a
OH YOU BEAUTIFUL DOLL (Version 2)	VIGO 137	Unissued	51a
ON MY MIND AGAIN	Col 40920	Unissued	24
ONE FADED ROSE	C 61908	Unissued	35
PEGGY SUE	Cr 002000	CDMSP 807	42
PEGGY SUE	*Pi 2221*	*CDMF 088*	*31b*
PEGGY SUE	Unissued	Unissued	45
PEGGY SUE	Cr 001000	Unissued	54
PEGGY SUE (Version 1)	VIGO 135	Unissued	31
PEGGY SUE (Version 2)	C 61885	Q 72293	31
PEGGY SUE GOT MARRIED	*C 62134*	*Q 72376*	*73a*
PEGGY SUE GOT MARRIED	*DRND 11260*	*MCD 11260*	*73e*
PEGGY SUE GOT MARRIED	*DXSE 7-207*	*FEP 2070*	*73c*
PEGGY SUE GOT MARRIED	MCA6-8000	CDMSP 807	70
PROMOTIONAL JINGLE (to tune of EVERYDAY)	Pr 102	Unissued	62
PROMOTIONAL JINGLE (to tune of PEGGY SUE)	Pr 102	Unissued	62
QUEEN OF THE BALLROOM	*Cr 002000*	*LVA 9227*	*08a*
QUEEN OF THE BALLROOM	Unissued	Unissued	08
QUEEN OF THE BALLROOM	Unissued	Unissued	11
RAINING IN MY HEART (mono mix)	C 62074	Q 72360	67
RAINING IN MY HEART (stereo mix)	C 757269	BH 7	67
RAVE ON (Take 1)	Unissued	Unissued	46
RAVE ON (Take 2)	Unissued	Unissued	46
RAVE ON (Take 3)	CRL 57210	Q 72325	46
READY TEDDY	CRL 57210	LVA 9085	29
REAL WILD CHILD (Version 1)	VIGO 137	Unissued	51a
REAL WILD CHILD (Version 2)	C 62017	Q 72341	51a
REMINISCING	*C 62329*	*Q 72455*	*64a*
REMINISCING	*CRL 757426*	*LVA 9212*	*64b*
REMINISCING	*Pi 2221*	*CDMF 088*	*64c*
REMINISCING	Unissued	Unissued	64
RIP IT UP	CRL 7/57450	LVA 9222	19
RIP IT UP	VIGO 134	ROLL 2013	19
ROCK AROUND WITH OLLIE VEE (fragment)	VIGO 134	Unissued	17
ROCK AROUND WITH OLLIE VEE (Take 12)	D 30434	CDLM 8038	18
ROCK AROUND WITH OLLIE VEE (Take 8)	DL 8707	O 5800	17
ROCK AROUND WITH OLLIE VEE (Take 8)	*Pi 1111*	*CDMF 088*	*17a*
ROCK ME MY BABY	*BL 54038*	*LVA 9081*	*38a*
ROCK ME MY BABY	Unissued	Unissued	38
ROCK-A-BYE ROCK	MCA 27059	MCM 1002	15
ROCK-A-BYE ROCK	*C 7/57426*	*LVA 9212*	*15a*
ROCK-A-BYE ROCK	*Pi 2221*	*CDMF 088*	*15b*
ROSE OF MONTEREY	Unissued	RCCD 3004	07
SEND ME SOME LOVIN' (version 1)	VIGO 135	Unissued	36
SEND ME SOME LOVIN' (version 2)	*BL 54038*	*LVA 9081*	*36a*
SEND ME SOME LOVIN' (version 2)	Unissued	Unissued	36
SHAKE RATTLE AND ROLL	CRL 7/57450	LVA 9222	19a
SHAKE RATTLE AND ROLL (incomplete)	VIGO 135	ROLL 2013	19
SLIPPIN' AND SLIDIN' (Fast version)	VIGO 136	Unissued	75
SLIPPIN' AND SLIDIN' (Fast version)	*C 757504*	*MUPS 371*	*75c*
SLIPPIN' AND SLIDIN' (Slow version 1)	VIGO 136	MUPS 371	75
SLIPPIN' AND SLIDIN' (Slow version 2)	*CRL 7/57426*	*Q 72459*	*75a*
SLIPPIN' AND SLIDIN' (Slow version 2)	PR 103	CDMSP 807	75
SMOKEY JOE'S CAFE	CRL 757504	MUPS 371	75c
SMOKEY JOE'S CAFE	VIGO 136	Unissued	75
SOFT PLACE IN MY HEART	CRL 7/577463	LVA 9227	05a
SOFT PLACE IN MY HEART	Unissued	Unissued	05
SOFT PLACE IN MY HEART 2nd version)	Unissued	Unissued	08
SPOKEN TRAILER FOR OFF THE RECORD	Unissued	Unissued	55
STARLIGHT	Pe 1002	Unissued	25
STAY CLOSE TO ME (7 false starts)	Unissued	Unissued	66
STAY CLOSE TO ME (Take 1)	Unissued	Unissued	66
STAY CLOSE TO ME (Take 2)	Unissued	Unissued	66
STAY CLOSE TO ME (Take 3)	Unissued	Unissued	66
STAY CLOSE TO ME (Take 4)	B 55115	CDSP 807	66
SUGARTIME (Version 1)	Unissued	Unissued	35
SUGARTIME (Version 2)	C 61908	Unissued	35
TAKE THESE SHACKLES FROM MY HEART	VIGO 134	Unissued	02
TAKE YOUR TIME	Unissued	Unissued	58
TAKE YOUR TIME (incomplete version 1)	VIGO 135	Unissued	51
TAKE YOUR TIME (incomplete version 2)	VIGO 135	Unissued	51
TAKE YOUR TIME (version 3)	VIGO 135	Unissued	51
TAKE YOUR TIME (version 4)	C 61985	Q 72325	51
TELL ME HOW	*B 54038*	*Q 72307*	*36a*
TELL ME HOW	Unissued	Unissued	29
THAT'LL BE THE DAY (fragment)	Unissued	Unissued	53
THAT MAKES IT TOUGH	CRL 572326	Q 72411	73b
THAT MAKES IT TOUGH	MCA6-8000	CDMSP 807	71
THAT MAKES IT TOUGH	*Pr 101*	*FEP 2070*	*73c*
THAT'LL BE THE DAY	B 55009	Q 72279	22
THAT'LL BE THE DAY	Cr 001000	Unissued	54
THAT'LL BE THE DAY	Cr 002000	CDMSP 807	42
THAT'LL BE THE DAY (Take 19)	D 30434	AH 3	17
THAT'LL BE THE DAY JINGLE (BILL RANDALL)	Unissued	Unissued	31
THAT'LL BE THE DAY JINGLE (BOB THEILE)	VIGO 135	Unissued	31
THAT'LL BE THE DAY JINGLE (MURRAY DEUTCH)	VIGO 135	Unissued	31
THAT'S MY DESIRE	*MCA-6 80000*	*Q 72483*	*46a*
THAT'S MY DESIRE	*Unissued*	*Unissued*	*46a*
THAT'S MY DESIRE (false start take 1)	VIGO 135	Unissued	46
THAT'S MY DESIRE (incomplete take 2)	VIGO 135	Unissued	46
THAT'S MY DESIRE (take 3)	MCA 27059	MCM 1002	46
THAT'S WHAT THEY SAY	*Cr 0020000*	*CPS 71*	*73c*
THAT'S WHAT THEY SAY	*Pi 2221*	*CDMF 088*	*73d*
THAT'S WHAT THEY SAY (Version 1)	Unissued	Unissued	69
THAT'S WHAT THEY SAY (Version 2)	*CRL 57326*	*LVA 9127*	*73b*
THAT'S WHAT THEY SAY (Version 2)	VIGO 136	Unissued	69
THE GOLDEN ROCKET	VIGO 137	Unissued	23
THINK IT OVER (false start version 1)	VIGO 135	Unissued	51
THINK IT OVER (false start version 2)	VIGO 135	Unissued	51
THINK IT OVER (version 3)	VIGO 135	Unissued	51
THINK IT OVER (version 4)	VIGO 135	Unissued	51
THINK IT OVER (Version 5)	*B 55072*	*Q 72329*	*51a*
THINK IT OVER (version 5)	VIGO 135	Unissued	51
THIS BOTTLE	Unissued	Unissued	11
TING A LING	Pi 1111	CDMF 088	17a
TING-A-LING (Take 7)	DL 8707	OE 9456	17
TITLES UNKNOWN	Unissued	Unissued	49
TRUE LOVE WAYS	Pi 2221	CDMF 088	67a
TRUE LOVE WAYS (mono mix)	CRL 57326	Q 72397	67
TRUE LOVE WAYS (stereo mix)	MCA6-80000	CDMSP 807	67
UNTITLED INSTRUMENTAL (aka BUDDY'S GUITAR)	VIGO 136	Unissued	75
VALLEY OF TEARS	CRL 57210	LVA 9085	29
VIVA LA MATADOR	Col 40920	Unissued	24
WAIT 'TIL THE SUN SHINES NELLIE	*C 62329*	*Q 72445*	*75b*
WAIT 'TIL THE SUN SHINES NELLIE	*CRL 757426*	*LVA 9212*	*75b*
WAIT 'TIL THE SUN SHINES NELLIE	VIGO 136	Unissued	75
WELL...ALL RIGHT	C 62051	Q 72346	50
WELL...ALL RIGHT	*LG 6006*	*CDMF 088*	*50a*
WHAT A YOU GONNA DO?	CI 55037	RCCD 3017	63
WHAT TO DO	*C 62448*	*Q 72469*	*73c*
WHAT TO DO	*CRL 57326*	*LVA 9127*	*73b*
WHAT TO DO	VIGO 136	Unissued	69
WHEN SIN STOPS (Take 1)	Unissued	Unissued	64
WHEN SIN STOPS (Take 2)	Unissued	Unissued	64
WHEN SIN STOPS (Take 3)	VIGO 137	Unissued	64
WHEN SIN STOPS (Take 4)	Unissued	Unissued	64
WHEN SIN STOPS (Take 5)	VIGO 137	Unissued	64
WHEN SIN STOPS (Take 6)	B 55130	CDSP 807	64
WISHING	C 62369	Q 72446	57
WISHING	*EC 81193*	*LVA 9227*	*57b*
WORDS OF LOVE	C 61852	LVA 9085	26
WORDS OF LOVE	Unissued	Unissued	24
WORDS OF LOVE	VIGO 135	Unissued	24
YOU AND I ARE THROUGH	Unissued	Unissued	09
YOU AND I ARE THROUGH	VIGO 134	Unissued	08
YOU AND I ARE THROUGH	*CRL 7/577463*	*LVA 9227*	*08a*
YOU ARE MY ONE DESIRE	*Pi 1111*	*CDMF 088*	*18a*
YOU ARE MY ONE DESIRE (false start)	Unissued	Unissued	18
YOU ARE MY ONE DESIRE (Take 2)	D 30166	OE 9456	18
YOU'RE THE ONE	CRL 57450	LVA 9222	74
YOU'RE THE ONE	*CRL 757504*	*MU 1059*	*74a*
YOU'VE GOT LOVE	*BL 54038*	*LVA 9081*	*38a*
YOU'VE GOT LOVE	Unissued	Unissued	38

DISCOGRAPHY

The following listings of US and UK releases by Buddy Holly and The Crickets gives details of record numbers, titles and release dates of all records of which we were aware at the time of going to press. The proliferation of such releases, both by MCA, their licensees as well as by 'bootleggers' has made the task of assembling complete listings of product difficult, and we would welcome any additions or amndements to the information contained. We have not attempted to list those various artist albums which contain one track by Buddy Holly, nor have we included separate listings for reissues of albums which are already listed (although the catalogue numbers appear, following the original album). It is regrettable, although hardly surprising, that counterfeit and 'bootleg' or unauthorised albums have appeared on the market in recent years to provide collectors with Buddy Holly and Crickets releases which have not been issued by MCA. It is also unfortunate that these bootleggers have often provided more attractive and informative packaging than MCA's. We do not intend our listing of such albums to legitimise or condone the producers of such material, especially since many of them have taken our material together with that belonging to MCA or the Holly Estate without permission. We have only listed those unauthorised releases which were at the time of issue, the first or only release of some or all of the material contained, and we have not listed counterfeit releases which in some cases have been passed off as originals. Collectors should beware when paying high prices for perfect-condition copies of hard to find albums—although genuine copies are still to be found, there are also fakes in the marketplace.

PART ONE: US RELEASES

SINGLES

Singles are listed in order of appearance on the American market. Dates are expressed in the British manner, i.e. day/month/year.

∅ denotes original release also available on 78 rpm single; □ denotes initial release in picture sleeve; ✠ denotes CD-only release
All releases credited to Buddy Holly or Buddy Holly & The Crickets except ● which denotes original release credited to The Crickets and ⊗ which denotes original release credited to Ivan.

D = Decca; B = Brunswick; C = Coral; MCA = MCA; PR = Prism

Record No.	Titles	Release date
D 29854 ∅	Blue Days, Black Nights/Love Me	16.4.56
D 30166 ∅	Modern Don Juan/You Are My One Desire	24.12.56
B 55009 ∅ ●	That'll Be The Day/I'm Looking For Someone To Love	27.5.57
C 61852 ∅	Words Of Love/Mailman, Bring Me No More Blues	20.6.57
D 30434 ∅	Rock Around With Ollie Vee/That'll Be The Day	2.9.57
C 61885 ∅	Peggy Sue/Everyday	20.9.57
B 55035 ∅ ●	Oh Boy !/Not Fade Away	27.10.57
D 30543 ∅	Love Me/You Are My One Desire	6.1.58
C 61947 ∅	I'm Gonna Love You Too/Listen To Me	5.2.58
B 55053 ∅ ●	Maybe Baby/Tell Me How	12.2.58
C 61985 ∅	Rave On/Take Your Time	20.4.58
B 55072 ∅ ●	Think It Over/Fool's Paradise	27.5.58
D 30650 ∅	Girl On My Mind/Ting-A-Ling	23.6.58
C 62006 ∅	Early In The Morning/Now We're One	5.7.58
B 55094 ∅ ●	It's So Easy/Lonesome Tears	12.9.58
C 62017 ∅ ⊗	Real Wild Child/Oh You Beautiful Doll	12.9.58
C 62051 ∅	Heartbeat/Well.. . All Right	5.11.58
C 62074	It Doesn't Matter Anymore /Raining In My Heart	5.1.59
C 62134	Peggy Sue Got Married/Crying, Waiting, Hoping	20.7.59
C 62210	True Love Ways/That Makes It Tough	29.6.60
C 62283	Valley Of Tears /You're So Square (Baby I Don't Care) (intended for release in the US but only issued in Canada)	9.61
C 62329	Reminiscing/Wait 'Til The Sun Shines Nellie	20.8.62
C 62352	Bo Diddley/True Love Ways	1.4.63
C 62369	Brown-Eyed Handsome Man/Wishing	29.7.63
C 62390	Rock Around With Ollie Vee/I'm Gonna Love You Too	6.1.64
C 62407	Maybe Baby/Not Fade Away	27.4.64
C 62448	What To Do/Slipping' And Slidin'	15.3.65
C 62554	Rave On/Early In The Morning	22.7.68
C 62558 □	Love Is Strange/You're The One	17.3.69
C 65607 ⊗	Real Wild Child/That'll Be Alright	0.69
C 65618	That'll Be The Day /I'm Looking For Someone To Love	0.69
MCA 60000	That'll Be The Day /I'm Looking For Someone To Love	0.73
MCA 60004	Peggy Sue/Everyday	0.73
MCA 40905 □	It Doesn't Matter Anymore/Peggy Sue	29.5.78
PR 100	Memories/A Message From Buddy's Parents	5.8
PR 101	That Makes It Tough/Norman Petty Talks About The Plane Crash	5.8
PR 102	You're The One/Everyday Jingle/Peggy Sue Jingle/KSYD Promo	5.8
PR 103	Slippin' And Slidin'/Dearest	9.81
MCA D 37295 □ ✠	That'll Be The Day/Oh Boy/Not Fade Away/Fool's Paradise	28.11.88
MCA D 37314 □ ✠	Peggy Sue/Rave On/Early In The Morning/It Doesn't Matter Anymore	3.1.89

EXTENDED PLAY 45 RPM SINGLES (EPs)

EB = Brunswick; EC = Coral; ED = Decca; HH = Holly House; SS = Solid Smoke.

All EP releases were in picture sleeves except HH

Record Number	Title	Release date
ED 2575	*That'll Be The Day*	27.11.57

That'll Be The Day/Blue Days, Black Nights/Ting-A-Ling/You Are My One Desire.

EB 71036 ●	The Chirping Crickets	12.1.58

I'm Looking For Someone To Love/That'll Be The Day/Not Fade Away/Oh Boy!

EB 71038 ●	*The Sound of The Crickets*	20.2.58

Maybe Baby/Rock Me My Baby/Send Me Some Lovin'/Tell Me How.

Record Number	Title	Release date
EC 81169	*Listen To Me*	14.4.58

Listen To Me/Everyday I'm Gonna Love You Too/Peggy Sue.

EC 81169	*The Buddy Holly Story*	20.2.59

Early In The Morning/Heartbeat/It Doesn't Matter Anymore/Raining In My Heart.

EC 81191	*Peggy Sue Got Married*	25.6.62

Peggy Sue Got Married/Crying, Waiting, Hoping/Learning The Game/That Makes It Tough.

EC 81192 ●	*The Crickets*	25.2.63

Great Balls of Fire (Earl Sinks, vocal) /Don't Cha Know (David Box, vocal)/It's Too Late (Buddy Holly, vocal)/Baby My Heart (Sonny Curtis, vocal).

EC 81193	*Brown-Eyed Handsome Man*	23.7.63

Brown-Eyed Handsome Man/Bo Diddley/True Love Ways/Wishing.

SS 8002	*Picture Record No 1* (12″ picture disc)	3.19.79

Peggy Sue/Brown-Eyed Handsome Man/Oh Boy!/Maybe Baby.

SS 8003	*Picture Record No 2* (12″ picture disc)	3.19.79

Rave On/Rock Around With Ollie Vee/That'll Be The Day/I'm Gonna Love You Too.

HH (no cat. number)	*Buddy Holly*	5.19.86

My Two Timin' Woman/I'll Just Pretend/Don't Come Back Knockin'/Brown-Eyed Handsome Man.

LONG PLAY ALBUMS (LPs, Cassettes and CDs)

Albums are listed in order of appearance on the American market.

BL = Brunswick; Cr = Cricket; CRL & CXB = Coral; DL & DXSE = Decca; GNW = Great North West; LG = Live Gold; MCA, DLMCA & MCAD = MCA; MSM = Pair; PA, PCD = Pick; VL = Vocalion; SE Silver Eagle; S = Silhouette; VCD = Varese Sarabande; VIGO = Vigotone

Coral catalogue numbers beginning with a 5 indicate mono releases; those with a 7 prefix are stereo or reprocessed stereo.

Record Number	Album Title	Release date
BL 54038 ●	*The Chirping Crickets*	November 1957

Oh Boy!/Not Fade Away/You've Got Love/Maybe Baby/It's Too Late/Tell Me How/That'll Be The Day/I'm Looking For Someone To Love/An Empty Cup/Send Me Some Lovin'/Rock Me My Baby.
(Re-released in 1962 as Buddy Holly and the Crickets CRL 57405/CRL 757405 and in 1987 as MCAD 31182)

CRL 57210	*Buddy Holly*	March 1958

I'm Gonna Love You Too/Peggy Sue/Look At Me/Listen To Me/Valley Of Tears/Ready Teddy/Everyday/Mailman, Bring Me No More Blues/Words Of Love/You're So Square/Rave On/Little Baby.
Reissued in 1989 as MCAD 25239)

DL 8707	*That'll Be The Day*	April 1958

You Are My One Desire/Blue Days, Black Nights/Modern Don Juan/Rock Around With Ollie Vee/Ting-A-Ling/Girl On My Mind/That'll Be The Day/Love Me/I'm Changin' All Those Changes/Don't Come Back Knockin'/Midnight Shift.
(Re-released in 1967 as The Great Buddy Holly, VL73811 with all of the cuts listed included, except for Ting-A-Ling and later renumbered as MCA20101 & MCA 737 and in 1988 as MCAD 31037)

CRL 57269/757269	*Hitsville*	January 1959

Various Artists album with one Buddy Holly track: Raining In My Heart (the only stereo release of this recording during Holly's lifetime)

CRL 57279/757279	*The Buddy Holly Story*	March 1959

Raining In My Heart/Early In The Morning/Peggy Sue/Maybe Baby/Everyday/Rave On/That'll Be The Day/Heartbeat/Think It Over/Oh Boy/It's So Easy/It Doesn't Matter Anymore.

CRL 57326	*The Buddy Holly Story, Volume 2*	March 1960

Peggy Sue Got Married/Well . . . All Right/What To Do/That Makes It Tough/Now We're One/Take Your Time/Crying, Waiting. Hoping/True Love Ways/Learning The Game/Little Baby/Moondreams/That's What They Say

CRL5 7426/757426	*Reminiscing*	February 1963

Reminiscing/Slippin' And Slidin'/Bo Diddley/Wait 'Til The Sun Shines, Nellie/Baby, Won't You Come Out Tonight/Brown-Eyed Handsome Man/Because I Love You/It's Not My Fault/I'm Gonna Set My Foot Down/Changin' All Those Changes/Rock-A-Bye Rock

CRL 57450/757450	*Showcase*	May 1964

Shake, Rattle and Roll/Rock With Ollie Vee/Honky Tonk/I Guess I Was Just A Fool/Ummm, Oh Yeah (Dearest)/You're The One/Blue Suede Shoes/Come Back Baby/Rip It Up/Love's Made A Fool Of You/Gone/Girl On My Mind.

CRL 57463/757463	*Holly In The Hills*	January 1965

I Wanna Play House With You/Door To My Heart/Fool's Paradise/I Gambled My Heart/What To Do/Wishing/Down The Line/Soft Place In My Heart/Lonesome Tears/Gotta Get You Near Me Blues/Flower Of My Heart/You And I Are Through.

CXB-8/ 7CXSB-8	*The Best of Buddy Holly*	April 1966

Peggy Sue/Blue Suede Shoes/Learning The Game/Brown-Eyed Handsome Man/Everyday/Maybe Baby/Early In The Morning/Ready Teddy/It's Too Late/What To Do/Rave On/True Love Ways/It Doesn't Matter Anymore/Crying, Waiting, Hoping/Moondreams/Rock Around With Ollie Vee/Raining In My Heart/Bo Diddley/That'll Be The Day/I'm Gonna Love You Too/Peggy Sue Got Married/Shake, Rattle and Roll/That Makes It Tough/Wishing

CRL 757492	*Buddy Holly's Greatest Hits*	March 1967

Peggy Sue/True Love Ways/Bo Diddley/What To Do/Learning The Game/It Doesn't Matter Anymore/That'll Be The Day/Oh Boy!/Early In The Morning/Brown-Eyed Handsome Man/Everyday/Maybe Baby

CRL 757504	*Giant*	January 1969

Love Is Strange/Good Rockin' Tonight/Blue Monday/Have You Ever Been Lonely/Slippin' And Slidin'/You're The One/Dearest/Smokey Joe's Cafe/Ain't Got No Home/Holly Hop

Record Number	Title	Release date

VL 73923   *Good Rockin'*   1971
I Wanna Play House With You/Baby, I Don't Care/Little Baby/Ting-A-Ling/Take Your Time/Down The Line/Now We're One/Words Of Love/That's What They Say/You And I Are Through.

DXSE 7-207   *Buddy Holly: A Rock And Roll Collection*   August 1972
Rave On/Tell Me How/Peggy Sue Got Married/Slippin' And Slidin'/Oh Boy/Not Fade Away/Bo Diddley/What To Do/Heartbeat/Well . . .All Right/Words Of Love/Reminiscing/Lonesome Tears/Listen To Me/Maybe Baby/Down The Line/That'll Be The Day/Peggy Sue/Brown-Eyed Handsome Man/You're So Square/Crying, Waiting, Hoping/Ready Teddy/It Doesn't Matter Anymore/*The Crickets Featuring Earl Sinks*: Love's Made A Fool Of You (Later renumbered as MCA2-4009)

Cr 001000   *Buddy Holly Recorded Live Volume 1*   March 1977
 Interview With Alan Freed/Learning The Game/Interview With Dick Clark/Flower Of My Heart/Live at London Palladium: (That'll Be The Day/Peggy Sue/Oh Boy!/Maybe Baby/Interview With Dale Lowery/Rip It Up/Love Is Strange/Gone/You're The One/The Crickets Live in New York c.1971: That'll Be The Day/Maybe Baby/Everyday/Keep-A-Knockin'/Well . . . All Right/Oh Boy!/Dearest
(Unauthorised release)

Cr 002000   *Buddy Holly In Person Volume 2*   December 1977
Newscast About The Plane crash/Tribute To Buddy Holly (Mike Berry)/That's My Desire/Good Rockin' Tonight/Stay Close To Me (Lou Giordano)/That'll Be The Day/Baby It's Love/Learning The Game/Rip It Up/Love Me/Queen Of The Ballroom/Rock Around With Ollie Vee/Peggy Sue/Interview With Ed Sullivan/That's What They Say/Down The Line/Crying, Waiting, Hoping/Newscast About The Plane crash
(Unauthorised release)

MCA 3040   *Buddy Holly/Crickets 20 Golden Greats*   May 1978
That'll Be The Day/Peggy Sue/Words Of Love/Everyday/Not Fade Away/Oh Boy!/Maybe Baby/Listen To Me/Heartbeat/Think It Over/It Doesn't Matter Anymore/It's So Easy/Well... All Right/Rave On/Raining In My Heart/True Love Ways/Peggy Sue Got Married/Bo Diddley/Brown-Eyed Handsome Man/Wishing

GNW 4014   *Visions of Buddy*   1980
Interview with Red Robinson (interspersed with Holly songs performed by The Crickets without Buddy Holly)

S 10003   *The Day The Music Died*   December 1980
Various artists album including the following Buddy Holly tracks: Interview With Alan Freed/Interview With Dale Lowery/Interview With Pat Barton/Interview With Red Robinson.
(Unauthorised release)

MCA 6-80000   *The Complete Buddy Holly*   February 1981
Gotta Get You Near Me Blues/Soft Place In My Heart/Door To My Heart/Flower Of My Heart/Baby It's Love/Memories/Queen Of The Ballroom/I Gambled My Heart/You And I Are Through/Gone/Have You Ever Been Lonely/Down The Line/Brown-Eyed Handsome Man/Bo Diddley/Good Rockin' Tonight/Rip It Up/Blue Monday/Honky Tonk/Blue Suede Shoes/Shake Rattle & Roll/Ain't Got No Home/Holly Hop/Baby Let's Play House/I'm Gonna Set My Foot Down/Baby Won't You Come Out Tonight/Changin' All Those Changes/Rock-a-Bye Rock/It's Not My Fault/I Guess I Was Just A Fool/Love Me/Don't Come Back Knockin'/Midnight Shift/Blue Days, Black Nights/Rock Around With Ollie Vee/I'm Changin' All Those Changes/That'll Be The Day/Girl On My Mind/Ting-A-Ling/Because I Love You/Rock Around With Ollie Vee/Modern Don Juan/You Are My One Desire/That'll Be The Day/I'm Looking For Someone To Love/Last Night/Maybe Baby/Words Of Love/Peggy Sue/Everyday/Mailman, Bring Me No More Blues/Listen To Me/I'm Gonna Love You Too/Not Fade Away/Ready Teddy/Oh Boy!/Tell Me How/Maybe Baby/Send Me Some Lovin'/Little Baby/Take Your Time/Rave On/You've Got Love/Valley Of Tears/Rock Me My Baby/(You're So Square) Baby I Don't Care/It's Too Late/An Empty Cup/Look At Me/Think It Over/Fool's Paradise/Early In The Morning/Now We're One/Lonesome Tears/Heartbeat/It's So Easy/Well . All Right/Love's Made A Fool Of You/Wishing/Reminiscing/Come Back Baby/That's My Desire/True Love Ways/Moondreams/Raining In My Heart/It Doesn't Matter Anymore/Peggy Sue Got Married/Crying, Waiting, Hoping/Learning The Game/That Makes It Tough/What To Do/That's What They Say/Wait 'Til The Sun Shines Nellie/Ummm, Oh Yeah (Dearest)/Smokey Joe's Cafe/Slippin' and Slidin'/Love Is Strange/Slippin' and Slidin'/Learning The Game/Crying. Waiting, Hoping/What To Do/That Makes It Tough/Peggy Sue Got Married/That's What They Say/Dearest/You're The One/Slippin' and Slidin'/Dearest/Love Is Strange/Peggy Sue Got Married/That Makes It Tough/Learning The Game/You're The One/Real Wild Child/Oh You Beautiful Doll/Jole Blon/When Sin Stops/Stay Close To Me/Don't Cha Know?/Interview With Dale Lowery/Ed Sullivan Show-That'll Be The Day/Peggy Sue/Interview With Ed Sullivan/Interview With Alan Freed/Interview With Dick Clark

SE 1005   *The Best Of Buddy Holly*   1982
Peggy Sue/It's So Easy/Maybe Baby/It Doesn't Matter Anymore/Oh Boy/Shake, Rattle and Roll/You Are My One Desire/Early In The Morning/Blue Suede Shoes/That'll Be The Day/Everyday/Raining In My Heart/Rave On/Think It Over/Ready Teddy/Send Me Some Lovin'/Slippin' and Slidin'/Love's Made A Fool Of You

MCA-27059   *For The First Time Anywhere*   February 1983
Rock-A-Bye Rock/Maybe Baby/Because I Love You/I'm Gonna Set My Foot Down/Changin' All Those Changes/That's My Desire/Baby Won't You Come Out Tonight/It's Not My Fault/Brown-Eyed Handsome Man/Bo Diddley. (Reissued in 1987 as MCAD 31048)

DLMCA 20260   *Words Of Love*   July 1985
Rock-A-Bye Rock/Peggy Sue/Well . . . All Right/Words Of Love/Reminiscing/Moondreams/Maybe Baby/Tell Me How
(Released on cassette tape only)

MCAD 5540   *From The Original Master Tapes*   October 1985
That'll Be The Day/Oh Boy/Not Fade Away/Tell Me How/Maybe Baby/Everyday/Rock Around With Ollie Vee/It's So Easy/I'm Looking' For Someone To Love/Peggy Sue/I'm Gonna Love You Too/Words Of Love/Rave On/Well . . . All Right/Listen To Me/Think It Over/Heartbeat/True Love Ways/Reminiscing/It Doesn't Matter Anymore
(Released on Compact Disc only, also numbered DIDX-203)

MSM2-35070   *Reminiscing*   1986
Rock-A-Bye Rock/Blue Days, Black Nights/Rock Around With Ollie Vee/Love Me/I'm Looking For Someone To Love/Rock Me My Baby/Tell Me How/You've Got Love/Peggy Sue/Look At Me/Ready Teddy/(You're So Square) Baby I Don't Care/Well . . . All Right/Take Your Time/Reminiscing/Moondreams

PA 1111   *Buddy Holly & The Picks*   1986
Love Me/Don't Come Back Knockin'/Midnight Shift/Blue Days, Black Nights/Girl On My Mind/Ting-A-Ling/Rock Around With Ollie Vee/Modern Don Juan/You Are My One Desire/The Picks: Buddy Holly Not Fade Away

MCA2 4184   *Legend*   September 1986
That'll Be The Day/Oh Boy!/Not Fade Away/Tell Me How/Maybe Baby/I'm Gonna Love You Too/Words of Love/Rave On/Well . . . All Right/Listen To Me/Everyday/Rock Around With Ollie Vee/It's So Easy/I'm Looking for Someone To Love/Peggy Sue/Think It Over/Heartbeat/Reminiscing/It Doesn't Matter Anymore/True Love Ways

VCD 47275   *Peggy Sue Got Married*   1989
Sountrack album featuring the undubbed version of Peggy Sue Got Married

Record Number	Title	Release date
LG 6006	*The Real Buddy Holly Story*	February 1992

Compilation album including the following Buddy Holly tracks: Interview With Red Robinson/Interview With Alan Freed/Interview With Dick Clark/KLLL Jingle (Everyday)/KLLL Jingle (Peggy Sue)/Interview With Dale Lowery/Interview With Pat Barton/Interview With Freeman Hover/The Picks overdubs: Well . . . All Right/(You're So Square) Baby I Don't Care/Heartbeat
(Unauthorised release)

PCD 2221	*The Voices Of The Crickets*	December 1992

True Love Ways/Everyday/Love Me/Don't Come Back Knockin'/You're So Square/Reminiscing/Heartbeat/Girl On My Mind/Ting-A-Ling/I'm Gonna Set My Foot Down/It's Not My Fault/Rock Around With Ollie Vee/Peggy Sue/Well . . . All Right/Midnight Shift/Blue Days, Black Nights/That's What They Say/Rock-A-Bye Rock/You Are My One Desire/Because I Love You/Modern Don Juan/The Picks: Words/You've Lost That Lovin' Feeling/Buddy Holly Not Fade Away

MCAD2-10883	*The Buddy Holly Collection*	September 1993

Down The Line/Soft Place In My Heart/Holly Hop/Blue Days, Black Nights/Love Me/Midnight Shift/Baby Won't You Come Out Tonight/I'm Changing All Those Changes/I'm Gonna Set My Foot Down/Rock Around With Ollie Vee/Girl On My Mind/Ting-A-Ling/Modern Don Juan/Brown Eyed Handsome Man/That'll Be The Day/I'm Looking For Someone To Love/Words Of Love/Not Fade Away/Everyday/Tell Me How/Ready Teddy/Listen To Me/Oh Boy/It's Too Late/Peggy Sue/I'm Gonna Love You Too/Look At Me/Little Baby/You've Got Love/Maybe Baby/Rock Me My Baby/(You're So Square) Baby I Don't Care/Rave On/Fool's Paradise/Take Your Time/Well . . . All Right/Think It Over/Early In The Morning/Heartbeat/It's So Easy/Wishing/Love's Made A Fool Of You/Reminiscing/True Love Ways/It Doesn't Matter Anymore/Raining In My Heart/Peggy Sue Got Married/Crying, Waiting, Hoping/Learning The Game/What To Do

MCAD 20425	*Oh Boy*	1994

Oh Boy/Heartbeat/You Are My One Desire/Listen To Me/Blue Days, Black Nights/I'm Gonna Love You Too/That's My Desire/It Doesn't Matter Anymore/Raining In My Heart/Early In The Morning

MCAD 11213	*Greatest Hits*	March 1995

That'll Be The Day/I'm Looking For Someone To Love/Words Of Love/Not Fade Away/Everyday/Oh Boy/Peggy Sue/I'm Gonna Love You Too/Maybe Baby/Rave On/Think It Over/Fool's Paradise/Early In The Morning/It's So Easy/Heartbeat/True Love Ways/It Doesn't Matter Anymore/Raining In My Heart

VIGO 134/137	*What You Been A-Missin'*	June 1995

My Two Timin' Woman/I'll Just Pretend/Take These Shackles From My Heart/Footprints In The Snow/Gotta Get You Near Me Blues/You And I Are Through/Memories/Baby Let's Play House/Down The Line/Baby Won't You Come Out Tonight/I Guess I Was Just A Fool/Love Me/Love Me/Don't Come Back Knockin'/Because I Love You/It's Not My Fault/Rock-A-Bye Rock/Rock Around With Ollie Vee/I'm Changing All Those Changes/That'll Be The Day/Ting-A-Ling/Rock Around With Ollie Vee/You Are My One Desire/Gone/Gone/Have You Ever Been Lonely/Have You Ever Been Lonely/Have You Ever Been Lonely/Brown Eyed Handsome Man/Good Rockin' Tonight/Rip It Up/Blue Monday/Honky Tonk/Blue Suede Shoes/Shake Rattle And Roll/Bo Diddley/Ain't Got No Home/Holly Hop/Bo Diddley/Last Night/Maybe Baby/Words Of Love/Not Fade Away/Peggy Sue/That'll Be The Day (Jingle for Bob Theile)/That'll Be The Day (Jingle for Murray Deutch)/Oh Boy/Send Me Some Lovin'/It's Too Late/Mona/Mona/Mona/That's My Desire/That's My Desire/Take Your Time/Take Your Time/Take Your Time/Fool's Paradise/Fool's Paradise/Fool's Paradise/Think It Over/Think It Over/Think It Over/Think It Over/Think It Over/Lonesome Tears/Now We're One/Love's Made A Fool Of You/Jingle for KLLL (Everyday)/Jingle for KLLL(Peggy Sue)/Promo for WACK/Promo for KSYD/Raining In My Heart/Moondreams/That's What They Say/What To Do/Peggy Sue Got Married/That Makes It Tough/Crying, Waiting, Hoping/Learning The Game/You're The One/Wait 'Til The Sun Shines Nellie/Slippin' and Slidin'/Slippin and Slidin'/Drown In My Own Tears (fragment)/Dearest/Dearest/Love Is Strange/Smokey Joe's Cafe/Leave My Woman Alone (Buddy's Guitar)/Newscast About Plane Crash/Newscast About Plane Crash/Interview With Red Robinson/Interview With Dale Lowery/Interview With Pat Barton/Interview With Alan Freed/Interview With Dick Clark/That'll Be The Day/Peggy Sue/Interview With Ed Sullivan/Oh Boy/That'll Be The Day/Peggy Sue/Oh Boy/Norman Petty Defends Himself/Message to The Dutch BHAS (Ella and Lawrence Holley)/Sonny Curtis: Because You Love Me/I'll Miss My Heart/Gary Dale: Go Boy Go/The Golden Rocket/Gone/I Overlooked An Orchid/Jim Robinson: Whole Lotta Lovin'/Whole Lotta Lovin'/Whole Lotta Lovin'/It's A Wonderful Feeling/Jack Huddle: Starlight/Believe Me/Fred Crawford: By The Mission Wall/Gary Dale: Look To The Future/Honey Honey/Charlie Phillips: Sugartime/Norman Petty Trio: Moondreams/Rick Tucker: Don't Do Me This Way/Don't Do Me This Way/Patty Baby/van: Real Wild Child/Real Wild Child/Oh You Beautiful Doll/Oh You Beautiful Doll/Oh You Beautiful Doll/Waylon Jennings: Jole Blon/When Sin Stops/When Sin Stops/Eddie Reeves: When Sin Stops/Lou Giordano: Stay Close To Me/Don't Cha Know/Sonny West: Oh Boy
(Unauthorised release)

ORIGINAL RELEASES BY OTHER ARTISTS RELEASES FEATURING BUDDY HOLLY

Artist	Title/s	Record Number	Year
JIM ROBINSON	A Man From Texas	Brill 2	1957
JACK HUDDLE	Believe Me/Starlight	Petsey 1002	1957
SHERRY DAVIS	Broken Promises/Humble Heart	Fashion 1001	1957
FRED CRAWFORD	By The Mission Wall	Starday ST 314	1957
THE NORMAN PETTY TRIO	Moondreams	Columbia 41039	1957
LOU GIORDANO	Don't Cha Know/Stay Close To Me	Brunswick 55155	1959
KEN JAMES	If I Had Known	Nor Va Jak 1321	1958
JIM ROBINSON	A Whole Lotta Loving/It's A Wonderful Feeling	Epic 9234	1957
WAYLON JENNINGS	Jole Blon/When Sin Stops	Brunswick 55130	1959
CHARLIE PHILLIPS	Sugartime/One Faded Rose	Coral 61908	1957
BILLY WALKER	Viva La Matador/On My Mind Again	Columbia 40920	1957

PART TWO: UK RELEASES
SINGLES

Releases are listed in order of appearance on the British market and dates are expressed in the British manner, ie day/month/year.

∅ denotes original release also available on 78 rpm single; □ denotes initial release in picture sleeve
All releases credited to Buddy Holly or Buddy Holly & The Crickets except ● which denotes original release credited to The Crickets and ⊗ which denotes original release credited to Ivan.

O = Brunswick; Q = Coral; HR = History of Rock; MU, MMU, BH; DMCA; MCA; MCAT; THAT = MCA; OG = Old Gold;;

Record No.	Titles	Release date
O 5581 ∅	Blue Days, Black Nights/Love Me	2.7.56
Q 72279 ● ∅	That'll Be The Day/I'm Looking For Someone To Love	10.9.57
Q 72293 ∅	Peggy Sue/Everyday	15.11.57
Q 72298 ● ∅	Oh Boy!/Not Fade Away	22.12.57
Q 72288 ∅	Listen To Me/I'm Gonna Love You Too	28.2.58
Q 72307 ● ∅	Maybe Baby/Tell Me How	28.2.58
Q 72325 ∅	Rave On/Take Your Time	6.6.58

Record No.	Titles	Release date
Q 72329 ● ∅	Think It Over/Fool's Paradise	4.7.58
Q 72333 ∅	Early In The Morning/Now We're One	8.8.58
Q 72341 ⊗ ∅	Real Wild Child/Oh You Beautiful Doll	31.10.58
Q 72343 ● ∅	It's So Easy/Lonesome Tears	31.10.58
Q 72346 ∅	Heartbeat/Well. . . All Right	21.11.58
Q 72360 ∅	It Doesn't Matter Anymore/Raining In My Heart	13.2.59
O 5800 ∅	Midnight Shift/Rock Around With Ollie Vee	5.6.59
Q 72376 ∅	Peggy Sue Got Married/Crying, Waiting, Hoping	28.8.59
Q 72392	Heartbeat/Everyday	18.3.60
Q 72397	True Love Ways/Moondreams	20.5.60
Q 72411	Learning The Game/That Makes It Tough	7.10.60
Q 72419	What To Do/That's What They Say	31.1.61
Q 72432	(You're So Square) Baby I Don't Care/Valley Of Tears	23.6.61
Q 72445	Look At Me/Mailman, Bring Me No More Blues	17.11.61
Q 72449	Listen To Me/Words Of Love	23.2.62
Q 72455	Reminiscing/Wait 'Til The Sun Shines Nellie	7.9.62
Q 72459	Brown-Eyed Handsome Man/Slippin' And Slidin'	8.3.63
Q 72463	Bo Diddley/It's Not My Fault	31.5.63
Q 72466	Wishing/Because I Love You	30.8.63
Q 72469	What To Do/Ummm, Oh Yeah (Dearest)	13.12.63
Q 72472	You've Got Love/An Empty Cup	24.4.64
Q 72475	Love's Made A Fool Of You/You're The One	4.9.64
Q 72483	Maybe Baby/That's My Desire	20.5.66
MU 1012	Peggy Sue/Rave On	22.3.68
MU 1017	Oh Boy!/That'll Be The Day	10.5.68
MU 1059□	Love Is Strange/You're The One	31.1.69
MU 1081	It Doesn't Matter Anymore/Maybe Baby	23.5.69
MU 1116	Rave On/Ummm, Oh Yeah (Dearest)	13.3.70
MMU 1198	That'll Be The Day/Well . . . All Right/Everyday	4.5.73
MCA 119	It Doesn't Matter Anymore/True Love Ways/Brown-Eyed Handsome Man	1.2.74
MCA 207	Oh Boy/Everyday	29.8.75
MCA 252□	True Love Ways/It Doesn't Matter Anymore/Raining In My Heart/Moondreams	3.9.76
MCA 253□	Peggy Sue/Rave On/Rock Around With Ollie Vee/Midnight Shift	3.9.76
MCA 254□	Maybe Baby/Think It Over/That'll Be The Day/It's So Easy	3.9.76
MCA 344□	Wishing/Love's Made A Fool Of You	13.1.78
HR 001	That'll Be The Day/True Love Ways	1.1.82
OG 9208□	That'll Be The Day/I'm Lookin' For Someone To Love	7.82
OG 9222□	Peggy Sue/Everyday	7.82
OG 9223	Oh Boy/Not Fade Away	7.82
OG 9224	Maybe Baby/Tell Me How	7.82
OG 9319□	Rave On/True Love Ways	4.83
OG 9325	It Doesn't Matter Anymore/Raining In My Heart	4.83

The following ten singles, BH 1– BH 10, were released in picture sleeves featuring winning artists in the 1984 Buddy Holly Week contest and contained in an outer box entitled The Portrait Series Buddy Holly Boxed Set (catalogue number BHB 1) which was reissued in 1985 with the same catalogue number but with a redesigned box.

BH 1□	That'll Be The Day/Rock Me My Baby	7.9.84
BH 2□	Peggy Sue/Everyday	7.9.84
BH 3□	Oh Boy/Not Fade Away	7.9.84
BH 4□	Maybe Baby/Tell Me How	7.9.84
BH 5□	Rave On/Ready Teddy	7.9.84
BH 6□	Think It Over/It's So Easy	7.9.84
BH 7□	It Doesn't Matter Anymore/Raining In My Heart	7.9.84
BH 8□	True Love Ways/Words Of Love	7.9.84
BH 9□	Reminiscing/(You're So Square) Baby I Don't Care	7.9.84
BH 10□	Brown-Eyed Handsome Man/Bo Diddley	7.9.84
THAT 1□	That'll Be the Day/I'm Looking for Someone To Love/ It Doesn't Matter Anymore/Raining In My Heart (7″ 45)	1.9 86
THATT 1□	That'll Be the Day/I'm Looking for Someone To Love/ It Doesn't Matter Anymore/Raining In My Heart (12″ 45)	1.9 86
MCA 1302□	True Love Ways/Raining In My Heart (7″ 45)	25.11.88
MCAT 1302□	True Love Ways/Raining In My Heart/Words Of Love (12″ 45)	25.11.88
DMCA 1302□	True Love Ways/Raining In My Heart/Words Of Love (3″ CD)	25.11.88
MCA 1368□	Oh Boy/Mailman Bring Me No More Blues (7″ 45)	11.9.89
MCAT 1368□	Oh Boy/Well . . . All Right/Mailman Bring Me No More Blues/Everyday (10″ 45)	11.9.89
OG 6147□	That'll Be The Day/Oh Boy/Maybe Baby (3″ CD)	2.6.89
OG 6154□	Peggy Sue/Everyday/Rave On (5″ CD)	2.11.90

EXTENDED PLAY 45 RPM RECORDS (EPs)

OE = Brunswick; FEP = Coral; OG = Old Gold; RCEP = Rollercoaster. All EP releases were in picture sleeves

FEP 2002	*Buddy Holly* (later re-titled *Listen To Me*) Listen To Me/Peggy Sue/I'm Gonna Love You Too/Everyday	Sep-58

NB Early sleeves feature a colour photograph, later copies are colour wash black & white

FEP 2003 ●	*The Sound Of The Crickets* Oh Boy!/Not Fade Away/Maybe Baby/Tell Me How	Sep-58

LONG PLAY ALBUMS (LPs, Cassettes & CDs)

AH = Ace of Hearts; CCSLP, CLACD = Castle; CRT = Cambra; CDX = Charly; CDLM, CDMSP, CP/CPS, LVA = Coral; VSOP = Connoisseur Collection; BOXD, PWKS, SHM, SSP = Hallmark/Pickwick; CDMF = Magnum Farce; IMP = Marks & Spencer; CMAD, DIDX, DMCA, DMCL, DMCM, MUP/S, MCBD, MCCD, MCL, MCLDD, MCM, MCF, CD = MCA; MSQ = Musiquarium; EMTV = EMI/MCA; MFP = Music for Pleasure; PLAT = Prism; 514 = Polygram; GBUD-A = Readers Digest; ROLL, RCCD = Rollercoaster; NEMCD = Sequel; SM = World Records; TSD = Telstar; UPLP = Union Pacific

Record Number	Title	Release date

LVA 9222   *Showcase*   June 1964
Shake, Rattle And Roll/Rock Around With Ollie Vee/Honky Tonk/I Guess I Was Just A Fool/Ummm, Oh Yeah (Dearest)/You're The One/Blue Suede Shoes/Come Back Baby/Rip It Up/Love's Made A Fool Of You/Gone/Girl On My Mind (Re-released in 1968 as He's The One, MUP/MUPS 315, in September 1986 as MCL 1824 and in 1993 as CLACD 306)

LVA 9227   *Holly In The Hills*   June 1965
I Wanna Play House With You/Door To My Heart/Baby, It's Love/I Gambled My Heart/Memories/Wishing/Down The Line/Soft Place In My Heart/Queen Of The Ballroom/Gotta Get You Near Me Blues/Flower Of My Heart/You And I Are Through (The first batch of albums pressed included, in error, 'Reminiscing' in place of 'Wishing'. Re-released in 1968 as Wishing, MUP 320)

AH 148   *Buddy Holly's Greatest Hits*   June 1967
Peggy Sue/That'll Be The Day/Listen To Me/Everyday/Oh Boy!/Not Fade Away/Maybe Baby/Rave On/Think It Over/It's So Easy/It Doesn't Matter Anymore/True Love Ways
(Re-released in 1969 as CP 8; (in 1974 as CDLM 8007 and in 1981 as MCL 1618 with the two additional tracks, Raining In My Heart and Peggy Sue Got Married)

MUPS 371   *Giant*   February 1969
Love Is Strange/Good Rockin' Tonight/Blue Monday/Have You Ever Been Lonely/Slippin' And Slidin'/You're The One/Dearest/Smokey Joe's Cafe/Ain't Got No Home Holly Hop
(Re-released in September 1986 as MCL 1825 and in 1992 as CLACD 307)

CP/CPS 47   *Buddy Holly's Greatest Hits, Volume 2*   May 1970
Early In The Morning/Well . . . All Right/Heartbeat/Peggy Sue Got Married/What To Do/(You're So Square) Baby I Don't Care/Words Of Love/Reminiscing/Brown-Eyed Handsome Man/Bo Diddley/Wishing/Love's Made A Fool Of You

CPS 71   *Remember*   September 1971
Maybe Baby/That Makes It Tough/Crying, Waiting, Hoping/Lonesome Tears/That's My Desire/Real Wild Child/Peggy Sue Got Married/Fool's Paradise/Learning The Game/That's What They Say/Reminiscing/What To Do

CDMSP 802   *Legend*   October 1974
That'll Be The Day I'm Looking For Someone To Love/Not Fade Away/Oh Boy!/Maybe Baby Tell Me How/Think It Over/It's So Easy/Peggy Sue/Words Of Love/Everyday/I'm Gonna Love You Too/Listen To Me/Rave On/Well . . . All Right/Heartbeat/Early In The Morning/Rock Around With Ollie Vee/Midnight Shift/Love's Made A Fool Of You/Wishing/Reminiscing/(You're So Square) Baby I Don't Care/Brown-Eyed Handsome Man/Bo Diddley/It Doesn't Matter Anymore/Moondreams/True Love Ways/Raining In My Heart/Learning The Game/Peggy Sue Got Married/Love Is Strange (Re-released in March 1982 as MCLD 606)

MFP 50176   *Rave On*   August 1975
Rave On/Love Me/It's Too Late/Take Your Time/That Makes It Tough/Gotta Get You Near Me Blues/Everyday/Baby Won't You Come Out Tonight/Dearest/I'm Looking For Someone To Love/Now We're One/Holly Hop

SM 301-5   *The Buddy Holly Story*   November 1975
Rock Around With Ollie Vee/Blue Days, Black Nights/Baby Won't You Come Out Tonight/It's Not My Fault/Love Me/Girl On My Mind/That'll Be The Day/I'm Gonna Set My Foot Down/Ting-A-Ling I'm Changin' All Those Changes/Midnight Shift/Don't Come Back Knockin'/You Are My One Desire/Modern Don Juan/I Guess I Was Just A Fool/Rock-A-Bye Rock/That'll Be The Day/I'm Looking For Someone To Love/Peggy Sue/Everyday/Oh Boy!/Not Fade Away/Listen To Me/I'm Gonna Love You Too/Maybe Baby/Tell Me How/Rave On/Take Your Time/Think It Over/Fool's Paradise/Early In The Morning/Now We're One/It's So Easy/Lonesome Tears/Heartbeat/Well . . . All Right/It Doesn't Matter Anymore/Raining In My Heart/Peggy Sue Got Married/Crying, Waiting, Hoping/True Love Ways/Learning The Game/What To Do/Reminiscing/Brown-Eyed Handsome Man/Bo Diddley/Wishing/Love's Made A Fool Of You/Words Of Love/Moondreams/Love Is Strange/You've Got Love/Dearest/Send Me Some Lovin'/Because I Love You/Look At Me/Rock Me My Baby/It's Too Late/You're The One/Valley Of Tears/Little Baby/Come Back Baby/Last Night/That's What They Say/Ready Teddy/(You're So Square) Baby I Don't Care/Slippin' And Slidin'/Blue Suede Shoes/Shake, Rattle And Roll/Rip It Up/Ain't Got No Home/Honky Tonk/Maybe Baby/An Empty Cup/Wait 'Til The Sun Shines, Nellie/Slippin' And Slidin'/Mailman Bring Me No More Blues/That's My Desire/That Makes It Tough/Holly Hop

CDLM 8038   *The Nashville Sessions*   November 1975
You Are My One Desire/Blue Days, Black Nights/Modern Don Juan/Rock Around With Ollie Vee/Ting-A-Ling/Girl On My Mind/That'll Be The Day/Love Me/I'm Changin' All Those Changes/Don't Come Back Knockin'/Midnight Shift/Rock Around With Ollie Vee (Re-released in 1983 as MCL 1754)

UPLP 004   *Blast From The Past*   1976
Various artists compilation album including the following Buddy Holly track:
Interview with Dale Lowery

CDLM 8055   *Western and Bop*   November 1977
Gotta Get You Near Me Blues/Soft Place In My Heart/Flower Of My Heart/Baby It's Love/Memories/Door To My Heart/Queen Of The Ballroom/You And I Are Through/Down The Line/Maybe Baby/Gone/Because I Love You/It's Not My Fault/I Guess I Was Just A Fool/I Gambled My Heart/Have You Ever Been Lonely

EMTV 8   *Buddy Holly Lives-Buddy Holly & The Crickets 20 Golden Greats*   February 1978
That'll Be The Day/Peggy Sue/Words Of Love/Everyday/Not Fade Away/Oh Boy!/Maybe Baby/Listen To Me/Heartbeat/Think It Over/It Doesn't Matter Anymore/It's So Easy/Well . . . All Right/Rave On/Raining In My Heart/True Love Ways/Peggy Sue Got Married/Bo Diddley/Brown-Eyed Handsome Man/Wishing
(Re-released in 1979 as MCTV 1 and in 1989 as DMCTV 1)

CPMSP 807   *The Complete Buddy Holly*   March 1979
Gotta Get You Near Me Blues/Soft Place In My Heart/Door To My Heart/Flower Of My Heart/Baby It's Love/Memories/Queen Of The Ballroom/I Gambled My Heart/You And I Are Through/Gone/Have You Ever Been Lonely/Down The Line/Brown-Eyed Handsome Man/Bo Diddley/Good Rockin' Tonight/Rip It Up/Blue Monday/Honky Tonk/Blue Suede Shoes/Shake, Rattle & Roll/Ain't Got No Home/Holly Hop/Baby Let's Play House/I'm Gonna Set My Foot Down/Baby Won't You Come Out Tonight/Changin' All Those Changes/Rock-a-Bye Rock/It's Not My Fault/I Guess I Was Just A Fool/Love Me/Don't Come Back Knockin'/Midnight Shift/Blue Days, Black Nights/Rock Around With Ollie Vee I'm Changin' All Those Changes/That'll Be The Day/Girl On My Mind/Ting-A-Ling/Because I Love You Rock Around With Ollie Vee/Modern Don Juan/You Are My One Desire/That'll Be The Day/I'm Looking For Someone To Love/Last Night/Maybe Baby/Words Of Love/Peggy Sue/Everyday/Mailman, Bring Me No More Blues/Listen To Me/I'm Gonna Love You Too/Not Fade Away/Ready Teddy/Oh Boy!/Tell Me How/Maybe Baby/Send Me Some Lovin'/Little Baby/Take Your Time/Rave On/You've Got Love/Valley Of Tears/Rock Me My Baby/(You're So Square) Baby I Don't Care/It's Too Late/An Empty Cup/Look At Me/Think It Over/Fool's Paradise/Early In The Morning/Now We're One/Lonesome Tears/Heartbeat/It's So Easy/Well . . . All Right/Love's Made A Fool Of You/Wishing/Reminiscing/Come Back Baby/That's My Desire/True Love Ways/Moondreams/Raining In My Heart/It Doesn't Matter Anymore/Peggy Sue Got Married/Crying, Waiting, Hoping/Learning The Game/That Makes It Tough/What To Do/That's What They Say/Wait 'Til The Sun Shines, Nellie/Ummm, Oh Yeah (Dearest)/Smokey Joe's Cafe/Slippin' and Slidin'/Love Is Strange/Slippin' and Slidin'/Learning The Game/Crying, Waiting, Hoping/What To Do/That Makes It Tough/Peggy Sue Got Married/That's What They Say/Dearest/You're The One/Slippin' and Slidin'/Dearest/Love Is Strange/Peggy Sue Got Married/That Makes It Tough/Learning The Game/You're The One/Real Wild Child/Oh You Beautiful Doll/Jole Blon/When Sin Stops/Stay Close To Me/Don't Cha Know/Interview In Topeka, Kansas/Ed Sullivan Show-That'll Be The Day/Peggy Sue/Interview With Ed Sullivan/Interview With Alan Freed/Interview With Dick Clark.
(Reissued in 1986 as CDSP/C 807, in September 1989 as DC/ LP CDSP 807. Listed for release as CD set in September 1989 but withdrawn)

Record Number	Title	Release date
IMP 114/2188/3008	*Heartbeat*	June 1980

Heartbeat/Send Me Some Lovin'/I'm Gonna Love You Too/Valley Of Tears/Love's Made A Fool Of You/True Love Ways/Maybe Baby/because I Love You/I'm Lookin' For Someone To Love/It's Too Late/You've Got Love/Raining In My Heart (Available only through Marks & Spencer retail stores during a short-lived experiment in record retailing)

SSP 3070	*Buddy Holly*	September 1980

That'll Be The Day/Tell Me How/Moondreams/You Are My One Desire/Baby Won't You Come Out Tonight/Rock Around With Ollie Vee/Well . . . All Right/It Doesn't Matter Anymore/Love Is Strange/Early In The Morning/(You're So Square) Baby I Don't Care/Everyday

MFP 50490	*Rock On With Buddy*	October 1980

Brown-Eyed Handsome Man/Rock Around With Ollie Vee/Ready Teddy/Rock Me My Baby/It's Too Late/Blue Days, Black Nights/Holly Hop/I'm Lookin' For Someone To Love/Crying, Waiting, Hoping/Peggy Sue Got Married/Rave On/Love Me/(You're So Square) Baby I Don't Care/Ting-A-Ling/Tell Me How/Love's Made A Fool Of You/Baby Won't You Come Out Tonight/Dearest/Slippin' And Slidin'/Everyday

MCF 3117	*Love Songs*	August 1981

True Love Ways/Everyday/Listen To Me/You've Got Love/Learning The Game/Send Me Some Lovin'/Love Is Strange/That's What They Say/Because I Love You/Raining In My Heart/Heartbeat/Moondreams/Take Your Time/Dearest/Look At Me/You're The One/Wishing/It Doesn't Matter Anymore/What To Do/Words Of Love
(Re-released in September 1982 as 20 Love Songs, MFP 5570, in 1984 with Greatest Hits as a twin cassette pack, catalogue number MCA 2117, in 1991 as DMCL 1717 and in 1992 as MCLD 19047)

CRT 008	*Buddy Holly*	January 1982

Peggy Sue/Slippin' and Slidin'/It's So Easy/Not Fade Away/Tell Me How/Crying, Waiting, Hoping/(You're So Square) Baby I Don't Care/Everyday/Rave On/Learning The Game/Well . . . All Right/Heartbeat/Blue Suede Shoes/Maybe Baby/Brown-Eyed Handsome Man/True Love Ways/It Doesn't Matter Anymore/Bo Diddley/It's Too Late/Oh Boy!/Moondreams/Wishing/That'll Be The Day/I'm Lookin' For Someone To Love/Listen To Me/Holly Hop/Love Is Strange/Words Of Love/Peggy Sue Got Married (Released on cassette tape only)

MCM 1002	*For The First Time Anywhere*	March 1983

Rock-A-Bye Rock/Maybe Baby/Because I Love You/I'm Gonna Set My Foot Down/Changin' All Those Changes/That's My Desire/Baby Won't You Come Out Tonight/It's Not My Fault/Brown-Eyed Handsome Man/Bo Diddley (Reissued in 1987 as CMCAD 31048, in 1991 as DMCL 1712 and in 1993 as MCLD 19185)

CR/T 123	*Buddy Holly & The Crickets*	May 1984

Raining In My Heart Baby Won't You Come Out Tonight/Modern Don Juan/Mailman, Bring Me No More Blues/Love's Made A Fool Of You/You've Got Love/Girl On My Mind/That'll Be The Day/Blue Days, Black Nights/Midnight Shift/I'm Gonna Love You Too/Don't Come Back Knockin'/Fool's Paradise/An Empty Cup/Rock Around With Ollie Vee/Think It Over/It's Not My Fault/I Guess I Was Just A Fool/I'm Gonna Set My Foot Down/Rock-A-Bye Rock/Because I Love You/You're The One/Ready Teddy/Send Me Some Lovin'/Lonesome Tears/Rock Around With Ollie Vee/Reminiscing/The Crickets featuring Earl Sinks: Love's Made A Fool Of You/When You Ask About Love/The Crickets featuring Sonny Curtis: Baby My Heart

CDX 8	*Buddy Holly Rocks*	May 1985

Gotta Get You Near Me Blues/Down The Line/Baby Let's Play House/I Guess I Was Just A Fool/Rip It Up Brown-Eyed Handsome Man/Bo Diddley/Holly Hop/Midnight Shift/Blue Days, Black Nights/Love Me/Don't Come Back Knockin'/I'm Changin' All Those Changes/Ting-A-Ling/Modern Don Juan/Rock Around With Ollie Vee/That'll Be The Day/I'm Lookin' For Someone To Love/Not Fade Away/Oh Boy/Peggy Sue/I'm Gonna Love You Too/Rock Me My Baby/Tell Me How/Rave On/(You're So Square) Baby I Don't Care/Think It Over/Love's Made A Fool Of You/It's So Easy/Early In The Morning/Maybe Baby It Doesn't Matter Anymore

MCM 5003	*Golden Greats*	July 1985

Peggy Sue/That'll Be The Day/Listen To Me/Everyday/Oh Boy !/Not Fade Away/Raining In My Heart/Brown-Eyed Handsome Man/Maybe Baby/Rave On/Think It Over/It's So Easy/It Doesn't Matter Anymore/True Love Ways/Peggy Sue Got Married/Bo Diddley (reissued in 1991 as DMCM 5003 and in 1992 as MCLD 19046)

DIDX-203	*From The Original Master Tapes*	November 1985

That'll Be The Day/Oh Boy!/Not Fade Away/Tell Me How/Maybe Baby/Everyday/Rock Around with Ollie Vee/It's So Easy/I'm Lookin' For Someone To Love/Peggy Sue/I'm Gonna Love You Too/Words of Love/Rave On/Well . . . All Right/Listen To Me/Think It Over/Heartbeat/True Love Ways/Reminiscing It Doesn't Matter Anymore (Originally imported from the USA by MCA as MCAD 5540. Reissued in 1986 as DMCMD 7003 and in 1993 as MCLD 19186)

ROLL 2013	*Something Special From Buddy Holly*	September 1986

Gone (2 versions)/Have you Ever Been Lonely (3 versions)/Brown-Eyed Handsome Man/Good Rockin' Tonight/Rip It Up/Blue Monday/Honky Tonk/Blue Suede Shoes/Shake, Rattle And Roll/Bo Diddley/Ain't Got No Home/Holly Hop

SHM 3199	*The Best Of Buddy Holly*	September 1986

That'll Be The Day/Maybe Baby/Peggy Sue Got Married/Rave On/True Love Ways/Bo Diddley/Oh Boy/Peggy Sue/Everyday/Think It Over/Brown Eyed Handsome Man/Heartbeat/Raining In My Heart/It Doesn't Matter Anymore (Reissued in 1987 as PCD 888 and in 1991 as PWKS 595)

GBUD-A-176	*The Unforgettable Buddy Holly*	September 1986

Peggy Sue/Maybe Baby/Rave On/Wishing/Oh Boy/Brown Eyed Handsome Man/Reminiscing/That'll Be the Day/It Doesn't Matter Anymore/Listen To Me/Think It Over/Valley Of Tears/Peggy Sue Got Married/Baby I Don't Care/Bo Diddley/Early In The Morning/Heartbeat/True Love Ways/Words Of Love/Crying, Waiting, Hoping/Look At Me/Dearest/Last Night/It's Too Late/It's So Easy/Raining In My Heart/Send Me Some Lovin'/Moondreams/Modern Don Juan/Girl On My Mind/Take Your Time/Everyday/Learning The Game/Love Is Strange/Ready Teddy/Love's Made A Fool Of You/Slippin' and Slidin'/Blue Suede Shoes/Rock Around With Ollie Vee/Rip It Up/Ain't Got No Home/Ting-A-Ling/Wait Till The Sune Shines, Nellie/Shake Rattle And Roll/Blue Days, Black Nights/Come Baby Baby/I'm Gonna Set My Foot Down/Rock Me My Baby/I'm Lookin' For Someone To Love/Rock-A-Bye Rock/I'm Changing All Those Changes/Baby Won't You Come Out Tonight/I'm Gonna Love You Too/Well . . . All Right/You've Got Love/That's My Desire/An Empty Cup (And A Broken Date)/Lonesome Tears/Because I Love You/Mailman, Bring Me No More Blues/Fool's Paradise/What To Do/Midnight Shift/It's Not My Fault/Not Fade Away/You Are My One Desire/That Makes It Tough/That's What They Say/Now We're One

MCL 1827	*The Stereo Album*	October 1986

True Love Ways/Moondreams/Raining In My Heart/It Doesn't Matter Anymore/Love Is Strange/Dearest/Peggy Sue Got Married/Crying, Waiting, Hoping/That Makes It Tough/Slippin' and Slidin'/You're The One/That's What They Say/What To Do/Learning The Game/Smokey Joe's Cafe/Wait Till The Sun Shines Nellie NB: Although test pressings were reportedly made for this album it was never made available commercially

MFP 5806	*Rock 'n' Roll Greats*	October 1987

That'll Be The Day/Peggy Sue/Listen To Me/Oh Boy/Rave On/Early In The Morning/Maybe Baby/Think It Over/Heartbeat/Not Fade Away/It's So Easy/Words Of Love/Everyday/I'm Gonna Love You Too

Record Number	Title	Release date

SHM 3221   *The Legendary Buddy Holly*   October 1987
Listen To Me/Words Of Love/You've Got Love/Learning The Game/Not Fade Away/What To Do/Early In The Morning/Wishing/Love's Made A Fool Of You/Love Is Strange/(You're So Square) Baby I Don't Care/Midnight Shift/Reminiscing/Valley Of Tears (Reissued as PWKS 523 in 1989)

CCSLP 172   *The Collection*   1988
Think It Over/That'll Be The Day/True Love Ways/ Words Of Love/Rock Me My Baby/Ready Teddy/I'm Gonna Love You Too/Love's Made A Fool Of You/Blue Days, Black Nights/Maybe Baby/I'm Looking For Someone To Love/Send Me Some Lovin'/Reminiscing/Listen To Me/ Well . . . All Right/Oh Boy/Wishing/Not Fade Away/Heartbeat/Moondreams/Raining In My Heart/Don't Come Back Knockin'/Peggy Sue/*The Crickets featuring Earl Sinks*: When You Ask About Love

PLAT/C 307   *True Love Ways*   May 1988
Peggy Sue/That'll Be The Day/Everyday/Oh Boy/True Love Ways/It Doesn't Matter Anymore/Raining In My Heart/Learning The Game/I'm Gonna Love You Too/Ready Teddy/Wishing/Well . . . All Right/Moondreams/Midnight Shift/Love's Made A Fool Of You/Reminiscing

VSOPLP 114   *The Legend*   February 1988
That'll Be The Day/Peggy Sue/Listen To Me/Because I Love You/Slippin' and Slidin'/Send Me Some Lovin'/Rave On/Heartbeat/Blue Days, Black Nights/Moondreams/Look At Me/Blue Suede Shoes/It Doesn't Matter Anymore/Midnight Shift/You Are My One Desire/Girl On My Mind/An Empty Cup (And A Broken Date)/Dearest/Oh Boy/Learning The Game/Love Is Strange/Take Your Time/Words Of Love/True Love Ways

TCD 2339   *True Love Ways*   February 1989
True Love Ways/Everyday/Heartbeat/Maybe Baby/You've Got Love/Peggy Sue Got Married/Reminiscing/Love Is Strange/Learning The Game/Think It Over/Raining In My Heart/It's So Easy/Words Of Love/Listen To Me/Wishing/Love's Made A Fool Of You/Because I Love You/Fool's Paradise/Crying, Waiting, Hoping/It Doesn't Matter Anymore

SHM 3294   *Moondreams*   April 1990
Moondreams/Because I Love You/I Guess I Was Just A Fool/Girl On My Mind/I'm Gonna Love You Too/You And I Are Through/Come Back Baby/You're The One/I Gambled My Heart/You Are My One Desire/Door To My Heart/Crying, Waiting, Hoping/Now We're One/Love Me/Soft Place In My Heart/Have You Ever Been Lonely (Reissued as PWKS 560)

BOXD 26   *Special Limited Edition 3-CD Box*   October 1992
Repackaging of three individual CDs, PWKS 523, 560 and 595, in outer numbered box (Reissued in 1995 in a 3-CD case and re-numbered BOXD 26T)

514 487-2/1   *Words Of Love*   February 1993
Words Of Love/That'll Be The Day/Peggy Sue/Think It Over/True Love Ways/What To Do/Crying, Waiting, Hoping/Well . . . All Right/Love's Made A Fool Of You/Peggy Sue Got Married/Valley Of Tears/Wishing/Raining In My Heart/Oh Boy/Rave On/Brown Eyed Handsome Man/Bo Diddley/It's So Easy/It Doesn't Matter Anymore/Maybe Baby/Early In The Morning/Love Is Strange/Listen To Me/I'm Gonna Love You Too/Learning The Game/Baby I Don't Care/Heartbeat/Everyday

CDMF 088   *The Picks—The Original Voices of The Crickets*   June 1993
True Love Ways/Everyday/Love Me/Don't Come Back Knockin'/(You're So Square) Baby I Don't Care/Reminiscing/Peggy Sue/Well . . . All Right/Midnight Shift/Blue Days, Black Nights/That's What They Say/Rock-A-Bye Rock/Heartbeat/Girl On My Mind/Ting-A-Ling/I'm Gonna Set My Foot Down/It's Not My Fault/Rock Around With Ollie Vee/You Are My One Desire/Because I Love You/Modern Don Juan/*The Picks*: Words/You've Lost That Loving Feelin'/Buddy Holly Not Fade Away

MCLDD 19242   *That'll Be The Day*   April 1994
I'm Gonna Love You Too/Peggy Sue/Look At Me/Listen To Me/Valley Of Tears/Ready Teddy/Everyday/Mailman, Bring Me No More Blues/Words Of Love/(You're So Square) Baby I Don't Care/Rave On/Little Baby/You Are My One Desire/Blue Days, Black Nights/Modern Don Juan/Rock Around With Ollie Vee/Ting-A-Ling/Girl On My Mind/That'll Be The Day/Love Me/I'm Changing All Those Changes/Don't Come Back Knockin'/Midnight Shift/Rock Around With Ollie Vee

MCBD 19506   *The Best Of Buddy Holly*   May 1994
That'll Be The Day/Oh Boy/Maybe Baby/Think It Over/Peggy Sue/Listen To Me/Rave On/Early In The Morning/Heartbeat/Midnight Shift/Peggy Sue Got Married/True Love Ways/Learning The Game/Everyday/Reminiscing/Brown Eyed Handsome Man/Bo Diddley/Wishing/Words Of Love/It Doesn't Matter Anymore

PWKS 4205   *The Crickets—The Singles Collection 1957-1961*   June 1994
That'll Be The Day/I'm Lookin' For Someone To Love/Oh Boy/Not Fade Away/Maybe Baby/Tell Me How/Think It Over/Fool's Paradise/It's So Easy/Lonesome Tears/*The Crickets featuring Earl Sinks*: Love's Made a Fool Of You/Someone, Someone/When You Ask About Love/Deborah/A Sweet Love/I Fought The Law/*The Crickets featuring Sonny Curtis*: Baby, My Heart/More Than I Can Say/*The Crickets Featuring David Box*: Don't Cha Know/Peggy Sue Got Married

MCCD 177   *Cover To Cover*   October 1994
Heartbeat/Listen To Me/Raining In My Heart/(You're So Square) Baby I Don't Care/Everyday/You've Got Love/I'm Gonna Love You Too/Mailman Bring Me No More Blues/Words Of Love/Well . . . All Right/Rock Around With Ollie Vee/Learning The Game/True Love Ways/Love Is Strange/*The Crickets Featuring Earl Sinks*: When You Ask About Love/I Fought The Law/Love's Made A Fool Of You/Ting-A-Ling/Time Will Tell/*The Crickets Featuring Sonny Curtis*: More Than I Can Say

MCBD 19522   *The Love Songs*   March 1995
Love Is Strange/Raining In My Heart/Valley Of Tears/You're The One/Baby It's Love/Baby Won't You Come Out Tonight/Because I Love You/You've Got Love/I Guess I Was Just A Fool/Love Me/Not Fade Away/I'm Gonna Love You Too/Send Me Some Lovin'/Lonesome Tears/Girl On My Mind/Now We're One/Crying, Waiting, Hoping/You're The One/Fool's Paradise/Blue Monday/Love's Made a Fool Of You/Love Is Strange

MSQ CD 002   *The Crickets with Buddy Holly—20 Of The Best*   April 1995
That'll Be The Day/Rave On/Peggy Sue/Words Of Love/Think It Over/Bo Diddley/Maybe Baby/Oh Boy/Blue Days, Black Nights/It's So Easy/You've Got Love/ Not Fade Away/Midnight Shift/Lonesome Tears/Brown Eyed Handsome Man/Early In The Morning/*The Crickets Featuring Earl Sinks*/Deborah/Love's Made A Fool Of You/I Fought The Law/*The Crickets Featuring Sonny Curtis*: Baby My Heart

ORIGINAL RELEASES BY OTHER ARTISTS FEATURING BUDDY HOLLY

Artist	Title/s	Record Number	Year
JACK HUDDLE	Starlight/Believe Me	CR 30236	1984
BEN HALL	*All From Loving You/Rose Of Monetrey*	RCCD 3004	1993
JACK NEAL	*I Saw The Moon Cry Last Night/I Hear The Lord Callin' For Me*	RCCD 3017	1996
JERRY ENGLER	What-A You Gonna Do?/I Sent You Roses	RCCD 3017	1966

CHARTS FILE

The following information is taken from charts published in the countries listed. The US charts were based on airplay and sales, generally other charts were based on sales information only. It is well known that singles charts in particular are susceptible to 'hyping' from record labels and other interested parties. There have been many attempts to compile charts which are impervious to such influences but it would seem that many lower region chart entries were not always reliable. In this context it is worth mentioning that *It's So Easy* appeared in the Record Mirror charts at position 19, while failing to make any impression on any other UK chart. The UK sales figures given here were taken from the Decca Record Company files and will therefore be of interest as they give a more reliable guide to the popularity—unfortunately the figure for *It's So Easy* was missing . . .

Title	US Billboard			US Cashbox			UK NME/RR			UK Sales	Australia		
	E	P	W	E	P	W	E	P	W		E	P	W
That'll Be The Day	8.57	3	22	8.75	3	20	9.57	1	15	431,000	10.57	2	16
Peggy Sue	11.57	3	22	10.57	2	20	12.57	6	17	259,000	2.58	2	13
Oh Boy!	11.57	10	20	11.57	13	14	12.57	3	15	331,000	2.58	2	13
Everyday				11.57	51	3					2.58	9	12
Listen To Me (Q 72288)							3.58	16	2	70,000			
Maybe Baby (Q. 72307)	3.58	17	14	2.58	11	11	3.58	4	10	293,000	3.58	15	10
I'm Gonna Love You Too				3.58	56	1					6.58	38	1
Rave On	5.58	37	10	5.58	56	2	6.58	5	14	150,000	858	29	1
Think It Over	7.58	27	9	7.58	42	10	7.58	11	7	86,000			
Early In The Morning	8.58	32	7	7.58	25	10	8.58	17	4	66,000	10.58	22	10
Fool's Paradise	8.58	58	1	7.58	73	1							
It's So Easy											1.59	8	19
Real Wild Child (Ivan)	9.58	68	5										
Heartbeat (Q.72346)	12.58	82	4				1.59	30	1	72,000			
Well . . . All Right											3.59	24	7
It Doesn't Matter Anymore	2.59	13	14	2.59	30	14	2.59	1	21	401,000	5.59	1	15
Raining In My Heart	3.59	88	2	2.59	88	1							
Midnight Shift							7.59	26	1	56,000	1.6	7	10
Peggy Sue Got Married							9.59	17	10				
Heartbeat (Q.72392)										38,000			
True Love Ways							5.6	25	1	44,000			
Learning The Game							10.6	28	2	38,000			
What To Do (Q.72419)							2.61	29	1	28,000			
Baby I Don't Care							6.61	14	10	121,000			
Listen To Me (Q.72449)							3.62	18	2	47,000			
Reminiscing							9.62	17	7	65,000			
Wait 'Til The Sun Shines Nellie											10.62	24	4
Brown-Eyed Handsome Man	10.63	113	2				3.63	3	12	159,000	8.63	10	5
Bo Diddley	4.63	116	4				6.63	8	10	130,000	5.63	5	9
Wishing							9.63	12	8	100,000			
What To Do (Q.72469)							12.63	27	8	56,000			
I'm Gonna Love You Too (reissue)											2.64	6	9
You've Got Love							5.64	40	6	30,000			
Peggy Sue (reissue)											8.64	34	4
Love's Made A Fool Of You							9.64	39	7	27,000			
Maybe Baby (Q.72483)							6.66	53	2	9,000			
Peggy Sue							4.68	32	9				
Love is Strange	4.69	105	3	5.69	94	3							
That'll Be The Day (THAT 1)							9.86	85	2				
True Love Ways (MCA 1302)							12.88	65	4				

The UK singles chart information was taken from New Musical Express top 30 charts up to September 1963 and from the Record Retailer/Record Mirror from that date when top 50 positions were given instead of top 20. Key: E = Month & year of 1st entry; P = Position; W = Weeks on chart; NME = New Musical Express; RR = Record Mirror/Record Retailer

UK EP CHARTS

No UK charts appear to have been printed for extended play records until the early 1960's. However, Buddy Holly and Crickets EPs were still popular and most remained in the record company catalogues until the general demise of the EP record in the late 1960's.

Title	Month entered chart	Peak	Weeks in chart
Listen To Me	3.62	12	17
Rave On	7.61	9	22
It's So Easy	1.62	18	1
Heartbeat	8.61	13	6
Buddy Holly No. 1	8.61	18	2
The Late Great	3.6	4	44
Four More	6.6	7	5

The UK EP chart information was taken from the Record Retailer/Record Mirror top 20 EP charts

US AND UK LP CHARTS

Title	Month entered US chart	Peak	Weeks in chart	Month entered UK chart	Peak	Weeks in chart
The Chirping Crickets				4.58	5	*
Buddy Holly				8.58	8	*
The Buddy Holly Story	4.59	11	181	5.59	2	156
The Buddy Holly Story Vol 2				10.60	7	14
That'll Be The Day				0.61	5	14
Reminiscing	3.63	40	17	4.63	2	31
Showcase				6.64	3	16
Holly in The Hills				6.65	13	6
Greatest Hits (AH 148)	7.67				9	40
Giant				4.69	13	1
Greatest Hits (CP8)				8.71	42	6
Greatest Hits (CDLM 807)				7.75	37	3
Buddy Holly Lives	8.78	55	12	3.78	1	20
Greatest Hits (MCL 1618)				9.84	100	1
True Love Ways				2.89	8	11
Words of Love				2.93	1	9

LP chart information is drawn from US Billboard and UK New Musical Express, Record Mirror or Record Retailer Long Play record charts. * weeks on chart not known

TOUR DATES

January 1956–February 1959

We have only included dates from the beginning of Buddy Holly's professional career, thus 'hometown' and similar appearances are not included. Tour dates are listed in date order and are taken from the original tour itinerary sheets prepared by booking agencies and from newspaper and magazine reports. Many dates were unconfirmed or open at the time itineraries were made at the beginning of each tour—consequently some have not been verified. Not all artists listed appeared on all dates of a tour. Blank dates are rest days or unknown. Any corrections or further information would be welcomed.

SONNY JAMES TOUR

Featuring: Sonny James, Faron Young, Tommy Collins, Wanda Jackson, Buddy Holly and the Two-Tones (Sonny Curtis & Don Guess)

April		May	
	dates and locations unknown	6	Oklahoma City, Oklahoma
		7	Tulsa, Oklahoma
			other dates and locations unknown

HANK THOMPSON TOUR

Featuring: Hank Thompson, Cowboy Copas, Hank Locklin, Mitchell Torok, Wanda Jackson, Glen Reeves, George Jones, Buddy Holly (with Sonny Curtis, Don Guess & Jerry Allison)

September	October
dates and locations unknown	dates and locations unknown

HANK THOMPSON TOUR

Featuring: Hank Thompson, Wanda Jackson, Mitchell Torok, Hank Locklin, Cowboy Copas, George Jones, Justin Tubb, Buddy Holly and the Two-Tones (Sonny Curtis & Don Guess)

January 1957			
9	Little Rock, Arkansas	16	Charleston, South Carolina
10	New Orleans, Louisiana	17	Ocala, Florida
11	Birmingham, Alabama	18	Miami, Florida
12	Jacksonville, Florida	19	Macon, Georgia
13	Tampa, Florida	20	Atlanta, Georgia
14	Unknown	21	Montgomery, Alabama
15	Savannah, Georgia	22	Pensacola, Florida
		23	Memphis, Tennessee

AUGUST, 1957 TOUR

Featuring: Clyde McPhatter, The Cadillacs, Edna McGriff, Otis Rush, Lee Andrews & The Hearts, Oscar & Oscar, The Crickets (and for the Apollo dates only, The G-Clefs)

August 1957			
2–8	Howard Theater, Washington, DC	16–22	Apollo Theater, New York
9–15	Royal Theater, Baltimore, Maryland	30	Brooklyn Paramount Theater, New York

BIGGEST SHOW OF STARS FOR 1957

Featuring: Paul Williams, Chuck Berry, The Spaniels, Johnnie & Joe, Tommy Brown, The Bobettes, Paul Anka, The Drifters, Frankie Lymon & The Teenagers, Lavern Baker, The Everly Brothers, Paul Williams, Jimmy Bowen, Clyde McPhatter, Sam "The Man" Taylor, Buddy Holly & The Crickets
(Buddy Holly & The Crickets, Paul Anka, The Everly Brothers and Jimmy Bowen did not appear on the dates marked * due to segregation laws then in force in those cities forbidding black and white acts on the same stage)

September			
1–5	Brooklyn Paramount Theater, New York	3	Heart of Texas Auditorium, Waco, Texas
6	Syria Mosque, Pittsburgh, Pennsylvania	4	Municipal Auditorium, San Antonio, Texas
7	The Mosque, Richmond, Virginia (possibly cancelled)	5	City Auditorium, Corpus Christi, Texas
8	Carr's Beach Ballroom, Annapolis, Maryland (possibly cancelled)	6	Sam Houston Coliseum, Houston, Texas
9	Municipal Auditorium, Norfolk, Virginia	7	City Coliseum, Austin, Texas
10	Akron Armory Auditorium, Akron, Ohio	8	El Paso Civic Auditorium, El Paso, Texas
11	Cincinnati Gardens, Cincinnati, Ohio	9	Municipal Auditorium, Albuquerque, New Mexico
12	Veteran's Memorial Auditorium, Columbus, Ohio	10	Catalina High Auditorium, Tucson, Arizona
13	Sports Arena, Hershey, Pennsylvania	11	Coliseum, Phoenix, Arizona
14	Maple Leaf Gardens, Toronto, Ontario, Canada	12	Mission Beach Ballroom, San Diego, California
15	Forum, Montreal, Quebec, Canada	13	Memorial Auditorium, Fresno, California
16	Onondaga Memorial Auditorium, Syracuse,New York	14	Rest day—Hilton Hotel, Los Angeles, California
17	War Memorial Auditorium, Rochester, New York	15	Shrine Auditorium, Los Angeles, California
18	Coliseum, Baltimore, Maryland (2 shows)	16	Rest day—Hilton Hotel, Los Angeles, California
19	Memorial Auditorium, Raleigh, North Carolina	17	San Jose Auditorium, San Jose, California
20	Memorial Coliseum, Winston-Salem, North Carolina	18	Auditorium, Sacramento, California
21	Coliseum, Charlotte, North Carolina	19	Civic Auditorium, San Francisco, California
22	Municipal Auditorium, Atlanta, Georgia	20	Matinee—Civic Auditorium, Stockton, California
23	*New Auditorium, Columbus, Georgia		Evening—Oakland Auditorium, Oakland, California (unconfirmed)
24	*Memorial Auditorium, Chattanooga,Tennessee	21	Oakland Auditorium, Oakland, California
25	*Memorial Auditorium, Birmingham, Alabama	22	Paramount Theater, Portland, Oregon
26	*Municipal Auditorium, New Orleans, Louisiana	23	Georgia Auditorium, Vancouver, BC, Canada
27	*The Auditorium, Memphis, Tennessee	24	Temple Theater, Tacoma, Washington
28	Municipal Auditorium, Tulsa, Oklahoma	25	Orpheum Theater, Seattle, Washington
29	Municipal Auditorium, Oklahoma City, Oklahoma	26	Orpheum Theater, Seattle, Washington
30	City Auditorium, Wichita Falls, Texas	27	Coliseum, Spokane, Washington
October		28	University of Idaho, Moscow, Idaho
1	New Auditorium, Dallas, Texas	29	Stampede Corral, Calgary, Alberta, Canada
2	Will Rogers Memorial Auditorium, Fort Worth, Texas	30	Edmonton Gardens, Edmonton, Alberta, Canada
		31	Exhibition Stadium, Regina, Saskatchewan, Canada

November

1	Arena Auditorium, Denver, Colorado
2	Forum, Wichita, Kansas
3	Municipal Auditorium, Kansas City, Missouri
4	Civic Auditorium Music Hall, Omaha, Nebraska
5	Auditorium, Topeka, Kansas
6	Kiel Opera House, St. Louis, Missouri
7	Indiana Theater, Indianapolis, Indiana
8	Coliseum, Ft. Wayne, Indiana
9	State Fair Coliseum, Louisville, Kentucky
10	Fox Theater, Detroit, Michigan
11	Sports Arena, Toledo, Ohio
12	Syria Mosque, Pittsburgh, Pennsylvania
13	Warner Bros. Theater, Erie, Pennsylvania
14	RPI Field House, Troy, New York
15	Boston Gardens, Boston, Massachusetts
16	State Theater, Hartford, Connecticut
17	Forum, Montreal, Canada
18	Auditorium Arena, Ottawa, Canada
19	Buffalo Municipal Auditorium, Buffalo, New York
20	Arena, Philadelphia, Pennsylvania
21	Unknown
22	Municipal Auditorium, Norfolk, Virginia
23	Coliseum, Charlotte, North Carolina
24	Mosque, Richmond, Virginia

ALAN FREED CHRISTMAS HOLIDAY OF STARS SHOW

Featuring: Fats Domino, Jerry Lee Lewis, The Everly Brothers, Buddy Holly & The Crickets, The Rays, Danny & The Juniors, Paul Anka and others

December
26–31 New York Paramount Theater

January 1958
1–6 New York Paramount Theater

EVERLY BROTHERS TOUR

Featuring:The Everly Brothers, The Royal Teens, The Rays, Buddy Holly & The Crickets, The Shepherd Sisters, Paul Anka, Margie Rayburn, Danny & The Juniors, The Tuneweavers, The Hollywood Flames, Jimmy Edwards, Billy Brown, The Mello-Kings, Al Jones, Sam Donahue & His Orchestra

January 1958

8	Coliseum, Charlotte, North Carolina
9	Venue unknown, Raleigh, North Carolina
10	Venue unknown, Winston-Salem, North Carolina
11	Venue unknown, Norfolk, Virginia
12	Mosque, Richmond, Virginia (2 shows)
13	Coliseum, Baltimore, Maryland
14	St, Joseph Armoury, Hazelton, Pennsylvania
15	Venue unknown, Youngstown, Ohio
16	Venue unknown, Columbus, Ohio
17	Venue unknown, Hershey, Pennsylvania
18	Venue unknown, Buffalo, New York
19	Auditorium, Rochester, New York
20	Location unknown
21	Syria Mosque, Pittsburgh, Pennsylvania
22	Venue unknown, Erie, Pennsylvania
23	Venue unknown, Cincinnati, Ohio
24	Venue unknown, Louisville, Kentucky

HAWAII

Featuring: Buddy Holly & The Crickets, Paul Anka, Jerry Lee Lewis, Jodie Sands

January
27 Civic Auditorium, Honolulu, Hawaii (2 shows)

AUSTRALIAN TOUR (LEE GORDON'S WORLD HIT PARADE)

Featuring: Paul Anka, Buddy Holly & The Crickets, Jerry Lee Lewis, Jodie Sands, Johnny O'Keefe

January

30	Sydney Stadium, Sydney, New South Wales
31	Newcastle Stadium, Newcastle, New South Wales

February

1	Sydney Stadium, Sydney, New South Wales (3 shows)
2	Rest day
3	Cloudland Ballroom, Brisbane, Queensland (2 shows)
4	West Melbourne Stadium, Melbourne, Victoria (2 shows)
5	West Melbourne Stadium, Melbourne, Victoria (2 shows)

HAWAII

Featuring: Buddy Holly & The Crickets, Paul Anka, Jerry Lee Lewis, Jodie Sands

February
9 Scofield Barracks, Honolulu

THE BIG GOLD RECORD STARS

Featuring: The Everly Brothers, Bill Haley & His Comets, Buddy Holly & The Crickets, Jerry Lee Lewis. Jimmie Rodgers was booked to appear on this tour, but did not do so.

February

20	Kellog Auditorium, Orlando, Florida (2 shows)
21	Ft, Hesterley Armory, Tampa, Florida (2 shows)
22	National Guard Armory, Jacksonville, Florida (2 shows)
23	Connie Mack Stadium, West Palm Beach, Florida (2 shows)
24	Dade County Auditorium, Miami, Florida (2 shows)
25	War Memorial Auditorium, Fort Lauderdale, Florida (2 shows)

THE BRITISH TOUR

Featuring: Buddy Holly & The Crickets, Gary Miller, The Tanner Sisters, Des O'Connor, Ronnie Keene & His Orchestra

March

1	Trocadero, Elephant & Castle, London (2 shows)
2	Gaumont State, Kilburn, London (2 shows)
3	Gaumont Theatre, Southampton, Hampshire (2 shows)
4	City Hall, Sheffield, Yorkshire (2 shows)
5	Globe Theatre, Stockton-on-Tees, Co, Durham (2 shows)
6	City Hall, Newcastle-on-Tyne, Northumberland (2 shows)
7	Gaumont Theatre, Wolverhampton, Staffordshire (2 shows)
8	Odeon Theatre, Nottingham, Nottinghamshire (3 shows)
9	Gaumont Theatre, Bradford, Yorkshire (2 shows)
10	Town Hall, Birmingham, Warwickshire (2 shows)
11	Gaumont Theatre, Worcester, Worcestershire (2 shows)
12	Davis Theatre, Croydon, London (2 shows)
13	Granada Theatre, East Ham, London (2 shows)
14	Granada Theatre, Woolwich, London (2 shows)
15	Gaumont Theatre, Ipswich, Suffolk (3 shows)
16	De Montfort Hall, Leicester, Leicestershire (2 shows)
17	Gaumont Theatre, Doncaster, Yorkshire (2 shows)
18	Ritz Theatre, Wigan, Lancashire (2 shows)
19	Regal Cinema, Hull, Yorkshire (2 shows)
20	Philharmonic Hall, Liverpool, Lancashire (2 shows)
21	Granada Theatre, Walthamstow, London (2 shows)
22	Gaumont Theatre, Salisbury, Wiltshire (2 shows)
23	Colston Hall, Bristol, Gloucestershire (2 shows)
24	Capitol Cinema, Cardiff, Glamorgan (2 shows)
25	Gaumont Theatre, Hammersmith, London (2 shows)

ALAN FREED'S BIG BEAT SHOW

Featuring: Jerry Lee Lewis, Chuck Berry, Frankie Lymon, The Diamonds, Billy Ford, Danny & The Juniors, The Chantels, Larry Williams, Screaming Jay Hawkins, The Pastels, Jo-Ann Campbell, Ed Townsend, Alan Freed Orchestra with Sam "The Man" Taylor

March
28	Paramount Theater, New York (2 shows)
29	Paramount Theater, New York (3 shows)
30	State Theater, Hartford, Connecticut
31	Loews Paradise Theater, Bronx, New York

April
1	Convention Hall, Philadelphia, Pennsylvania
2	Coliseum, New York
3	Coliseum, Baltimore (2 shows)
4	Memorial Hall, Dayton, Ohio
5	Auditorium, Grand Rapids, Michigan
6	Public Hall, Cleveland, Ohio
7	Memorial Hall, Canton, Ohio (2 shows)
8	War Veterans Memorial Auditorium, Columbus, Ohio (2 shows)
9	The Arena, Windsor, Ontario, Canada (2 shows)
10	The Arena, London, Ontario, Canada
11	The Auditorium, Kitchener, Ontario, Canada
12	Sports Arena, Toledo, Ohio
13	IMA Auditorium, Flint, Michigan (2 shows)
14	Cincinnati Gardens, Cincinnati. Ohio
15	Kiel Auditorium, St, Louis, Missouri
16	Municipal Theater, Tulsa, Oklahoma (2 shows)
17	Municipal Auditorium, Oklahoma City, Oklahoma (2 shows)
18	The Forum, Wichita, Kansas (2 shows)
19	Auditorium, Kansas City, Missouri

20	Auditorium, Omaha, Nebraska
21	Civic Centre, Bartlesville, Oklahoma (2 shows)
22	Waterloo Auditorium, Waterloo, Iowa
23	Orpheum Theater, Madison, Wisconsin (3 shows)
24	Riverside Theater, Milwaukee, Wisconsin (3 shows)
25	Municipal Theater, Minneapolis, Minnesota
26	Civic Opera House, Chicago. Illinois (2 shows)
27	Afternoon—Memorial Coliseum, Fort Wayne, Indiana
	Evening—Civic Centre, Lansing, Michigan
28	Central High School Auditorium, Kalamazoo, Michigan (2 shows)
29	Unknown
30	Auditorium, South Bend, Indiana

May
1	Syria Mosque, Pittsburgh (2 shows)
2	Buffalo, New York (2 shows)
3	Toronto, Ontario, Canada (2 shows)
4	The Forum, Montreal, Quebec, Canada (2 shows)
5	Lewiston, Maine
6	Boston Garden, Boston, Massachusetts
7	The Arena, Providence, Rhode Island (2 shows)
8	Cancelled
9	The Arena, Hershey, Pennsylvania
10	Cancelled

SUMMER DANCE PARTY

Featuring: Buddy Holly & The Crickets, Tommy Allsup's Western Swing Band and in some cases, locals artists as the opening act.

July
4	Angola, Indiana
5	Spring Valley, Illinois
6	Mushegon, Michigan
7	Unknown
8	Electric Park Ballroom, Waterloo, Iowa
9	Matters Ballroom, Decorah, Iowa

10	Delwein, Iowa
11	Duluth, Minnesota
12	Rothschild Pavilion, Wausau, Wisconsin
13	Crystal Rock Ballroom, Rhinelander, Wisconsin
14	Unknown

THE BIGGEST SHOW OF STARS FOR 1958—AUTUMN EDITION

Featuring: Frankie Avalon, Bobby Darin, The Olympics. Dion & The Belmonts, Bobby Freeman, The Elegants. Jimmy Clanton, The Danleers, Duane Eddy, Clyde McPhatter, Buddy Holly & The Crickets, Jack Scott, The Coasters, Sil Austin Orchestra

October
3	Worcester Auditorium, Worcester,Massachusetts
4	State Theater, Hartford, Connecticut
5	The Forum, Montreal, Quebec
6	Memorial Centre, Peterborough, Ontario
7	Memorial Auditorium, Kitchener, Ontario
8	Sports Arena, Toledo, Ohio
9	Indiana Theater, Indianapolis, Indiana
10	Unknown
11	Veterans Memorial Auditorium, Columbus, Ohio

12	Unknown
13	Syria Mosque, Pittsburgh. Pennsylvania (2 shows)
14	Unknown
15	Community War Memorial Building, Rochester, New York
16	Catholic Youth Center, Scranton, Pennsylvania
17	Municipal Auditorium, Norfolk, Virginia (2 shows)
18	Park Center, Charlotte, North Carolina
19	Mosque, Richmond, Virginia

WINTER DANCE PARTY

Featuring: Buddy Holly, The Big Bopper, Ritchie Valens, Frankie Sardo, Dion & The Belmonts, Debbie Stevens

January 1959
23	George Devine's Million Dollar Ballroom, Milwaukee, Wisconsin
24	Eagles Ballroom, Kenosha, Wisconsin
25	Kato Ballroom, Mankato, Minnesota
26	Fournier's Ballroom, Eau Claire, Wisconsin
27	Fiesta Ballroom, Montevideo, Minnesota
28	Promenade Ballroom, St, Paul, Minnesota
29	Capitol Theater, Davenport, Iowa

30	Laramar Ballroom, Fort Dodge, Iowa
31	Duluth Armory, Duluth, Minnesota

February
1	Riverside Ballroom, Green Bay, Wisconsin
	(Afternoon appearance at Cinderella Ballroom, Appleton, Wisconsin cancelled, probably due to bad weather and failure of tour bus)
2	Surf Ballroom, Clear Lake, Iowa

Following the deaths of the three major artists on the show, Frankie Sardo and Dion & The Belmonts continued to the end of the tour. Bobby Vee made his first professional stage appearance with his group The Shadows at the date for February 3. For the remainder of the tour, Jimmy Clanton and Frankie Avalon were engaged as headliners, and Holly's backing group rejoined the tour with Ronnie Smith as lead singer, The remaining dates were as follows:

February
3	The Armory, Moorhead, Minnesota
4	Sioux City, Iowa
5	Val Air Ballroom, Des Moines, Iowa
6	Danceland Ballroom, Cedar Rapids, Iowa
7	Les Buzz Ballroom, Spring Valley, Illinois
8	Aragon Ballroom, Chicago, Illinois

9	Hippodrome Auditorium, Waterloo, Iowa
10	Melody Hill, Dubuque, Iowa
11	Memorial Auditorium, Louisville, Kentucky
12	Memorial Auditorium, Canton, Ohio
13	Stanbaugh Auditorium, Youngstown, Ohio
14	The Armory, Peoria, Illinois
15	Illinois State Armory, Springfield, Illinois

USEFUL ADDRESSES

It is usually appreciated when writing to any of these contacts to enclose return postage in the form of a stamped addressed envelope in your own country, or an International Reply Coupon (available from Post Offices) if writing to an address overseas.

Buddy Holly Appreciation Society Australia
21 Brookside Street
Upwey
Victoria 3158, Australia

Buddy Holly & The Crickets Fan Club
142 Burns Avenue
Feltham
Middlesex TW14 9HZ, England

The Buddy Holly Memorial Society
PO Box 6123
Lubbock
Texas 79493-6123, USA

The British Buddy Holly Society
"Bramwell"
Roke
Near Benson
Oxfordshire, England

Crickets File Magazine
412 Main Road
Darnall
Sheffield S94QL, England

The Crickets
8455 New Bethel Road
Lyles
Tennessee, 37098, USA

John Beecher
c/o Rock House, London Road
St. Mary's, Stroud
Gloucestershire, GL6 8PU, England

Holly International Magazine
45 Westfield Road
Tickhill
Doncaster, DN11 9LB

Larry & Travis Holley
Holly House Records
4803—17th Street
Lubbock 79416, USA

MCA Records Ltd
139 Picadilly
London W1V 0AX

MCA Records Inc./Uni Dist.Corp.
10 Universal City Plaza
Universal City
California 91608, USA

INDEX